D1520561

Rhetoric and Reality in Plato's
Phaedrus

SUNY Series in Ancient Greek Philosophy
Anthony Preus, EDITOR

RHETORIC AND REALITY IN PLATO'S
P H A E D R U S

DAVID A. WHITE

STATE UNIVERSITY OF NEW YORK PRESS

Published by
State University of New York Press, Albany

©1993 State University of New York

For information, address the State University of New York Press,
State University Plaza, Albany, NY 12246

Production by Bernadine Dawes
Marketing by Fran Keneston

Library of Congress Cataloging-in-Publication Data

White, David A., 1942-
    Rhetoric and reality in Plato's Phaedrus / David A. White
        p.   cm. — (SUNY series in ancient Greek philosophy)
    Includes bibliographical references and index.
    ISBN 0-7914-1233-4 (alk. paper) : $54.50. — ISBN 0-7914-1234-2
(pbk. : alk. paper) : $17.95
    1. Plato. Phaedrus.   I. Title.   II. Series.
    B380.W48   1992   91-43967
    184-dc20   CIP

10   9   8   7   6   5   4   3   2   1

To

Mary Jeanne, Daniel and Colin

BRIEF CONTENTS

Acknowledgment xv

Introduction: Principles of Interpretation 1

Chapter 1. Myth and Rhetorical Inspiration (227a–237b) 11

Chapter 2. Socrates' First Speech (237b–244a) 35

Chapter 3. The Metaphysics of Madness and
the Nature of Soul (244a–247c) 65

Chapter 4. Soul and Truth (247c–250d) 107

Chapter 5. Beauty and the Capture of the Beloved (250d–257b) 139

Chapter 6. Rhetoric and Truth (257b–262c) 175

Chapter 7. Rhetoric and Dialectic (262c–266d) 203

Chapter 8. Nature and the Art of Writing (266d–274b) 229

Chapter 9. Writing and Wisdom (274b–279c) 251

Epilogue: Method and Metaphysics in the *Phaedrus* 277

Notes 293

Bibliography 319

Index 331

EXPANDED CONTENTS

Acknowledgment   xv

Introduction: Principles of Interpretation   1

Chapter 1. Myth and Rhetorical Inspiration (227a–237b)   11

Leisure and Love   11

Socrates and Phaedrus   14

The Problem of Mythic Explanation   17

Socrates and the Possibility of Self-knowledge   20

Beauty and the Nourishment of Discourses   22

The Speech of Lysias   24

The Conditions of Praiseworthy Discourse   25

The Inspiration of Socrates   28

The Premise of Socrates' First Speech   290

Phaedrus' Threat and the Socratic Character   30

Chapter 2. Socrates' First Speech (237b–244a)   35

Socrates' First Speech: Invocation   35

Rhetorical Setting   37

Argument and Definition   37

Division between Lover and Nonlover   38

Desire and Predication   41

A Definition of Love   42

Socrates and the Inspiration of Madness   42

The Speech Continued   45
Beloved and Intellect   45
Beloved and Pleasure   46
Reversal of Lover and Beloved   47
Socrates and Poetic Possession   50
Socrates and Truth   52
Phaedrus and the Propagation of Discourse   52
Socrates the Seer   53
The Need for Recantation   55
Shame and Recantation   58
The Audience for the Palinode   60
Remark   61

Chapter 3. The Metaphysics of Madness and the Nature of Soul
      (244a–247c)   65

The Human Origin of the Palinode   65
The Metaphysical Origin   66
The Madness of Prophecy   67
The Madness of Poetry   70
The Metaphysics of Madness   71
Wisdom and Nature   75
The Nature of Soul—Self-motion   78
The Form of Soul   87
The Powers of Soul   89
Soul and the Good   93
Mortality and Immortality   95
The Nature of Soul's Wings   100
The Divine Ascent to Reality   101

Chapter 4. Soul and Truth (247c–250d)   107

Poetry and Truth   107
Reality and Divine Soul   108
Reality and Human Soul   111
Destiny and Fallen Soul   114
The Afterlife of Human Soul   117

Recollection: The One and the Many   120
Madness and Participation   124
Metaphysics and Mystery   128
Mystery and the Good   130

Chapter 5. Beauty and the Capture of the Beloved
        (250d–257b)   139

Beauty and Wisdom   139
The Vision of Beauty   140
The Experience of Beauty   142
The Poetic Vision of Love   143
The Divine and the Choice of Beloved   146
Love and Participation in Divinity   147
The Education of the Beloved   148
The Happiness of Love   149
The Form of the Horses   151
The Vision of the Beloved   156
Beauty and Memory   157
The Training of the Evil Horse   158
Love and the Good   160
Love and Desire   162
Love and Friendship   164
Love and Philosophy   165
The Blessings of Friendship   169
The Socratic Recantation: Summary   170

Chapter 6. Rhetoric and Truth (257b–262c)   175

The Unity of the Phaedrus   176
Writing and the Love of Honor   178
The Problem of Writing   180
The Story of the Cicadas   183
Rhetoric and Truth   191
The Challenge of Opinion   192
The Art of Speaking: Rejoinder and Criticism   193
The Definition and Scope of Rhetoric   194

Rhetoric and Opposition   196
Rhetoric and Truth   199

Chapter 7. Rhetoric and Dialectic (262c–266d)   203

The Synoptic Perspective   203
Truth and Inspiration   204
The Art of Rhetoric: Agreement and Division   206
Definition and Inspiration   208
The Critique of Lysias' Speech   209
Socrates' Speeches: Recapitulation and Madness   210
The Art of Rhetoric: Principles and Definition   213
Collection and Division   215
Division and Nature   218
Socrates—the Lover of Method   223
Love and the Unity of the Phaedrus   226

Chapter 8. Nature and the Art of Writing (266d–274b)   229

The History of Rhetoric   229
Art and the Preliminaries of Rhetoric   230
Art and Nature   232
Nature and Totality   236
The Structure of Nature   240
Teaching the Art of Rhetoric   241
Practicing the Art of Rhetoric   243
Probability and the Good   245

Chapter 9. Writing and Wisdom (274b–279c)   251

The Problem of Writing   251
The Prophecy of Thamus   252
The Character of Writing   254
The Gardens of Letters   256
Lysias Revisited   260
The Legacy of Composition   268
Socrates Prophesies   270

The Prayer of Socrates   271
Concluding Comment   275

Epilogue: Method and Metaphysics in the *Phaedrus*   277
Collection   277
Division and Nature   278
Nature   279
   The Range of Nature   279
   Nature and the Forms   280
   Simplicity and Complexity   280
   Active and Passive   284
   Nature and Totality   285
   Nature and Division   287

Notes   293
Bibliography   319
Index   331

A C K N O W L E D G M E N T

I wish to thank the American Council of Learned Societies for a Fellowship that helped support this study.

Principles of Interpretation

The *Phaedrus* was the first dialogue Plato wrote. This belief, arising in antiquity, did not die quickly—a relatively recent exponent was Friedrich Schleiermacher. As a statement of Platonic chronology, this view no longer receives credence. However, Schleiermacher's reasons for this determination are worth examining. He thought that the sources and methods of philosophizing for Plato were intimately interwoven throughout the *Phaedrus*, and that subsequent dialogues were extensions and refinements of these principles. Thus, the *Phaedrus* is the first dialogue written because it is the first to project the fundamental Platonic questions.

Schleiermacher's grasp of the thematic sweep of the *Phaedrus* remains sound. The concern for the practical matter of rhetoric and the defense of the philosophical life recalls the *Apology*, and the theory of rhetoric continues the investigation begun in the *Gorgias*, although from a different perspective. The interest in language brings to mind the *Cratylus*, in particular seeing sense in etymology and determining the relation between words and things. Reflections on the nature of soul evoke the *Phaedo* and the *Republic*. The speculative cosmology anticipates the *Timaeus*, and the extensive myth, embodying a complex account of reality, looks backward to the *Phaedo* and the *Republic*. The inspired states attributed to the poet evoke the *Ion* and the *Republic*.

I

The epistemology of anamnesis continues the concern of the *Meno* to make contact with reality. The doctrine of collection and division extends the inquiry into method, which began in earnest in the *Phaedo* and *Republic*, and is a precoursor of the sustained reflections on method in the *Sophist* and the *Statesman*. The oratorical interest in love consummates the primary focus of the *Lysis* and the *Symposium*. In short, the *Phaedrus* shines its many rays throughout Plato's early, middle, and late dialogues.

I

W. V. Verdenius, writing in the 1950s, described the *Phaedrus* as a "step-child" of classical scholarship—a trope intended to highlight the relative lack of attention given to the dialogue. This observation can no longer be made. In addition to a fairly steady stream of journal literature, there have been a number of books on the *Phaedrus*, new translations, and an extensive (and seminal for some) article by Jacques Derrida— all within the last two decades. Much may be learned from this body of work. But more may yet be said.

The wealth of themes developed in the *Phaedrus* implies the possibility of various viable perspectives for interpreting the dialogue. One of its particularly striking features, recognized since antiquity, is the stark contrast between the series of three speeches on love (231a–257c) that reaches a pinnacle in one of Plato's most resplendent myths, and the apparently dispassionate inquiry into the nature and methodology of rhetoric (257a–279e). This contrast has engendered the problem of "the unity of the *Phaedrus*."

The approach taken in this study is based on the premise that the *Phaedrus* can be read as an account of reality, and of how human nature must confront that reality in order to speak, and to live, as wisely and well as possible. Thus, one way in which the unity of the *Phaedrus* becomes apparent is to read the dialogue as a variegated exercise in—to use a non-Platonic word—metaphysics, the Platonic concern to describe "the things that are." This approach is not without drawbacks. To sustain it throughout a convoluted dialogue means that some aspects of the *Phaedrus* will receive scrutiny only as they bear on the structure of reality animating the dialogue as a whole. But the unavoidable loss of interpretive discussion that results will, I feel, be more than compensated for by situating these issues within a more articulated metaphysical position. The *Phaedrus* has yet to receive its due as a concentrated discourse on metaphysical considerations, both in substance and method. The following study is a tentative first step in that direction.

II

It has been asserted that the *Phaedrus* and the *Parmenides* are "near neighbors" to one another in order of composition.[1] The two dialogues appear to be polar opposites, both stylistically and in terms of content. But is there a subtle apposition between them?

At the conclusion of his commentary on the introductory portion of the *Parmenides*, F. M. Cornford observes that this dialogue is "written throughout in the plainest conversational style," with one isolated stylistic exception—Parmenides' comparison of himself to the veteran chariot-horse described in a poem by Ibycus (137a), a reference that "stands out like a single patch of colour on a grey background" (p.64). Why did Plato choose this one brief moment to loosen the discursive tautness of the *Parmenides*?

The chariot-race image occurs at a crucial juncture in the *Parmenides*. The young Socrates has confidently advanced a version of the theory of Forms. This theory is then criticized by the elder Parmenides. After Parmenides admits that the Forms are necessary for all thought and discussion, he advises Socrates that before attempting to define particular Forms, Socrates should undergo a "preliminary training" (135d). Parmenides offers a brief sketch of a method based on an earlier suggestion by Zeno, but then he begs to be relieved of the burden of illustrating the method more fully. However, Zeno himself presses the company in attendance to urge Parmenides to do what is, he claims, a heavy task for one of Parmenides' age. Parmenides replies (Allen's translation):

I must do as you ask. Yet really, I feel like the old racehorse in
Ibycus, who trembles with fear at the start of the race because
he knows from long experience what lies in store. Ibycus compares himself, forced as an old man to enter the lists of love
against his will. When I remember how, at my age, I must
traverse such and so great a sea of arguments, I am afraid.
Still, I must oblige you, especially since, as Zeno says, we are
alone among ourselves (137a–b).

The rest of the *Parmenides* follows, a singularly searching exercise in
metaphysical inquiry.

The "single patch of colour" links the statement and critique of the
theory of Forms with the extended training which must be undergone
before the Forms can be adequately defined and related to one another.
This brief description marks the structural pivot of the entire
dialogue—what precedes states the problem and what follows is the
propaedeutic for answering that problem. If, however, Cornford's assessment of the *Parmenides'* style is correct, then the "grey background" of the dialogue cannot explain why this dash of color appears
where it does, much less why it appears at all. But an explanation,
speculative yet significant, does emerge once this interlude is read in
conjunction with the *Phaedrus*, the near neighbor to the *Parmenides*.[2]

Here in C. M. Bowra's translation in the *Oxford Book of Greek
Poetry in Translation*, is the Ibycus poem cited by Parmenides:

> Lo, Love again with glancing eyes
> That melt from under lids of jet
> Drives me with manifold sorceries
> Into the Cyprian's boundless net.
> Ah, how I tremble when he comes on.
> Like an old champion chariot-horse,
> Who drags the light car, when youth is gone
> Unwittingly to the course.

Parmenides has compared himself to a racehorse rather than to the
driver of that horse. The suggestion is that although he is capable of
moving toward a goal, he may not be able to display the guidance a

competent driver could provide. Who then is the driver remaining in the poetic shadows?

Parmenides sees himself not only as a racehorse, but as an old racehorse (i.e., he has been running on this type of course for many years). Furthermore, his animal sense of awareness includes anticipation, since he starts to tremble even before this running of the race begins. Why do his memories affect him so powerfully? What forces Parmenides, an aging horse, to enter again the "lists of love?" If love is more hardship than joy, why not simply decline to participate in the contest? Why is one forced to love?

If love means something other, and higher than, a form of carnal expression, then one might be forced to love in order to become intimate with the objects of this more fundamental type of experience. The labor of love may well require a metaphysical exercise essential for realizing the nature of love in its highest sense. Parmenides as racehorse remembers past efforts at running this course. But are these memories solely of his own rigorous efforts or are they also of the cause of such rigor? In the *Phaedrus*, memory as anamnesis refers to what soul saw by participating in the vision of the Forms when all soul, both divine and human, was a union of winged horses and a driver. Could Parmenides also be hinting at the metaphysical dimension of memory and the fact that describing memories of Forms on a high level of generality is an especially taxing exercise?

So far, Parmenides has followed the flow of imagery in Ibycus' poem. But, suddenly, he concludes the description of his memories by noting how frightened he is to "traverse such and so great a sea of arguments." No reference to the sea appears in Ibycus' poem. Furthermore, this image disrupts the consistency in Parmenides' application of the poem to his own situation. How can a chariot race for love be run on the sea? It cannot, at least not in the natural order of chariot racing. But such a race can be run *over* the sea. The horse capable of this racing will be special—he will be winged, just as the horses and driver of soul in the *Phaedrus* are winged. The Platonic Parmenides has subtly shifted the context of imagery from earthbound horses running chariot races for erotic prizes to horses who can race through the heavens, perhaps toward true reality where the prizes are visions beheld by those capable of such vision.

Finally, Parmenides does accede to the wishes of the company, because "we are alone among ourselves." The *Phaedrus* concludes with Phaedrus quoting the Pythagorean adage "friends have all things in common." Parmenides will undertake the arduous voyage into the realm of the Forms because he is among a small community of kindred spirits. The *Phaedrus* goes to considerable pains to demonstrate the true nature of friendship (i.e., the relation between human beings bound to one another by the highest degree of reality)—thus, the conversants in the *Parmenides* pick up where the friends in the *Phaedrus* conclude. In the *Phaedrus*, true love is ultimately defined in terms of friendship with the Forms, and the task of elucidating the nature of the Forms binding us to them in friendship is begun in earnest in the *Parmenides*.

The fact that Parmenides, via Ibycus, has referred to elements crucial to the mythical portion of the *Phaedrus* suggests that the problems explicitly raised in the *Parmenides* were already implicit in the *Phaedrus*, in particular defining the Forms and determining how they are related to one another. In the *Phaedrus*, the "lists of love" concern the various contests waged by the lover—of a beautiful human, of the Form beauty, of all Forms—against attractive appearances which threaten to deflect love from its proper ends. Parmenides' seemingly offhand remarks intimate that the struggles he is about to inaugurate with unity and other abstract terms are no less relevant for the lovers of the Forms in the *Phaedrus* than they are for those students of the *Parmenides* who desire to embrace the Forms.

Once the philosophical love developed in the *Phaedrus* reaches its limits, then the advocate of that love meets a multitude of intricate metaphysical problems. These problems, rendered poetically and mythically, are the lists of love. What the *Phaedrus* has engendered metaphysically amidst one of the most intense of human experiences, the *Parmenides* carries into the most rarified realm of metaphysical speculation. The brief interlude of stylistic color in the *Parmenides* is not an isolated poetic surge; it thematically links the *Phaedrus* and the

Parmenides, showing the relevance of philosophical love to abstract reflections on the nature of the Forms.

The most explicit reminder of this dimension in the *Phaedrus* occurs at 261d–e, when Socrates, characterizing rhetoric at a high level of generality, cites Zeno, the "Eleatic Palamedes," with his reknowned skill for making "the same things appear to his audience to be like and unlike, one and many, at rest and in motion." Phaedrus agrees that Zeno's discourses must indeed be included as part of rhetoric, an agreement elevating rhetoric into a decidedly metaphysical context. By implication then, the method for finding the truth, a method which will apply most immediately to the public types of rhetoric prominent in the *Phaedrus*, will also apply to determining the nature of terms of utmost generality. These are the same terms which, when Zeno read his speech in the *Parmenides*, evoked the theory of Forms from the young Socrates, a theory he was then unable to defend because, as Parmenides might have put it, he had not been tested in the lists of love.

In addition to direct metaphysical concerns, the *Phaedrus* deals with a variety of other topics, a fact about its structure noted since antiquity. One of these topics is the nature of rhetoric. As part of its treatment of rhetoric, the *Phaedrus* develops a theory of the philosophical significance of writing. This theory enunciates principles for producing good writing. The *Phaedrus* is a written document. But is it good writing?

The argument of the *Phaedrus* sanctions the relevance of this question. The problem of good (and bad) writing is posed at 258d. There Socrates asks Phaedrus whether they should question anyone who has ever written or who will ever write anything, regardless whether the author is a poet or an ordinary person. Later, when the inquiry into the nature of writing has been concluded, Socrates says that the preceding account will hold for anyone who has ever written anything, regardless of its form (277e). Thus, even if the *Phaedrus* as a dialogue does not fall neatly into the classes of poetry or prose, it remains an example of writing. The *Phaedrus* may therefore be assessed in light of the principles advanced in the *Phaedrus* itself.

The first and most important condition for good writing advanced in the *Phaedrus* is that the writer must know the truth about the subject matter treated (277b). The speaker or writer must know what is truly real in such a way that it can be defined and then divided exhaustively into its constituent kinds (277b–c). Thus, the writer's knowledge of truth entails knowledge of the method for arriving at truth. Furthermore, this methodological stance must be seen in light of what Socrates says in his second speech, when he dares to speak the truth since "the truth" is his theme (247c). Now if the *Phaedrus* illustrates good writing, it will have unity—i.e., it will be formed with head and suitable limbs (264c), its unity analogous to that of a living organism. On this analogy, the head of the *Phaedrus* will be the truth. Therefore, the problem of the unity of the *Phaedrus* involves showing how the parts of the dialogue depend on truth—i.e., the nature of reality described in the *Phaedrus*—for their structure and development.

Two cautionary remarks should be made: first, the metaphysical principles developed from the structure and detail of the dialogue are in some cases inchoate; hence the need for the Epilogue to this study, in which the elements of this metaphysics are codified and problems noted (and there are many). Second, the complexity of the *Phaedrus* is such that it admits many worthwhile interpretations, their value depending on the centrality of the approach taken and the consistency in which these approaches are developed. Thus, existing studies of the *Phaedrus* focusing on, e.g., self-knowledge, psychology, and moral inquiry should be taken not as rivals to what is attempted below, but (when appropriate) as complements. The claim here is not that the *Phaedrus* is just a covert dry as dust tract in metaphysics, but that its structure includes this dimension and that developing this dimension is a legitimate interpretive approach.

The *Phaedrus* is written; as such, it is little more than an artefact unless it is read. But one of the primary dangers inherent in the written word is its indiscriminate publicity, i.e., it can be read by anyone free to do so. However, as the *Phaedrus* itself points out, some writing should not be read by people who lack the capacity for understanding what they read (275e). This danger is also voiced, although more subtly, in the *Parmenides*. When Zeno agrees to read his treatise in defense of the doctrine of Parmenides, he remarks that the treatise had been "stolen" and, as a result, had gained a certain notoriety such that it now is taken as a definitive treatment of Zeno's views following Parmenides. Zeno adds that it had been written when he was a young man, suggesting that the work might not have received such notice if, over time, he could have studied it, perhaps revising, perhaps never making it public at all. As things turned out, Zeno never had these options. But such are the dangers of putting words into print. Despite this reservation, however, it seems true to say that if Socrates does lead Phaedrus to the truth—if truth it be—then the reader of this remarkable mythic and metaphysical adventure will also be led to the truth once all phases of the *Phaedrus* are coordinated to achieve that end.

The interpretation offered below follows the dialogue as narrated and is divided into nine chapters according to the dialogue's "natural joints," i.e., those junctures which allow the importance of metaphysical considerations to become most readily apparent. Burnet's text is used; the translations, based on Hackforth, Fowler, and Rowe, are my own.

CHAPTER 1

Myth and Rhetorical Inspiration
(227a–237b)

The *Phaedrus* begins with Socrates speaking to Phaedrus: "Dear Phaedrus, where are you from and where are you going?" The form of address indicates an intimacy between the two men, whether of easy acquaintance or something more remains to be seen. Socrates' question suggests that Phaedrus is headed somewhere out of the ordinary, thus arousing Socrates' interest in both where he has been and his intended destination. The presence of motion and an aura of impending strangeness animate this question, elements which will characterize the subsequent conversation until, when it concludes, Socrates will say to his lone companion "let us be going" (279a). Socrates will then return with Phaedrus to a place of mutual concern and relative safety, both men having won greater understanding both of themselves as individuals and as friends, as well as the structure of reality underlying this understanding.

Leisure and Love

Phaedrus tells Socrates that he has just been with Lysias, the well-known writer of speeches currently visiting Athens, and that he is going for a walk "outside the walls," since Acumenus, a physician and friend of both Phaedrus and Socrates, has advised that recreation is less fatiguing on roads than on city streets. Thus, Phaedrus is en route away from the city and from the protection provided by its walls. Socrates agrees with the ostensible reason for this venture, i.e., advice, presumably wise, concerning the relative well-being to the body of walks on roads rather than on streets. However, he will soon question whether pursuing such exercise was Phaedrus' real motive in determining his present destination.

Socrates asks what Phaedrus had discussed during the morning, then answers his own question by asserting that Lysias doubtless entertained Phaedrus and the rest of the company with his speeches. Socrates' surmise is true, and Phaedrus is anxious to tell what he has heard. Phaedrus tells Socrates he will recount the morning's discourse if Socrates has leisure to walk along and listen. Socrates replies that hearing the conversation with Lysias will, quoting Pindar, be a greater thing than "business."

This last remark may be taken as a chance quip borrowed from a great poet, but it also has serious undertones. Socrates' business is not to traffic in merchandise in the agora, but to talk to his fellow Greeks in the attempt, as he will say shortly, to know himself (229e). The subtle presence of opposition should be noted, since exploring the boundaries of opposition as a metaphysical notion will become one of the controlling concerns in the dialogue. In this case, however, business (ἀσχολίας) is not an opposite to leisure (σχολή), although it may appear to Athenian business people that Socrates' business was leisure, since all he did was talk about matters of scant practicality. If Socrates temporarily gives up his business to hear a report of a discussion between Lysias and Phaedrus, then this report promises to be serious business. Notice that Socrates wants to hear the conversation Phaedrus had with Lysias—not just Lysias' speech, i.e., he wants to hear what Phaedrus said (Socrates thus assumes Phaedrus spoke) as well as what Phaedrus heard. Socrates continues then to ply his "business," although in this case he believes he will passively hear a conversation rather than, as is his wont, actively participate in one.

Both men have the requisite leisure to rehearse this narration, and Phaedrus notes that Socrates is especially suited to hear what was said, for the subject of the conversation was, in a way, a speech about love. Lysias had described one of the beauties (καλῶν) being tempted, but— and here, Phaedrus says, is the pretty thing—not by a lover. The speech contended that the beauty's favors should be granted to the nonlover rather than to the lover. Socrates' aptness for hearing his speech reminds us of his predisposition toward matters amatory, and the more abstract possibility (already outlined in the *Symposium*) that beauty and the love of beauty may lead toward the highest reaches of reality. However, Phaedrus himself does not now seem particularly susceptible to these long-range possibilities, since although he had been with Lysias for an extended period (227a), the principal attraction of the speech was its prettiness, a characteristic doubtless extolled during the morning's discussion. Yet Phaedrus is nonetheless quick to recall that Socrates is preeminent in the matter of love.

At this point, Socrates knows nothing of the detail of Lysias' pretty oratory, but he wishes aloud that if this speech advanced the claims of love on behalf of the poor and the old—conditions Socrates shares with "most of us"—then it would have become truly useful and widely democratic (227d). One the one hand, Socrates' irony indicates that the thesis of this speech strikes him as, at best, farfetched; on the other hand, the intended scope of the remark reveals his concern that the effect of love should apply to the broadest base of humanity, as if love was in some sense a constant, a metaphysical necessity for all.

Socrates enjoins Phaedrus to report the speech, but he is reluctant; after all, he, Phaedrus, is but a private citizen and could hardly recite from memory what Lysias, the cleverest writer of the day, had taken a long time to execute at his leisure. Phaedrus found this speech to be pretty, and now he says that Lysias the man is unparalleled in cleverness. Prettiness and cleverness index Phaedrus' current receptivity to rhetoric. If a clever writer is also wise, then Socrates' interest in his work will be justified; but if Phaedrus' allegiance to such writing is restricted to its cleverness, then it will be difficult for him to follow the proof-structure of Socrates' second speech. In this speech, Socrates

will show that the madness of love is given by the gods for our greatest
well-being, a proof prefaced with the warning that it will be accepted
only by the wise and disbelieved by the "clever" (245c). Phaedrus must
show that he has the capacity to move beyond what he currently values
as cleverness in rhetoric in order to see the sense in what Socrates eventually says about love, and about discourse in general.

Socrates and Phaedrus

As a preamble to his next remarks, Socrates asserts that if he is unmindful of Phaedrus then he has forgotten himself, but that neither of these
is true. Socrates feels certain that Phaedrus heard the speech of Lysias
many times, a repetitive task Lysias was only too willing to perform. In
fact, Socrates sees Phaedrus borrowing the text of the speech and reviewing the parts he especially liked. He occupied himself in this way
until, growing tired, he went for a walk. Socrates also infers that
Phaedrus has already memorized the speech, unless it was rather long,
and that he intended to practice declaiming it while outside the walls.
Then, meeting by chance a man who was "sick" to hear discourses,
Phaedrus resolved that Socrates share in his "Corybantic revel." But
when Socrates, the "lover of discourse," requested him to speak, he
played coy, as if he did not desire to speak. Socrates insists, however,
that Phaedrus would have declaimed Lysias' speech in any case, even if
those who happened along the road did not want to hear it (228b–c).

This passage shows the extent to which Socrates interprets the
character of Phaedrus in light of what Phaedrus has revealed about his
activities on this day, as well as Socrates' understanding of himself
when in the presence of someone of Phaedrus' nature. This knowledge
is of practical importance now, and its generalization will be of theoretical importance later, when discussion turns to achieving success in
rhetoric, for such success presupposes knowing one's audience and the
kinds of discourses that will persuade them.

In this case, Phaedrus is an audience of one, and in his preliminary
assessment, Socrates shows how far he has seen into the character of
that audience. The picture of Phaedrus that emerges is of an individual

with an intense but, perhaps, undisciplined appreciation of the powers of discourse.[1] Phaedrus has been enthralled by Lysias' speech, and had it repeated often. But even such repetition was inadequate. Since Phaedrus has already revealed that he is particularly impressed by the prettiness and cleverness of this speech, the parts he read and reread were doubtless those which, in his mind, displayed the flashiest rhetoric. If so, then Phaedrus, at least at this point, values style over substance. This inference becomes all the more telling if Phaedrus wants to become a mirror image of Lysias in the sense of reciting the speech verbatim—hence his trip outside the walls and into the open for declamatory practice.

The emphasis then shifts from Socrates' analysis of an unreflective Phaedrus in the presence of attractive discourse to a precis of Socrates' knowledge of self in the same context. When Phaedrus chanced upon Socrates, he met someone sick with desire to hear discourses. As evidence of this sickness, Socrates has expressed great interest in hearing Lysias' speech even before he knows what that speech is about—his sickness is so pervasive that its cravings must be fed regardless of the content of those speeches. Furthermore, Socrates is aware that listening to Phaedrus echo the speech will cause a frenzy simulating the practice of the Corybantic rites.[2] Socrates envisions Phaedrus becoming consumed by this condition and, perhaps surprisingly, feels that he also will share in it. In fact, Socrates' sickness leads him to accompany Phaedrus outside the walls of Athens, a venture which, as Phaedrus will note, is decidedly out of character for the city-loving Socrates. If therefore such is the natural consequence of this Socratic sickness, then Socrates' soul may not be driven by an unalloyed vision of pure reality.

To Socrates, Phaedrus acted coyly in refusing to speak when Socrates, the lover of speeches, desired him to do so. Phaedrus' conduct thus reflects what the speech has counseled, withholding favors from a lover (i.e., a lover of discourse) and bestowing them on someone else. Although in Phaedrus' mind the speech's fine language was its principal attraction, his behavior toward a living embodiment of love realizes the very content of the speech which he wants to keep from Socrates.

This reaction illustrates the insidious effect that such "fine" discourses can have on those who are attracted to them for, perhaps, the wrong reasons. We shall see that Socrates, sick with his own love of discourse, will in a sense also fall prey to the darker side of its blandishments when he competes with Lysias for Phaedrus' rhetorical favor.

Phaedrus now knows that he will have to speak, or (more accurately) read, for he realizes that Socrates will not leave his side until he does so. Socrates says that Phaedrus, in this realization, sees him as he truly is (228d), indicating that Phaedrus has some of the kind of knowledge of others that Socrates has displayed of him. In this case, Phaedrus has just testified that Socrates is an adept in matters of love, implying that Phaedrus knows something important about Socrates and that Socrates also realizes it about himself. As Socrates says in the *Symposium*, love is the one thing he understands (177e), a remarkable admission from one usually professing to know only that he does not know. The *Phaedrus* will teach that if Socrates does indeed understand love and its metaphysical origins—the highest sense of love—then he knows all that a human being need know.

Despite his uncritical fervor for certain forms of discourse, Phaedrus shows a degree of percipience in assessing the nature of another human; in fact, Phaedrus the man will be limned as not without philosophical sophistication. However, he has not thought through this awareness to see its implications for his own life, particularly in assessing the truth and practical consequences of what he hears in the rhetorical arena.

Phaedrus insists that he lacks memorized knowledge of the entire speech—instead, he proposes that he repeat the "sense" of the speech, how the lover and the nonlover differ, summarizing the major points from the beginning. Phaedrus believes that he has fully understood the content of the speech in relation to its structure even if he has not yet committed every word of it to memory. This belief will, however, measure the inadequacy of Phaedrus' notion of rhetorical structure if the speech has no structure, with no real beginning (as Socrates will demonstrate). The fact that Phaedrus refers to sense (διάνοιαν) of this speech then becomes unintentionally ironic, especially if the form of the speech is such that its apparent meaning is threatened by incoherence. That Phaedrus conceives of the speech in terms of its sense is nonetheless significant; he believes he is capable of construing and formulating a discourse according to its discursive content. It will become evident, however, that the true dianoetic content of a speech entails much more, particularly with regard to metaphysical content, than Phaedrus currently thinks is essential to produce a good speech.

In the end, Socrates does know Phaedrus, and as he presses his advantage, Phaedrus admits defeat, suggesting that they find a suitable place for reading the speech. Now outside the walls, they wade at the edge of the Ilissus, with Phaedrus noting that he is fortunate in being barefoot whereas Socrates is always unshod. Phaedrus sees a very tall plane tree, with shade and a grassy swell on which to sit or, he adds (perhaps flirtatiously), to lie upon (229b). It is summertime, the sky is bright with the sun, the heat of the day approaches—concurrent conditions suggesting that the time is ripe for fruition, both in nature itself and in the derivative discourses concerning reality about to unfold.[3]

The Problem of Mythic Explanation

As the two men prepare for the reading, Phaedrus recalls the current belief that they are in the vicinity where Boreas seized Oreithia. He wonders whether the place by the river is the actual spot, since it is pure and clear and fit for girlish romps. No, Socrates says, this event occurred further downriver; it is marked by an altar to Boreas, an altar which Phaedrus has never noticed (presupposing that Phaedrus has passed this way before). Phaedrus then asks, apparently amazed, whether Socrates believes that this mythic tale is true. Socrates answers that if he disbelieves the myth, as the wise do, then he would not be out of the ordinary, a response linking this popular reaction to Phaedrus' implicit skepticism. Then, endowed with such wisdom, Socrates could readily proffer a rationalistic explanation for a myth, e.g., that Boreas, the north wind, blew the maiden off the rocks as she was playing and that, dying in this way, she could be said to have been "carried off" by Boreas (229d). Thus, the seizure of the maiden was merely an accident of nature, an event then invested with mythic garb around a personified Boreas acting from unrequited passion.

Such explanations are attractive, but, for Socrates, they are produced by a clever and not entirely enviable person. The reason: after this explanation, the rationalist must necessarily explain the form of the Centaurs and then that of the Chimaera, as well as the corresponding forms of the Gorgons, Pegasus, and a host of other legendary natures. Someone attempting with a "rustic sort of wisdom" to explain them according to probability will need a great deal of leisure to accomplish this task (229e).

R. Hackforth has posed the problem of the "organic significance" of the Boreas myth in the *Phaedrus* as a whole. His answer: "it is inserted in order to preclude any question that might arise later on about the local divinities who inspire Socrates: Phaedrus, and the reader too, are not to attempt to rationalise what Plato makes Socrates say about them any more than they should rationalise the rape of Oreitheia." Verdenius objects, against Hackforth, that "this was not a real danger" and that what Socrates had in mind were "the subsequent myths on the soul and on love. These will have to be interpreted allegorically, but Socrates already warns us that allegorical interpretation should always be directed by self-examination." Verdenius also claims that Socrates objects to the current form of allegorizing because the "art of allegorical interpretation is still in its infancy, so that it works slowly and laboriously."[4]

Hackforth has raised a crucial problem; in fact, the Boreas myth and Socrates' reaction to it establish a theoretical foundation for the entire dialogue. Hackforth's understanding of the organic significance of the early myth is, however, inadequate, and in this regard Verdenius' reading, which connects the Boreas myth to the later accounts of love and soul, is more to the point. But Verdenius' subsequent observation concerning the fact that allegorical interpretation is still in its infancy is itself wide of the mark. For it would follow that if this type of explanation matured, it would be less laborious and time-consuming and, presumably, more relevant because it would require less time away from the study of self. This consequence reveals that Verdenius has not reproduced the real objection Socrates has against this type of explanation.

Socrates asserts that the allegorist has reduced the Boreas myth to an event explainable as a natural cause, and that such an explanation is produced by clever people who are "not to be envied." They are not be envied because, having begun this kind of allegorical reduction, they must then "necessarily" reveal the "form" of the Centaurs and Chimaera and a host of other such beasts and monsters. Note, however, that no thematic connection exists between the Boreas story and this list of mythic monsters. Why then does Socrates insist on the necessity to explain these esoteric and fabulous phenomena?

This necessity derives from the fact that Socrates construes the putative explanation of the Boreas myth to involve a principle of some sort. This principle must therefore be applicable to other instances of mythic phenomena, since for Socrates it is not possible to explain one myth without that explanation being derived from a principle which would also produce explanations for other myths—indeed, all myths. Notice then the difference between the Boreas story and the other examples Socrates cites—i.e., the Centaur, the Chimaera, the Gorgon, the Pegasus, and all other beings of this sort. The Boreas myth is an event involving living beings, whereas the other examples are simply living things as such. The supposed explanation of the Boreas myth replaced a supernatural tale with a clear (although rare) instance of natural cause and effect. If the requisite explanations run parallel in principle, then the accounts of the living things should also identify their origins in nature. But at this point the complexity of the problem emerges.

Socrates asserts that the allegoricist must explain the form of the Centaur, etc. But the Centaur is half-man half-horse. How then will it be possible to explain this polymorphous being in terms of its natural origin? Furthermore, the other examples given also share this characteristic, i.e., all are unnatural combinations of naturally self-subsisting beings. The appeal to explaining the form (εἶδος) of these beings should therefore be understood not just as a description of their physical

shape, but of shape as a nature (φύσεων). Socrates uses both locutions,
form and nature, to underline the fact that an appropriate explanation
will reveal what constitutes these beings both metaphysically as well as
physically.

Socrates then concludes that those who attempt, with a rustic sort of
wisdom, to explain each of these things "according to probability" will
require considerable leisure—and Socrates does not have such leisure
(although he is sufficiently leisured to listen to Phaedrus repeat a Lysian
speech). The sense in which the allegoricist is clever but unfortunate
now becomes clearer. He is clever in having seen that something in nature can explain something depicted mythically; he is unfortunate, however, both because the appeal to nature and its processes can result only
in probability and because the need to explain all mythical stories and
beings in this way will mean that an allegoricist who wants to display
consistency and completeness must thoroughly explore the thickets of
probability in order to accomplish this herculean task. Assaying this
task is a rustic form of wisdom—wisdom, because based on a vision of
what, more broadly, underlies mythical beings and events; rustic, because restricted to explanations which, since they appeal to aspects of
nature, are not themselves metaphysically fundamental.

The fulcrum of this kind of hypothetical explanation is probability;
only likenesses can be adduced when pursuing such explanations. Socrates will address the factor of similarity and differences more explicitly
at the outset of his reflections on the various rhetorical discourses spoken to that point (261eff). For now, we are alerted to the fact that in trying to explain an account in mythic form, probability will be the best
that can be achieved. If therefore the cleverness of this kind of explanation parallels the cleverness of Lysias' speech we are about to hear, then
it is equivalent to an account which is superficially attractive but without requisite metaphysical depth.[5]

Socrates and the Possibility of Self-knowledge

Socrates does not have the leisure to pursue this kind of investigation
because he does not yet, as the Delphic motto has it, know himself. It

is, in fact, ridiculous to examine these things; instead, Socrates accepts what is "customary" concerning them and investigates a more fundamental question: whether Socrates is a "beast" more complex and furious than the Typhon or a gentler and simpler "animal" naturally sharing in a "divine" destiny (230a–b). Consider how Socrates describes the two extremes—(a) he may be a beast like the Typhon, a hundred-headed monster of hybrid origin (in this respect similar to the Gorgon, etc.), blown up with pride in self, who was eventually conquered by Zeus and thrown into Tartarus.[6] In the *Republic* (IX, 588c), the lower part of man's nature is compared to a many-headed monster, some heads resembling tame creatures and others wild ones. The multiplicity of heads indicates that this diversity is guided by some kind of intelligence, but the wildness of the appetites controlling some of the heads suggests that the creature is, as Socrates has already said, essentially a beast (θηρίον). But if a beast, then how can Socrates, a human being (indeed, a philosopher!), include this as a real possibility for determining his own nature? (b) At the other extreme, Socrates sees himself as perhaps an animal, a living thing (ζῷον) sharing in a divine destiny. This possibility represents a polar extreme to that of (a). Thus, the divine aspect, whatever its precise character, establishes a hierarchy with this end uppermost and the other end at the nadir.

Note, however, that neither extreme is specifically human—the low end is represented as a beast, the high end as a living thing. This point is important because it suggests that these terms are metaphysical *termina* for a continuum of possibilities. The beast is a human beast just as the living thing is a living human thing, but Socrates wants to emphasize that both are extreme possibilities, hence his use of more inclusive terms to name them.

When therefore Socrates says that he accepts the Boreas myth, and presumably all other existing myths, according to what is customary, he does not mean either that he ignores these myths or that he does not believe in allegorizing them. What he means is that only if he knows himself in a certain way—between the extremes of beast and living thing—will he be able to confront a myth to see what the myth conveys according to a fundamental metaphysical configuration in light of which all such narratives should be assessed. Socrates is pointing to the fact, only inchoate at this point in the day's conversation, that the capacity to know nature in all of its forms ultimately rests on how much soul can recoup of the knowledge that (as the palinode will explain) was bestowed on soul prior to birth. Socrates accepts what is customary about the myths as the point of departure for systematic scrutiny based on a knowledge of reality and how that knowledge may require transmutation into a mythic dimension when soul becomes the animator of body. In sum, the introduction of the Boreas myth and its connection to the need for self-knowledge, when seen in an appropriate metaphysical context, effectively circumscribes the vast narrative boundaries of the *Phaedrus* as a whole.

Beauty and the Nourishment of Discourses

As soon as Socrates and Phaedrus arrive at the place Phaedrus has suggested for reading the speech, Socrates bursts into praise of its natural beauty. This description, carefully arranged from sky to earth and divided according to the external senses, is characterized, as De Vries notes (pp. 56–7), by a great display of rhetorical finesse. The majestic plane tree spreads its branches, an adjacent willow is "very beautiful" and issues a "most fragrant" scent. The spring flowing by the tree is very pleasing and the water is "very cool" to the touch of Socrates' foot. Also, the place seems sacred, belonging to some nymphs and Achelous, since there are statues to them nearby. The air is lovely in its breeziness and with the sound of the cicadas and their chirruping music. But the "most pleasing" feature is the grass, "perfectly fine" for reclining one's head for reading. Socrates congratulates Phaedrus for his most excellent guidance to this wondrous place (230b–c).

The beauty of this setting is vividly portrayed. A tall willow now complements the plane tree visible from some distance away, and the willow provides beauty of fragrance. The feel of the water on Socrates' foot is also refreshing, and with the breeze and the sound of the cicadas, the setting radiates beauty to the senses of sight, touch, and hearing. This sensory suffusion of beauty quickens Socrates' inborn sensitivity to this quality (although, as we shall see shortly, it is a sensitivity with certain limitations). Socrates may be a relative stranger to the wonders of nature, but he is no stranger to beauty, whatever form its sensible manifestations may assume. The omnipresence of beauty provides a continual sensory counterpoint to the progressively more elaborate and elevated mythic and philosophical discourse that will mark the advance of the day's discussion.

Phaedrus remarks that Socrates seems more like a stranger than a native; in fact, it seems to Phaedrus that Socrates does not go outside the walls at all. Socrates explains that he is a "lover of learning" and that country places and trees do not teach him anything, whereas people do. Nonetheless, Phaedrus seems to have found the "drug" which will entice Socrates away from the city and its inhabitants. Just as hungry animals are led by leaves or fruit, so Socrates is attracted by speeches "in books," to the point of following their lead all over Attica (230d–e).

Socrates has just said that he does not yet know himself (230a); now, however, he describes himself as a lover of learning. To love learning and to love wisdom are often taken as synonymous, but in view of Socrates' avowed lack of self-knowledge, we should understand the love of learning as the desire to become aware of what must be known to be wise. In short, love of learning is a necessary condition for love of wisdom.

A distinction of this sort is further suggested by Socrates' next remark, i.e., that he is like an animal lured by speeches in books. If Socrates is a lover of learning, then he can also be "drugged" by the appeal of written discourse, so much so that he is reduced to the level of an animal. This metaphor takes on added meaning in view of the range of possibilities Socrates had just introduced in his supposed lack of self-knowledge, a range bounded by lower animate beings. Thus, even if he is a lover of learning, his own nature is sufficiently complex to encompass an animal-like desire for speeches. The fact that these speeches are conveyed in books, i.e., in writing, renders this desire all the more antagonistic to the love of learning given the strictures against writing which Socrates will lay down later, after the heat of the rhetoric has subsided. To crave speeches is one thing, to crave written records of speeches is quite another—Socrates is seemingly affected with both desires.

It is not the case, as Phaedrus' remarks suggests, that Socrates has never left the city,[7] but the fact that Socrates has done so now additionally proves how his sickness for discourses has dislocated his habitual behavior. Socrates, lover of discourses, has been led to a place of great natural beauty by the promise of hearing a speech about love read to him. The rhetorical arena has been defined, and Socrates is about to enter the first engagement in the lists of love waged in the *Phaedrus*.

The Speech of Lysias

The speech of Lysias is, in one sense, the structural pivot of the dialogue. Socrates will compete with it rhetorically, recant this speech with another one, much longer and considerably more complex, then stand back from these rhetorical displays and analyze how rhetoric in general should be pursued if all such efforts are to be true and successful.

Whether or not this speech is in fact by Lysias has been debated since antiquity. It is obvious, but nonetheless worth noting, that Plato—the Shakespeare of classical letters—could imitate virtually any style (as the *Symposium* well attests). But whatever the truth may be in this regard, the relevant question for interpreting the *Phaedrus* is how the speech fits the structure of the dialogue. For even if the speech is by Lysias, it must cohere organically with the other parts of the *Phaedrus* if the dialogue as a whole is to display the unity incumbent upon a work of good writing.[8]

The speech may be summarized as an attempt to show an individual who is the object of erotic desire that he should grant sexual favors to someone who does not love him rather than to someone who does. A number of reasons are presented to justify this thesis. These reasons, randomly deployed (according to Socratic principles of rhetoric), are narrowly pragmatic, deriving from a notion of the beloved's well-being calculated in terms of the social and economic utility of love.[9]

Lysias' speech is philosophically arresting as much for what it does not say, i.e., its unconsidered assumptions, as for what it does. This foundational instability reveals the lover (posing as a nonlover) articulating various courses of action which bespeak rationality, or at least a kind of calm practicality, while counseling consent to desires which are, as a rule, unique in their intensity. Thus, from the standpoint of principles, the speech of Lysias is based on a fragmented understanding of the relation between rationality and desire. We shall see Socrates ground this relation more securely—but still inadequately—in his first speech; he will then complete the metaphysical underpinning for this relation in his great second speech. Later, Socrates will note that some points in Lysias' speech warrant further study (once the initial premise of the speech has been altered). These points will be cited, whenever possible, in subsequent discussion of Socrates' speeches.

Although this sketch of Lysias' speech clearly does not do justice to either its length or its apparently feasible counsel, it must suffice from the standpoint of treating it as a protometaphysical document.[10]

At the start of the day's discussion, Socrates had requested to hear the conversation between Phaedrus and Lysias; the fact that Phaedrus recounts just Lysias' speech suggests that Phaedrus himself asked few if any questions, but simply had the speech reread and then acquired a copy of it for his own future recitation. The implication is that Phaedrus found the content satisfactory, perhaps persuasive. Socrates does not share this reaction, and his response to the speech is subtle and complex.

The Conditions of Praiseworthy Discourse

Phaedrus glows with pleasure as his recitation of Lysias' speech concludes. Is it not marvelous, he asks, especially in its language? More than that, Socrates says—the speech is miraculous, indeed quite overwhelming. However, this reaction was caused by Phaedrus reading the speech, not by the speech itself. Socrates assumed that Phaedrus knew more than he about speeches, and simply went along with him, following the divine spokesman in this "Bacchic" rhetorical frenzy (234d).

Phaedrus is bemused, as it were, by the supposed excellence of Lysias' speech. But the feature of this speech which aroused his condition is its language, its names (ὀνόμασιν). Phaedrus has been more affected by the choice of vocabulary than by the way that vocabulary was ordered and, more importantly, by how that vocabulary represents "the truth." Socrates would have us see him—Phaedrus' audience—even more swept away, so much so that his description of the narration appeals to divinity as a primary factor in causing this reaction. It was, literally, the "divine head" (θείας κεφαλῆς) of Phaedrus which led Socrates to share in a kind of Bacchic frenzy, recalling his apt prediction that Phaedrus would lead him with discourse in a Corybantic revel (228c) and anticipating the mythic description of soul's "head" as, in company with a god, it peers above the rim of the heavens to see "the things that are" (248a). If Socrates is not wholly ironical here, the point illustrates his self-analysis that he is indeed sick with love of discourse, since he can be so affected not just by discourse, but also by its reciter, especially if the speaker is rapturously enthusiastic for that speech.

Phaedrus is put off by Socrates' bantering, and challenges him in the name of the "god of friendship" to tell whether he thinks any of the Greeks could speak better or longer on the same subject (234e). Phaedrus believes that the speech of Lysias excels in every relevant respect, i.e., both in length and quality. Furthermore, this challenge encompasses not only Athenian orators, but anyone in Athens or indeed any of the Greeks. If Socrates can surpass this speech, then Socrates will best not only Lysias but anyone aspiring to rhetorical excellence. For Phaedrus, the speech of Lysias sets the standard for such excellence; to improve on it would, apparently, require a superhuman effort—precisely the kind Socrates will provide.

Surprised by the intensity of Phaedrus' reaction, Socrates asks whether the speech should be praised because its author has said what he ought or because the words are "clear and well-turned and elegant." If the latter, then Socrates will grant the point, but only on Phaedrus' word, since Socrates himself did not notice what, for Phaedrus, constituted the special fineness of the language. Socrates was attending only to the sense of the speech's rhetoric. And, he says, even Lysias would not think this sense adequate. For, unless Phaedrus wants to disagree, Lysias said the same thing two or three times, as if he could not think up many things to say about one topic and as if he were showing off a youthful ability to say the same thing in two different and stylistically impressive ways. The shocked Phaedrus says that Socrates speaks nonsense. For in fact, Lysias has omitted nothing that belongs to the subject; as a result, no one could speak on that subject longer or more worthily (235a–b).

Phaedrus has said that the speech was especially fine in its language. If, however, Phaedrus has misinterpreted the sense of the speech in terms of what it "ought" to have said, then the language of the speech might not have the pretty properties which Phaedrus believed it possesses and which Socrates, interpreting Phaedrus' reaction to the speech, has made explicit. Socrates' evaluation implies that sound must be wedded to sense in order for the whole speech to be truly fine. Socrates shows that he has a facility for specifying the rhetorical attributes of supposedly "good" speaking, but his assessment suggests reservations concerning Phaedrus' own conviction.

Socrates' attention was directed only to the sense of the speech "with respect to its rhetoric." The sense of the speech is its *nous* (νοῦν) while the counterpart dimension which Phaedrus had offered earlier to relate to Socrates as a surrogate for reciting the entire speech is its *dianoia* (διάνοιαν—228d). Although sense here may be taken as a popular expression indicating only that Socrates knows what the speech means, there is a subtle philosophical dimension present as well. The suggestion is that Socrates has seen further into the speech than Phaedrus even though he has heard it but once, the extent of his more profound vision reflecting the epistemological contrast between *nous* and *dianoia* (as implied in the *Phaedo* and developed more explicitly in the *Republic*). The fact that Socrates was analyzing Lysias' rhetoric from this perspective thus raises the possibility that he can situate all that usually passes for rhetoric in relation to more fundamental metaphysical concerns (even if they must be developed in a mythic mode). This contrast between Socratic *nous* and Phaedrean *dianoia* describes two distinct approaches to the meaning of one speech, and anticipates a related development in the metaphysical hierarchy presented in the mythic portion of Socrates' second speech.

When Socrates offers his initial critique of the speech's rhetoric, he says that Lysias himself would not think it sufficient in this regard. But how can Socrates attribute such a patently self-destructive assessment to Lysias if in fact Lysias wrote the speech? Surely if Lysias, one of the premier rhetoricians in Greece, would not have thought that its rhetoric was adequate, then he would have either withdrawn this speech or written another one. It appears then that this implication tells against the supposed authenticity of the speech. This is shown by having Socrates say that if Lysias (i.e., the real Lysias) were to examine the speech (attributed to Lysias but actually written by Plato), then even he would not agree that its style was rhetorically sound. This interplay encompasses Lysias as author and Lysias as critic, with Plato serving as both author (in the manner of Lysias) and critic (in the persona of Socrates). It may also be inferred that Plato did not intend to demean the real Lysias' reputation as a rhetorician, since if the speech were indeed as formally inadequate as Socrates will designate, then the real Lysias would hardly promulgate such a poor effort.

The Inspiration of Socrates

Phaedrus' disagreement with Socrates' criticism is unequivocal—no one, he says, could speak abut Lysias' topic more or better, i.e., with respect to both the length and the quality of the discourse. But Socrates does not agree with this evaluation. He feels certain that wise men and women from the past have spoken and written about these things in a way which will refute Lysias' speech. Phaedrus wants to know who they are and where Socrates has heard such discourse. Socrates cannot answer directly, but he insists that he must have heard something, either from Sappho "the beautiful" or Anacreon "the wise" or from some of the prose writers. His justification is that he senses his bosom swelling with another speech, different from Lysias' but no less good. And since Socrates knows his own ignorance, he could not have formed the speech himself; he must have been filled with it through his ears, like a pitcher, from another source. But because of his denseness, he has forgotten how and from whom he heard it (235b–d).

Hackforth remarks (p. 36) that the identification of Socrates' inspiration as Sappho or Anacreon or a prose writer is "not to be taken seriously."[11] But this dismissal is premature, since although the precise historical authorship may not be intended seriously, the matter of the origin of speeches, i.e., their inspiration and sanctioning power, will be important in determining the soundness of Socrates' own speeches and, ultimately, of the possibility of achieving truth in rhetoric.

Socrates has acknowledged that he is a lover of learning (φιλομαθής) but at this moment he professes his ignorance (ἀμαθίαν) of the matters dealt with in Lysias' speech. The burgeoning speech Socrates feels has filled him through his ears, as if his mind were little more than an empty pitcher awaiting substance of some sort. This ignorance may be seen to follow from his lack of self-knowledge confessed to at 229e, an implication rendering the speech he is about to declaim all the more detached and impersonal, since it could hardly have come from someone afflicted with such ignorance. Furthermore, if Socrates knew what was said in the past about love, he could do so either from hearsay, by a sort of oral tradition, or (more likely) from some written record. The latter possibility testifies to the importance of writing in preserving past language, and signals the dependency of speech on writing insofar as writing stabilizes language as a record of discourse.

The Premise of Socrates' First Speech

Phaedrus does not care where this speech comes from, but he definitely wants to hear a better speech than the one in the book, a speech no shorter and different. However, Socrates hastens to note that Lysias has not failed entirely, a possibility which, he adds, would not befall even the worst writer. If, for example, one were to argue, as Lysias has, that the nonlover should be favored over the lover, then praising the nonlover's wisdom and blaming the lover's unreason are necessary arguments. In this case, only the formal arrangement of the arguments would be laudatory, not their invention. But for arguments not required by a given premise and thus hard to invent, both invention and arrangement would deserve praise. Phaedrus agrees with this qualification and, as a result, he allows Socrates to begin with the premise that the lover is "more sick" than the nonlover (235d–236b).

Phaedrus cannot change the original premise of the speech altogether, for then there would be no basis for comparing Lysias' speech with that of Socrates to determine which was better. Thus, Socrates must be granted a concession in order to produce at least some different arguments than those offered in Lysias' speech. Socrates is now in a position both to invent new arguments to support Lysias' thesis and to rearrange the arguments that appeared in that speech in order to strengthen their rhetorical persuasiveness. And, in fact, Socrates will not only reorder Lysias' speech, but he will also establish a rudimentary methodology, psychology, and metaphysics as a basis for that reordering and for the new notions developed in his own speech.

Phaedrus' Threat and the Socratic Character

Socrates now reacts as if Phaedrus has been taking him seriously. But, Socrates insists, he has been only teasing Phaedrus and would never attempt to surpass the "wisdom" in Lysias' speech with something "more colorful." Phaedrus immediately challenges Socrates to speak as well as he can, lest the two fall into the game of *tu quoque* and Phaedrus be compelled to taunt Socrates with the same accusations Socrates had aimed at him prior to Phaedrus reading him the speech of Lysias.

This reversed opposition recalls the reversal when Phaedrus led Socrates outside the walls and then Socrates led Phaedrus along the banks of the Ilissus. Now Phaedrus compels Socrates to speak, just as earlier Socrates had compelled Phaedrus to repeat Lysias' speech. The notion of opposition, a crucial underpinning in the metaphysics of the *Phaedrus*, is also central to its dramatic interplay. Zeno could show that opposites go one way, then the other, and Plato stages the drama according to the same oscillating opposition. Phaedrus' compulsion and the reference to the *tu quoque* game have an aura of play, just as opposites can, at a conceptual level, "playfully" (and confusingly) be made to become their own opposites. But Phaedrus is serious about this game, no less serious than the attempt to ground opposition in a more comprehensive and stable metaphysical reality.

Phaedrus warns Socrates that he must make up his mind to speak what he felt in his breast or Phaedrus, younger and stronger, will take advantage of their solitude and literally wrest the words from him. Socrates insists that he, an amateur, will make himself ridiculous if, without preparation, he attempts to compete with a master writer on the same subject. Phaedrus now makes his final move. He will force Socrates to speak by swearing an oath, not by a god, although he momentarily intimates he might do so, but by the plane tree nearby. The oath is that unless Socrates speaks, Phaedrus will never read Socrates another speech or tell him about one. Socrates acts shaken, admitting that his intense love of discourse could never endure such a destiny. Therefore, since Phaedrus has sworn this oath and Socrates would never give up these feasts, he agrees, but on condition that he keep his head wrapped in order to get through the speech as quickly as possible and not look at Phaedrus and feel shame. Phaedrus readily accepts these conditions, for they are of little consequence to him, and he urges Socrates to speak (236b–237a).

At first, Socrates refuses to repeat the speech welling inside him, just as Phaedrus refused to repeat the speech of Lysias to him. Even when Phaedrus threatens physical force, Socrates remains unpersuaded. This reticence, not sharing what one is naturally attracted to rhetorically, should be contrasted with the closing sentiment of the dialogue, when it is said that "friends have all things in common." In true friendship, there would be no need or inclination for the coyness characterizing the relation between Phaedrus and Socrates in their early exchanges on rhetoric; it is a measure of the distance separating Phaedrus and Socrates from true friendship that they initially bandy these speeches about in this way.

The final inducement eliciting Socrates' speech is an oath Phaedrus takes. Phaedrus is flippant in identifying the support for the oath—i.e., first "some god" but finally the plane tree sheltering their resting place. This tree has been described as tall and resplendent (230b); presumably these properties represent the sanctioning power behind Phaedrus' oath. If so, then Phaedrus has replaced the divine, i.e., an indeterminate deity, with an oath based on a natural—and quite beautiful—object. In a sense then, the oath driving Socrates to fashion for his friend the speech heard from some unknown mortal source derives from Socrates' respect for, and love of, beauty.

Socrates accepts the oath by admitting that he is a lover of discourse (236e). Compelled by such love, Socrates will utter a speech, cut it short halfway through, and then, later, severely criticize it as saying nothing true or healthy (242d–e). But if Socrates were truly a lover of discourse, then he would not have allowed this love to compel him to utter such a speech. At this point, Socrates' love of discourse is unrefined, so to speak, and in this sense he continues to exemplify the fact, stated earlier, that he does not yet know himself. For if he knew himself, he would not put himself in a position where his love of discourse would result in a sin against love itself. Socrates' self-analysis shows that his lack of self-knowledge includes precisely the subject of the day's speeches. Socrates, by his own admission (in the *Symposium*) a master of the intricacies of love, must move toward a still better understanding of love in order to realize the forms of discourse worthy of love.

That Socrates nonetheless has a certain presentiment of what his speech will entail can be seen from his ploy of declaiming that speech with his head wrapped. This dramatic gambit has both active and passive repercussions. Actively, Socrates will not see Phaedrus—his audience, friend, and an exemplar of youthfulness and fine appearance, nor will he see the natural beauty abounding in their locale. Socrates therefore speaks about love in a certain way while concurrently shutting off his vision, the main sensory avenue toward the recognition of beauty, the primary instigator of love (cf. 250d). Passively, the face of Socrates will not be seen by Phaedrus, and the resulting speech will come floating from, in a sense, an anonymous source (reflecting its unknown origin of inspiration). If another traveler chanced by, only the discourse itself could be heard, with presumably all attention focused on that speech—and its merits and weaknesses—rather than on the identity and personality of its speaker. Socrates is afraid of making a bad showing, but only because of the derivative degree of inspiration which moved him to make the challenge in the first place. He knows this wisdom will be better than that embodied in Lysias' speech, but he has presentiments that it will not do justice to its subject matter—love.[12]

Given his masqueraded lack of identity, why then does Socrates feel shame? According to Hackforth, "the shame that Socrates really feels is, as transpires later (234B), due to having been forced to adopt an unworthy conception of love" (p. 35, n4). But at this point (237a), Socrates does not know that the conception of love is unworthy. When the speech is over, Socrates will describe (242c–d) how his natural ability as a seer had made its presence felt from the inception of the speech, and that something troubled him throughout its declamation. But only after his *daimon* warns him does Socrates realize the nature of that wrong—a sin against love. Thus, the reason for Socrates' shame must be pursued anew, for at this point Socrates did not know that he would sin this way.[13]

Socrates agrees to give what will turn out to be a sinful speech because Phaedrus threatened to cut off his supply of speeches. For Socrates, this consequence is unthinkable (or so he would have us believe). By his own admission, Socrates can be carted around Greece like a hungry animal before a carrot if volumes of speeches are dangled before him (230d–e). He is, in a word, "sick" with love of discourse (228b). I suggest therefore that Socrates' shame is caused by the fact that he has allowed his love of discourses to overpower his natural modesty as far as being a competent, much less skilled, speechmaker. Socrates has said that he feels he can speak a better speech than that of Lysias; but just because it is better, it does not follow that the speech is any good, i.e., that it says the truth. By risking such a speech (thereby preserving his potential store of speeches from Phaedrus), Socrates has reduced himself to the level of an animal hungrily seeking sustenance, an exemplar of the lower end of the spectrum of possibilities registering the presently indeterminate character of Socrates' nature (230a).

It should be emphasized that this reduction will follow *regardless what Socrates says in his speech*; the mere consent to give it renders him animalistic in his own eyes. Such a decision is singularly inappropriate from a man who (according to Socrates) Phaedrus believes is wise (237b). Socrates is not wise in consenting to give the speech, and realizing that he has been driven to give it anyway is why he now feels shame. Furthermore, Socrates does not want to shame the beauty in Phaedrus and nature, nor does he want to shame Phaedrus as friend and philosopher—as it happens, both beauty and friendship will be violated by the letter of what he is about to say concerning love.

CHAPTER 2

Socrates' First Speech (237b–244a)

The first speech of Socrates will be, according to his self-critique, a sinful exercise. But what Socrates says of Lysias' speech also applies to his own rhetorical effort, i.e., much in it is worth considering. In fact, much in it is worth imitating once the appropriate metaphysical perspective has been secured and extended. This chapter presents the key metaphysical features of the speech.

At 266a, in discussing the need for method in rhetoric, Socrates says that his first speech followed the method of collection and division in defining a "left-handed" kind of love. The fact that this speech embodies a method justifies analyzing it in light of that method (as subsequently described) in order to show how the speech's structure and content anticipate the more expanded metaphysics underlying that method (and developed in Socrates' second speech). If read in this way, the first speech becomes—even as it sins—considerably more metaphysically perceptive than it appears initially.

Socrates' First Speech—Invocation

Socrates begins his speech by invoking the Muses, in the same breath offering some etymological speculation concerning whether the name for the clarity they bestow comes from the form of their song or from

the race of the Lygians, who were reportedly very musical.[1] This
etymology anticipates the related discussion in the second speech,
when Socrates speaks of those in the past who gave names to things
(244c). In that speech, Socrates criticizes the current changes in names
from those given by the ancients, implying that it is somehow important to preserve the original names—if they indicate the truth. In the
case at hand, Socrates wavers concerning the origin of the word describing the clarity of the Muses. Note, however, that the appeal is
either to the form (εἶδος) of their song or to the race (γένος) of the Ly-
gian people, i.e., in either case, to general characteristics. The suggestion is that correct etymology must be based on relations between
words and realities of a certain metaphysical shape.

Socrates asks the clear-voiced Muses only to go "with" him to aid
in narrating this speech. Strictly speaking then, the Muses may not be
Socrates' sole source of inspiration. And since the Muses are not invoked before the second speech, it may be that their powers of inspiration are limited because a discourse about love in the highest sense
must be inspired by a source altogether higher than the Muses.[2]

In this introduction, Socrates describes the entire speech as a myth
(μύθου—237a), and he will use the same designation when the speech
concludes (μῦθος—241e). By comparison, only part of the second
speech is identified as mythic. This concerted description of the first
speech is significant in view of the earlier discussion of the Boreas
myth. Socrates said then that he accepted myths in their customary
sense until such time as he had secured knowledge of self. Thus, the
sense of the first speech, as a myth, will depend on the extent to which
Socrates has achieved self-knowledge before, and during, its presentation. And there is evidence that he has not mastered himself in this regard, since he ventures this speech only because Phaedrus swore to cut
off the nourishment Socrates receives from discourses, whether read or
declaimed. Also, Socrates has agreed to repeat what he felt to be wisdom from an unrecollected source—but he will soon admit that this repetition contributed to his shame. The level of wisdom tapped by this
speech is therefore more inchoate than explicit. By calling the first
speech a myth, Socrates alerts us to the need to examine it, and to iden-

tify whatever "wise" notions in that speech will require additional analysis.[3]

Rhetorical Setting

The characters in Socrates' speech are sketched in a preamble, apparently essential to the whole speech.

There was once a boy, or young man, of great beauty, who had many lovers. Among these lovers was an individual of singular slyness who, although as much in love with the boy as any of the other lovers, had made the boy believe that he was not in love with him. He then attempted to persuade the boy that his favors would be granted to the nonlover rather than to the lover (237b). This strategy is tactically shrewd. If the loved one is persuaded to favor only the nonlover, then he will favor that *one* of his lovers who has appeared in the guise of a nonlover. This lover will then win the prize over all other lovers precisely by posing persuasively as a nonlover.

But the paradox underlying this set of circumstances quickly becomes evident: the beloved will be loved by a "nonloving" lover. In making explicit what is implicit in the setting of Lysias' speech, Socrates brings out the falseness of the situation, a falseness which may be connected to the rhetorically haphazard manner in which the Lysian lover attempted to make his case. Viewed abstractly, the nonlover is a living embodiment of the unity of opposites, i.e., loving and nonloving, since his words espouse nonlove over love while his nature and (if his speech is successful) his actions exemplify being in love (i.e., the "nonlover's" understanding of love).

Argument and Definition

Addressing the "dear boy" in the guise of the nonloving lover, Socrates insists that there is only one way to begin to converse well. One must know what the counsel incorporated into the conversation concerns. Most people lack such knowledge, but do not realize that they lack it. As a result, they are not in concert from the beginning of their inquiry, and they end up agreeing neither with each other nor with themselves. To avoid such confusion, Socrates suggests that they agree on a definition of love, what it is and its power, and keep it in view throughout their investigation of whether love brings advantage or harm (237c–d).

The first speech introduces the need for methodological considerations essential for successfully pursuing reasoned discussion. Failing to establish a definition at the outset results in disagreement not only between the views of the discussants but also within each participant. Such disagreement will tell against success in inquiry, since the contesting views do not meet on common ground. And, more fundamentally, this lack of agreement entails that each participant will have internally incompatible views (quite apart from any incompatibility arising between views of two people).

Division between Lover and Nonlover

Socrates begins to define love by asserting that "it is evident to all" that love is a desire and it is also just as clear that nonlovers desire beautiful things. How then, Socrates asks, to distinguish between lover and nonlover? Socrates grounds this distinction by claiming that in each of us there are, necessarily, two ruling principles which we follow wherever they lead. The first is the natural desire for pleasure, the second is acquired opinion which intends the best. Sometimes these principles, varying in power in relation to one another, agree and sometimes they disagree (237d–e).

In the recapitulation of his two speeches, Socrates asserts that the first speech divided "madness" (*paranoias*) until, eventually, it found a left-handed type of love (266a). The implication is that the definition of this kind of love required a series of divisions; if we examine the speech at this point, however, we discern a series of collections as well. This should not occasion surprise. The recapitulation at 266a is only the barest outline of how collection and division animated Socrates' rhetoric, and closer study will demonstrate the complex presence of the method in the first speech.[4]

Love was spoken of in terms of desire (ἐπιθυμίας) at the very out-set of Lysias' speech (231a). Socrates borrows this notion, but not without significant amplication; first, he situates love as a (τις) desire, suggesting that other types of desire may exist, and second, he prefaces this claim with the proviso that "it is evident to all." Although Socrates' claim is stronger than Lysias since it is a view which, we are told, everyone maintains, the fact that it is an opinion immediately suggests that whatever will be inferred from this claim can never reach beyond opinion. It is equally evident, Socrates then contends, that nonlovers also desire what is beautiful. This claim, no less universal than the first, is also qualified as an opinion. But this qualification does not hin-der Socrates from juxtaposing both opinions, then inferring that this juxtaposition requires distinguishing between the lover and the non-lover. What forces this distinction? It is precisely the "gathering of dis-persed particulars," i.e., the opinions, shared by all, concerning the nature of love and nonlove. And what is discerned from such gathering is desire—the feature common to both opinions. The subsequent in-quiry will therefore focus on desire as the reality, tantamount to if not explicitly understood as a Form, which must be analyzed in order to secure a definition of love. And Socrates has also shown something about opinion—that stockpiled opinions may become subject to incon-sistency. A higher mode of knowledge based on a higher kind of reality must be secured in order to avoid this difficulty.

In order to establish the difference between love and nonlove, Soc-rates must divide something to show how the desire of a lover differs from the desire of a nonlover. The next step then is another collection, i.e., Socrates gathers dispersed pluralities "in each of us" to secure a range of reality universal in scope and appropriate for distinguishing between the desire of lover and nonlover. The necessity in seeing (νοῆθαι) these characteristics is required because Socrates is now ex-amining something, human nature, that possesses a structure with a unity analogous to that of a Form, and he must "see" this kind of unity in order to be capable of dividing it in such a way as to distinguish love from nonlove. The necessity is dictated by the collection phase of the method; the seeing is the kind of cognition that discerns unity from gathering dispersed particulars. The presence of implied methodology thus continues to be felt.

What Socrates sees "in us" are two principles, the inborn desire for pleasure and an acquired opinion aiming for the best. To translate *idea* as principle seems appropriate, since each *idea* is multifold and involves generation of some sort. There is, however, an important metaphysical dimension in the term which should not be overlooked. For Socrates is, in fact, dividing that unity which is human nature, what is "in us," according to the technical sense of nature defined at 270d.[5]

An initial clue that Socrates is pursuing the technical sense of nature appears in his description of the desire for pleasure as inborn or ἔμφυτος, a cognate of nature, *phusis*. Second, the fact that Socrates names each of the principles in us as an *idea* conveys the high degree of generality on which this division has been secured. These principles are realities which, although complex, are definite and in some respects unchanging, thus resembling Forms. Third, Socrates has divided human nature into two *ideas*, again following the procedure given at 270d, which states that the various parts of a thing's nature must be enumerated. Finally, the next step asserts that the two principles sometimes agree, disagree, and vary in power—in short, Socrates outlines how they act and are acted upon with respect to each other, another essential characteristic in determining a thing's nature (270d).

The fact that the desire for pleasure is inborn whereas opinion leading toward the best is only acquired suggests that the pleasure principle is more fundamental than the epistemic principle, a decidedly unplatonic position and a clue that this characterization of human nature is fundamentally incomplete. And if we take into account the objects of pleasure Socrates will mention shortly—food, drink, etc.—the reason for this incompleteness becomes clear, for the human nature Socrates is analyzing here is essentially embodied. But in his second speech, Socrates will define a human nature strictly in terms of soul, apart from any relation to body. The point is apparently that pleasure is inborn to us, if the "us" in question is soul-cum-body. If, however, human nature can be understood as just soul, then it is possible that the pleasures sought for will, for metaphysical reasons, differ from those attracting the human being as embodied.

Desire and Predication

Socrates now contrasts the functions of the two principles. When opinion leads toward the best through reason, then its name is temperance; when desire leads against reason toward pleasure and rules in us, its name is "excess." Excess itself has many names, for it has many parts and many Forms. Whichever Form chances to be dominant gives its name, a name neither beautiful nor worthy, to the individual who has it. If, for example, desire for food prevails over the best and the other desires, the one who has this desire is called a glutton; similarly, it is obvious what to call someone tyrannized by desire for drink. And, Socrates concludes, it is very obvious what names will always be given when desires such as these begin to rule (238a–b).

This phase of the speech produces two new realities—temperance and excess. These realities result from collecting the two principles in us and then examining the collection in terms of characteristics defined by the technical sense of determining the nature of something. The emphasis on naming should also be noted; Socrates continues to analyze desire and its relation to love in terms of the predicational mode, i.e., on a level of formality. Thus, the type of excess which is dominant "gives its name" to the one who has it—drunkenness gives its name to a drunkard—thereby confirming, by predication, the reality of that Form of excess on the being who participates in it.

Temperance and excess have been established by way of collection and nature, and Socrates continues to apply methodological considerations, now by dividing excess. According to Socrates, excess has many Forms and many parts. The distinction may be explained as follows: Excess is itself a Form. If excess is divided, then the results of this division are parts of excess. Thus, gluttony is part of excess, drunkenness is part of excess, etc. Excess, as one Form, will have as many parts as there are types of excess capable of being divided from that unity. Now gluttony exists as a part (of excess); but gluttony can also exist in its own right. In this sense then, gluttony is also a Form, itself capable of being divided. When therefore Socrates says that *hubris* has many parts and many Forms, he is referring to divisions of a Form from two distinct perspectives. The results of division constitute the many parts of the Form divided; but these parts are Forms when they are considered by themselves.

Hubris thus illustrates what the *Phaedrus* will refer to as a nature, i.e., a formal unity with a complex metaphysical constitution. The present distinction between Forms and parts anticipates the doctrine of natures articulated later, in the discussion of rhetoric; in fact, drawing this distinction illustrates an essential feature of that doctrine at an especially crucial juncture. For it is the nature of *hubris* that will determine the definition of love on which the rest of Socrates' first speech depends.[6]

A Definition of Love

The rationale for what has been said before is clear, Socrates says, but all things are more evident when said than when unsaid. With this proviso in mind, he now defines love: desire without reason which pursues the pleasures of beauty and, mastering opinion striving for the right, has been strengthened by other desires akin to it to seek bodily beauty—this strength gives that desire its name, love (238c). According to this definition, the desire for pleasure and beauty is connected to other desires like it—e.g., the desire for the pleasure of food and drink—and the resulting strength, a merger of all such desires, gives its name to the desire for one kind of reality—the beauty of bodies. If true, this merger would help explain the often overwhelming intensity of that kind of physical desire, and also the quality of its pleasure when fulfilled.

Socrates and the Inspiration of Madness

But at precisely the point when Socrates has defined love, he interrupts the speech to ask Phaedrus whether it seems to him, as it does to Socrates, that he is possessed by a divine condition. Socrates insists that their location by the Ilissus is filled with the divine, so that his discourse will often seem inspired, especially since he is already voicing dithyrambs. Phaedrus is the cause of this rhetorical excess, or so Socrates claims, and Socrates adjures him to listen silently in the hope that perhaps the attack will be stayed—assuming that god cares to effect things in this way. And with this, Socrates returns to his initial exercise in rhetoric (238d).

Later in the discussion, Socrates describes himself as mad during both his first and second speeches (265a). But how was he mad in his first speech? Socrates has warned Phaedrus to expect an inspired frenzy, given that he is already speaking dithyrambically. The word for frenzy is νυμφόλυπτος, and the allusion to the Nymphs reappears in what turns out to be the end of the first speech, when Socrates tells Phaedrus that he has transcended dithyrambs, slid into hexameters, and that if he proceeds to praise the nonlover, he will be "possessed by the Nymphs" to whom Phaedrus has exposed him (241e). Also recall that at the outset of the speech, Socrates invoked the assistance of the Muses. If therefore the first speech can be connected with the Muses, then Socrates' description of himself as mad while uttering that speech is justified, since the Muses are listed in the second speech as one of the divine sources of madness.

It would appear then that the reason for the interruption was to show Phaedrus that Socrates was inspired by poetic madness. Note, however, that according to the second speech, the madness of poetry is only one type of madness. Three other types of madness are also distinguished in that speech.

a. The first division of madness is that of prophecy (244b–d). Now at 238d, during his interruption of the first speech, Socrates predicts that he will be in an even greater poetic frenzy. Furthermore, Socrates says later (242c) that he is a prophet—although not a very serious one. Therefore, Socrates verifies possessing the first type of madness, since he will fulfill his prediction by moving from dithyrambs (238b–c) to hexameters (241a).

b. The second type of madness is that of purification from illness or excess through prayers and services to the gods (244e). And at the same moment in the interruption (238d), Socrates calls on god to act lest he be overtaken by the possession which has already seized him. This appeal is certainly prayerful, if not itself a prayer. As such, it illustrates awareness of the efficacy of the second kind of madness, and Socrates' hope that this condition will be instilled in him as he continues to speak.

c. As we have seen, Socrates is also poetically inspired insofar as poetry depends on the Muses, thus illustrating that he has the third type of madness distinguished in the second speech.

d. Finally, Socrates interrupts the speech immediately after he has defined love. But this definition was secured after applying collection and division, an application explicitly identified by Socrates during his recapitulation of the speeches at 266a–b. Now the fourth type of madness analyzed in the second speech will be the madness of love. And being possessed by this madness includes the ability to collect dispersed perceptions under one idea, or Form. If therefore Socrates was inspired in the second speech and if this inspiration resulted (in part) in the statement and application of collection and division, then Socrates was also inspired by the same type of madness in his first speech when he applied that method to determine (albeit sinfully) the nature of love.

The reason Socrates interrupts the first speech where he does now becomes more evident. Socrates completes his definition of love at 238c4. The interruption concludes at 238d6. Between 238c4 and 238d6. Socrates has given examples of all four types of madness to be introduced and discussed later, in the second speech. Thus, the first speech—including the interruption—anticipates the complete range of madness derived in the second speech. From this standpoint, even if Socrates has violated rhetorical canons by interrupting his first speech, Plato repairs this structural rift by integrating that interruption into the larger context of madness insofar as madness grounds the divisions of the second speech within an extended metaphysics. The first speech, when read as part of the whole dialogue, is therefore no less organically whole than the second.

The Speech Continued

The subject of deliberation has been defined and now, Socrates says, we will concentrate on that definition in order to determine what advantage or harm will likely come from lover and nonlover to the one granting them favors (238e). The subsequent discussion is based on joint pairs of opposites—favors granted to lover and nonlover in terms of advantage and harm. This structure also reflects the method of determining a thing's nature, since the beloved will act by bestowing favors and then be acted upon by the lover (or nonlover), either to advantage or harm. The following three sections discuss excerpts from the first speech relevant to the metaphysics underlying this speech.

Beloved and Intellect

Anyone who is ruled by desire and is a slave to pleasure will necessarily make his beloved as pleasing to him as possible. To one who is "sick" in this way, everything not opposing him is pleasant, everything better or equal to him is hateful. Thus, the lover will, if possible, always make the beloved weaker and inferior. Now, in general, the ignorant is inferior to the wise, the cowardly to the manly, the poor speaker to the eloquent, the dull-witted to the bright. Such evils and still greater than these in the intellect of the loved one will necessarily give pleasure to the lover if placed in the beloved by nature; if they are not naturally present, the lover must instill them or be deprived of immediate pleasure. Finally, the lover is necessarily jealous and keeps the beloved from what would make him most wise. This is "divine philosophy" and the lover must keep the beloved from it so that the beloved will not learn to loathe the lover. The beloved must be kept in a condition of ignorance, and as a result, he must depend on the lover for everything, and become most pleasing to the lover and most harmful to himself. With respect to the intellect then, Socrates concludes that the lover is not a worthy guardian (238c–239c).

The primary reason for the harm to the beloved is that the lover will keep the beloved away from divine philosophy, a study from which the beloved will learn to despise the lover. This position has intriguing consequences. If the nonlover argues that the beloved should not go with the lover because the lover will keep him from divine philosophy, the implication is that the nonlover will permit (if not urge) the beloved to pursue philosophy. But if the beloved should discover the truth through studying philosophy, then it would appear that the beloved would indeed despise the lover, but only because the beloved realizes that the individual named as a lover (by the nonlover) was acting as a (true) nonlover would act. In addition, however, the beloved would surely challenge the nonlover to explain why he called himself a "nonlover" when in fact he would be acting as a lover should act in urging the pursuit of philosophy. It is testimony to the ingenuity of Socrates' sinful first speech that the treatment of divine philosophy not only exposes the fundamental falsity of the nonlover but also indirectly demonstrates to the beloved that love, truly understood, is better than its opposite.

Beloved and Pleasure

Socrates begins this phase of the speech with the principle that many other evils await the beloved in addition to those indicated for intellect, body, and property, but "some daimon" has mixed them with a transitory pleasure. Thus, nature has given to the flatterer, who does great harm, a pleasure not without charm; in the same way, a courtesan is pleasant but nonetheless injurious, and many other individuals and practices display such temporary pleasure.

However, the lover is not only harmful but in all respects unpleasant to the beloved. Thus, the beloved cannot anticipate even the ephemeral pleasantness characterizing the mixed types of pleasure just mentioned. Consider, Socrates says, the old adage about like things attracting, that those of the same age will share pleasures and thereby an acquired friendship. But this adage may be countered with "familiarity breeds contempt;" in these cases, such society quickly palls and the friendship so formed disappears. Furthermore, the lover, although unlike the beloved, nonetheless exhibits the strongest compulsion toward him. Driven by need, the lover, who is old, wants always to be near the beloved, who is young, so that youth may pleasure age in every sentient way. But what pleasure or assuagement can the lover give as the beloved gazes at a face stripped of beauty, youth, and other things unwholesome to hear about, much less to be compelled to come in contact with? The uncomely appearance of the lover is paralleled by the suspicious watchfulness accorded the beloved in all ways, as well as the beloved having to hear untimely yet fulsome compliments when the lover is sober and tiresome, and disgusting speech when he is awash with drink (240b–e).

The type of activities Socrates describes are, apparently, not intrinsically evil, since they have a patina of pleasure granted by a daimon. A godlike being has thus transformed evil into a good by blending pleasure with these activities. The point suggests that pleasure is itself a good, an inference derivable from the pleasure principle as part of human nature and reinforced here, when we learn that a divine agent contributes to the character of the acts in question. If, however, a daimon represents derivative divinity, then the pleasure so advocated may be correlatively derivative.

Socrates had been challenged by Phaedrus to improve formally on Lysias' speech. Lysias had mixed the disadvantages of the lover with the advantages of the nonlover; in contrast, Socrates separates these two types of reactive phenomena—his actual speech outlining the former while the unstated second part would have addressed the latter. Furthermore, Lysias presented this mixture of reactions in no set order; Socrates proceeded systematically in his treatment of topics—intellect, body, property, pleasure, and (as we shall see) dismissal of the beloved by the lover. This pattern suggests that the topics moved from most to least important, culminating in the beloved's recognition that consort with a lover (i.e., a loving "nonlover") was a mistake from the outset. The proof of this error is now stated.

Reversal of Lover and Beloved

The lover is harmful and disgusting; but when his love ends, he is false to the beloved, who hoped to receive many good things by virtue of the lover's oaths, prayers, and promises. When the time comes to discharge these promises, the lover is ruled by sense and temperance instead of love and madness, a change of which the beloved is ignorant. The beloved requests favors for what he has given, reminding the lover of what was said and done, as if conversing with the same man. The lover cannot, from shame, announce that he is now changed, nor can he keep the promises made while under a mindless rule, given that he has recovered his senses and, if continuing to act as he had, would become what he was before. He flees these things, becoming necessarily a defaulter. The beloved did not know from the start that he should not yield to a lover necessarily without sense but rather to a nonlover with sense; if the beloved did not choose in this way, the beloved would necessarily surrender himself to one harmful to him in property, body, and above all to the education of the soul, than which nothing is in truth more important, whether to humans or to gods (241a–c).

Why does Socrates say that sense and prudence replace love and madness when the lover was originally described not as mad but as sick? In reviewing his two speeches, Socrates claims that "we said that love is a kind of madness" and that there are "two kinds of madness"— (a) those arising from human sickness and (b) those from a divine release from customary habits. Thus, when Socrates says that mind and prudence replace love and madness, he means love and madness understood at this point according to (a), love as that kind of madness falling under human sickness. In terms of the psychology advanced in the first speech, this sickness is the consequence of the natural desire for pleasure overwhelming opinion aimed at the best. The subtle shift from sickness to madness does not so much anticipate the content of the second speech (as Verdenius maintains, p. 99), but rather collection and division (which, of course, partially structures the second speech). Socrates must already have in mind, if not collection and division itself, then that phase of the method which shows that the sickness he has been analyzing is a type of madness.

Mind and temperance in the reversed relation between lover and beloved are pivotal in what turns out to be the conclusion of Socrates' first speech. According to Hackforth, "it looks at first sight as though the mere dying out of passion automatically involved moral goodness and the highest level of cognition or intelligence which Plato normally—or at all events frequently—calls *nous*." Hackforth rejects this possibility as "incredible" and opts instead for reading the terms at a "popular level" of meaning (p. 48), i.e., the lover has simply come to his senses concerning the lack of wisdom in the carnal exercise he has been singlemindedly pursuing.[7]

However, these terms may be understood to represent more precise philosophical functions or capacities. The lover has changed in that he no longer loves the beloved (in the lover's original sense of love). Is this change a simple loss of desire for the beloved? If so, then it would not follow necessarily, as Socrates asserts, that the lover no longer wants to be what he was before; rather, he may well simply transfer his desire from this beloved to another one. That the lover does not want to be what he once was implies that mind and temperance must have content of some sort; the lover must know now something he did not know before, when he desired the sexual favors of the beloved, to realize that if he takes up with another beloved he becomes indistinguishable from what he was prior to this realization.

When Socrates concludes that the beloved should have chosen a nonlover with *nous* rather than a lover without it, he implies that the unstated second half of his speech would have shown how the nonlover would be preferable precisely because of behavior based on the possession of *nous*. The consensus among commentators has been that *nous* here, as elsewhere in the first speech, should be taken as "good sense" in some popular vein. Yet consider that Socrates concludes his recapitulation of the first speech by asserting that if the beloved makes the wrong choice, he must submit to someone who will have the "most harmful" effect on the education of his soul, than which in truth there neither is nor will be anything more important, whether to humans or to gods (241c). By parity of reasoning, the care of the nonlover, pursued under the aegis of *nous*, will be attentive to the education of soul in the most fundamental sense. Socrates notes that even the gods must be educated in this respect, a claim presupposing that gods have souls (a fact about their nature elaborated in the palinode), and that the care of their souls depends on what divine soul sees of *nous*. How then can the *nous* of the nonlover accomplish such an important end if it is merely random "good sense"? *Nous* must be defined therefore in a way assuring the beloved that converse with such an individual is to his ultimate well-being. This definition is not supplied in the first speech—in fact, Socrates abruptly concludes the speech at this point. But we shall see that *nous*, understood from the standpoint of the lover, will become the primary avenue of cognition—for the souls of gods as well as other types of soul—when Socrates redresses the sinful first speech with his palinode.

Socrates and Poetic Possession

These things, Socrates says to the boy, his audience, must be kept in mind; furthermore, it must be known that the lover does not undertake friendship with good will, but merely to fulfill an appetite. To illustrate the point, Socrates breaks into verse—"as the wolf loves the lamb, so the lover loves the beloved." And, suddenly, he stops. "There it is," he says to Phaedrus, enjoining his auditor not to listen to him any more and to let the speech end there. Phaedrus is surprised at this sudden conclusion, since he thought Socrates would have said as much in praise of the nonlover as he said in criticizing the lover. Socrates explains that he stopped because he had moved beyond mere dithyramb and into hexameters. If he started to praise the nonlover, what sort of poeticisms would he begin to essay? He could fall prey to the nearby Nymphs to whom Phaedrus had exposed him. Socrates then summarizes the rest of his speech—the nonlover possesses all the good traits opposed to those found in the lover. Why, he adds, make a long speech? Let his "story" end here, and at this point Socrates insists that he will cross the Ilissus rather than allow Phaedrus to impose another such rhetorical necessity upon him (241c–242a).

Later, Socrates will say that his first speech sinned against love. Now, however, the speech is arrested for another reason. Socrates has poetized that the wolf will love the lamb by consuming, thus destroying it; the parallel is that the love of this kind of lover will also destroy the beloved, at least in spirit, perhaps corporeally as well. However, in moving from almost dithyrambic discourse at the beginning of the speech into hexameters, Socrates does not want to continue the speech because of how he will speak, i.e., the purely formal mode of his discourse; presumably whatever would be said in this mode is not directly taken into account.[8]

Since Socrates does not want to risk discourse while teetering on an ungrounded level of inspiration, he summarizes the remainder of his speech. This summary is a terse exercise in opposites. And, in fact, Socrates' first speech is a study in opposites. Thus, the true lover's advantages are precisely the opposite of what Socrates ascribes to the (false) lover in his first speech. If the first-speech lover acts to the disadvantage of the beloved, then the implication is that the original definition of love really defines nonlove. The speech, in short, enunciates what a (true) lover would *not* do. To condemn the lover, as Socrates has done aping Lysias' speech, becomes to condemn the nonlover. Therefore, Socrates does not detail praising the nonlover (determined as such according to the original definition of love) because he would be, from the standpoint of truth, praising true love under the name of nonlove. If Socrates were to complete his speech following its present structure, he would consummate the reversal of opposites—his speech would, as a finished whole, condemn the lover (instead of praising the lover) and praise the nonlover (instead of condemning the nonlover).

The speech ends as it began, by Socrates calling it a *muthos*. As already noted, a discourse of this sort requires analysis and amplification, a task all the more pressing if the speech has been sinful. And his concluding threat, to cross the Ilissus rather than be forced by Phaedrus to continue, testifies to the seriousness of Socrates' intent. Their stroll to the edge of the Ilissus was initiated on the city side of the river. Thus, if Socrates were to cross the river, he would be taken further from the city than he is already, sending him away from the potentially educational presence of humanity and toward even more remote—and, perhaps, frenetically divine—locales. The concerted use of opposition, both in dramatic detail and in rhetorical foundation, converges here, at the culmination of Socrates' first speech.

Socrates and Truth

The inspiration for Socrates' reply to Lysias is from a derivative source. It should come as no surprise then that the content of the speech is derivative—indeed, given the character of true love (as developed in the palinode), it has been sinful. The implied methodology leading to these results is, however, partially reliable, at least in principle, and in this respect Socrates has not only bested Lysias in purely rhetorical terms but he has also begun to lead Phaedrus toward the truth. The first speech achieves this introduction through Socrates' application of collection and division, his grasp of formal realities, and the subtly evinced presence of mind and the good during the description of the moral transition in the loving nonlover. The complete metaphysical hierarchy, more fully developed in the second speech, is already present here. The first speech is therefore a glimpse of the truth. In moving away from the city in order to hear a speech about love, Socrates has moved toward a more fully articulated account of the truth about love. But before that journey is completed, Socrates must reorient the distortions in what has been said about love so far.

Phaedrus and the Propagation of Discourse

Phaedrus responds to Socrates' threatened departure by noting that it is almost noon; as a result, they should stay until the heat of the day is past and discuss what has been said. Then, when it is cooler, they can leave their resting place by the Ilissus. Socrates exclaims that Phaedrus is "divine" and simply wondrous concerning discourses; in fact, no one in Phaedrus' lifetime has produced such discourses, whether by speaking them himself or by compelling others to speak them. Socrates excludes in this regard "Simmias the Theban," but Phaedrus is far ahead of the rest (242a–b). Discounting the implications of the day's heat, Socrates focuses on what Phaedrus has mentioned as a worthwhile pastime while they wait until the day moves on. Socrates will indeed speak again and then discuss that speech at some length.

The reference to Phaedrus as a propagator of discourse recalls the

Symposium, in particular that Phaedrus led Eryximachus to propose that the assembled company pay homage to love.[9] Just as Phaedrus instigates a series of speeches on love in the *Symposium*, so also does he excite the Socrates of the *Phaedrus* to voice a pair of speeches, and on the same subject. If, however, this implicit allusion between dialogues is sanctioned by referring to Phaedrus' "divine" powers of rhetorical inspiration, then the explicit comparison between Phaedrus and Simmias should receive equivalent consideration. And if this comparison includes the inspirational function of Simmias in the *Phaedo*, then Plato alludes to the *Phaedo* as well as to the *Symposium*.

At *Phaedo* 85c, Simmias initiates challenges to Socrates' discussion of the nature of soul. To answer these challenges, Socrates will find it essential to articulate an extremely complex *logos* blending autobiography, sustained reasoning on abstract metaphysical matters, and a sweeping eschatological myth. If Phaedrus is less inspirational than Simmias—but only marginally so—then we may anticipate that the *logos* Socrates is about to deliver will be only slightly less complex in structure than that produced in the *Phaedo*. Furthermore, the *Phaedo* account depicted reality by appealing to myth at certain crucial junctures. Socrates' second speech will occupy the same complex plane of significance. Finally, the discourse Socrates spoke in the *Phaedo* included references to mind and the good. To what extent these notions belong to the structure of reality developed in the *Phaedo* is disputed;[10] if, however, mind and the good are essential to the metaphysics of the *Phaedo*, then this antecedent discussion sanctions the possibility that the same components will also animate the metaphysics of the *Phaedrus*. From this perspective, the allusion to Simmias shapes not only the length of Socrates' second speech—it will be long indeed—but also its content. Plato is alerting his audience to recall the *Phaedo,* and to expect an analogous rhetorical voyage extending over vast and to a certain extent uncharted metaphysical territory.[11]

Socrates the Seer

Phaedrus wants particulars about this speech Socrates has promised to deliver, and Socrates reveals that as he was about to cross the stream, "the daimon and sign" that usually comes to him did in fact appear. Socrates believes he heard this daimon warning him to absolve himself before going away, as if he had somehow sinned "against deity." Now, Socrates says, he is a seer, not a serious one but, as bad writers say, sufficient for his own purposes. How prophetic is soul, Socrates exclaims to his friend. For during the entire time he was delivering the speech, something was bothering him: Socrates quotes the poet Ibycus to express the sentiment—he was distressed to buy honor from men by sinning against the gods. But now he has seen his error (242c–d).

The Socratic daimon, mentioned in earlier dialogues, performs an admonitory function. In this case, the daimon warns Socrates to absolve himself since he had sinned against deity. The impersonality of the aggrieved party—deity (θεῖον)—suggests that Socrates has sinned not so much against one specific deity, e.g., the god of love, but that in sinning against love Socrates has sinned against the entire divine dimension of reality.

The divine voice has informed Socrates that he must absolve himself by making his peace with the divine. But note that Socrates' own powers of divination—his own ability as a seer (μάντις)—revealed to him the precise nature of the offense. The daimon told Socrates that he was doing wrong; the prophetic function of Socrates' soul revealed what this wrong was. Socrates' abilities as a seer in this sense have not always been understood. De Vries notes that Socrates "compares himself with someone who knows just enough of reading and writing to muddle through" (p. 106). But Socrates intends a more complex meaning. First, Socrates can, by his own admission, be lured all over Greece with speeches in books (230e), a kind of temptation which suggests, by its strength, more than muddling conversance with the contents of books. Second, Socrates has apparently read a good number of books, for later in the dialogue he displays almost encyclopaedic knowledge of existing manuals of rhetoric (266d–268a). Finally, the *Phaedo* Socrates tells how he devoured (and understood) the works of Anaxagoras as part of his quest for the good (98b). Could someone who just muddles through in reading do so with such breadth and depth?

For Socrates, to act as a seer results from possessing a form of madness. Thus, Socrates knows why his speech was offensive because he is, in a real sense, inspired to know. Although Socrates does not himself write (with exceptions noted in the *Phaedo*), he is a seer when he sees why the speech he has recited is in error. He is justified in identifying himself as not a very good seer if he can only recognize the presence of the error without adequately responding to it. Being a mediocre seer should be seen therefore not as a sign of Socrates' membership in the class of muddling literates, but rather as illustrating part of the structure of madness (about to be analyzed in the second speech) and, as such, anticipating the metaphysical vision to be provided by another, and higher, form of this madness.

The Need for Recantation

The speech Phaedrus brought with him and Socrates' reply to that speech were "terrible" in being foolish and somewhat impious. Socrates asks Phaedrus whether he believes that love is the son of Aphrodite and "a god." Phaedrus replies "so it is said," suggesting that his beliefs in this matter might not coincide with the popular view. In any case, Socrates insists that love does not appear this way in Lysias' speech nor in his own response. For if love is "a god or something divine," then love cannot be evil—but the two speeches said that love is evil (242d–e).

Socrates asserts, axiomatically, that love is a god or something divine. In the *Symposium,* the goddess Diotima tells Socrates that love is a daimon, intermediate between the divine and the mortal; thus, "through love all the intercourse and converse of god with man" is carried on (202e). But in the *Phaedrus*, love is elevated from a condition intermediate between god and humanity to a god or something divine.

The significance of this shift may be measured by situating the divine in the metaphysical hierarchy of the *Phaedrus*. First, note the difference between love as a god or as something divine. If love is a god in the usual sense, then love is an anthropomorphic entity endowed with a stock of personal characteristics, e.g., preferences and dislikes commonly associated with deities. But if love is something divine, understood as a property shared by all deities and not reducible to any one of them, then its anthropomorphic dimension is diminished, if not eliminated, and love becomes assimilated to whatever is common to deity. And, in the mythic section of the second speech, Socrates will address this commonality. He says there that the vision of the reality beyond the rim of the heavens makes the gods divine (249c). Love in the *Phaedrus* thus continues to be an intermediary—just as love in the *Symposium* unites humans with the gods, so love in the *Phaedrus* unites the gods to the Forms, and, by implication, humans to the Forms, all the Forms, through the agency of the gods. The relation between humans and gods is therefore not metaphysically fundamental; when humans love, they love, ultimately, the Forms through the mediating agency of the gods.

The speech of Lysias and Socrates' rhetorical reply sinned against love, saying "nothing healthy or true" if we accept, as Phaedrus has, the claim that love cannot be evil. As a result of the admonition of the daimon combined with his abilities as a seer, Socrates now realizes that he must purify himself. There is an ancient purification, Socrates says, unknown to Homer but known to the poet Stesichorus. When Stesichorus was blinded for speaking badly of Helen, he knew the reason, unlike Homer, because he was "skilled in music." To counteract the cause of his blindness, Stesichorus wrote poetry saying that Helen did not go onto the ship nor to the walls of Troy. Once this poem, the "palinode," was completed, he immediately regained his sight. Socrates contends that he will be wiser than both these poets. Before he suffers as they did, he will atone for his sin with his own recantation, this time with a bare head rather than one covered because of shame (242d–243b).

Both the speech of Lysias and Socrates' reply contained nothing "healthy or true." Recall here the importance of life as a crucial element in Socrates' proof of soul as indestructible, the final phase of the last proof of soul's immortality in the *Phaedo* (106d–e). From this standpoint then, a healthy discourse does not merely point to its positive status as an organic whole, but suggests a relation between that whole and the fundamental metaphysical source—life—through which all living things are what they are. This brief allusion shows how Socrates has situated the self-critique of his speech in a broad metaphysical context apposite to that opened up by the interrogation of Simmias in the *Phaedo*.[12]

The appeal to the ancient purification appropriate for those who have sinned concerning mythology points to the revisionist strain in Socrates' approach to poetry as a type of rhetoric which, in theory, should fall under the sway of the truth. The poet Stesichorus goes blind (thus losing the capacity to experience visual beauty, the most precise sensory avenue to the most manifest Form) because his poetic discourse contained lies about Helen—the paradigm of feminine beauty. However, Stesichorus recanted his mythological error by writing a poem denying that Helen went to Troy. Once this poem was complete, his sight returned. Homer, in contrast, went blind (as tradition has it) and remained blind. Socrates attributes the cause of this condition to Homer not recognizing his sin against mythology.

Consider the implications: according to Socrates, it is a lie to say that Helen went to Troy. Both Stesichorus and Homer promulgated this lie. But for Homer, this lie became the basis for the plot of the entire *Iliad*. Thus, if Homer would have realized his lie and acted upon that realization, he would never have written the *Iliad* (assuming, of course, that Homer would have wanted to keep his sight). As a result, one of the greatest Greek poems is based on a lie, should therefore never have been written, and its author lacked the wisdom to recognize it as a lie. Presumably Homer could have regained his sight with a complete second epic based on a denial of the thesis of the *Iliad*. That only a finished poem would have accomplished this end is implied by the fact that Stesichorus regained his sight only after finishing his own palinode.

Some commentators have taken the point here to be that Stesichorus is a better poet than Homer because he is more inspired, and that Socrates must therefore be playfully ironic, since Homer is obviously the superior poet.[13] But the point does not concern the aesthetic value of the poetry; it concerns the relation between poetry as mythology and truth. The fact that Homer is revered as a poet does not justify what Homer has poetized with respect to the truth, and therefore with respect to its ultimate effects on his audience.

The fact that Socrates believed Homer to lack wisdom (and in this respect to be inferior to Stesichorus, who had greater respect for the truth) is shown at the end of the day's discussion, when Socrates enjoins Phaedrus to go and tell Homer (or any other poet) what Socrates and Phaedrus had heard about knowing the truth and being able to defend what one has written in light of that knowledge. What would be the point in having Phaedrus relay this report to Homer if not that Socrates sees the *Iliad*, indeed the entire Homeric corpus, as shot through with utterances that could never be justified if Homer were resurrected and made to defend the rightness of what he wrote? The groundwork for this bold challenge to Greek poetry is laid in the juxtaposition of Stesichorus and Homer, and what Socrates learned from how they handled myth in their work.

Shame and Recantation

Phaedrus is pleasantly surprised at the prospect of yet another Socratic discourse, but Socrates wants to impress on him the shameful character of the two speeches already uttered. He describes what would happen if a noble and gentle man, either in love with someone of the same character or loved by such a person, had happened to hear what was said about love in these speeches (e.g., that lovers become violent over trivia and are consumed with jealousy). Such an individual would refuse to agree with this censure of love, for he would know better. Phaedrus agrees, and Socrates emphasizes his own shame before this hypothetical audience, not to mention his fear of having offended love. He intends therefore to cleanse the brine from his ears—the conduits for the speech he had purportedly heard from a source of long ago and which he has repeated, albeit unwillingly, to Phaedrus—with a sweet discourse. And Socrates advises Lysias to write as soon as he can that the lover should be favored over the nonlover, everything else being equal. Phaedrus takes up the challenge for Lysias, and he tells Socrates that he, Phaedrus, will compel Lysias to write another speech on the same topic. Socrates says he believes Phaedrus will do this, as long as "you are what you are." Phaedrus then tells Socrates to speak—and at this point the Socratic palinode begins (243c–244a).

Why does Socrates introduce this hypothetical observer as an additional member of the audience? The observer is described as either loving someone like himself or having been loved by someone of this sort—presumably then this individual would remain noble and gentle come what may in the matter of love. This kind of person would refuse to agree with the Lysian/Socratic censure of love just because he is the kind of person he is, i.e., noble and gentle. The implication is that Phaedrus is not such an individual because he accepted the Lysian/Socratic thesis without demur, indeed with unlimited enthusiasm, and that Socrates is also lacking in this regard in that he allowed himself, if only temporarily, to be lured into mouthing a rhetorical position coincident with that thesis. This appeal to someone endowed with a certain character suggests that only the right kind of person will be properly receptive to the full force of love. As we shall see, this uniqueness is also crucial in identifying the nature of successful rhetoricians.

After Phaedrus announces his intention to force Lysias to write another speech on the same subject, Socrates says he believes Phaedrus will do this, as long as he remains the type of person he is now. Phaedrus continues to view this kind of rhetorical exchange as a competition, and he presumes that however good Socrates' next speech may be, Lysias will still be capable of competing with, perhaps even surpassing, it in value. If, however, Phaedrus changes during Socrates' coming speech, then he may no longer be interested in promoting such competition—assuming this change alters Phaedrus' attitude toward what rhetoric is and does.

As things turn out, Socrates is no less prophetic here than he was earlier. Phaedrus does learn from Socrates' second speech, and the evidence for this change appears immediately after that speech, when Phaedrus claims that Lysias will make a poor showing *if* he attempts to compete with Socrates' speech (257c). Phaedrus has just proclaimed that he would necessarily compel Lysias to write another speech; after the palinode, however, Phaedrus will leave such competing up to Lysias—and he is certain of the outcome if the competition occurs. Phaedrus no longer needs to help engage Lysias in these rhetorical lists of love, implying by this decision that he is no longer the same person he was prior to the onset of the second speech. For this speech will change his philosophical attitude toward rhetoric and, perhaps, toward love itself.

The Audience for the Palinode

Before he begins the palinode, Socrates asks the whereabouts of the "youth" to whom he was speaking, since he must hear the coming speech lest he choose a nonlover rather than a lover. Phaedrus responds "here he is," ready whenever Socrates wishes. Socrates then begins the speech proper (243e–244a).

The response by Phaedrus has stirred discussion concerning the extent to which he should be understood as the intended audience for this speech.[14] For Hackforth, this interchange is "playful," given that Phaedrus has not been shown as inclined to favor the nonlover in practice, "whatever he may think of it in theory" (p. 53, n1). But what Phaedrus has or has not done in fact is not Socrates' present concern; what concerns him is Phaedrus' admiration for a speech which counsels yielding to a nonlover, an admiration which could be transformed into future action precisely according to these misguided lights. This is a real danger, one Socrates is anxious to prevent.

Internal evidence indicates that Phaedrus' age is about forty,[15] so it would be somewhat unseemly for him to refer to himself as a youth. Why then does he do so? Perhaps because he realizes that rhetoric, especially about love, is not just a verbal exercise—words for the sake of words. It can affect how one leads one's life. Thus, he sees himself as on a par with the youth being addressed in the sense that he realizes how impressed he is with the cleverness of the thesis that such an individual should favor the nonlover rather than the lover. In this respect then, and despite his "advanced" age, Phaedrus and the youth are identical. Notice also, however, that in so binding himself to the upcoming speech, Phaedrus suggests that he possesses whatever it takes to comprehend that speech. The "youthful" Phaedrus is philosophically disposed, however attractive he might, at this juncture, find the Lysian thesis, a thesis which runs counters to that Socrates is about to argue. Whether or not Phaedrus will negotiate the lists of love is impossible to say. But it is a testament to Phaedrus' capacity as a potential philosopher that Socrates must go to considerable rhetorical (and philosophical) heights in order to make certain that his palinode not only addresses his own sin against love, but that it does so in a way which will persuade Phaedrus, his audience, of the truth of this matter.

Remark

The interlude between the two Socratic speeches has a structural function similar to the interruption dividing the two sections of Socrates' first speech. For during this interlude, Socrates again illustrates various forms of madness comprising the divisions of madness to be made in the second speech.

Socrates has said he is a so-so seer. His cry "how prophetic (μαν-τικόν) soul is" shows Socrates' soul manifesting the prophecy (μαν-τικῆ —244b) of the Sibyl and all others who prophecy. This is the first type of madness identified in the second speech. In this case, Socrates' soul was prophetically aware—at the very outset of his speech—that what was to be said would be sinful. Presumably he was not aware, however, how sinful it would be, and this lack serves as evidence for his own assessment of himself as not a very serious seer. For surely if he had seen how sinful that speech would become, he would not have allowed himself to speak it.

Once Socrates fully realized that his speech sinned against love, he was not at a loss to know how to proceed. He must purify himself, and he is aware of an ancient purification which Stesichorus knew but which Homer did not. The purification (καθαρμὸς) is the palinode, a speech exemplifying the purifications (καθαρμῶν) mentioned at 244e, in the discussion of the second type of madness. This madness absolves those with an ancient (παλαιῶν) guilt; in this case, Socrates' speech was based on the ancient (παλαιοι) wisdom of the wise men and women who had addressed the question of love (235b). Thus, Socrates' palinode will not only redress his own sin, but also the "sinful" wisdom of which he was the progressively unwilling mouthpiece.

Socrates knows about this purification because he is possessed by the second type of madness listed in the palinode. And, it may be noted, Stesichorus originally knew it because he was "educated in the Muses." This explanation anticipates the function of the Muses described later, at 259b–d, when Socrates discourses on the singing cicadas and their intermediary role between mortals and the Muses. Stesichorus knew the appropriate purification not because he was a better poet than Homer, but because he was more closely in touch with all the Muses, especially those with a special function in matters pertaining to philosophical truth.

After Socrates reveals that he had been distressed throughout his speech, he quotes a passage from the poet Ibycus to express his feelings. If this is inspired poetry (and recall that Ibycus' work was cited at a crucial juncture in the *Parmenides*), then it was inspired by poetic madness, the third type of madness designated in the second speech. Socrates also remembers the relevant passage from the Stesichorean palinode (243b), which must also have been inspired to accomplish the requisite purification for Stesichorus.

Socrates does not poetize himself here, as he did briefly at the end of the first speech and as he will, extensively, during the palinode. Yet his appeals to these brief but appropriate poetic excerpts show Socrates sharing that inspiration by recalling the passages and connecting them to his own situation. One must be susceptible to poetic madness to allow existing poetry to emerge within one's thoughts, especially at a point when the "wise" Socrates is confessing that his attempt at rhetorical wisdom has been sham and, as a result, that it threatens his self-sufficiency as a human being.

Socrates was affected by all four forms of madness in his first speech, and he continues to be possessed, at least occasionally and to a degree, by three of the four types during the period between the sinful first speech and its purificatory palinode.[16] The interruption in Socrates' first speech and the interlude between the first speech and the palinode are therefore identical in being structured on the fourfold division of madness Socrates is about to reveal. As such, these episodes illustrate the reality of madness as found, in diminished yet palpable degrees, in the less dramatic periods of human intercourse. And it is fitting to the grandeur and seriousness of Socrates' task that he again embody these manifestations of madness. There is, in fact, a complex metaphysics of madness pervading Socrates' personality as well as his immediate physical surroundings, an omnipresence finely suited to the far-flung metaphysical reaches essayed in the palinode to come.

CHAPTER 3

The Metaphysics of Madness
and the Nature of Soul
(244a–247c)

Socrates begins his palinode by insisting that the fair boy keep in mind that the prior discourse was by Phaedrus, son of Pythocles of Myrrhinus, but that the speech he is about to deliver is by Stesichorus, son of Euphemus of Himera. Socrates then asserts the main premise of the speech: it is not true that when a lover is present a nonlover should be more favored because the lover is mad while the nonlover sane. If madness were an evil, then this claim would be well-said; in fact, however, the greatest of "good things" come from madness when it is sent as a gift from the gods (244a).

The Human Origin of the Palinode

The first speech is by Phaedrus in the sense that he threatened to cut off Socrates' supply of discourses unless Socrates responded in kind to Lysias' speech. The second speech is by Stesichorus in the sense that Socrates, wishing to atone for his sinful first speech, will follow the successful example of Stesichorus by declaiming a palinode. But why add the name and birthplaces of the fathers of these individuals?

65

According to H. N. Fowler, Pythocles means "eager for fame," Myrrhinus "myrrhtown," Euphemus "man of pious speech," Himera "town of desire." Hackforth admits the significance of the last two names, Euphemus and Himera, but he adds that "to find significance in the other four is a task best left to Neoplatonic subtlety" (p. 56, n1).[1] For Hackforth, Plato's etymologizing is "sometimes serious, sometimes playful in this matter" (p. 59). But what does Plato want to accomplish in those cases when he *is* serious? A pattern of etymologizing emerges in the *Phaedrus*, beginning at 238c, when love takes its name from the words for the force of desire, and reaching a concerted peak in the discussion of the first type of madness (244bff). The function of etymologizing, here and in general, will be addressed when Socrates discusses the metaphysics of etymologizing in his analysis of the first type of madness.

The Metaphysical Origin

The strategy of the second speech may be described thus: Socrates will divide madness, *mania*, in order to show how a "manic" lover can also have *sōphrosynē*, a kind of wisdom which, in its most complete form, encompasses a perspective on the principles of all reality. As we shall see, this reconstitution will relate *eros* to *nous* so that the two become compatible—indeed essential—to one another. Whereas Socrates' first speech ended with the beloved realizing that it is preferable to accept a nonlover with *nous*, the second speech will show that it is even better for a beloved to embrace a lover with *nous*. In fact, it will be shown that to love in the highest sense is to exercise our abilities to know, guided by *nous*, what is most real.

    If Socrates is inspired by madness from the outset of the second speech and if that madness is (at least partially) the madness of love, then the metaphysics which Socrates will advance in this speech should reflect the extent to which love allows us to see reality. Notice then that the effects of madness are referred to as the greatest of good things (ἀγαθῶν). Thus, the initial characterization of madness defines benefits to human beings in light of the good. The same appeal to the good as a fundamental metaphysical principle will apply to the gods when Socrates describes the nature of divine soul (246b).

The types of madness established here are subsequently shown to be derived by division, a phase of the method of collection and division (265b–266b). Now if division presupposes something collected as its subject, then the process of division is being directed toward the good insofar as the good underlies situations where madness, in the sense under study, comes into play. The fact that this division produces a collection of "goods" implies that the good is coextensive with the Forms of madness so divided.

The Madness of Prophecy

The first type of madness is exemplified by the prophetess at Delphi and the priestesses at Dodona who, when inspired, have bestowed many fine benefits on Greece, both in public and in private. When they were sane, however, few or no benefits were conferred. And if we speak of the Sybil and all others who by prophecy have foretold many things to many people, thereby improving them, it would be necessary to speak for a long time.

It is worth noting, Socrates adds, that the ancients who invented names did not think madness shameful, for otherwise they would not have connected the word *mania* with that one "finest art," the art of foretelling the future. They name this art *mania* thinking that madness, coming as it does from the gods, was a "fine" thing. Now, however, people have rudely inserted a "t," calling it the *mantic* art. In the same way, the ancients, considering that art which rationally investigates the future by examining birds and other signs, called it the "oinonistic" art, since this art combines "thought" (*oiesis*) with "mind" (*nous*) and "information" (*historia*). Here again, the moderns have interjected another letter, changing the "o" in "oionistic" from short to long, thus making the word sound more elevated. In sum, just as prophecy for the ancients is higher than augury, both in name and in fact, so also the madness which comes from a divine source is higher than human sanity (244b–d).

Discussion of the first kind of madness is dominated by an appeal to the etymology underlying the ancients' way of naming. The ancients seem to have had insight inspiring them to represent at least part of the reality denoted by the name through the very name itself. For example, in naming prophecy "madness," they in effect equated madness as such with one of the arts madness inspired. When the moderns then named prophecy *mantikē* rather than *mania*, this shift changed madness in the sense that that one art, prophecy, was now distinguished from madness as such. What for the ancients was a whole (*mania*) became for the moderns reduced to a part (*mantikē*).

By changing the orthography of the original word, the moderns not only showed tastelessness, but also a kind of metaphysical short sightedness.[2] The significance of this shift emerges once it becomes clear why prophecy is, as Socrates says, the "finest" art, i.e., why the ancients were correct in equating it with madness as such. The reason emerges from the etymology of augury, or the oionistic art. Socrates asserts that in practicing this art, human intellect was supplied by thinking with mind (νοῦν) and information through the study of birds and other such signs. Commentators insist that *nous* here means, e.g., "to realize that something is definite" (Verdenius, p. 175). But "definite" according to what standards of reality?

The word may be taken in a more determinate sense. Note the contrast in this etymology between intellect (διανόιας) and *nous* implying that two distinct modes of cognition are present. Note also the parallel between this etymology and the description of the lover's return to *nous* and wisdom in Socrates' first speech (241b). These considerations suggest that if *nous* stands for a more fundamental type of cognition than *dianoia*, then this sense anticipates a development of *nous* in the second speech which is crucial in grounding the cognition of what will be characterized as ultimate reality. There is reason to think then that the ancient etymology of oionistic is given in metaphysical and epistemological ultimates, as if the ancients had intuitively recognized that etymologizing, rightly done, specifies words so that their origins indicate primary elements in the structure of reality.

Prophecy is the finest art therefore because its practitioners are placed in contact with *nous*, i.e., with what (following the technical sense of the term sketched in earlier dialogues—and reappearing shortly in the palinode) controls the regularity of the cosmos. The prophet, having a glimpse of *nous*, realizes what will happen by seeing how mind underlies the principles which control whatever happens. Of the arts, prophecy requires the most sensitive and concerted interplay between *nous* and *dianoia*, producing only a "story" in the case of prophecy, since prophetic utterance is, necessarily, futural.

A rationale for this "playful" treatment of etymologizing now becomes apparent. The claim that the ancients believed that prophecy *is* madness (coupled with the etymology of augury, a lower yet metaphysically significant type of prophecy) implies that the ancients realized the extent to which prophecy put them in touch with fundamental metaphysical principles. Other arts existed for the ancients, just as they do for Socratic modernity—but only one art, then and now, is so revelatory of reality, hence the ancestors' insight in naming that art with the word which represented the source of all divine inspiration for the arts. The implication is that all arts derive, in some sense, from an interplay of *dianoia* and *nous*.[3]

In theory, the moderns can see just as well as the ancients—if they realize where and how to look at things and at words naming things. The pattern of etymologizing throughout the dialogue follows this perspective. Socrates etymologizes in the *Phaedrus* to show how certain key words reflect their metaphysical heritage by bearing relations to other words of the same fundamental sort. There would then be no significant difference between the common nouns explicitly etymologized in the dialogue and the proper nouns inviting such speculation at the outset of the palinode. The proper names are no more, but no less, significant than any words so etymologized—they are pointers toward regions of reality rather than referential exhibitors. But if this pattern of etymology does relate primary meanings of words to more fundamental cognates, then, as the *Cratylus* teaches, we as speakers must study the reality suggested by these etymologies rather than rest content with whatever nuances are detected and articulated in such linguistic exercises.

The Madness of Purification

The second type of madness concerns those situation when, as a result
of some ancient guilt, "diseases and the greatest woes" have beset certain families. The "prophetic" power of this type of madness discerns
how to relieve those so afflicted by having them take refuge in prayer
and service to the gods; purification and rituals thus safeguard the possessor of this madness both for the present and the future. Those
"rightly" possessed are released from current troubles (244d–245a).

Socrates will illustrate this kind of salvation from a distinctive
species of sickness—the sickness of love for another person. In this
case, the purification required for success will not be said in the language of mysteries; it will, however, require considerable self-under-
standing and self-control in order that the individual so afflicted can
see how such salvation can be achieved.[4]

The Madness of Poetry

The third type of madness, explicitly identified as "third," taking hold
of a pure and gentle soul, awakens and inspires it to songs and other
poetry, and by glorifying the untold number of deeds of the ancients,
educates those who are to come. Without the madness of the Muses,
someone approaching the gates of poetry confident of becoming an
adequate poet by art will fail; poetry of sanity vanishes when compared
to poetry of madness (245a).

For Verdenius, it appears from this discussion that "Plato recognizes the existence of good poetry" (p.276), an implication apparently
running counter to the critical treatments of poetry in the *Republic* and
other dialogues. There is, of course, considerable poetry to come in the
palinode, explicitly designated as such by Socrates at 257a; therefore it
would be anomalous—if not inconsistent—to incorporate poetry into
the speech if poetry, by its very nature, was bad or ill-formed. In fact,
however, suitably inspired poetry designated for certain ends is one of
the benefits which madness confers upon mortals. Furthermore, the

claims made for poetry here are compatible with those made in the *Republic*. In Book X, Socrates admits that hymns to the gods and praises of famous men are acceptable poetic themes. In the *Phaedrus*, Socrates cites the countless deeds of the ancients as the proper subject of poetry, as long as the deeds are poetized to educate posterity. Thus, if the deeds of the ancients are included among those which result in the praises of famous men, then the *Phaedrus* is only stating what is implied in the *Republic*. The *Phaedrus* does not criticize matters of poetic style as does the *Republic*, but instead concentrates on the content of the poetry, leaving it to the wisdom of the poet to know how to present this content for maximum educational effect.

The fact that the art of poetry will not, by itself, confer success on its practitioners suggests that whatever rules or procedures comprise this art—and, perhaps, any art—are insufficient to achieve the desired effects on an audience. The poetic art will produce a poem, but that poem, however formally well-constructed it may be, will not compare to the results achieved when these canons are enlivened with divine inspiration. The limitations of art in this regard will become one of the primary themes in the second phase of the *Phaedrus*, particularly in discussing the art of rhetoric.

The Metaphysics of Madness

As noted, Socrates will assert later (265b) that four divisions of divine madness were made in the palinode. These divisions are cited at that point to illustrate the method of dialectic. So far we have examined each of the first three divisions. However, we may also learn about the metaphysics grounding this method by examining these divisions from the standpoint of what Socrates later says about this particular application of the method.

At 265b, Socrates contends that these divisions produced classes (εἴδη). Now if madness is a Form, then it may be assumed that division of a Form produces classes which are themselves Forms. And, in fact, the classes of madness are developed to display features characteristic of Forms: Substantive—pertaining to the specific content of each type of madness; Formal—pertaining to each type of madness as a class, itself part of a Form.

Substantive

Each of the first three types of madness begins with a reference to the ancients (παλαιὸι), then traces the repercussions of that madness into the future. It was the ancients who named prophecy (presupposing that prophecy was practiced then) and, when successful, prophecy foretells what happens in the future. Purification deals with ancient curses and, again when successful, protects the recipient in the present and the future. And poetry treats the deeds of the ancients in order to educate posterity (i.e., those who live afterwards). The efficacy of these types of madness traverses time, beginning with what is old and continuing into and through the future. The onset of madness is, of course, in the present, but the circumstances underlying its efficacy encompass all three temporal dimensions. Each type of madness has the capacity to establish such pervasive temporality. These characteristics reflect the fact that the Forms are eternal; thus the effects of madness display a temporality analogous to the eternality enjoyed by a Form.

   Each type of madness also produces a certain sort of cognition. Prophecy reveals the future; purification establishes rights (i.e., modes of action, for curing curses), poetry educates all who attend to it. The type of cognition differs in the activities producing it, but all types are the same in securing knowledge—those who hear the priestess know the future, those who hear the rites of purification know what to do to be cleansed from guilt, those who hear the poets know what can be learned from ancient deeds. The human media for such knowledge, duly inspired, may or may not be aware of the import of these utterances, but this is irrelevant to their cognitive status for those who hear them and, perhaps, act upon what they hear.

   Finally, however intense it may be, the inspiration of madness issues in discourse—the prophetess must utter prophetically, the purified must pray reverently, the poet must sing eloquently. Again, differences will obtain between, say, the language of an oracle and the reflections of an Odysseus, but there must be language as a necessary condition for determining these three types of madness.

Formal

Prophets and priestesses confer benefits when duly inspired, but "few or none" when they lack such inspiration. Those seeking purification must be rightly possessed to secure the correct rites to be saved from past sins. And the poet poetizing through art alone cannot rival the poet properly inspired by the Muses.

For each type of madness, Socrates establishes a contrast between true inspiration and a lesser degree of that condition. The contrast is not complete polarity, of pure presence and absence. The uninspired prophet can, occasionally, utter a beneficial prophecy; the uninspired poet does not cease to be a poet altogether, i.e., in the sense of being incapable of inscribing a single hexameter line. Such a poet makes poetry, but of quality inferior to inspired poetry. The range of this contrast is important, for it suggests that madness is marked by degrees of efficacy. A continuum of success or failure characterizes each type of madness; thus, acting from madness is a complex and dynamic affair, subject to limitations depending on the degree of madness as well as the nature of the individual possessed by it. Madness must take hold in the right way and to the right degree—otherwise there will be either limited results, or no result at all.

The various types of madness, construed as processes from the standpoint of those who participate in them, may be subject to degrees. But, it will be maintained, this characteristic can hardly apply to madness insofar as it admits of types (i.e., Forms of madness). For surely degrees of more or less cannot pertain to the various divisions of madness as a Form.

This possibility cannot, however, be dismissed out of hand. The first type of madness is prophecy. The practitioners of this madness include the prophetess (προφῆτις) at Delphi. The second type of madness enters by prophetic power (προφητεύσασα) to release an ancient guilt by means of purifications and rites. Hackforth has noted that the second type of madness "is really a particular sort" of prophecy (p.59).

In other words, the power to prophesy a correct purification is, it seems, just one application of the more inclusive capacity to prophesy about anything. The implication (not mentioned by Hackforth) is that a part/whole relation emerges between the first two types of madness. Thus, the second type of madness is related to the first type as the first and second types, taken individually, are related to madness as such.

This special intimacy also emerges from the fact that neither the first nor the second type of madness is enumerated, whereas both the third and fourth types are so designated. Later, at 270d, Socrates asserts that determining the nature of something requires numbering its constituent Forms. At the moment, Socrates is determining the nature of madness—the "third" type is the madness of poetry, the "fourth" type is the madness of love. The fact that the initial division of madness does not number the first two Forms of madness suggests that this division may not have been executed with requisite precision. At 265b, Socrates does enumerate each of the four types. But even if these types have been cleanly divided, as the later passage suggests, the original division raises an important question concerning the nature of a Form *qua* divided.

After concluding the description of poetic madness, Socrates says that many more fine results of madness coming from the gods could be mentioned (245b). Does this disclaimer refer to additional benefits from the three types of madness distinguished so far, or to additional types of madness—as yet unspecified—from which other benefits may be described? If the former, then the division of madness is exhaustive; omitted are only some benefits provided by these three types. But if the latter, then the division is incomplete and the first three types represent only a partial division of the Form madness. Socrates will designate a fourth kind of madness, that of love. But the relevant question is whether the set of four represents an exhaustive division of madness, a possibility important in light of the final review of the method of collection and division, when Socrates asserts that a subject of inquiry must be divided exhaustively before knowledge of it is possible (277b).

If further divisions of madness are possible, then Socrates' application of method here in the palinode is incomplete as it stands. But if so, then there is nothing misleading about the list of four types—it simply must be completed by exhaustive division. However, the unenumerated first two types suggest that the list may not be complete because such completion may not always be possible. In other words, if part of a Form can yield another part of itself, then perhaps such division has no attainable limit. A Form thus becomes a kind of continuum, with a potential infinity of parts. If the passages where Socrates enumerates the parts of madness are emphasized, then the *Phaedrus* seems to conceive a Form as a unity capable of exhaustive division by a set of enumerable parts. But given that the *Parmenides* allows the other sense of unity serious consideration, the nature of Form in this regard may not be as established as the *Phaedrus* would lead us to think.

But even if the division of madness into four types does represent a partial listing of an enumerably exhaustive set, how are these divisions made? What principle (if any) guides such division?

As noted, the fourth type of madness, love, is the best and the highest (249e, also 265b). Since love is determined in this way only in relation to the other three divisions of madness, this characteristic suggests that the types of madness have been divided according to a hierarchy. Thus, if love is the best then the other three types of madness are somehow inferior to love. And the first three types of madness may themselves be arranged hierarchically. In sum, the attribution of "best" to one type of love suggests that the good will be a factor in dividing a Form into its constituent parts. (This important feature of the good will be examined in the Epilogue.)

Wisdom and Nature

The palinode continues. Socrates insists that we should not let others frighten us by saying that a reasonable friend should be preferred to someone who is inspired. For if it can be shown that love is not sent from the gods for the advantage of lover and beloved alike, the individual arguing this will receive the prize of victory. The problem can be stated thus: we must prove that the relevant inspiration, the fourth type of madness, has been given by the gods for our greatest good fortune. This proof, Socrates adds, will be believed by the wise but not by the clever.

It is necessary, first, to know the truth about the nature of divine and human soul by seeing how it acts and is acted upon. Socrates now introduces the proof's fundamental principle—the famous discussion of soul's immortality based on self-motion (245b–c).

Socrates has shown that three types of madness confer benefits on human beings. Now he must prove that love, also a type of madness, is given to us by the gods not just as a benefit, but for our greatest good fortune. The full scope of this problem must be kept in mind, for it will control critical assessment of the subsequent discussion. The account offered by Socrates will not be complete until the madness of love has been shown to provide both lover and beloved with their greatest happiness. In order to preserve the structural unity of the palinode, the parts of this account must be examined in relation to one another, and as elements within one complete proof-structure, until that conclusion has been established.

The fact that the proof will be complex, and in unforeseen ways, is hinted at when Socrates advises that the clever will reject and the wise accept it. Cleverness (δεινοῖς) has been exemplified in the speech of Lysias (228a) and also, in an avowedly negative sense, by Socrates' own first speech (242d). Phaedrus, impressed with both speeches, seems to be particularly susceptible to such cleverness, along with its hidden dangers; as a result, he may not possess the wisdom required to accept the forthcoming proof. The extent to which wisdom differs from cleverness will be measured by what Phaedrus (and the reader) must bring to bear in order to follow the second speech from start to finish. If, e.g., the proof incorporates an involuted myth, then the exercise of wisdom will include the ability to interpret a myth in conjunction with whatever discursive content the proof may contain.

The proof proper begins with determining the truth about the nature of soul, divine and human, by understanding its active and passive properties. This step is, as Socrates says, only the first phase of the proof; it represents the proof's fundamental principle, its *archē*, but it does not constitute the proof. As a result, the wisdom required to accept the proof includes not only seeing the sense of this principle, but also connecting that sense to what follows, a difficult task given the stark shift between the principle's terse style and the soaring grandeur of the subsequent myth.

The discussion from 245c to 246a is commonly understood to prove the immortality of soul. But this reading is misleading, and undue emphasis on this discussion as self-contained reasoning about a property of soul will misrepresent both the account and its function in the proof as a whole. Strictly speaking, Socrates is not proving the immortality of soul—he is doing precisely what he says he is doing, i.e., beginning to describe the nature (φύσεως) of soul,[5] a nature which will characterize both divine and human soul.

The nature of soul is not equivalent to the immortality of soul, one property of that nature. Soul's nature is, as Socrates explicitly says at this point, what soul does and what happens to soul, i.e., all its active and passive properties. Later, at 270d, Socrates will formalize this study of soul by asserting that in considering the nature (φύσεως) of anything, it must be determined whether (a) the thing is simple or complex and (b) how, in either case, the thing then acts or is acted upon. When therefore Socrates insists, at 245c, that the truth about the nature of soul must be known in a certain way, he is invoking the technical specifications for determining a thing's nature laid down later as essential for producing methodologically correct rhetoric. As we shall see, determining the full nature of soul—how it acts and is acted upon in relation to true reality—is more complex than demonstrating soul's possession of immortality.[6]

Truth in this context, i.e., about the nature of soul, should be taken in the sense defined shortly, at 247c–e, when Socrates insists that he will speak the truth about the truth. This perspective on truth becomes crucial because in that discussion, Socrates describes a metaphysical vision—of realities, i.e., Forms, in relation to mind and the implied presence of the good—which continues the concern for mind and the good shown in the *Phaedo* and the *Republic* and, later, in the *Philebus*.

That truth will be metaphysically complex is anticipated by the two contrasting types of cognition involved in comprehending the nature of soul. Socrates says that we "know" the truth concerning soul's nature by "understanding" its active and passive properties. Knowing (νοῆραι) the truth is the higher form of cognition, given that the structure of truth (to be stated shortly in mythic context) will include mind, the good, and the Forms. But understanding (ἰδόντα) the active and passive properties of soul can be more discursively presented, since this kind of awareness presupposes only the ability to make distinctions based on formal components. The same cognitive contrast between knowing and understanding occurs again, at 246d, in a pivotal context concerning the nature of deity. These two levels of cognition thus reflect the first two levels of knowledge identified in the divided line in the *Republic*, corresponding to *nous* and *dianoia* respectively. They are introduced at this crucial juncture to anticipate the interwoven mythic and discursive modes of discourse structuring the proof as a whole, thereby highlighting the complex wisdom required to believe that proof.

The Nature of Soul—Self-motion

The subsequent interpretation of 245c–246a follows the narrative order developing the principle, the *archē*, underlying the proof of soul's nature.

1. The *archē* begins: "all soul is immortal." There are two main problems here, one arising immediately (a), the other (b) depending on the logic of this assertion in the account as a whole.

(a) the classic question—should "all soul" be taken collectively, distributively, or, perhaps, in both senses? We know at this point that "all" must encompass both "divine and human soul," since Socrates indicated this distinction in his statement of the problem. In this sense, all soul must eventually be divided in order to account for the difference between these two types of soul. Even after this division is secured, however, the same question may still arise, pertaining then to all [human] soul and all [divine] soul. This issue is pertinent to certain features of soul, the most obvious being personal immortality. However, the generality of the approach to soul's nature may reduce, if not eliminate, the relevance of this issue. In other words, the ambiguity may be intentional because what the account as a statement of principle asserts about soul does not require that such a distinction be drawn at this juncture. This interpretation gains support from discussions of soul appearing later in the proof, when the collective/distributive distinction is clearly observed. For if Socrates is aware of this distinction later, it may be supposed that he is aware of it now.

(b) If the purpose of the account is to demonstrate that soul is immortal, then the account begins with a statement of the demonstrandum. But the conclusion of the account reads that soul is necessarily ungenerated and immortal (246a2). Strictly speaking then, the account must show not only that soul is immortal, but also (i) that soul is ungenerated and (ii) that it is necessarily the case that soul is both ungenerated and immortal.

(i) A sound proof that soul is immortal would seemingly imply that soul is ungenerated, since if soul is not subject to death then it would appear that soul must always have existed, and if it always existed then it could never have been generated. But if synonymy between immortal and ungenerated obtains, then that part of the subsequent discussion dealing with soul as ungenerated becomes otiose. We may recall, however, that the *Phaedo* supplements the final proof of soul's immortality by proving soul's imperishability, clearly implying that possessing immortality does not guarantee that soul is also imperishable. So if, in the *Phaedrus*, immortal soul is not imperishable by virtue of being immortal, then immortal soul may also not be ungenerated.

If therefore immortal and ungenerated are not synonymous, then Socrates must offer additional evidence to indicate that soul is also ungenerated. This logical complexity introduces the possibility that the "all soul is immortal" at the head of the discussion is a premise rather than a conclusion. Socrates asserts the immortality of soul as a claim either already established by prior argumentation or as a plausible assumption (cf. *Meno*, 81c). According to this line of thought, Socrates does not intend to show that soul is immortal; rather he wants to show

how soul is immortal—by self-motion—in order to infer, with additional argumentation, that soul is ungenerated. The interpretation offered below will keep this possibility in mind.

(ii) The appeal to necessity at the conclusion of the discussion may be taken as a form of emphasis rather than as a distinctive logical modality. Even so, it should be possible to indicate why this emphasis appears, especially given the terseness of the account as a whole. As we shall see, it is because soul is immortal and ungenerated in certain ways that soul is necessarily immortal and ungenerated.

2. "For that which is always in motion is immortal, but that which moves something and is moved by something, if its ceases to move, ceases to live."

After asserting that "all soul is immortal," Socrates next contends that "that which is always in motion is immortal." Now if Socrates were to infer that all soul is always in motion by combining the claims that (1) all soul is immortal and (2) what is always in motion is immortal, then he is guilty of an undistributed middle. But Socrates need not be reasoning fallaciously because he may not be reasoning at all. He could be merely pointing out a feature about what is always in motion, i.e., that it is immortal, an indication which is clearly relevant to soul because of the common predicate—immortality. The relation between immortality and self-motion has therefore yet to be determined.

The claim about the immortality of continual motion (ἀεικίνητον) could refer (in Greek) either to some thing always moving or to the property of self-motion as such, apart from whatever thing may possess that property. Since soul is not explicitly mentioned again until 245e3, toward the very end of the account, the emphasis is perhaps more on the property of continual motion than on the substantive sense; in other words, Socrates is exploring characteristics insofar as they may pertain to soul rather than itemizing soul's attributes, as if it were a fully cognizeable substrate ready at hand.

Socrates now considers the property of moving something else and being moved by something else. He asserts that a thing in this condition will, if it ceases to move, also cease to live. Notice the complexity introduced in this point. Instead of considering continual motion as immortal, we are to examine something both moving and being moved. Continual motion, as such, does not presuppose a relation to something other than itself, but the active/reactive type of motion does; at this point, the relevance of the technical sense of nature becomes prominent, since to move something else is to act and to be moved by something else is to be acted upon. The subsequent analysis may therefore exemplify such a nature and illustrate the underlying method for knowing that nature.

Something both moving and being moved is not necessarily always moving. But Socrates' claim, that if something moving and moved ceases to move then it ceases to live, does not seem to follow. Consider B moving C and being moved in turn by A. Why, if B no longer moves in moving C, must B cease to live? Could not B remain alive as being moved by A without necessarily having to demonstrate agency as alive by acting upon something other than itself?

The answer to this question depends on how life is to be understood in this context. Socrates' assumption seems to be that life, as predicated of B, means that a thing lives when it moves something else and when it is moved by something else. In other words, life names a complex relational state of affairs marked by both activity (e.g., B moving C) as well as passivity (e.g., B moved by A). It would follow that everything alive is involved, necessarily, in both active and passive relations with things other than itself.

It then becomes essential for the continuation of motion—and for the continuation of life—to posit a source of motion itself continually moving. If, e.g., B derives its motion solely from the activity of A and A were to cease such activity, then both A and B will cease to move and therefore cease to live. Now A is either moved by something else or it is not. If the former, then how does A begin moving (and, in general, anything begin moving)? If the latter, then A is in self-motion and the origin of motion is not a problem. Yet if something self-moving were to cease moving, then not only that thing would cease moving but it will be possible for anything in self-motion to cease moving. And if one thing (or one kind of thing) were self-moving in a way which set in motion all other things which moved, then if that thing (or, again, that type or thing) ceased moving, all motion would be terminated. Therefore, there must be continual motion, or something continually moving, otherwise a cessation of motion encompasses all instances of activity and passivity and the result will be stasis, the complete absence of life in what had been permeated by life. According to this interpretation, life is intimately related to nature—it is, in fact, defined by the technical sense of activity and passivity advanced later in the *Phaedrus*.

3. "Only that which moves itself, since it does not leave itself, never ceases moving, but is itself the source and principle of motion in everything else that moves."

The identification of continuous motion as a self-motion which never leaves itself may appear mere circumlocution. But the point takes on more consequence if seen in the context of determining the nature of soul. For if, following the active/passive rubric, self-motion were to "leave," then the self-moving thing would be destroyed either because the thing was acted upon by something other than itself or if the thing acted so that its self-motion somehow ceased. This characteristic of self-motion is therefore appealed to on principle, following from the technical sense of nature as applied to soul.

Socrates generalizes the character of continuous self-motion so that it becomes the "source and principle" of motion for all things which move. Thus, the motion evident in things depends on what is always in self-motion. The analysis has moved from whatever is always in self-motion to a dependency relation encompassing the motion of all things which move. That this step is crucial becomes evident when translated into active and passive terminology—those things which act so that they move must themselves be acted upon by something which (a) produces motion in all other things which move while (b) not being acted upon so that its own motion ceases.

Socrates is careful not to say that all things move, but only that self-motion is essential for all things which are defined by motion. The existence of things without motion, and how they depend, or are related to, things with motion is left unspecified at this point. The active and passive character of this relation is not discussed here, although it will be considered in due course.

4. "But the principle is ungenerated." It has been asserted that what is always moving is immortal and that what is self-moving is always moving. What is self-moving is therefore immortal. But if soul is self-moving, then soul is immortal and it would appear that Socrates could conclude the demonstration. Discussion continues because something essential must be added in analyzing the nature of a principle. This requirement is due to the relation between soul, as self-moving, and what is other than soul—e.g., body—and the extent to which body can be acted on by soul. The active/passive factor is, again, of fundamental importance.

If soul is related to body, then even if soul is self-moving, is must be shown that the action of soul in moving body is not, and cannot be, a kind of motion which would cause soul to stop moving. From this perspective, the introduction of the notion of a principle or a beginning of motion is essential to the nature of soul, if it is the case that soul exists in continual interaction with body.

5. "For everything that is generated must be generated from a principle, but the principle is not generated; for if it were it would not be generated from a beginning."

The argument is general, i.e., it is about any principle. Socrates shows that a principle, with respect to its origin, is entirely active and in no sense passive. In other words, a principle produces activity and is not passively produced by something else, under pain of losing contact with itself, i.e., becoming self-contradictory and thus nonexistent.

This argument has been characterized as supplementary or secondary, but according to the line of interpretation pursued here this is not true. Recall that the discussion concludes that soul is necessarily (immortal and) ungenerated. Socrates must establish a connection between the putative immortality of soul and the fact that soul has been identified as a principle, i.e., as a source or a beginning, in order to conclude the argument as stated.

6. "Since it is ungenerated, it must also be indestructible; for if the principle were destroyed, it could never be generated from anything nor anything else from it, since all things must be generated from a principle."

A first principle cannot be acted upon in such a way as to be destroyed. If a principle were destroyed, then, obviously, it could never act to reestablish its existence. Nor could anything else be produced if this lack of activity eventuated, since all things depend for their existence on the activity of a first principle. As a result, this self-motion is the principle of motion and it cannot be either destroyed or generated, otherwise everything that comes to be would stop and never have another source of motion.

This phase of the argument extends the scope of self-motion with respect to activity. The principle of self-motion now not only guarantees the continual motion of all other things which move, it also guarantees the continued generation of those things, i.e., their existence as things capable of motion. This is the force of the indirect proof inferring what would transpire for the entire universe and all things in it which are generated if the principle of self-motion were itself subject to destruction or generation. Self-motion acts so that it provides both the motion and the continued existence of everything which, by itself, can display motion.

7. "Thus that which moves itself is the principle of motion. And it can be neither destroyed nor generated, otherwise all the heavens and all generation must collapse and stop, never again having a source of motion or origin."

When Socrates reasons that the heavens and all generation must stop and never again have any motion, it would follow that the heavens cease to exist as moving and thus, presumably, sink into a state of nonexistence. Now if generation refers strictly to the production of living things, then the cessation of generation would not affect the existence of nonliving things. However, Socrates will soon say (at 246b8) that soul "takes care of" all things soulless. If therefore soul somehow ceased to exist, then all that is soulless would become subject to whatever transpired without soul's guidance. Presumably all that is soulless would not instantly vanish, but gradually wear away until, perhaps, complete annihilation were approached. The active/passive rubric is specially prominent here, since soul acts not only to bring life and motion to all bodies which have life, but it also acts so that all bodies without life are directed by what soul decrees. The passive dependence of the soulless on soul is essential to the ordered existence of the soulless.

It has been asserted that this claim about self-motion is based on the impossibility that the heavens could ever cease moving—"it seemed unthinkable that the regular rotation of the heavens and the continued process of generation should suddenly cease."[7] But this observation does not specify the relevant impossibility. Is it unthinkable that a functioning universe would somehow cease to function, or even that the universe should not exist at all? If Plato did envision these possibilities, then the point is not simply that certain states of affairs are unthinkable, but rather, more fundamentally, that these states could readily be thought of but would never happen because if they could have happened at some point in the duration of the universe then they would have happened before now. The fact that they have not yet happened justifies, for Socrates, the claim that they never will—and never could.

8. "But since that which is moved by itself has been seen to be immortal, someone who says that this self-motion is the essence and account of soul is not disgraced."

The *ousia* of soul is said to be self-motion. Later at 247c8, *ousia* names the most fundamental degree of reality existing beyond the heavens. If therefore *ousia* designates the ultimate reality of a thing, then the ultimate reality of soul is self-motion.

Two important implications follow: (a) if self-motion defines soul's reality, then soul cannot be a Form, since Forms are not in motion. The dispute concerning the relation between soul's metaphysical character and the Forms typically arises from the final proof for the immortality of soul in the *Phaedo*, and although the complexity of that argument might support the thesis that soul is a Form, the careful account of soul's nature in the *Phaedrus* tells against it. (b) Also, if soul is essentially in motion but motion, of whatever sort, represents a derivative degree of reality, then soul must be related to a higher degree of reality in order to establish the possibility of its existence. (Throughout this discussion of soul's nature as self-motion, no mention is made of the Forms or any other kind of reality—except that of "body.")

That Socrates is fully aware of this metaphysical requirement is indicated by the fact that he has the souls of the gods move up to the rim of the heavens in order to be nurtured by the vision of reality beyond the heavens. The point is made explicit at 249c, where it is asserted that the gods are divine only because their souls see this reality. The souls of mortals accompany, to the best of their ability, the souls of the gods, and to this extent all souls depend on the reality beyond the heavens for their nature as continually and necessarily self-moving. Presumably soul is coeval with this reality, since soul is both immortal and ungenerated.[8] But an ontological dependency obtains, since soul could not maintain itself as self-moving without beholding realities which, in principle, never move.

To conclude that attributing this essence to soul would not disgrace one who held this position brings out the fact that the argument has been directed at human and divine soul. The argument has entered into the sphere of divinity; nonetheless, the given reasons justify that what has been said about soul adequately portrays its essence. Thus, the argument has not been a disgraceful venture into this especially impenetrable region of thought and discourse.

9. "For every body which derives its motion externally is soulless but that which has its motion within itself is besouled, since that is what soul is. . . . "

The reference to "every body" (πᾶν · · · σῶμα) parallels in form the earlier reference to "all soul" (ψυχὴ πᾶσα). In this case, however, there is a clear distinction (with a distributive sense) between every body which is acted upon in order to move and every body which, ensouled, acts by moving. Some bodies are ensouled, some bodies are not. The former, e.g., a human body, has its motion within itself in that soul is "inside" the body and acts by quickening the body with life. The latter comprises all inanimate objects which, to the extent that they have the capacity for motion, move because they are acted upon by soul (or, more accurately, by ensouled bodies).

10. "but if this is true—that that which moves itself is nothing else than the soul—then soul would necessarily be ungenerated and immortal."

When Socrates asserts that "no other thing" but soul is capable of self-motion, this fact confers necessity on soul being "ungenerated and immortal." Why? It has been shown that all bodies either derive motion from without or from within. The former cannot be in self-motion because their motion has been received from another; the latter cannot be in self-motion if body acts on soul in a way causing the whole to cease moving. Thus, if self-motion is proper to such a body, it is only because the body has a soul. Now soul is immortal if it is in the nature of soul to be in self-motion. And soul is ungenerated if soul is the only thing in self-motion; for if the principle of soul as self-moving is something other than soul, then soul would not be ungenerated, i.e., it would come from something other than itself.

The importance of the argument showing the character of a principle now becomes clear; it is in virtue of this argument that Socrates can infer the necessity of soul's being ungenerated. The conclusion of the whole discussion is therefore a conjunction of the conclusions of the two phases of the *arche*.

It remains to show how these active and passive properties of soul are related to the "form" of soul. Now if soul depends for its nature (in part) on the Forms and the Forms are many and complex, then this dependency is also diverse and heterogeneous. If, however, we have seen and grasped the sense of soul's properties as stated in the *arche*, then we may be receptive to the kind of knowledge required to know the nature of soul, whether it is simple or complex, and however soul may be related to things other than itself. For as we shall see, because the soul's *ousia* is immortality as self-motion, the active and passive properties of soul—its "form"—must be expressed mythically.

The Form of Soul

Socrates concludes that enough has been said concerning the immortality of soul. But concerning the form of soul, it is necessary to speak as follows: to say what it is in all respects would require a divine and very long narrative, but it is humanly possible to say briefly what it is like, and this is how Socrates shall speak. Let soul be likened to the compos-

ite nature of powers in winged horses and driver. The horses and drivers
of the gods are all "good and from the good," while those of the others
are mixed. And first of those others, the driver of our soul guides a pair
of horses, one fine and good and from fineness and goodness, the other
the opposite and from these opposites. For us, therefore, driving is
"necessarily" difficult (246a–b).

The initial phase in the analysis of soul's nature was terse and
taut—as if pure reason were marching confidently in carefully measured strides toward a recognizably attainable goal. But suddenly, Socrates begins to soar far and wide, wielding the image of winged horses
and their drivers to represent something like the truth about soul. Why
this sudden shift in rhetorical style?

Recall that specifying a thing's nature includes an accurate and
comprehensive description of whether that nature is simple or complex. So far Socrates has shown only that the nature of soul includes
self-motion, and that soul is the principle of motion for all other things
capable of motion. This *archē* does not mention whether soul, either by
itself or in relation to body, has parts in any sense. Therefore, the statement of the *archē* leaves open whether soul is simple or complex.

If, at this point, soul's nature is only partially determined, then
when Socrates begins to describe the powers of a nature so determined,
his extended rhetorical figure merely reflects this indeterminacy. Whatever the image of winged horses and driver may reveal concerning
soul's nature, these revelations depend on the reliability of the initial,
only partially articulated nature of soul. This covert methodological
message with respect to soul's nature must be kept in mind. The substance and much of the detail of the palinode—from 246a, when Socrates concludes his account of soul's immortality, to 257a, when he
announces the completion of the recantation of his sinful first speech—
receives dramatic and philosophical import from the image of soul as
winged horses and driver. When, during their subsequent reflections,
Socrates tells Phaedrus that the second speech was "really sportive
jest" (265d), he excludes from this assessment those parts of that
speech which adumbrated the method of determining truth by collection, division, and determining a thing's nature. The jest may then refer

to the splendid mythic panorama of this speech, engendered only after
incompletely applying the method for securing truth in rhetoric. But it
remains vital to interpret the myth according to the problem for the sake
of which this myth has been introduced.

The Powers of Soul

The interpretation advanced here of the winged horses/driver image
has not been presented in the literature, as far as I know. As a propaedeutic for this reading of the text, it will be necessary to examine
critically—and at some length—the standard interpretation.

Hackforth reaffirms a long-standing tradition when he asserts that
it is "of course obvious that the charioteer with his two horses sym-
bolizes the tripartite soul familiar to us from *Rep.* IV"—a composite of
a reflective or calculative part, a spirited or passionate part, and an appetitive part. He immediately adds, however, that "there is much in the
present section and in the pages which follow that cannot be so translated, and that Plato does not intend to be translated . . . " (p. 72).[9] A
comparison of *Republic* IV with relevant portions of the *Phaedrus* myth
does reveal several similarities. But there are more differences than
similarities, and some differences are so striking and crucial that one
must question whether what is obvious to Hackforth et al. is really so
obvious.

Hackforth has aligned the triplicity of the *Phaedrus* account with
the tripartite character of soul in *Rep.* IV as follows:

charioteer = calculative part
good horse = spirited part
evil horse = appetitive part

But there are a number of problems with this schematic:

1. If the good horse corresponds to the spirited part of soul, then
the standard interpretation permits the inference that love is necessarily evil. For in *Rep.* IV love is a type of desire (439d). But desire flows
from the appetitive function. And in the *Phaedrus*, the appetitive function is represented, in part, by the evil horse. But the *Phaedrus* will

demonstrate that love, at least the right kind of love, is ultimately directed by mind (*nous*) and is good.

2. In the *Phaedrus*, the image of soul as winged horses and driver encompasses both divine and human soul. But divine soul has no evil horse—its horses are "good and from the good." How then can the tripartite structure in *Rep.* IV accommodate this mythic fact? Hackforth remarks: "I think the implication is that, whereas the tripartition of *Rep.* IV was deduced from the fact of moral conflict, we may still postulate three parts of soul when there is no question of such conflict" (p. 76). But this appeal is unpersuasive. Why should we posit three parts of divine soul when its mythical differentiation comprises only a charioteer and good horses? In *Rep.* IV, three distinct parts of the soul are proposed—what would be the corresponding third part in divine soul?

3. *Rep.* IV concerns soul existing in a human body. But the mythical account in the *Phaedrus* concerns soul existing prior to its animation of bodies, human or otherwise. Thus, the functions of the appetitive part of soul refer to desires originating when soul is affected by body—thirst, hunger, the sensual phase of love, etc. But no such appetites are or can be found in the initial account of soul in the *Phaedrus* because triplicity is part of its nature prior to any "entombment" in body. The only appetitive drive ascribed to the evil horse during this phase of the myth is the yearning to move away from what the good horse and driver actively seek to see (248a–b).

4. Later, in commenting on the more detailed description of the two types of horse given at 253c–e, Hackforth says (p. 107): "The description of the two horses, with which this section opens, conforms to the psychological analysis of *Rep.* IX (580–581) rather than to that of *Rep.* IV." Now if the *Republic* shifts in describing the nature of soul's triplicity, then of course Hackforth has license to follow that shift. Apparent discrepancies between IV and IX are Plato's, not Hackforth's. However, the *Phaedrus* myth remains constant despite such shifts in the *Republic*. And Hackforth's correlation of that myth with *Rep.* IX results in problems as serious as those stated above.

a. Although each of the three parts of soul has its own specific object of desire in *Rep.* IX, only one of these three parts desires love, the appetitive part (580e). But in the *Phaedrus*, the "whole" soul loves (253e).

b. In *Rep*. IX, each part of soul has its own object of desire. But in the *Phaedrus*, the driver and good horse share the same desire (254a). Hackforth admits this identity, and comments as follows:

> the charioteer and the good horse are so much one in purpose and function that their distinction can hardly be maintained if we seek to go behind the imagery. The most that we can say is that continence is conceived as in one aspect intellectual, its source being knowledge or recollection of ideal beauty, and in another as emotional (107).

Two criticisms may be made:

(i) According to this account, the good horse provides the "emotional" aspect of love's subjugation. Now examination of *Rep*. IX reveals, first, that emotion as such is never named as essentially related to desire; and, second, that the desires likely to include emotive elements—thirst, hunger, love—follow from the appetitive part of soul. But in the *Phaedrus* the appetitive part is represented partially by the evil horse, not by the good horse alone.

(ii) The good horse is the spirited part of the soul. In *Rep*. IX, the spirited element is described as "wholly set on predominance and victory and good repute" (581a). But in the *Phaedrus* myth, there is no indication that the good horse is set on predominance and victory. But if the good horse represents the spirited part of the soul in *Rep*. IX, then why is its presence in this regard so muted in the *Phaedrus* myth?

(c) If the evil horse in the *Phaedrus* myth is, as Hackforth puts it, "evil from the start" (p. 108), then surely its counterpart in *Rep*. IX is equivalently evil. But this equivalency implies that everything pursued by the appetitive part of soul—"food and drink and love"—must also be evil, or at least contribute to the satisfaction of evil appetition. *Rep*. IX requires only that these appetites be controlled, hardly implying that the appetites are inherently evil.

Hackforth faces this problem by asserting that Plato's "real purpose is not to propound a psychological doctrine for its own sake," but to contrast divine Eros with that which is evil (266a); Hackforth then adds that Socrates makes what the *Republic* calls desire intrinsically evil—not merely evil when in excess—chiefly because he can thereby bring evil love "most vividly before us" (p. 108).

Again, however, the explanation is unpersuasive. First, the discrepancy between what is intrinsically evil (the evil horse) and what is evil only in excess (the appetites of soul) cannot be slid over as neatly as Hackforth tries to do. Furthermore, Hackforth's reason for this escape ultimately undercuts his whole interpretation of the *Phaedrus* myth. He claims that at 253c, Plato's "real purpose is not to propound a psychological doctrine for its own sake." But if Plato is not doing this at 253c, then he is not propounding psychology for its own sake at 246a, the start of the account of soul as tripartite. How then can Hackforth proclaim, in commenting on 246a, that the *Phaedrus* allegory is obviously the psychology at *Rep.* IV?

For one, perhaps several, of the discrepancies just sketched, the Hackforth interpretation could perhaps be justified by appealing to the fluidity of mythical language and the fact that assigning neat and comprehensive correlations between doctrine and mythic detail is impossible. But the cumulative force of these problems suggests that the triplicity of soul in the *Phaedrus* myth cannot be based solely (if at all) on the psychology adumbrated in the *Republic*.

This conclusion may be bolstered by the following considerations. At the point where triplicity of soul is introduced in the palinode, Socrates has concluded that soul is immortal by reason of its perpetual self-motion. But the argument for this conclusion did not mention soul having parts. Why then should we import an analytic account of soul's nature found in another dialogue as the ultimate rationale of the allegorical account of soul's nature in this dialogue? Furthermore, and even more damaging, if allegorical language is intrinsically imprecise by virtue of its poetic quality, why should Socrates cloak the nature of soul in mythic details in the *Phaedrus* when elsewhere, i.e., an earlier dialogue, he has discursively revealed that very nature? Hackforth's version of the standard interpretation assumes that the *Phaedrus* allegory must approximate an account of soul given in another dialogue, and that psychological function alone determines the sense of this allegory. But why must this be so? Let us assume instead that the sense of the image should be derived simply from the *Phaedrus* as a whole.

Soul and the Good

Why does Socrates insist that it would take a god to describe soul's form? And why would the description be lengthy? One reason the account will be lengthy is that the nature of soul is difficult to determine. Socrates will say shortly that there is divine as well as nondivine soul. Therefore, to describe the form of soul completely is to describe both divine and nondivine soul. Recall, however, that such types of distinctions of soul did not appear in determining soul's nature as self-moving. But this description of soul's nature was nonetheless held not to disgrace whoever maintained it, implying that self-motion is perfectly proper to divine soul.

Determining how such motion pertains to the form of divine soul would also be a very complex matter if divine soul can experience things which nondivine soul cannot (or not to the same degree). Only a divine soul could then describe the form of soul as such (since, as noted, the form of soul includes both a divine and nondivine component). This implication suggests that the form of soul will be determined by a range of reality which, in its intrinsic complexity, is in some sense closed off from human cognition. For this reason therefore, the human Socrates must use a "figure" to describe this aspect of soul. The reality in question can be articulated—but only if a god or divine emissary speaks; a human speaker can only approximate this reality. In sum, the relation between soul as self-moving and the complex metaphysical setting within which soul moves is the essential backdrop for determining the sense of the allegorical treatment of soul's form.

The figure Socrates introduces includes two differentiations—soul has a team of horses and a driver, typically of a chariot, and both horses and driver are winged. Thus, soul will have capacities with respect to this metaphysical complexus insofar as it displays properties of a driver as well as properties of horses (of different character), and also insofar as the organic unity of these properties is winged.

Socrates says that the horses and drivers of the gods are "good and from the good." According to Hackforth, this phrase is probably a stereotype, meaning no more than "wholly good" (p. 69, n2).[10] But if a literal sense is preserved, then the point is both that all aspects of divine soul are inherently good and that these aspects are also "from the good" in the sense that the good is not exhausted by those features of it animating divine soul. This reading suggests a kind of participation relation between divine soul and the good, a relation which establishes the good as not only real in itself, but occupying an especially high place in the metaphysical hierarchy, given that divine soul depends on it for its own reality. Note then that the phrase "good and from the good" will appear again, at 274a, in a context of similar generality, where the same contrast applies.[11]

After differentiating the soul according to the horse/driver image, Socrates distinguishes soul's powers insofar as they pertain to the gods and "the others." Does "the others" mean just the plurality of those others who are human beings or does it mean, more inclusively, all things ensouled other than the gods? If the latter, then there are various classes of ensouled thing, and the "form" of the soul of these classes is constituted in different ways. That this is the intended sense is suggested when Socrates says "first" in referring to the specific configuration of powers in human soul, as if the "mix" of human soul represented just one type of soul among other types of living things. In addition, after stating that driving is, for us, difficult because of the mixed lineage of our horses, Socrates states that the next topic is to determine why a "living being" is called mortal or immortal. Although the subsequent analysis describes a living kind of thing which is human, the account is sufficiently broad to encompass any seemingly self-moving thing. Thus, the image of soul's powers contrasts human and divine soul, but the image also covers a broader class than just human beings. Additional evidence for this inclusion appears later in the palinode, when nondivine soul alternates between animal and human life (249b).

Human soul, our soul, is driven by a pair of horses, the one "fine and good," the other from the opposite properties. For us, therefore, driving is necessarily painful and troublesome. The horses of human soul are opposites, and there is no indication that either opposite could be eliminated from the nature of human soul. Driving, for us, is necessarily painful and troublesome because part of our soul is necessarily the opposite of fine and good. This feature of human soul is therefore crucial to our nature, especially in terms of its active and passive capacities.

The above considerations indicate that determining the form of soul as depicted through the figure of horses and driver will encompass a metaphysical perspective which includes the good, and whatever regions of reality are affected by the good. Socrates will enunciate this perspective in due course, when he attempts to speak "the truth about the truth" (discussed in the next chapter).

Mortality and Immortality

At this point, Socrates proposes to discuss why living beings are called mortal and immortal. First, soul, considered collectively, takes care of all that is soulless, and it traverses the entire universe, existing in various forms at various times. When soul is perfect and completely winged, it ascends, governing the cosmos. However, when soul loses its wings, it is borne along until it lands on something solid, whereupon it adopts an "earthly body" which seems to move itself because of the power of soul. This unity of body and soul is called a living thing, and named mortal. "Immortal," in contrast, is not said by any rational process, but we, neither understanding nor sufficiently knowing deity, imagine "something immortal" having soul and body naturally united "for all time." Socrates does not insist on the rightness of this phase of the account, leaving god to decide how "dear" it will be (246b–d).

It is necessary to explain why things are named mortal and immor-

tal because soul is now determined to take care of "the soulless." The
types of reality falling under the category of soulless are not specified,
but if everything bodily or material is included, then soul will have a relation to body insofar as soul cares for body. Thus Socrates is analyzing
the nature of soul in terms of what soul acts on, i.e., everything that
lacks soul. This description of the active powers of soul will be complemented by showing how soul is acted on by body while soul acts by
caring for body.

The original reference to all soul is ambivalent between a collec-
tive and distributive sense of soul, but here the sense appears to be col-
lective, since all soul takes care of the soulless regardless which of the
forms soul assumes. But it is also evident that soul admits of differentiation, since soul appears in distinct forms (εἴδεσι). Such differentiation need not, by itself, preclude soul existing distributively. In the
Phaedrus, there is human soul, divine soul, and (later) animal soul—
all these are forms of soul in which, presumably, certain properties are
constant. But of course the soul of Zeus is not identical to the soul of
Hera, the soul of Socrates need not be indistinguishable from the soul
of Phaedrus, etc.

At this point, soul is not divided into human and divine—its only
characteristics are that it is perfect and fully winged. Only soul fully
winged can mount upward, thereby being capable of universal governance. This kind of motion implies that the closer soul gets to the limits
of the heavens, the more perfect soul becomes; the perfection of soul
admits of degrees, depending on the distance between soul and whatever is upward. Soul's perfection depends on how it is acted upon by
what is at—or (as we shall see) above—the heavens, and only the dimension of soul closest to this reality will be capable of governing the
cosmos. Socrates will develop this implied metaphysics when he
speaks "the truth about the truth."

Soul is, however, subject to the loss of its wings—from which it
does not follow that soul has lost the capacity to regrow them. This loss
nonetheless shows that a specific nature can be acted upon and suffer
privation of a sort. Now without wings, soul is borne along, continuing
to float in accordance with its natural tendency to ascend toward the

heavens, until it fixes on something solid. This "something" thus possesses a degree of existence prior to being visited by soul, implying that entities exist, as material, without the presence of soul. It follows then that matter, as the principle underlying these indetermine things, is no less primordial than soul. No argument is given to show that matter and soul are coeval; but if they are, surely matter will relate to soul in ways no less fundamental than soul's motion in relation to matter.

The principle reality of soul is self-motion, established in the *archē* introducing the analysis of soul's nature. We now have the two poles, as it were, defining the limits of soul's self-motion. On the one hand, fully winged soul can move up and thereby rule the cosmos, implying that soul must involve itself in this kind of motion if soul is to be perfected. On the other hand, soul without wings will move down toward what is solid, a motion which, although running contrary to soul's perfection, is no less proper to soul's nature if soul can no longer move in the opposite direction. The self-motion of soul is controlled by two types of reality—whatever exists above, attracting soul toward realizing its perfection, and material things, drawing soul downward when soul lacks wings.

This portion of the palinode thus exemplifies describing the nature of soul in the technical sense, i.e., how soul acts and is acted upon. That soul possesses continuous self-motion can be demonstrated by reasoned discourse; what directs soul's motion is of sufficient metaphysical complexity to require a mythic figure for its specification. But in either case, the analysis is dictated by the theory of determining a thing's nature. It is vital to keep this methodological aspect of the account in mind when determining the sense of the figure representing the form of soul.

Once soul makes itself at home in the solid thing, that thing becomes an earthly body, i.e., an entity which, as moving, is qualitatively different from what it was as simply material. This thing seems to be moving itself, but it appears that way because soul has the power to transform a material thing into an earthly body. The appeal to power (δύναμιν) is important in showing that Socrates continues to analyze soul according to the technical specification of determining a thing's nature. Thus it is in the nature of soul—even soul bereft of its wings—to have the power to move something other than itself. Notice that if the earthly bodies referred to here include (what we call) plants and animals, then all these things are living by virtue of a principle of life which is by nature winged. All living things thus retain a measure of receptivity to whatever allows soul, when fully winged, to govern the universe.

The highest manifestation of soul occurs at the level of divinity. Notice, however, that the gods necessarily display a derivative reality if their existence depends on soul, since soul is, by nature, a principle of self-motion. The self-motion of soul may be no less eternal than the eternality of the Forms, but the fact that the gods are in motion means that the gods have diminished reality when compared to the realities existing beyond the heavens.

Whether or not the gods possess body as well as soul is left undecided. Socrates implicitly leaves the matter open when he entreats god to find his words on this matter as "dear" as possible. In any event, a mortal can neither understand nor know an immortal, if immortality refers to a type of soul existing solely by itself. The contrast between this pair of cognitive approaches to the divine should be noted. To deny that we can understand (ἰδόντες) the divine nature covers the kind of knowledge pertaining to formal reality; to deny that we have sufficiently known (νοήσαντες) this nature represents a higher kind of awareness, one which, as the word itself suggests, is accessible to a higher function of intelligence. The suggestion is that we do in fact know something about the divine nature, but that this knowledge was not sufficiently mastered when it was originally acquired.[12] Socrates will emphasize the contrast between these two types of cognition shortly, when the distinction is drawn between mind and intellect.

We are now in a position to continue the analysis of the figure of soul's horses and driver from the standpoint of the complex metaphysics underlying the determination of soul's nature. Consider again the word ἡνιόχου, usually translated as "charioteer." A charioteer requires a chariot, even when the charioteer is divine. But this particular charioteer seems to be without a chariot. For in the initial statement and development of soul's powers, applicable to both divine and human soul, Socrates is describing just soul—not the composite of soul and body. Thus, the ready inclination to identify this function of soul as equivalent to a charioteer must be suppressed, since being a charioteer presupposes driving a chariot, and at this point in the figure there is no chariot. How then does the chariot fit into this mythic figure? Hackforth quickly disposes of this concern. His answer—it does not fit in; the chariot "has no symbolic value . . ." (p. 77).[13] For Hackforth, the mythic chariot can never go anywhere in its symbolic travels with soul.

But are we to believe that Plato, crafting one of his most powerful mythical statements on matters of great moment, should be so heedless of structural detail as to introduce an element into a crucial allegory and then leave it symbolically unattached to anything else in that statement? Since the relation between charioteer and chariot is not identical to the relation between the soul and body of the charioteer, we "weigh down" this portion of the palinode unnecessarily if, at this juncture, we burden soul with towing around an inanimate chariot. Recall again that the original distinction between mortal and immortal was based on a division of *living being*—and the chariot as such is lifeless and therefore an inappropriate element in the structure of the figure representing soul's power.

Translating ἡνιόχου as "charioteer" anticipates the fact that it is part of the nature of soul to be related to something other than itself. Furthermore, this something resembles a chariot in the sense that both exist as lifeless. But it is not a chariot—it is body and, at this point, not a particular body but body in the broadest sense, i.e., matter attracting part of soul's nature and (in the case of a particular human body) capable of being moved by soul's power of animation. Strictly speaking then, at this point in the second speech, ἡνιόχου is not a charioteer; it is a driver whose function is to control the horses of soul and whatever powers and capacities belong to the nature of soul—including the capacity of soul to be affected by the body which it, soul, may—or, importantly, may not—come to animate.

The importance of seeing soul's driver in this more fundamental sense rather than in relation to a chariot (construed as a determinate body) becomes even more prominent during the next phase of the figure.

The Nature of Soul's Wings

It is the natural power of the wing to lift what is heavy and soar to the place where dwell the race of the gods. More than anything else bodily, the wing shares in the divine. Now the divine is beautiful, wise, good, and all such things. By these the wing of soul is fed and grows; by their opposites, ugliness and evil, the wing is wasted and destroyed (246d–e).

Socrates continues to couch the discussion of soul's wings in terms of its nature. Thus, wing acts by lifting what is heavy upwards, toward the race of the gods, and is acted upon by vileness and evil, which can damage or even destroy the wing. Presumably the destruction of soul's wings would not affect the continued existence of soul, for then soul would not be immortal. If therefore soul's wings were destroyed, then soul retains its self-motion but no longer has the capacity of lifting anything toward the divine realm. This implication would account for the soul of a human being becoming so enmeshed in evil that in its next life cycle it animates a lower animal rather than another human, i.e., its wings have been destroyed and thus it cannot lift an animal toward the gods.

In having the capacity to lift what is heavy toward the divine, the wing shares in the divine more than anything else pertaining to the body. The language of sharing (κεκοινώνηκε) recalls the participation relation. The implication is that the body as such participates in the nature of the divine, since the wing, as a bodily feature, shares in the divine more than anything else belonging to the body. But if so, then body is not intrinsically evil, since if it were then it could not share in the divine at all. Presumably body is evil only to the extent that as a type of entity having weight, it exists at one end of a metaphysical spectrum with pure reality at the other extreme. This feature of the wing's nature is important in locating body on the same metaphysical plane as soul (in terms of implications drawn from mythic imagery).

The wing shares in the divine. But the divine itself shares in true being. When Socrates characterizes the divine as "beautiful, wise, good, and all these thing," he is describing what is common to all the gods (although not all gods may see all these things), hence the terms "race" (γένος) of the gods and the "divine" (θείου). But the point now is the intimate connection between divinity and the Forms, for this connection will be developed later in the speech.

The Divine Ascent to Reality

The great leader in heaven is Zeus, who leads, driving a winged chariot, arranging and caring for all things. He is followed by an army of gods and daimons deployed, in order, in eleven squadrons, with Hestia alone remaining at the home of the gods. Of the other deities, each of the twelve gods designated as rulers is assigned a certain task. There are many blessed and divine orbits within the heavens, and the gods are happily nourished on these sights, each of them doing the task assigned. Any deity, if willing and able, can always follow another deity, for jealousy is absent from the divine choir.

When the gods go toward a feast and a banquet, they mount upward toward the top of the heavens. The chariots of the gods, well-guided and tractable, easily make the ascent, but the others have difficulty. For the evil horse, having weight, pulls toward the earth all drivers who have not trained this horse well—and here the extremity of toil and effort awaits these souls. But when the souls called immortal reach the summit, they go outside, standing on the surface of the heavens, and having taking their positions, the revolution of the heavens carries them all the way around while they gaze at "the things" beyond the heavens (246e–247c).

The gods are now expressly seen as embodied—yet still immortal in the sense explained above. Only at this point does Socrates add that Zeus drives a winged chariot, thus reinforcing the interpretation that in the initial description of soul's powers, ἡνιόχου should be rendered "driver" rather than "charioteer" in order to emphasize that the soul as such, apart from any direct relation to body, is capable of motion in opposed directions.

Zeus arranges and cares for all things. This care (ἐπιμελούμενος) recalls the care (ἐπιμελεῖται) provided by soul for the soulless when all soul (considered collectively), is fully winged, traversing the heavens and appearing in a variety of forms (246c). If Zeus represents the deomorphic equivalent of all soul, then all as the object of Zeus' care refers to everything, whether living or nonliving—including all the other gods. Thus, the various tasks performed by the subordinate leader gods have been assigned by Zeus, and the demarcation of gods and daimons into twelve groups, arranged in sequence according to a principle of hierarchy, reflects the order Zeus has imposed on the divine establishment on the basis of what each god has seen of the reality beyond the heavens. Presumably the daimons include souls of deities less divine than the gods proper (recall that Eros in the *Symposium* is a daimon).

Only two of the ruling deities are named at this point—Zeus and Hestia, who, it is said, remains in the house of the gods. The suggestion is that the motion of the gods throughout the heavens, attending to their various obligations, is only part of their nature. Thus, the gods must rest as well as labor. Hestia, goddess of the hearth—who swore on Zeus' head to remain a virgin—is apparently the most earthlike of the gods, and in this respect is the divine counterpart to Zeus. Since the divine nature includes residence in a home, it is fitting that a deity have the function of preserving that home, thus guaranteeing this aspect of divinity. It is also fitting that Socrates refers to the race (γένος) of the gods, since the lineage from Zeus to Hestia describes a genus of sorts, a kind of continuum ranging from most to least divine. Thus, in staying home while the other gods travel about the heavens, Hestia establishes an analogy to the earth, and to matter in general, in the sense that the gods, necessarily seen as embodied, must satisfy whatever requirements are placed on them by having such a nature. Finally, the fact that the gods' house is within the heavens suggests that they regularly experience less reality when discharging their duties than when they ascend to rest on the surface of the heavens. The extent to which the home of the gods represents their natural habitat, so to speak, is the extent to which the gods embody a derivative degree of reality.

It is also important to note that the gods, as a race, derive happiness from the blessed sights in the heavens in conjunction with performing their function. In the preamble to the discussion of love as the fourth type of madness, it was said that love was given to us for our greatest good fortune. Thus, the blessed sights the gods witness in the heavens—the divine counterpart to appearances of the Forms experienced by human souls when these souls become incarnate—are combined with "practical" affairs; in this regard, their mode of existence reflects the life of mortal happiness, harmonious interplay of pure knowledge and activity guided by that knowledge.

To affirm that the gods can follow each other to the extent that they see fit derives from the fact that the gods' functions are fixed. And the lack of jealously among the gods reveals that however they become related to one another, no deity ever questions or reacts negatively to this fixedness (in this regard, the chorus of gods is somewhat removed from the typical philosophy department). Socrates notes that the gods travel in orbits throughout the heavens, suggesting that each god eventually circumscribes the heavens, seeing as much as it is possible to see from that particular vantage point. Given such glimpses of true reality, how could any god ever be jealous of any other god? There is, however, an appetitive factor in divine nature, since the gods move about if they so wish. The fact that they must have the power to do so implies that the nature of the gods is complex, including an element of privation.

But the gods must not only leave their home to execute their duties and to follow their peers—they must leave the heavens as well. Even divine soul requires wings in order to ascend within the heavens to secure attendance at their feast and banquet. One property of body, weight, is shared by both mortal and immortal living beings. The gods thus possess a type of symbolic weight resulting from the union of divine soul with body. As a result, even the gods must be carried up in order to govern and, ultimately, to be in a position to receive the sustenance by virtue of which they are divine (cf. 249c). Hence the need for divine wings.

This section of the palinode is devoted almost exclusively to an account of the divine ascent to reality. There is, however, one brief but significant excursus dealing with nondivine soul. In contrast to divine soul, the other souls have great difficulty in making the ascent. These types of soul all have, by nature, an evil horse. Socrates then describes the core sense of evil in this context, a description crucial for determining the allegorical sense of the figure representing the form of soul.

The reason for the difficulty of the other souls is that their evil horse, having weight, draws the chariots of these souls down toward earth. The weight (βρίθει) which the evil horse shares in should be contrasted with the weighted (ἐμβριθὲς) condition which it is the natural purpose of wing to lift toward the dwelling place of the gods (246d). The primary function of the evil horse concerns the phenomenon of weight; this horse has, or, more literally perhaps, participates in (μετέχων) weight. As such, the evil horse represents the natural capacity for motion away from the vault of heaven, just as the winged part of soul has the capacity for motion toward this region. The imagistic figure contrasting divine and nondivine soul again exemplifies the methodological requirement for analyzing a thing's nature, i.e., showing how it can act and be acted upon (movement toward the heavens and away from the earth, or vice versa).

The evilness of the evil horse is not the mere presence of matter. Rather, as Socrates explicitly says, the evil is weight, i.e., the *attraction* of something that "participates in" matter toward a central material locus, in this case the earth proper. If matter itself were evil, then the mere fact that soul had a propensity to matter would make soul ineradicably evil and presumably imply that soul's attraction toward the earth is not just a capacity, but a capacity bound to be actualized. At this level of mythic representation, however, evil becomes the attraction for whatever may draw soul away from what soul as a whole desires to experience.[14]

Nonetheless, soul has a natural disposition for evil in this sense, since the attraction of the evil horse for the earth is exercised prior to soul losing its wings. Socrates is careful to note that the whole soul can counteract the sway of the evil horse, on condition that the charioteer "train" this horse. But the evil horse is in soul by nature, and no amount of training will eliminate its presence. The disposition for evil can be controlled, not extirpated.

This dimension of evil, in conjunction with the divine ascent to the banquet of truth, represents the metaphysical basis for interpreting the figure of soul's form. The picture that begins to emerge of human soul (as one kind of nondivine soul) is of a principle of life with complex natural powers simultaneously drawing soul toward mutually opposed realities. Note that in this typification of evil, no mention is made about soul's desires, or strategies for the satisfaction of carnal appetites. If the image of soul as winged horses and driver is interpreted just as developed so far, then Socrates is envisioning soul as moving, and moving eternally, within an eternal universe defined by bipolarity—at one extreme is the reality which, as we shall see, is beyond the heavens, at the other extreme is the earth, no less fundamental in reality, and all that is earthly, material, and characterized by weight. Socrates will amplify the character of each of soul's three components; for now, the driver of soul directs it toward reality, the good horse provides the motion toward that destination, the evil horse is attracted toward matter, the other extreme. Indeed, the allegory is basically metaphysical, and the psychological analogues defining soul's nature are based on this metaphysical perspective.

The gods are about to partake of the divine feast. First, however, we are reminded that the gods are immortal only in the sense that "we call" them immortal; the word "immortal," which as defined earlier incorporates an essential connection between body and soul, reflects a mode of apprehension befitting the limits of human nature. When these immortals reach the top of the heavens, they stand there and the heavens revolve in such a way that the gods behold the things outside the heavens.

Although motion is proper to the gods while they pursue their assigned functions *within* the heavens, once they have ascended to the upper *surface* of the heavens, they remain motionless. The gods then witness what is beyond the heavens, not because of any agency on their part but, more primordially, because the heavens themselves rotate.

The gods thus become one with the heavens, suggesting that the very possibility of cosmic motion is governed by whatever is beyond the heavens. This striking image resists literal paraphrase, since whatever was outside the heavens would exist both outside of space (and therefore be incapable of being seen) as well as time (since the heavens themselves define the limits of time if time is dependent on motion, particularly the motion of the heavens as such).

The things outside the heavens beheld by the gods are denoted only by the neutral plural article, leaving open the precise nature of these things. In one sense, the things seen are the Forms; the implication that what exists there is outside of space and time coheres with the properties of the Forms given in other dialogues. Also, the lack of motion characterizing the gods once they are atop the heavens reflects the stability of the reality they are witnessing. But it would be premature to conclude that the gods behold just the Forms. The metaphysical character of the divine vision is more complex, as we shall see in the next chapter when Socrates dares to speak "the truth about the truth."

CHAPTER 4

Soul and Truth (247c–250d)

The gods have taken their place on the rim of the heavens, beholding what is beyond. For Socrates, this region was never, nor will ever be, worthily hymned by any earthly poet. It is, however, as Socrates shall now say, since he must "say the truth" because his speaking concerns "the truth" (247c).

Poetry and Truth

Socrates asserts confidently that poetry has limits if employed to describe reality. However, to divorce what Socrates is about to say from the range of poetic production does not mean that Socrates' own pronouncements are not, at least in part, poetically inspired. At the conclusion of the palinode (257a), Socrates refers to the "poetical language" he had to employ; if such language comes into play at 247c, then Socrates is indeed poetizing about the truth. But Socrates is an earthly poet, and would seem precluded by that fact from attaining the required bardic heights. The inspiration required to speak the truth about "the truth" must therefore come from a source other than the Muse of poetry. But what source? The answer depends on the truth, since if Socrates does say the truth about what is true, he does so through language with, perhaps, a poetic dimension, but which is ultimately sanctioned by a source other than that allowing all earthly poets, however inspired they may be, to poetize.

Reality and Divine Soul

The inspired Socrates says that the regions above the heavens hold the colorless, formless, and intangible truly existing being, the subject of all true knowledge, a place discernible only to "mind, the pilot of soul." Now the divine intellect is nourished on "mind and pure knowledge," as is every soul which cares to receive its proper food, thereby rejoicing in "seeing reality" for a certain length of time. While it beholds truth, soul is nourished and prospers until the revolution of the heavens brings soul again to the same place. During this revolution, soul sees justice itself, temperance, and knowledge—not knowledge with a genesis, varying in relation to the things we now call reality, but knowledge of what exists in true being. In the same way, soul beholds and is nourished by all other truly real being. After receiving this sustenance, divine soul moves through the heavens and goes home. There the driver places the horses of divine soul in the stable, feeding and watering them with ambrosia and nectar (247d–e).

This "hymn" on the regions above the heavens is important not only for defining the boundaries of the metaphysics animating the *Phaedrus*, but also in grounding the unity between the account of love in the palinode and the theory of rhetoric advanced in the discursive phase of the dialogue. Socrates is now speaking in mythic terms—he will make this characteristic explicit at 253c8. But the distinctions developed in this section should still be taken seriously, with the proviso, discussed earlier, that any myth must be subjected to analysis before its content can be properly interpreted.

Note the contrast in this passage between mind, *nous*, and intellect, *dianoia*. Mind has been characterized as the pilot of soul. But if divine intellect is fed on mind (and pure knowledge), then mind and intellect are not identical. According to the figure for soul's nature, the driver of soul becomes a combination of mind and intellect, each presumably performing different cognitive functions. The gods, animated by a type of soul with this structure, must therefore ratiocinate as humans do, but with the crucial difference that their deliberations are always directed by mind, whereas other types of soul do not have that guarantee.

If mind pilots soul, it must do so on the basis of what mind discerns when viewing the region beyond the heavens, i.e., the truth. This region is described, first, in terms of three negations—it lacks color, shape, and any kind of tangible existence. The third characteristic, intangibility, gathers together the first two descriptions and then generalizes their sense; in no respect does truth display perceptual properties. Next Socrates describes the truth in positive terms—it is the "really existing being" (οὐσία ὄντως οὖσα). At this point, the nature of this being receives no additional determination. It would be premature then to infer that this complex reference to being meant just the Forms.[1] This is so for two reasons: first, Socrates has various terminology available for naming the Forms in the abstract (as he will do presently); why then call the Forms *ousia* and not, e.g., *ta eidē*? Second, really existing being might include a reality other than and not reducible to the Forms; in this case, an extremely general locution would be required to represent this metaphysical complexity.

The divine intellect is fed on mind and pure knowledge. This reference to knowledge appears again when divine soul is described as seeing the truth during one of its cycles on the rim of the heavens. Such knowledge, Socrates says, is not of things we call real, but of realities abiding in real being. Justice and temperance are also mentioned, befitting their role as paramount realities in the political and moral order. However, the inclusion of knowledge, *epistēmē*, as a member of this trio is curious, for it does not seem parallel to justice and temperance.[2] Presumably there is a Form of knowledge, as there are Forms of justice and temperance. But knowledge is broader than either justice or temporance (or any single Form) in naming whatever can be understood about any Form.

I suggest therefore that Socrates cites knowledge at this point to emphasize that kind of cognition capable of assimilating everything that exists insofar as it belongs to the truth, i.e., justice, temperance, all other Forms—and any other dimension of reality. From this perspective, the inclusion of knowledge is, again, a kind of generalization after particular objects of knowledge have been identified. The intellect is fed on such pure knowledge, pure if unmixed with experience of particular beings and encompassing everything that knowledge is capable of comprehending.

When Socrates describes the truth as really existing being, and then specifies two realities later identified as Forms, it may appear that being, *ousia*, is what is common to all the Forms taken collectively. But there is another possibility. Socrates describes the really existing being as what holds (ἔχει) the region beyond heavens. In the *Phaedo*, the Anaxagorean theory of causality is criticized for overlooking that which "embraces and holds together all things" (99c). What holds together all things would presumably hold each Form together with all other Forms so that not only each Form could be known as such, but also all relations possible between and among Forms. In the *Phaedo*, what holds together all things is "the good," *to agathon* (99c). If the object of pure knowledge is not just the Forms as such, but the Forms as coexisting with each other within the universal bonding of the good, then the implied presence of the good sanctions the appeal to mind, *nous*, as essential to knowledge, and necessitates using an extremely general term, *ousia*, to describe such reality. (This chapter will conclude by defending this interpretation of the seminal importance of the good in Socrates' account of the "mysteries" in relation to truth.)

The Socratic evocation of true reality concludes with an especially vivid detail—the driver of divine soul puts up the horses at the manger, feeding them ambrosia and giving them nectar to drink. The implication is that the horses of divine soul are not themselves nourished by the vision of reality outside the heavens; if they were, there would be no need to provide special sustenance for them within the heavens. Ambrosia and nectar are, of course, the standard fare for the gods while in their heavenly abode; the fact that here the horses of the gods' souls receive this food illustrates the distinction between the divine charioteer and the divine horses.

Since the horses are essential to divine soul, the different types of nourishment establish that divine soul is complex insofar as it partakes of different degrees of reality. The highest fare bestowed on the gods (from the perspective of Greek poetry) becomes the sustenance of the lowest phase of the divine nature (from the standpoint of mythic truth). A standard poeticism is preserved, but transformed into a minor key by virtue of the main metaphysical theme and the unique role played by the divine charioteer in apprehending the degrees of reality which inhabit the regions beyond the heavens. The fact that divine soul is partly constituted by horses implies that the nature of divine soul can be affected by a dimension of reality less real than that which is related to the driver of divine soul. And we shall see that the differentiation and implied ranking of the parts of divine soul are paralleled in human soul.

Reality and Human Soul

In contrast to the life of the gods, the life of the other souls may be described thus. Of these souls, the best type follows the gods, lifting the driver's head into the outer region, riding on the revolution of the heavens. But they are beset by their horses, scarcely (*mogis*) seeing the realities. Another type of soul now rises, now sinks, its unruly horses allowing it to see some realities but not others. All other souls follow, straining for but unable to attain the upper reaches. They follow around the revolution from below, trampling and colliding with one another in trying to pass their neighbors. Much confusion and rivalry result— many souls are lamed, their wings broken due to the incompetence of souls' drivers. These souls, after expending great effort, leave without seeing reality; they then feed on opinion.

This intense desire to see truth rests on the fact that the best part of soul is fed there, with the nature of soul's wings, which elevate soul, nourished by what is seen. Destiny decrees that a soul, following god and seeing any of the "truths," will not be harmed until the next period of heavenly traversal; if it always secures this vision, soul always remains unharmed. But if soul cannot follow a god, then it cannot see, and when by accident it is filled with heaviness and evil, becoming weighty, it falls to the earth (248a–c).

Socrates divides soul into divine and others. He then describes those of the other souls who follow god, the best souls, in terms of their ability to lift the head of the driver into the outer region. If the other souls include those prospectively animating both humans and nonhuman living things, then when Socrates says that all souls seek to follow god, the implication is that all souls—regardless what kind of thing soul may subsequently animate—have the capacity to know a measure of reality. Thus, an animal soul, insofar as it is soul, remains to some extent guided by the desire to behold reality. Furthermore, if plants have souls, then they too, *qua* soul, would share in the same fundamental desire. Animals are mentioned in the *Phaedrus* as ensouled; plants are not. But the picture that emerges is of a dimension of life cutting across generic differences and enabling anything alive to receive direction from mind as the fountainhead of all purposive activity.

The imperfect vision of those souls achieving the rim of the heavens is caused by the behavior of their horses. They trouble soul, so the realities are only partially beheld, or they are unruly, with soul seeing only some realities and not others. The first type of soul apparently sees all the realities that its attendant deity sees, but not as clearly as the accompanying divine soul because of the pressure in the other direction caused by the troublesome horses. The second type sees some realities (presumably also with less than perfect clarity) but does not see others at all, in this case because the unruly horses occasionally drag soul altogether beneath the rim of the heavens. The contrast is therefore between qualitative and quantitative differences in beholding reality, between how well reality is known and how much reality is known. Note also that the first type is, apparently, the best that human soul can do; thus if this type of soul accompanied Zeus, then it would see all the realities (assuming that Zeus saw all the realities), but its vision of any one reality would be blurred. The point is, however, that at least one type of human soul has partial cognizance of all reality.[3]

Those souls not seeing any realities are held back by the incompetence of their drivers. The suggestion is that soul always retains the possibility of seeing reality as long as the driver of soul properly steers the whole soul. Without such direction, souls become rivals with one another, jealously results, conflicts ensue, and soul's wings are broken, with consequent inability to make the ascent with a deity toward the truth. Unlike the souls of the gods, for whom jealousy does not exist (247b), the souls of humans fall prey to concern for what other souls are doing, and to the desire to upstage their peers. Note, however, that this rivalry is not for the acquisition of wealth, power, or fame—nor does it derive from the pressure of body on soul, for at this point soul has not yet fallen and is still without body. The conflict is based on a fundamental desire for a closer view of reality. The implication is perhaps that all subsequent forms of rivalry, once soul has become beset by human body, originate from concern for reality, or at least what soul, with body, takes to be real, a construal which may take various tangible but skewed forms—fame, power, wealth, carnal pleasure, etc. Those souls failing to see any part of reality go away, sustaining themselves on "opinion" (in Hackforth's striking phrase, the "food of semblance"). It appears then that opinion is no less eternal, and necessary, as truth, assuming that all forms of soul's nourishment are as necessary as the various degrees of success found in soul's quest for reality. If so, then objects of opinion must exist—and, by implication, exist eternally—to balance the objects of knowledge represented by the realities. This presupposition anticipates the fundamental importance of the earth, and of matter in general, as grounding the existence of objects of opinion.

A soul seeing any of the truths will be safe until the next traversal of the heavens, and if this soul always secures such a vision, then soul will always be safe in this respect. It is not necessary therefore that soul must eventually inhabit some kind of body; soul can always exist just as soul, on condition that soul successfully achieves vision of at least one of the realities. This point is essential in determining the relevance of evil insofar as it defines, and affects, the nature of soul. The immediate implication is that soul's driver always remains a driver, since soul never loses its various capacities, but may never become a charioteer, since it is not necessary that soul must inhabit a body.

Destiny and Fallen Soul

Some souls fall away from the vision of reality, are somehow filled with forgetfulness and evil, grow heavy, and then sink to the earth. Destiny decrees that the first birth of such a soul will not animate the body of an animal, but rather that kind of being which is human. Socrates then enumerates a ranked series of callings and avocations based on the extent to which the souls of these types of human life have beheld the truth (248d–e). The first type—representing the soul that has seen "the most"—comprises the birth of one who is to be "a philosopher or a lover of beauty or one of a musical and loving nature." Hackforth's remark (p. 83) on this first life typifies scholarly opinion: "The first life needs no comment, save that the *philokalos*, *mousikos*, and *erotikos* are not persons others than the *philosophos*, but denote aspects of him. . . ."[4] Hackforth denies that real distinctions occur among these three types, even though he admits such distinctions on several of the lower levels—e.g., the third level has "a politician or man of business or a financier," where three distinct types are intended. But this denial, asserted without argument, is premature, and an examination of the first level will show that it is a questionable reading.

Hackforth contends that the lover of beauty and the person of a musical and loving nature are virtually identical. But such synonymy clashes with implications from other texts in the *Phaedrus*. Later in the palinode, Socrates distinguishes between the awesome love which wisdom and the rest of the Forms would inspire if they were visible and the privileged status of beauty, the clearest and most loved of the Forms (250d–e). It would follow then that the lover of wisdom, the philosopher, is distinct from and in fact higher than the lover of beauty simply because beauty is the most accessible Form and therefore the most receptive to love, while wisdom and all other Forms require concentrated intellection before they yield their own distinctive natures. Presumably a lover of wisdom is also a lover of beauty, since the soul of the philosopher has seen the most reality and beauty is the most palpable Form (cf. 250d). But a lover of beauty is a lover of wisdom (and the other Forms) only if the manifest availability of beauty could be transmuted into a similar appreciation of all less visible

Forms. Thus, a lover of beauty who did not also love temperance would remain distant from the love of the philosopher, who loves both realities. Therefore, the philosopher is both distinct from and higher than the lover of beauty.

It may also be inferred that the lover of beauty is higher than the lover of the Muses. The lover of the Muses loves nine deities, i.e., the various products these deities inspire. But these deities, as deities, receive their being from the visions of reality they behold (a point Socrates will make clear at 249c). Thus a lover of beauty loves the Form beauty, but a lover of the Muses loves a set of beings who receive their reality from the Form beauty (and all other Forms). Now the individual with a musical and loving nature would, as a loving enthusiast for the products of the Muses, be naturally attracted to what all the Muses represent, including philosophy proper. However, this individual must work through the "aesthetic" (understood in the Greek sense) level of reality embodied in the products inspired by the Muses, a passage potentially treacherous, as attested to (albeit mythically) by the destiny of those early humans who become cicadas because they could not orient the lambent song of the Muses with other, more mundane human concerns (cf. 259b–e). Therefore, loving the Muses becomes a derivative degree of love following from the derivative character of its object.

In general, the various levels of soul are both internally differentiated and ordered—the philosopher is higher than the lover of beauty, and the lover of beauty is higher than the lover of the Muses. The order of lives thus contains two types of differentiation: the difference between any two levels is one of kind and is apparently discrete, the difference between (or among) the members identified within each level is one of degree and is continuous, since each level is defined by the same amount of reality seen.

The order of lives is based on the premise that all types of soul arranged in this hierarchy have seen some of the truth. This condition is clear when Socrates asserts that no soul having seen any of the truths will enliven a beast at soul's first birth. Thus when soul falls into the nine types of human life, each type is animated by a soul which has seen some truth during one of the cycles round the heavens with an attendant deity. The degrees of truth will vary; the soul of a poet has seen more reality than the soul of a craftsman but less reality than the soul of a prophet. The ordering of the hierarchy is not justified,[5] and perhaps this is one phase of the palinode which, as Socrates will say in assessing the speech as a whole, has veered away from the truth (265a). It may be noted, however, that the list is enumerated, a feature suggesting that Socrates is confident such a list can be accurately produced, since enumerating the types of a thing is one of the essential steps involved in knowing the nature of that thing (cf. 270d).

At the low end of this soul-spectrum, the tyrant, the type of soul most opposed to that of the philosopher, has therefore seen some of the truth, from which it may be inferred that no tyrant is all bad, or, more accurately perhaps, that the soul of even the basest tyrant had, at one point, seen something of the truth. The highest level of soul, the philosophical, has seen the most reality. Recall, however, that such vision was vouchsafed to this kind of soul during a previous cycle. Thus, even the soul of a philosopher can—indeed does—become forgetful, since this condition must affect soul in order for it to fall and begin to animate a specific type of human being. It is important to emphasize this aspect of the account, for it vividly conveys how even the greatest philosopher is evil simply by virtue of the fact that the soul of this philosopher must have fallen victim to mischance and evil in order to take up residence in an embodied being. However much reality that soul saw during any one cycle upon the rim of the heavens, there was a subsequent cycle when it beheld nothing of this reality, suffered from an incompetent driver, was thereby compelled to feed on opinion, became heavy, and fell toward the source of weight. The philosophical life, lived by a human being with other human beings, is a type of existence which, although the highest in its accessibility to reality, remains fraught with peril and the chance for error and other forms of misadventure.

It is vital to note that this evil besets soul before soul becomes related to a specific type of body. Socrates has left open the possibility that soul may never enter a body, a state of perfection secured as long as soul, when accompanying a god, sees something of truth. Some souls do fall, however, implying that soul has the capacity to be affected by reality other than the reality beyond the heavens. When this capacity is actualized, soul moves toward this lower reality, a motion producing soul's evil and weight.

But why is this evil propensity activated? The account offers no explanation other than to appeal to mischance, a notion which may mean that it just happens to some souls but perhaps not to others. In addition, the usage of destiny in this passage suggests fundamental questions concerning the nature of soul in relation to the control, or lack of control, exhibited by this power. If. e.g., soul is in the hands of destiny, would it also follow that truth and destiny are equally fundamental, and equally powerful? The question is no less tantalizing as it is unanswerable, given that the text—a myth, we will recall—merely hints at the status of destiny in this regard.[6]

The Afterlife of Human Soul

For all types distinguished in the hierarchy of lives, those who live justly fare better than those who live unjustly. Each soul returns to the place where it came in ten thousand years; such time must pass before soul regains its wings. Only the guileless philosopher or the philosophical lover of youths can become rewinged in less time, for if they have chosen such a life for three consecutive periods of a thousand years, they become winged in the three-thousandth year and fly away. The other souls, having completed their first life, are judged, then go either to places under the earth for punishment or are raised by justice into a heavenly abode, there to lead a life worthy of the life they led while "in human form." For both classes of soul, the passing of a thousand years brings them to a choice of their second life, each soul choosing as it will. At this point, a human soul can enter the life of an animal, and a soul which once animated a human and then enlivened an animal can become again the soul of a human. Only the soul having never seen "the truth" can not pass into human shape (248e–249b).

The appeal to degrees of justice should be noted. If a philosopher loves wisdom, then a philosopher love justice if justice is a part of wisdom. But loving justice does not guarantee that one will be just. Even a philosopher can be unjust, or perhaps more in the spirit of philosophy as the highest life, some philosophers are more just than other philosophers. It would also follow that one tyrant may be less unjust than another tyrant. The fact that each of the nine kinds of life is marked by degrees of justice continues the pattern of the continuum in terms of soul's participation in reality. And, finally, the state of soul after death is directly dependent upon the activity of soul while participating in human life.

So much may be safely inferred. However, at this point, the palinode enters a speculative realm where it is difficult to maintain one's metaphysical bearings. But consider several tentative implications which pertain to the relation between soul and reality. (It may be noted that the following discussion, as indeed the overall approach to this phase of the palinode, is conservative in its demythologizing strategy. Doubtless additional layers of significance will be discernible to commentators studying the *Phaedrus* from different perspectives.)

Socrates says that all souls (with two exceptions discussed below) are judged after their first life, and are either rewarded or punished; then, after a thousand years, they freely choose their second life. After ten thousand years, these souls return to whence they came. Each thousand-year cycle thus comprises the human life span, including those years soul spends by itself after death, i.e., separated from body. After ten of these cycles, soul returns, apparently with its wings fully restored. The important point here is that soul, having lost its wings, will, in due time, always regain them. Whatever soul did during all ten of its thousand year cycles does not matter in this respect; regardless whether soul was animating the most unjust tyrant for ten consecutive periods, that soul will regain its wings, no less than the souls of those who lived higher lives in the highest accord with justice.

The fact that soul is not entirely dictated by destiny in the history of soul's ten-thousand-year cycle becomes clear when Socrates emphasizes that every soul is allowed to choose each of its ten lives during the complete cycle. Such choice is extremely open-ended, however, since the soul of a human can choose the life of an animal, and the soul of an animal—a soul which once animated a human—can choose to become a human again. One can readily imagine a human life so horrendous that the soul having borne that life would willingly choose to become an animal rather than risk another round of unspeakable torment. However, it is difficult to visualize, even mythically, the soul of a horse choosing to become the soul of a charioteer, since the soul of an animal would have to preserve some human characteristics while enlivening that animal just to be in a position to make a choice at all, much less to choose to become a human rather than, say, an animal higher or lower than a horse.

In addition, these implications render understanding human soul as the bearer of personal immortality difficult to maintain. The sheer magnitude of the duration—ten thousand years—suggests that any individuating elements adhering to a human soul during one of its thousand-year periods would be purged over such a span of time, and that this soul would eventually return to an aboriginal winged state ready to begin again another millennia-long cosmic drama. It would appear then that the individual human being is only an occasion for human soul to fulfill its nature as winged, as something that loves and desires communion with true reality.

The sole exceptions to the ten-thousand-year regimen are those ascribed to the souls of the guileless philosopher and the philosophical lover of youths. Hackforth asserts that "these are not two different persons" (p. 85, n2). But, I suggest, these are two different types of person. The first type, a guileless philosopher, is one who pursues the love of wisdom precisely for its own sake, without regard for whatever personal favor that life might bestow. But a lover of youths, one who does so with philosophy (μετὰ φιλοσοφίας), is that individual who loves youths with a view toward maximizing the inherent drive toward wisdom in both himself and that youth. By implication, the first type of philosopher loves wisdom without necessarily loving a youth, suggesting that one need not love another human being in order to be a philosopher—the philosopher must love only wisdom. But if a philosopher does love another human being, it must be done properly and justly.

It does not follow, of course, that a philosopher of the first type is not attracted to other humans, but this attraction would be strictly to what, in humans, is conducive to the love of wisdom. The strict lover of wisdom does not become attached to a particular youth in the way that philosophers of the other type do. The latter approach wisdom through the pursuit of youths, or, more accurately, through pursuing the qualities pertaining to wisdom which, for this type of philosopher, are acquired initially (and, perhaps, necessarily) through the love of a particular human being. The guile or fraudulence that could beset the first type of philosopher is in a sense a more serious threat than the various forms of excess, already well documented, that confront the philosophic lover of youths, for deception could emerge in any of this philosopher's interactions, whether with things, events, or people. The contrast then is between exponents of what might be called pure and dependent philosophy, between the individual who can approach wisdom through experience with anything and the individual who will follow a definite humane course in seeking wisdom. Both approaches intend to the same destination, but they follow different paths in order to reach it.[7]

Recollection: The One and the Many

After stipulating that the soul of every human being has seen some of the truth, Socrates lays down as a necessary condition for displaying this vision that a human being must understand and reason according to a Form, moving from many perceptions into one by means of reasoning.

Socrates says into one (εἰς ἕν), without specifying what kind of unity he has in mind. But since Socrates continues in the same sentence to describe this unity as a remembrance of "those things" soul saw when it journeyed with god and rose into "real being" (249c), the unity must be that of each of the realities. And the plural should be noted— the human soul apparently saw more than one of the realities during its trip with the gods around the heavens.

A human being sees such unity by studying perceptions, which may differ from each other in various respects, and then by remembering the identity between what it sees within this set of perceptions and what it saw when it beheld the reality as a unity. The study of perceptions is controlled by reasoning (λογισμ ῷ), i.e., by drawing inferences from claims reporting what has been perceived. We see the unity of the reality by working through the various implications derived from our perceptions of what is around us. Once in command of this kind of recognition, we can reason according to a Form (κατ' εἶδος), i.e., we can make judgments based on what soul has remembered of the nature of that Form, the rightness of these judgments depending on the extent to which soul has seen this unity as derived from the multiple perceptions instigating the original remembrance of the Form. This is the first time the realities are named using the terminology of Forms (εἴδη); note then that the context concerns the realities insofar as they have become the object of knowledge for soul inhabiting a body.

Only the philosopher's intellect is winged, for the philosopher is always, as far as possible, in contact through memory with those things through which a god is divine (249c).

The philosopher's intellect is directly conversant with the level of reality on which the Forms reside. This contact may vary—Socrates qualifies the philosopher's access as so far as possible, but the philosopher's intellect is always in such contact whereas other souls may never recoup that pristine metaphysical experience. The variations concern the degree to which the remembrance of the philosopher approaches the pure vision of philosophical soul untrammeled by body. Also, the fact that the philosopher's intellect is winged does not imply that the philosopher's entire soul is winged; if the intellect is the driver, then either or both horses of this soul may remain unwinged, thereby keeping the philosopher's converse with reality unavoidably earthbound. The philosophical intellect is not restricted to the remembrance of beauty—it recalls "those things" (i.e., an indeterminate number of the realities). Many individuals, including the philosopher, are naturally sensitive to beauty, but only the philosopher is sensitive to other realities as well, whether moral, mathematical, or mundane.

The nature of the realities recalled by the philosopher is particularly crucial in this context, for Socrates asserts, in the same sentence, that these realities account for why a god is divine. Socrates has already admitted that we must invest the gods with an anthropomorphic form. Now, Socrates affirms that the gods are what they are only because they are related to the realities. This relation may be taken to mean that the gods are merely names representing different collections of Forms. As such, the gods would have no independent reality. To follow Zeus, e.g., is to follow whatever Forms may properly be attributed to the leader of the divine choir. The same would hold, *mutatis mutandis*, for all other deities. On this reading, whereas Socrates was convicted of inventing gods, Plato would effectively destroy the gods altogether.

But there is no need to insinuate such a drastic meaning into the text. Assume that the gods maintain an independent existence, apart from both the realities and mortals. It is asserted that their existence is defined by the relations they bear to the realities. This metaphysical dimension will determine the nature of the gods in a way very different from the characteristics which human being have typically attributed to these gods. Thus, Zeus may be depicted to a human audience as, say, a philanderer, but Zeus as deity (and regardless how his nature appears anthropomorphically) is determined by his converse with the realities. This is the case if the gods, no less than human, must derive nourishment from these realities.

What becomes crucial therefore is the relation joining deity to the realities. Consider: either the gods exist or they do not. Now if the realities and the gods are not the same, then if the gods do not exist, the realities as such are unaffected and may be directly approached by mortals. And even if the gods do exist (as Socrates certainly thinks), mortals must pay heed to them as higher beings—but only because the gods are "good and from the good," and in this respect naturally closer to the truth. Thus, later, when Socrates speaks of following a god, or of making someone resemble a god, he should be understood as advocating an educational process based primarily on the realities metaphysically defining that god rather than on the anthropomorphisms mythically attributed to it.

A further inference may be drawn. Since human souls follow divine soul, then the same realities that activate and energize the gods also perform the same function for human soul. Therefore, with respect to soul's immortality, the distinction between divine and human soul is one of degree, not of kind. Divine soul has continuous and straightforward access to the realities, while human souls' access to them is discontinuous (save for the philosopher) and difficult (for all)—but the same realities animate both types of soul.

Socrates now speaks of the need for a man to employ the memories of the realities rightly, and thereby to be initiated into the perfect mysteries and to become truly perfect. This initiation will, however, alienate such an individual from the many, who will consider him mad rather than inspired (249c–d).

The fact that the many treat the inspired person as deranged is neatly ironic. The philosopher's actions are indeed out of the main stream of normal behavior, and the many are correct to note this fact. But the philosopher does not possess a madness detrimental to one's well-being, as the many believe; quite the contrary, the philosopher is gifted with a vision that places a properly mundane perspective on worldly affairs and lifts the soul of the philosopher into the realm of the truly real. The irony in this situation is that none of the many want to be mad in the way the philosopher is mad; however, if the many were somehow to embrace this madness, they would realize that the philosopher's life is far preferable to theirs. They would then avidly court the madness they now deride.

It is also not just a matter of remembering what soul saw when soul existed prior to birth. A human being must achieve such memories rightly (ὀρθῶς). The nature of this rightness is not specified at this point, but it may be argued that Socrates is anticipating the doctrine of collection and division as the right way to recoup soul's original vision. If so, a direct correlation exists between the prosaicness of this method and the appeals to mysteriousness and initiation into perfection Socrates mentions at this point. The more correctly the method is applied, the less mysterious becomes the process of initiation into perfection.

Madness and Participation

Socrates concludes the account of the fourth type of madness by observing that when one sees an earthly instance of beauty, one is reminded of the true, and one's wings begin to grow. The observer of this
beauty longs to fly but cannot, and for this reason gazes upwards, like
a bird, and, neglecting the things below, is accused of being insane. It
has been shown, Socrates says, that of all inspirations this is the best
and from the best, both for those who have it and for those who share in
it; whoever shares in this madness, loving one of the beautiful things,
is called a lover. For every soul of a human being has seen, by nature,
the realities, otherwise it would not have entered this type of loving
thing. But it is not easy for souls to recall these realities, either those
who saw them only briefly or those who, after falling to the earth, had
the misfortune to establish evil connections and turn to wickedness,
forgetting the holy visions they once beheld (249d–250a).

An individual inspired by the fourth kind of madness, when seeing
something beautiful, remembers "the true" and feels soul's wings
begin to grow. Translations typically read the true beauty. But Socrates
says "the true" (τοῦ ἀληθοῦς)—not true beauty. And there is an important metaphysical reason to take him at his word.

At 247c, Socrates said that in this portion of the palinode, the truth
will be his theme; at 248c, he said that soul attaining a vision of any of
the truths will not fall into body; at 249b, he said that only a soul which
had beheld the truth could enter a human being. Truth is an appellation
for the highest reality, that truly existing being which shines forth for
the benefit of divine and all other forms of soul. Thus, when Socrates
says that seeing a particular instance of beauty puts us in mind of the
true, he does not mean merely that this sight lifts soul toward beauty as
such, but rather that it directs soul to the true, i.e., the entire realm of
reality of which true beauty is one element.

Socrates is now concluding his account of the fourth type of madness, and the madness of love encompasses all the realities, not just the
reality of true beauty. Although the soul of the philosopher is explicitly
asserted as having seen the reality of beauty as such, it is possible that

a human soul in transit with the soul of a god saw the realities of, e.g., justice and circularity—but not the reality of beauty. Yet since beauty is the most palpable Form, this soul, seeing a beautiful thing, could be lifted into the true—that dimension of the truth including just what that soul saw—by experiencing an instance of a Form which that soul did not see during its vision of the realities. This transition is possible because true beauty is the same as true justice, true circularity, etc., in that all are realities accessible to a properly initiated soul.

The point is anticipated in the *Meno*. Socrates cites wise men and women who told of things divine, e.g., that because soul is immortal and has been born many times, it "has beheld all things in this world and the world beyond"; furthermore "the whole of nature is akin" and "there is nothing" soul has not learned (81b–c—Allen's translation). In the *Phaedrus*, the soul of the philosopher has seen only "the most" but the *Meno* passage reinforces taking "most" to mean that the philosopher's soul has seen all the realities, but with incomplete comprehension of this totality.

Socrates has said in the *Phaedrus* that the Forms beauty, prudence, wisdom, justice, temperance, e.g., are dear to souls in providing the happiness human soul seeks. However, does this qualification imply that some Forms are not dear to soul? If so, then when the mature Socrates of the *Phaedrus* becomes the young man of the *Parmenides*, this crucial metaphysical restriction will result in his discomfiture. The young Socrates will deny that dirt, mud, and hair have Forms, and the sage Parmenides cautions him that once he matures as a philosopher, he will no longer scorn the Forms of such entities.

The *Meno* implies that soul will be as happy as possible since soul knows (or knew) everything possible to know. If this implication holds for the *Phaedrus*, then the philosopher cannot rest content with knowing the most about the Forms—the philosopher must continually strive for something like polymath status, for only in knowing as much about everything as a lifetime will allow can the philosopher's soul be projected toward reunion with all the realities, the source of true happiness. It would appear then that all Forms should be precious to soul (as the Platonic Parmenides suggests), not just the Forms with manifest moral effect.

This interpretation of beauty in relation to all other Forms is important in determining the sense of the contrast Socrates has introduced between having and sharing love. Hackforth says (p. 94) that this contrast refers to the lover and the beloved, respectively. But this cannot be correct.

Consider *A* loving *B* and *B* being loved by *A*. According to Hackforth, *B* would share in the love of *A* to the extent that *B* reciprocates the love *A* has for *B*. Now if *B*'s love for *A* is either greater or less than *A*'s love for *B*, then an unbalanced love-relation results. But this imbalance is surely incompatible with the state of commensurate love described later in the palinode when both lovers, having conquered the desires spurred by their souls' evil steeds, enjoy a life of happiness and harmony here on earth (265b). If *B*'s love is either greater or less than *A*'s love, then we must conclude that Socrates established an apparently significant contrast between having and sharing only then to describe an ideal relation between two lovers in which, as Hackforth himself says, "the good of the lover and of the beloved are one and indivisible" (p. 94).

It is essential to determine what having and sharing are having and sharing of. Socrates has just said that his account from 245b till now has concerned the fourth kind of madness. Therefore, when he adds in the next sentence that this is the best type of inspiration, for anyone who has it or shares in it, the contrast concerns the difference between having and sharing madness,[8] not a difference between two individuals, one a lover and the other a beloved. The purpose of the contrast is to distinguish between different modes of being affected by the fourth type of madness. Therefore, since all realities capable of being seen by soul constitute the true object of madness, the distinction between having and sharing concerns different aspects in soul's experience of the truth. Socrates asserts that the fourth type of madness is "of the highest origin" because it is engendered by the realities themselves, and by all the realities as they comprise fully existing being.

I suggest then that having madness indicates the extent to which each level of soul in its present embodied life has access to whatever realities, whatever truth, that level of soul beheld during the period when it existed without body. Thus, having madness exists on as many levels as there are levels of soul, with each successive level experiencing proportionately fewer or less of the realities. This hierarchical sense of madness implies that the nine levels of soul taken as a set do not represent a simple part/whole schema. In other words, the philosophical level of soul is not the only one which "has" madness while each of the succeeding eight levels merely "shares" in it. There are, so to speak, nine different part/whole relations, with the content of each whole determined by the appropriate vision of the realities, the truth, which each level of soul has experienced. Thus, sharing madness refers to the fact that conditions must be fulfilled in order for soul— whether the soul of a philosopher or that of a tyrant—to realize the full extent of the madness which it naturally has in view of its original vision. These conditions are usually more approximated than actualized, and it is to maximize the sharing of madness that Socrates will institute the method of collection and division. We note again the importance of reading the high-flown rhetoric of the palinode from a mere prosaic, but also more practical, metaphysical perspective.

The fact that each of the nine levels of soul is itself differentiated into types suggests that sharing madness will imply the possibility of movement up—or down—within each level. Thus, for example, a philosopher can become infatuated with either a work of art or a human lover and consequently lose sight of the Forms (thereby ceasing, at least temporarily, to be a philosopher in the true sense). And it is possible for a lover to the Muses to see, with appropriate methodological training, all that a lover of beauty and a lover of wisdom can see. The placement of this kind of lover on the highest type of love is therefore fully justified. Viewed in this way, the appeal to the Muses at the outset of Socrates' first speech (237a) becomes more than a formalistic invocation—it attests to the uniform function proper to the Muses in providing tangible entry to the truth. Given this common function, a lover of the Muses should be, by implication if not in fact, a lover of all the Muses. And a lover of one beautiful human can ascend from that love to the love of the Form beauty, and from there to recognizing the relations between that Form and all other Forms, a recognition to which the

philosopher alone has privileged access. Only on the ninth and lowest
level is such movement impossible. Apparently a tyrant must remain
fixed, since on that level of soul the tyrant is the sole occupant.

In sum: having madness refers to the limiting condition that stipulates the degree of truth a given embodied soul can attain based on that
soul's prior vision of the realities; sharing madness refers to the extent
to which that soul has actualized this capacity depending on its success
or failure in employing correctly and justly the memories of the original vision. Having and sharing madness are decidedly metaphysical,
indicating essential and complementary factors in determining the nature of soul with respect to the Forms.

Metaphysics and Mystery

Few souls are left who retain an adequate memory of these visions, and
these few, when they see any of the likenesses to the realities in the
other world, are amazed and can no longer control themselves. But
they do not understand their condition because they do not adequately
perceive. In the earthly likenesses of justice, temperance, and the other
realities "dear" to souls, no light shines, but only a few of us, using our
darkening sense organs, can approach these images, seeing what is
common in their resemblances. In contrast, beauty was seen shining
brightly when, in company with the happy chorus, the souls of humans
saw the blessed sight and vision, we with Zeus, others with another
god. This vision initiated these souls into what is rightly called the
most blessed mysteries, when we lacked experience of the evils to
come. Perfect and simple and calm and happy were the appearances we
saw in the pure light, ourselves being pure and not entombed with what
we carry about and call a body, a condition akin to being imprisoned
like an oyster in its shell (250a–c).

The identity of the "we" in this passage has been disputed.
Hackforth, for example, claims that Plato is referring to himself, and
not to Socrates (p. 93, n2). This is prima facie implausible, since the
"we" is a plurality—who then would accompany Plato on this voyage
of metaphysical discovery? Furthermore, there are textual reasons im-

plying that the reference is to Socrates and Phaedrus. First, toward the conclusion of the palinode, Socrates observes that the speech had to include poetic diction for Phaedrus' sake (257a). Thus, if Socrates knew during the palinode that he was speaking to Phaedrus, an audience of one, then he would not have said "we" unless both Phaedrus and Socrates—or, more accurately, their souls—had been on this voyage with Zeus. And second, the reason Phaedrus' soul could inhabit this vision will be given later, when Socrates describes Phaedrus as a lover of the Muses (φιλόμουσον—259b). Phaedrus thus belongs to the first level of soul, i.e., of a musical or loving nature (248d). And since he is on that level, he can see, in company with Socrates and following the lead of Zeus, what the philosopher can see when resting on the rim of the heavens. Socrates recognizes philosophical possibilities in Phaedrus that may not be apparent, especially given his early excess for Lysian rhetoric.[9]

Few souls on earth remember the realities they saw prior to the fall. The likenesses to the Forms they do see here are so disconcerting because the viewer fails to place these likenesses properly in mind, to see the relation between a given particular and the Form grounding this particular. This condition, or *pathos*, is part of their nature as an ensouled being, and Socrates is careful to employ the technical terminology for determining the nature of something (described at 270d).

The majority of souls fail to make these recognitions because their *organon* are not as sensitive as those belonging to the properly philosophical, individuals who can see dim vestiges of reality where others cannot. Hackforth says (p. 95)[10] that the "dull organs" are "in fact the inadequate reasoning powers of man." But there are reasons to suggest that this identification is not entirely accurate. First, Socrates is speaking about the *organon* of philosophers as somehow privileged, the reaction of the few who see the earthly likenesses of the realities. They do so now with difficulty, although in that other world we, following Zeus, saw the blessed sight of beauty shining by itself. But the souls of philosophers did not reason to this vision of the realities—they simply *saw* or intuitively grasped them, as did the soul of Zeus. And second, the failure to understand why such vision is so disconcerting results from a failure to perceive (διασθάνεσθαι) sufficiently what is being experienced. Later, Socrates will add in clarification that the experience of beauty in particulars shines most clearly through vision, the clearest of our senses (αἰσθήσεων). It seems then that the *organon* are, or at least include, the avenues of perception, with sight the most precise and the other senses less acute in their abilities to behold.

Although Hackforth's identification of the *organon* as reasoning powers is, I believe, incomplete, an important element of rationality should be incorporated into the kind of experience Socrates is describing. The word for perceiving used as 250b, διασθάνεσθαι, has the sense of seeing through the appearance of the thing and into, as it were, the thing's metaphysical structure. Socrates is referring to the sense organs, but not just insofar as they place soul in immediate contact with perceptible things. The senses, especially vision, juxtapose soul with the stuff of things in such a way that soul, when perceiving the thing, can see in that perception the presence of a Form. Such vision would presumably be a skill of the philosopher, particularly one well-versed in the appropriate methods. Thus, human soul perceiving an instance of beauty parallels soul by itself seeing beauty as a reality. A "percept" of a beautiful thing, if separated from the metaphysical ultimate which engendered it, becomes an unnatural abstraction for this approach to perception. Furthermore, the concerted appeals to light during this passage (250b–c) suggest that what the soul of the philosopher perceives is not just the presences of the Form beauty as an isolated reality, but also the relations between beauty and all other realities insofar as the realities are illuminated by the good.[11] For it is precisely at this point that Socrates concludes his description of memory, doing so by noting that the vision of the realities is an initiation for us into the mystery of mysteries.

Mystery and the Good

The immediacy of the perceptual experience of beauty is directly relevant to the concluding section of this portion of the palinode, a soaring rhetorical song about the joyousness of soul when it sojourned with true reality. This joy resulted from participation in the "most blessed mysteries." Earlier, Socrates had also referred to initiation into the mysteries, then with respect to properly employing remembrances of true reality (249d). To what extent are these mysteries open to articulation?

Interpretation of this section is complicated by the fact that Socrates borrows terminology from the mystery cults. Hackforth's only comment is to note the passage's "mystery-symbolism taken probably from Eleusis" (p. 95). De Vries (p. 151) echoes Hackforth's claim about the mystery terminology, but he quotes Thompson as rightly pointing out that "here the transposition" of a mystery terminology is momentarily interrupted, with the passage referring to the Forms "rather than to the Eleusinian images." The precise analogues to the Eleusinian images will probably never be known. But even if these analogues were known, it would not follow that their metaphorical relevance to the metaphysics developed in the *Phaedrus* could be determined just from that information. As we shall see, it is possible to sketch an outline of these mysteries by considering other passages in the *Phaedrus*.[12]

Socrates describes the vision he had of beauty "shining" brightly. This vision is just one of the apparitions which soul had when it accompanied divine soul to the rim of the heavens. These apparitions are, Socrates says, "perfect and simple and fixed and happy." Earlier, Socrates described how soul had seen "justice itself" and "temperance itself" (247e). These are named "the realities" (*ta onta*). Presumably beauty itself is also one of the realities. If therefore *ta onta* are the Forms and beauty shining brightly is one of *ta onta*, then the apparitions Socrates refers to at 250c are apparitions of the Forms (although, importantly, Socrates does not name them as such here).

We, that is, the souls of Socrates and Phaedrus, were initiated into the most blessed mysteries when we existed just as soul, without a body. The superlative suggests that mysteries admit of degrees, i.e., that some mysteries are more mysterious than others. This highest level of mystery was experienceed by soul existing alone, prior to any entombment of soul in a mortal body. This is an important point. Socrates

has just spoken of the difficulty in discerning the light in the likeness of
such realities themselves that is most mysterious—not the experience
of trying to detect the presence of the realities in earthly copies. In
other words, what is called the problem of participation may be one of
the mysteries, but it cannot be the most mysterious mystery; the problem of participation concerns the Forms in relation to particulars
whereas Socrates is now speaking of the Forms as such, apart from any
instantiation of them.

It is possible to indicate, in broad outline, the character of the most
mysterious mystery. Consider that Socrates speaks of beauty shining
(λαμπρόν), the apparitions of all realities soul say in pure light (ἐν
αὐγῇ), and the lack of light (φέγγος) in the earthly likenesses of the
various precious realities. This consistent pattern may be dismissed as
mere imagism lacking any philosophical import. However, the concerted light imagery should have determinable significance with respect to the realities, otherwise this poetic phase of Socrates' attempt
to speak the truth about the truth may lead his audience astray.

Let us review briefly the account of soul's nature presented so far.
At 246a, Socrates asserted that telling what the form of soul is like
would require a long discussion only a god could provide, hence the
need to approximate this discussion through a human figure. As noted
above, a god would be required presumably because divinity can enter
a dimension of reality closed off to lesser, mortal beings.

Two clues help to determine the relevant features of the divine nature with respect to this dimension. First, divine soul is comprised of
functions which are "good and from the good" (246b), whereas all
other types of soul have a mixed composition, i.e., a combination of
good and the disposition for evil. The phrase "good and from the good"
is often taken as merely intensive, lacking special metaphysical import. However, in view of the perspective on totality offered to divine
soul, the phrase suggests that the nature of divine soul is receptive to
the good because this type of soul is itself good in all respects. Therefore, if divine soul is from the good, then divine soul is closer to the
good because it itself is entirely good. Furthermore, the fact that divine
soul is not only good, but also "from the good" suggests that the good

as such is more inclusive than that phase of it which resides in divine soul.

This fundamental aspect of the good with respect to the gods echoes in Socrates' description of the madness of love as "the best and from the best" (ἀρίστη τε καὶ ἐξ ἀρίστων—249e). Note that the balanced phrasing here parallels the description of divine soul with respect to the good. We may infer that the highest division of love is best and from the best because it is derived directly from the good, just as divine soul is derived directly from the good. Thus when we love in the highest sense, we love what is best (i.e., the good), and the extent to which we can produce a method for realizing that love amid the complex character of the reality in which we now find ourselves is the extent to which our love is "from the best."

The second clue is that the divine soul is nourished by the highest kind of reality, a reality which holds all its components and which is visible only to mind (247d). Thus, the divine soul has a greater insight into the ways in which mind can comprehend the underlying structure of the good, the highest level of reality. In the *Republic*, the analogue to the good is the sun, with sunlight tangibly representing the enlightening and fructifying power of the good. In the *Phaedo*, the good, what holds all things together, anticipates the sense in which, for the doctrine of truth advanced in the *Phaedrus*, the most real being holds the region yielding pure knowledge, a type of knowledge accessible only to mind. Again in the *Republic*, mind represents the faculty responsible for attaining the highest kind of knowledge, an approximation of the good. Thus the parallel characteristics of divine soul developed in the palinode suggest that the good and mind are essential elements in the *Phaedrus* structure of reality. The dimension of the good is preserved in the concerted appeals to the light essential to experience the realities beyond the rim of the heavens. Divine soul sees these realities because, so illuminated, they can be seen. And this light, although less dramatic in its mythic presentation in the *Phaedrus*, is the same light that, in the *Republic*, streams from the good.

When Socrates says that beauty and the apparitions of the realities are seen to shine when experienced by human soul in concert with divine soul, he means that this vision is mysterious not just because it is difficult to know the realities per se, but because it is even more difficult to know the realities in their fundamental relations to mind and the good. The extent to which the good remains ineffable is precisely the extent to which knowledge of the realities will, and perhaps must, remain mysterious.

It is significant therefore that during this section of the palinode—which, upon its conclusion, Socrates describes as a long account in praise of memory and the joys of the other time (250c8)—the Forms, approached as they are from the standpoint of divine soul, are consistently referred to as the realities, "the things that are" (*ta onta*). The lone exception occurs at 249c, when Socrates describes the necessary condition for being human as understanding according to a Form (κατ' εἶδος). The standard Platonic terminology for the Forms, *eidos* and *idea*, will occur consistently later, after the palinode, in the discussion of the method of collection and division. This linguistic shift suggests that the Forms are only truly real when seen as divine soul sees them, in the immediacy of their relations to mind and the good. When the Forms are seen in light of the good, they are the realities; when the Forms are seen with this relation dimmed, they are "the Forms" or "the ideas". Human soul sees the realities as Forms, especially when human beings must approach and refine the presence of the Forms through a complex methodology. To the extent that the Forms are not seen with respect to the good, the Forms display a diminished degree of reality.

Socrates has said that the most blessed of the mysteries, which we knew when we were perfect and fully initiated, concerned the experience of the appearance of the realities. These appearances were perfect and simple and fixed and happy. But why does Socrates refer to appearances (φάσματα) of the realities rather than, more directly, to the realities?

This question may be answered by considering the four properties ascribed to these appearances:

Completeness

The first property of the appearances is also found earlier in the same sentence listing the four properties. There human soul is said to celebrate these appearances in a state of completeness (ὁλόκληρα). Human soul is complete when it beholds the realities. But human soul is, at that time, without experience of subsequent evils (250c). If evil besets human soul, then it will no longer be complete in the sense that it was while dwelling in the ambience of the realities. Therefore, completeness, when said of human soul, refers to a condition which, under certain circumstances, can become altered. By parity of reasoning, completeness as predicated of an appearance of a reality means that the appearance can undergo alteration. The difference is that in this case, the capacity for an appearance to undergo alteration does not affect the character of what that appearance is of—the reality as such does not change. The sense in which appearances of realities differ from realities is conveyed by the next property of these appearances.

Simplicity

The second property of appearances is simplicity (ἀπλᾶ). Later, at 270b, Socrates says that whenever we want to know the nature of anything, we must first consider whether that thing is simple (ἀπλοῦν) or complex and then, in either case, inquire what power of acting it possesses and of being acted upon and by what. I suggest that Socrates is using this sense of simplicity in describing the appearances of the realities. By way of illustration, consider 254b, when the driver gazes at the radiant face of the beloved and finds his memory borne back to the nature of beauty (τὴν τοῦ κάλλους φύσιν), which he sees standing with modesty upon a pedestal of chastity. The imagery here should not conceal the relevant point; strictly speaking, beauty— the reality beauty—has a nature, and the nature of beauty is such that it has appearances that can be acted upon by the appearances of chastity and modesty. Simplicity thus refers to the extent to which an appearance can act and be acted upon by other appearances of other realities. Beauty and chastity do not change, but the appearances of beauty and chastity can be said to change in that they become involved in relations to realities other than the realities of which they are appearances.

Fixity

The third property may be translated as fixed (ἀτρεμῆ). This is the only property of the four listed which does not have a cognate occurring elsewhere in the *Phaedrus* (according to Ast, this is the only instance of the word in the Platonic corpus). But an appropriate analogue emerges at 277b, when Socrates presents another version of the method for knowing the truth about whatever is said or written. After defining the thing in question, the seeker of truth must divide that thing according to its Forms "until further division is impossible." The first two properties of appearances, the first implicitly, the second explicitly, have intimated that the appearances of realities are subject to alteration of a certain sort. But even in the midst of such alteration, the appearance of a reality retains an essentially fixed character. The third property reasserts that important characteristic. It is placed third in the sequence in order to allow the relevant aspects of communion between and among appearances of realities to receive their due emphasis. But the appearance of a reality is still the appearance of a reality, and shares with that reality at least one sense of invariability.

Happiness

The fourth and final property is happiness (εὐδαίμονα). This property clearly shows that the appearances of realities are intermediaries, directed from the realities as such to divine and human soul. While the nature of the appearance of a reality can be described as complete, simple, and fixed, it is not obvious how happiness can be predicated of that appearance. However, happiness can be said of the appearances of realities in that these appearances cause happiness in the soul beholding them. Furthermore, the property of happiness illustrates the property of simplicity, since it must belong to the nature of an appearance to act upon divine or human soul in such a way as to cause soul to be happy.

When, immediately after this section of the palinode, Socrates apologizes for its length, he notes that his excess was caused by yearning for the joys of that time (250d). This admission informs Phaedrus, and the reader, that the joys (μακρότερα) so ardently desired are precisely the most joyous (μακαριωτάτην) visions of the realities Socrates has just mentioned (250c). Furthermore, these are the same joyous (μακάριαι) sights which give happiness (εὐδαιμόνων) to the divine souls as the gods move about the heavens attending to their various duties (247a). Both gods and humans are made happy by the same kind of reality. Socrates thus confirms that his own soul did experience these joys, implying that Socrates knows full well that he is a philosopher and that, despite his avowals of ignorance, he is one of those few earthly mortals who have seen "the most." It also would follow that Socrates is a happy man, at least in the technical sense advanced here in the palinode.

The fact that appearances are described as "happy" suggests that all appearances are uniform in this respect. But how do the Forms of, say, mud and horse pertain to human happiness? The relevance of the good becomes apparent at this point. For if the reality of every Form encompasses its relation to the good, then all Forms are identical to one another in this one respect. If therefore a penumbra of the good animates each Form, then to know any one Form as a reality, regardless of any relations to particulars, is to be in the presence of the good shared by that reality. Thus, it is good for the philosopher to know *any* Form. Certain Forms are indeed "dear" to the philosopher in that their instances bear directly on producing the happiness proper to social contexts. But the extent to which knowing the full nature of reality constitutes human happiness is the extent to which all Forms are dear to the philosopher.

This section of the palinode concludes with a brief coda depicting a human imprisoned in the body as an oyster in a shell. The contrast produced by these two motifs is jarring, and is strongly reminiscent of the *Phaedo*, where the imprisonment of soul in body is also emphasized (81e) and human beings are compared to frogs around a pond (109b). The often cited Platonic Orphism may well sound here. But in concert with the metaphysical dimension described above, the images reinforce the sense in which the mystery terminology in this portion of the palinode recalls the complex metaphysics of the *Phaedo*, in particular mind and the good. The good is the culminating metaphysical element in Socrates' attempt to speak the truth about the truth. The extent to which the good can be related to the metaphysics of the Forms advanced so far in the palinode and articulated in the coming descriptions of collection and division is the extent to which the mythic appeals to the mysteriousness of the truth become somewhat less mysterious.

CHAPTER 5

Beauty and the Capture of the Beloved (250d–257b)

The inspired Socrates has said the truth about the truth. He now returns to earth, as it were, and, still inspired, he relates this soaring sense of truth to more mundane dimensions of experience.

Beauty and Wisdom

Socrates has concluded that portion of his speech concerning memory, a topic considered at length because he longed to relive the joys felt at that time. One of the realities, beauty, shown among these joyous visions and, since we have been on earth, it shines most clearly through sight, the clearest of our bodily senses. Prudence is not seen—if it were visible in this way, it would rouse awesome love, as would all other "lovely" realities. But beauty alone has this privilege, since it is the clearest seen and the most beloved (250d–e).

The embodied Socrates reminds us that he is speaking of the metaphysical memory of realities experienced when soul had not yet fallen into a body. Socrates has prolonged present discourse to satisfy, however inadequately, his desire for the joys of that vision. The fact that Socrates approximates these joys in speaking about them testifies to the strength of his present inspiration and, perhaps, to the accuracy of his account of the truth. In fact, just speaking about these joys—thereby sharing them with Phaedrus—is part of what makes Socrates happy in such discourse.

Beauty is special in producing such joy, but no reason other than the inherent clarity of vision is given to explain beauty's privileged position in the sensible world. We have suggested that the clear radiance of visible beauty opens a special receptivity to the good, since beauty must be no less—or more—intelligible than any other Form *qua* Form. Socrates does not restrict beauty's effect to one type of beauty; apparently a beautiful inanimate thing can engage someone with an immediacy equivalent to that of a beautiful human—e.g., Socrates expressing to Phaedrus his excitement concerning the natural beauty of the Ilissus (230b–c). Of course, beauty embodied in a human being is the highest form of this immediacy, perhaps because of how the experience of such beauty leads to seeing the truth.[1]

Equally significant is the assertion that prudence—as well as the other lovely (ἐραστᾷ) Forms—would cause awesome love if it were as visible as beauty. The awesome (δεινοὺς) love generated by prudence is emphasized because that love would curtail the pursuit of those carnal pleasures which now so beleaguer soul. But prudence is only one reality capable of producing this reaction. For if all Forms are lovely, then all particulars dependent upon the Forms could be the subject of the same intense reaction as a beautiful person is now. A truly wise philosopher therefore loves everything, since everything is capable of leading the philosopher back to "the things that are." To show the way toward achieving this metaphysical end, Socrates will soon enunciate the method of collection and division in tandem with the method of determining the nature of things.

The Vision of Beauty

The individual not recently initiated or corrupt does not ascend quickly from this world to beauty itself when seeing some particular named for beauty here. This individual yields to pleasure and, beast-like, pursues lust and procreation. He makes excess his companion and neither fears nor is ashamed to seek pleasure against nature. In contrast, the newly initiated, who had beheld "many sights," seeing a godlike face or bodily form which provides a good remembrance of beauty, first shudders and then is awed, as of old. In fact, had he not feared being thought mad, he would worship the beloved as an image of a god (250e–251a).

The distance between the thing named beautiful and beauty itself is prominently, if negatively, displayed when the newly initiated or corrupt person makes excess ($\H{\upsilon}\beta\rho\epsilon\iota$) his guiding light. The pursuit of such pleasure is thus connected to the springs of action described in Socrates' first speech, when love was defined as a type of excess. Here in the palinode, the image of this kind of soul moving with excess as a companion becomes a negative simulacrum of soul in company with a god, seeing what is truly real. Excess leads to a distinctively carnal fulfillment; however, the slighting reference to begetting need not repudiate the act of procreation per se, but merely indicates that this kind of soul has lowered its practice of Eros to the point where it can fructify itself only as animals do. To seek such pleasure is against nature ($\pi\alpha\rho\grave{\alpha}$ $\phi\acute{\upsilon}\sigma\iota\nu$), a claim anticipating how determining the nature of soul will show that such pleasure damages both soul and the person soul animates. What is unnatural is not the sheer desire for another person, but rather an inappropriate reaction to the presence of, and expression of love for, a particular type of beautiful thing.

The newly initiated experiences beauty by seeing a face reminiscent of a god. The divine thus serves as an intermediary between the visible appearance of the physical thing and the goodness of the memory of beauty as such. An index of the newly initiated's lack of education is that he does not worship this person as an image of a god because he fears being thought mad by the many. For it the newly initiated were fully initiated, he would not act or fail to act in ways controlled by the possible reaction of the many. He would not care whether the many thought him mad, since he knows both that he is mad and that it is good for him—or anyone—to be in this condition.

The Experience of Beauty

Socrates now begins a long and detailed description, based on the image of soul as winged, of the effect the sight of the beautiful person has on the newly initiated. Two dimensions of imagery are at work here, one physical with unmistakable erotic overtones, the other more abstract and metaphysical.[2] The soul Socrates is about to describe presumably belongs to the highest class of soul, since Socrates says it has seen many sights (πολυθεάμων) at that time (i.e., when it existed apart from body and accompanied deity to the rim of the heavens). Thus the resulting psychology may have to be adapted when souls with less metaphysical vision encounter a beautiful human being.

The beholder, shuddering, feels warmth as emanations of beauty enter the eyes. The parts holding the feathers, once hard, now soften, and as nourishment from radiating beauty flows into him, the quills from the feathers swell and grow from roots over "all the form of the soul," for soul was once all feathered (251b).

If soul's form is composed of parts or functions, then all parts of soul are affected by beauty. And if it is natural for feathers to lift the wing toward true reality, then the fact that the whole soul is feathered—or was feathered at one point—suggests that the whole soul can still lift itself from the depths, however profound those depths may be, and meet true reality once again. To feather the evil part of soul is not to eradicate it as evil, but to render it capable of moving into the presence of true reality.

This experience is felt by the whole soul, and just as the gums of those cutting teeth are irritated and sore, so also the soul suffers when its feathers begin to grow, and it becomes fevered, itchy and uncomfortable. Then, beholding the beauty of the boy, soul receives the particles that flow toward it—particles called "longing"—and becomes warm and moist, its pain ceasing and joy surging forth. When soul is alone and apart from the boy, however, the feather passages become dry and closed. Each growth then pricks the place where it is growing, and the whole soul all around stings with pain. When remembering the beautiful one, however, soul rejoices. Because of this mixed pleasure and pain, soul is troubled; it is maddened and in this state can neither sleep at night nor stay in one place during the day, and it is filled with desire and hunger to be in a place to see the one "having beauty." Seeing him and bathing in the waters of desire, the feather passages of soul are opened again—soul's pain is now eased and the consequent pleasure is the sweetest possible at that time (251c–e).

The emanations of beauty are nourishment for the beholder, recalling the image of the food partaken of by soul when it saw the truth (247d). The etymological link between the particles (μέρη) of beauty entering the eye of the initiate and the longing (ἵμερος) felt from the action of these particles illustrates the kind of etymologizing referred to earlier in the palinode. And the image of flowing mythically represents the process of participation, i.e., the passage between the Form beheld and the observer reacting to and knowing that Form. Soul is without shape, but envisioning it as circular (or spherical—κύκλῳ) recalls the revolution (κύκλῳ) in which divine soul beheld the absolute (247d). Each human soul thus becomes a monad with perspective on truth, a miniature metaphysical universe in its own right. Beholding an instance of true beauty renders soul open to all other realities accessible to that type of soul.

Soul's pain is assuaged by remembering, as Socrates carefully puts it, the one "having beauty." What soul remembers is the beauty in the boy, not the boy as such; note also that the pain is removed not by actually seeing the beauteous boy, but merely by remembering him. This memory causes the soul to rejoice, just as the memory of beauty and all other realities will cause a much more concentrated and fundamental joy to a soul properly tuned to those memories.

The Poetic Vision of Love

Socrates now recalls the "beauteous boy" who is the supposed audience for the palinode, and he concludes that the condition he is describing is called love by mortals, but the gods call it something which, because of the boy's youth, may seem laughable. Socrates then cites a pair of verses on love from, he says, Homer's spurious works, one verse of which is excessive and not entirely metrical:

> Mortals call him winged love,
> But immortals the winged, because he must grow wings.

His audience may believe or disbelieve these verses, but the condition of lovers and the cause of love are as Socrates has said (252b–c).

The use of poetry at this crucial juncture recalls the third type of madness, poetic inspiration. If the lines Socrates cites are not by Homer, they may be Plato's, attributed to a Homeric source for the sake of artistic authority.[3] But in a sense the question of authorship is not crucial; what is crucial is that the madness of poetry conveys what it does about love. Furthermore, Socrates has just said that the soul beholding the one having beauty (252b1) is healed of its greatest ills (μέγιστον πόνων). Recall that the second type of madness, purification, also resulted in alleviating the greatest ills (πόνων . . . μεγίστων). The fact that both types of pain are designated in the superlative suggests that the vision of beauty will heal the soul of the beholder from the unique metaphysical pain involved in longing for the joys of that former time, just as the right purification will heal someone suffering from a familial guilt incurred long ago.

This particular instance of the third type of madness is, despite its relevance, metrically flawed, as Rowe points out (p. 185). But just as the madness of poetry is incomplete in producing flawed verse, so the madness of love will be incomplete if it does not transport soul to the point of seeing, and articulating, the outermost reaches of reality described during the highest pitch of inspiration in the Socratic palinode. The lines nonetheless illustrate how poetry can depict the metaphysical truth about love. Love must grow wings, just as the word for love (ἔρωτα) must grow by adding a prefix ("pter-") indicating how it should grow (πτέρωτα), i.e., by adding wings for the ascent to the truth. Socrates' extended and graphic description of the cause and condition of lover and beloved concludes with the poetic insight that this state must be elevated into the highest metaphysical reaches before Eros can be seen as it truly is.

What then does this embodied form of love fly toward once soul's wings are grown? Since the gods recognize the need for Eros to become winged, it must be toward what the gods saw when on the rim of the heavens. But what the gods saw was the truth. And the truth encompassed the realities held together by the good. Gods are closer to the full range of reality Eros is naturally attracted to; mortals are further away from that reality, thus further away from the word more correctly describing the route to that reality.

The ultimate cause of Eros will be what attracts human beings toward a level of reality transcending carnal interests and providing the souls of both lover and beloved with the highest available degree of happiness. This type of love is not erotic in the way that love of one beautiful human can be. But if love is understood as a form of possession involving all our faculties, both perceptual and intellectual, then this comprehensive experiential medium aptly names the entry into what, for Plato, constitutes true reality. In this sense then, love is a constant. Individual souls vary in their abilities to ascend toward the realities accessible to their level of soul, but the process contouring this ascent remains identical, regardless who is loving or what Form is being loved.

How can love, conceived of in this sense, exercise such a distinctive metaphysical function? Plato uses the good in a number of crucial places in the *Phaedrus* to remind his audience that the good remains integral to the metaphysical vision described in that dialogue. From this perspective, the teaching about the nature of Eros in the *Phaedrus* specifies a process which, when fully and successfully practiced, functions according to the same universal parameters as the notion of *to agathon*. Thus, if soul were to love all the Forms, then soul would be good in the most complete sense, i.e., soul would see how any one Form is related to every other Form. Soul would be held together with all the realities through soul's love for these realities, just as soul was at one with all the realities accessible to soul when viewing them in the company of a god. Love becomes a kind of process equivalent of the good; it represents an attempt to translate the rarified and esoteric doctrine of the good in the *Phaedo* and the *Republic* into a realm of experience which can be more readily understood, applied (through the method of collection and division) and, perhaps, even perfected.

The Divine and the Choice of Beloved

Those who had been followers of Zeus can bear a heavier weight from Eros, the winged god. However, those who serve Ares and followed him, whenever love seizes them and they think injustice has been done to them by the beloved, are ready to sacrifice both themselves and the beloved. Each of the followers of the other gods acts in the same way, i.e., as far as possible honoring and imitating that god while this follower remains uncorrupted and lives his first life here. In this way he acts and conducts himself toward the beloved and all others. Each chooses the one loved from among the beautiful according to character, treating the beloved as the image of his god, adorning the beloved, honoring and worshiping him (252d–e).

The lover adorns his choice like a statue in order to honor and worship the beloved. To picture the beloved as a statue calls to mind the divine statuary mentioned at the beginning of the dialogue in Socrates' description of their resting place (230c), and it anticipates the description of soul remembering how it saw the reality of beauty sitting with modesty on a pedestal of chastity (254b). When transferred to a human subject, the image of a statue depicts a living, changing being not quite as subject to the vagaries of life by virtue of participating in the degree of reality represented by the god. The adornment (κατακοσμεῖ) given by lover to beloved has, as the word suggests, a cosmic dimension, as if the beloved were arrayed in appearances of whatever realities the appropriate god beheld during the journey on the rim of the cosmos. This adornment is not mere costumed finery, but the kind of education guided by the most comprehensive metaphysical vision.

It is vital in this context to understand why the lover is attracted to the beloved in the first place. According to Martha Nussbaum, these lovers love one another not "as exemplars of beauty and goodness," but strictly as individuals (*Fragility*, p. 220). Recall, however, that the newly initiated one is moved by seeing a godlike face, a vision causing him to "offer sacrifices to his beloved as to an idol or a god" (251a). The reason for this is that each human soul follows in the train of a god and lives, so far as possible, "honoring and imitating that god" (252d).

When a beloved is chosen, the lover chooses him "from the ranks of the beautiful" and adorns and fashions him as though he were his god (252e). And Socrates will go on to say that those without experience must search within themselves to find the nature of their god; if they do, they grasp him "by memory" and receive character and habits "so far as it is possible for someone to share in god" (253a).

The implication from these passages is clear—when the lover is attracted to someone, he sees traces of the divine in a human form. But now recall two passages from the myth. At 249c, Socrates says that the intellect of the philosopher only has wings, for he is always, as far as possible, in communion through memory with those things the communion with which causes god to be divine. In other words, what makes the gods divine are the visions they behold when they rest on the rim of the heavens and view true reality. And, at 246e, Socrates clearly states the content of those visions: "but the divine is beauty, wisdom, goodness, and all of these things." Therefore, if the lover is attracted to the beloved because the lover sees an image of the divine, then what the lover loves in the beloved is precisely the beloved's personal manifestation of what makes the gods divine—"beauty, wisdom, goodness, and all of these things." In short, lover loves beloved for precisely the reasons—e.g., the possession of beauty and goodness—that Nussbaum denies. To recognize what the lover truly loves in the beloved is crucial, since the object of this love determines how the lover acts toward the beloved insofar as the beloved is a human being.

Love and Participation in Divinity

The followers of Zeus desire that the soul of the beloved be as much as possible like Zeus, so they seek someone of a philosophical and ruling nature. When they find and love this kind of person, they do whatever is possible to make him resemble this divine standard. Those who have not had experience in such tutelage learn from whoever can instruct them, and they also seek such knowledge in themselves; when they seek the nature of their god in themselves, they are successful because they were compelled to focus on the god. And remembering this god, they are inspired, receiving from him character and habits as far as it is possible for an individual to share in a god (252c–253a).

Socrates is careful to describe the sought—for soul in terms of its nature (φύσιν), again linking this section of the myth with the technical sense of nature. But to know thyself in the sense of knowing how to educate the beloved is not in all instances an immediately solvable exercise. Those who do not have the requisite knowledge should learn from all who can teach them anything. The example of Socrates in the agora comes to mind, talking to anyone about matters of moment. With the assistance of the oracle, Socrates had learned that his wisdom was in knowing that he did not know. But the Platonic Socrates wanted to know about almost everything. Pursuing such knowledge is thus a type of love—in fact, philosophical love. Thus to lead another toward a Zeus-like character is to engage that individual in the most comprehensive sort of philosophizing.

The Education of the Beloved

The lover thinks the beloved causes the intensity of his recognition of the divine; as a result, the lover loves him even more. If, for example, this lover is inspired by Zeus, he responds to the beloved's soul in the same way as the Bacchants, trying to inspire and fashion that soul as much as possible like the god. Those who followed Hera seek a kingly sort, and when they find one they act in the same way toward him. This pattern is followed for all gods who provide models for human love; each type of lover seeks a youth who by nature corresponds to the appropriate deity. Then the lover imitates the god, persuading and educating the beloved so that the form of the beloved's soul is as much like the god as possible. There is no jealousy toward the loved one and the lover tries to lead the beloved to be as much as possible like the god they revere (253a–c).

The lover persuades and educates the beloved in matters of reality by speaking. Later, at 261a, Socrates will define rhetoric as leading the soul by means of words. And this is precisely what the lover must do for the beloved, i.e., lead the beloved toward becoming a Zeus-like nature (if they are both philosophical). Therefore, the lover will persuade the beloved by using one kind of rhetoric directed toward a specific end, and he will educate the beloved in the truth—in the realities and their formal relations to one another. This appeal to persuasion and education establishes a direct link between the palinode and the second half of the *Phaedrus*. For if persuasion requires discussion and discussion requires rhetoric and rhetoric requires method to secure certitude, then the account of collection and division, an essential factor in rhetoric, will show, in broad outline, how the lover should speak to the beloved to produce the likeness of Zeus—and the realization of philosophy in an earthly setting—in another human being.[4]

All souls on each of the nine levels had seen varying degrees of truth while in the company of a deity. It appears then that the gods differ in their respective visions of reality, since Zeus, having seen the most reality, is placed first in heaven, followed by eleven squadrons of divinities placed in order (247a). Presumably this order is based on what each god had seen of the truth. If so, then it is apparently accidental why a given human soul rises to the rim of the heavens with Zeus—eventually becoming a philosopher, or with Hera—eventually becoming a king. Whatever determines soul's initial link with a certain deity will ultimately define the extent to which soul sees the truth and, by mythic implication, what kind of life that soul will lead if it eventually falls from the company of the divine.[5]

The Happiness of Love

The desire of those who love "truly" and the initiation which they teach, if achieved, is, as Socrates has said, beautiful, causing happiness to pass from the lover who is inspired to the loved one. But such happiness transpires only if the loved one is captured by the lover. Socrates then begins to describe this capture, returning to the details in the original image of soul's powers characterized in terms of a driver and horses (253c).

The desire of the lover is now for the proper initiation and educa-

tion of the beloved into the mysteries of love. These mysteries are the
apprehension and comprehension of "the truth," the highest kind of reality, and the fulfillment of this desire brings happiness from the lover
to the beloved. During the brief preamble before the discussion of love
as the fourth type of madness, Socrates says the he must prove that love
has been sent for our greatest "good fortune" (245c). At 253c, the lover
has happiness, i.e., the lover is thoroughly possessed by the madness
of love. If therefore Socrates can show how the lover captures the beloved, then the happiness of the lover will be shared by the beloved. It
is good fortune for one's soul to have seen something of reality; but it is
happiness when that soul can recoup this vision and instill it into a
kindred spirit.

To say that this union of allied souls is beautiful (καλή) is not just
to attribute beauty as such to it; rather, this predication encompasses
the relation between beauty and all other realities existing beyond the
heavens (depending, of course, upon the extent to which the pair of
souls saw that reality). Furthermore, the fact that the lover must initiate
the beloved recalls the complete metaphysics of truth described at
247c–e, including the penumbra of the good surrounding each of the
realities and establishing relations between and among all the realities.
To be properly initiated is therefore not just to know as much as possible about the realities present in the formal nature of sensible things,
but also to know as much as possible about the good as it allows these
things to be related to as many other realities as possible.

This level of kinship, if achieved, will enable the lovers to share
as much reality as possible. Beauty, the most palpable Form, doubtless appears in their experiences and in their discourse about these
experiences, but other Forms are present as well, a communal metaphysical vision spanning all levels of human soul. It remains true,
however, that the happiness of philosophical lover and beloved will
be more intense, or higher, than the happiness of a kindred pair, since
philosophical souls had seen more of the truth than pairs of soul belonging to any of the other levels of soul.[6] But even a philosopher must
struggle intensely to capture a similar soul, as Socrates will now vividly show.

The Form of the Horses

Socrates' description of the capture of the beloved by the lover, the final phase of the palinode, continues as in part a paradigm for the cognitive process. In this process, staged in a distinctively Platonic theater, lover is to beloved as knower is to Form or instance of Form, and to the implied presence of the good. The erotic and the metaphysical continue to be portrayed in intimate allegiance with one another.

In the beginning of the myth, each soul was divided into three parts—two had the form of horses, the third the form of a driver. Socrates says that this division will be retained in what follows: Let us now address the goodness of the good horse and the evil of the evil horse (253d).

Only at this point does Socrates make explicit that the description of soul's form, begun at 246a, initiates that part of the palinode which is a *muthos*. Just prior to the onset of this myth, the discursive demonstration of soul's nature had concluded that its nature is essentially self-motion. Now if Socrates continues to follow the methodology of 270d–e for determining a thing's nature, then the next step would number the constituent Forms and describe how they act and are acted upon. Therefore, when Socrates says that he divided soul into two (δύο) forms and a third form (εἶδος τρίτον), this step both follows the methodology of 270d–e and implies that soul is complex, at least in terms of this mythic figure. And since Socrates says that "each" (human) soul has been so divided, then all soul ("all" taken distributively) is complex.

If human soul is tripartite at 253c, then logically it is also tripartite at 246a. But the implied appeal to methodology offers an important clue in explaining why Socrates only now feels capable of defining the goodness of the good horse and the evil of the evil horse. Socrates describes goodness and evil because he has articulated the nature of the good in the course of his true account about the truth (247c to 250d). Thus, to know about the good is a necessary condition for describing the goodness and badness of a particular thing—especially the various functions of soul. Yet this account of soul's form, avowedly mythical, must be analyzed and clarified. In this case, however, the mythic description of soul's powers contains its own interpretive guidelines.

The horse standing on the nobler side is upright and clean-limbed in form, has a high neck and aquiline nose, is white with dark eyes. He is a "lover of honor with temperance and modesty" and a "companion of true opinion." He needs no whip, and is led only by command and by discourse. The other horse is crooked, heavy, malformed, with a short thick neck, flat nose, dark color, and grey bloodshot eyes. He is a companion of excess and pride, is shaggy-eared and deaf, and is averse to whip and spurs (253d–e).

This remarkable description details the "form" of each kind of horse. Although the initial characterization refers to physical properties, it would be premature to understand form just in its root sense of shape or outward appearance. For each description includes a relation between the horse and an epistemic or moral absolute—the good horse as a "companion of true opinion," the evil horse as a "companion of excess and pride." Now if form (εἶδος) meant only physical shape, then these relations would be purely arbitrary; if, however, form means shape in conjunction with the reality or power consonant with this shape, then these relations are appropriately grounded in the metaphysics of the truth. Recall that the primary purpose of this image is to represent the synthesis of natural powers incorporated into the form of soul—the soul as a unity—both divine (without the evil horse) and human. Let us attempt to translate the physical characteristics attributed to the horses according to guidelines provided by this metaphysical framework.

The good horse is a companion of true opinion and the evil horse a companion to excess. I suggest that the object of the good horse's friendship, true opinion, should be correlated with the opinion striving "for the best" advanced in Socrates' first speech (237e), and that the excess consorted with by the evil horse parallels the excess naming the subversion of opinion aiming at the best by the pursuit of pleasure, also described in the first speech.[7]

The characteristics concluding the description of the form of the two horses thus accentuate the differences between the accounts of soul in Socrates' two speeches. In the first speech, the type of opinion was "in us"—not in that part of us which is our soul—with no provision made for any knowledge higher than opinion. Also in the first speech, opinion aimed at the best. This stipulation suggests that the higher mode of knowledge advanced in the palinode via intellect and mind, the driver or soul—a power of soul absent from the speech—will have the same destination, i.e., the good as illuminating all realities existing beyond the heavens.[8]

Recall also that both human and divine soul are drawn by horses. But divine soul is led by horses which are always good. If therefore the goodness of divine soul is identical in kind to the goodness of human soul, then the reason why divine soul is always good will be the same as the reason why human soul is as good as it is. Divine soul is determined by its relation to the reality beyond the heavens. Since divine soul has no capacity for anything more real than the object of that vision, its goodness originates in the continuous impetus to see this reality. Thus, the good for both divine and human soul gives to such soul the capacity to experience the highest degree of reality.

But human soul is drawn by both good and evil horses. According to this line of interpretation, evil would be the counterpart of good not merely in that it halts motion toward the highest degree of reality, but also because it actively reverses the direction of movement, i.e., away from reality. If the evil horse dominates soul as a whole, then soul's vision of reality would recede to the point that its capacity for animating a human would be reduced to that of a soul enlivening only a lower being—wolf, bee, etc.

This approach to determining the import of the good horse may also be applied to its purely physical characteristics. Thus, the good horse is clean-limbed, i.e., its features are sharply distinguished from one another—as are the properties of something correctly divided according to its nature (by collection and division). He carries his neck high—so that the horse's head will be closer to the light of the sun, and to the reality existing (mythically) beyond the heavens. He has an aquiline nose—a feature of beauty fitting for an animal approximating formal beauty. He is white with dark eyes—the polar contrast in color

suggesting the kind of opposition which, although seemingly fundamental to metaphysical reflection, can nonetheless be superseded by a
higher kind of reality, just as the good horse will help lead the whole
soul to that reality by seeing it as clearly as possible.

The good horse is a friend to honor, which suggests that soul is
naturally sensitive toward attaining and maintaining the good standing
one may have in the eyes of other human beings; notice, however, that
such honor is guided by temperance and modesty—honor is not bought
at any price, but only if it coheres with a pair of primary virtues. Finally, the good horse is a companion of "true opinion." In the account
of soul's vision of the truth, the souls unsuccessful in achieving this vision had to retreat below the rim of the heavens and there feed on opinion (248b). The intimacy between the good horse and true opinion illustrates the highest cognitive level that the good horse can achieve. But
just as there is a higher virtue than honor, so also there is a higher
knowledge than true opinion. The good horse represents the motion in
the soul toward realizing these approximations of soul's perfection.
But of course the good horse is controlled by the driver, who is capable
of leading soul toward its perfection through the apprehension of wisdom and truth.

The physical appearance of the evil horse may be similarly interpreted. This horse is crooked, heavy, and scarcely natural in the arrangement of its parts, i.e., its weight draws its bulk toward the earth or
toward matter, and its parts do not cohere well with one another, thus
showing that the attraction of the material has a detrimental effect on
the horse as a unity, as a sum of parts. The short thick neck accentuates
the horse's stubbed appearance, compressing the head, the seat of intelligence, into the rest of its bulky frame. The dark color of the horse—in
stark contrast to the whiteness of the good horse—reflects the absence
of light, or intelligibility, endemic to matter. His eyes are bloodshot,
perhaps from the exertion of attempting to draw the whole soul away
from true reality and toward the carnal; the eyes are also grey, a color
which, as Aristotle points out (*Meta* 1018^{a}25), is a mixture of black and
white, thus indicating the interplay between the inherent clarity provided by vision and the fact that such clarity is, for the evil horse, made

murky by his propensity toward the inherently obfuscatory character of the material. The unkempt condition of the evil horse's ears are external signs of the horse's deafness; it cannot hear the dictates of the charioteer and scarcely obeys harsher forms of persuasion (i.e., whip and spurs), but wants simply to go its own way whenever an object of desire appears.

This way of reading the description of the two horses is, of course, an interpretation. But if these equine appearances are understood from this perspective, then the purely physical characteristics of the horses display a rationale coincident with the metaphysical dimension underlying this portion of the palinode.

Furthermore, it is now possible to account for the silence concerning the physical appearance of soul's charioteer. The charioteer is soul's direct link to the realities, and to the good, and represents soul's capacity for actualizing the extent to which reality is intelligible for that soul. According to the hierarchy of lives, there are nine distinct types of soul (i.e., nine different levels at which soul has assimilated the truth). The fact that definite descriptions are offered of the good and evil horses of soul suggests that all nine levels of soul have the same type of goodness and evil as represented by the accounts of the good and evil horse. However, since there are nine distinct ways in which soul drives its horses with respect to the truth it has seen, it would falsify the complexity of the highest function of soul to label it with a physical description of some sort, thereby suggesting a sameness which the nature of soul in this regard precludes. As a result, Socrates says nothing about the physical properties of soul's charioteer.[9]

The tripartite form of soul developed according to the image of driver and winged horses, and interpreted in light of the methodology for determining a thing's nature, may be summarized as follows:

A. *Driver (and, when animating a body, Charioteer)*—soul as mind (*nous*) and intellect (*dianoia*). The capacity of soul to be acted upon by the presence of the truth—the realities and the good—in all their instances, and to act in order to direct soul toward unity with the highest degree of reality accessible to that level of soul.

B. *Good Horse*—capacity of soul to initiate and complete motion toward unity with the truth. When soul is not incarnate, the white horse assists in regulating all other capacities of soul; when soul is incarnate, the white horse helps the charioteer control whatever desires attend soul when it coexists with body and leads soul toward achieving a level of honor and opinion so that soul, once properly trained, can see the truth.

C. *Evil Horse*—capacity of soul to be affected by all that is other than the truth (i.e., matter and whatever desires of soul are consequent upon the existence of matter and the possession of body), and to initiate and, if possible, to unify the whole soul with whatever is other than truth understood as the highest reality.

The Vision of the Beloved

The human soul, "formed" in this way, now approaches human beauty. When the charioteer sees the face of the person inspiring love, a sensual warmth is diffused throughout the soul, with the charioteer of soul pricked with the feelings of desire. The horse obedient to the charioteer, restrained then as always by modesty, holds himself back and does not leap upon the beloved. But the other horse, no longer obeying spur or whip, rushes forward and causes all forms of travail to his fellow horse and to the charioteer, compelling them to go toward the loved one and reminding them to pursue the pleasures of carnal love (254a).[10]

The charioteer combines the act of seeing the beloved's face, and perhaps the special glow in the eyes of the beloved, with the spreading of sensuous excitement throughout the whole (πᾶσαν) soul. The fact that the charioteer instigates this reaction implies that this ardor has an intelligible base, since the other components of soul depend on the charioteer for the capacity to receive and react to this vision. However, the lower functions of soul are fed, as it were, through a sensory channel, recalling that soul as unity—the whole soul—has an essential link to the material realm. The fact that the charioteer of soul, i.e., the source of soul's capacity to know, feels warmth and is affected by desire shows that the natural response to corporeal beauty is felt, in a decidedly carnal vein, by the purely rational function of soul. Thus, desire has an inherent degree of rationality and rationality includes an element of desire. Note also that the good horse, in natural obedience to the charioteer, always acts with modesty, reinforcing the fact that the appetitive function represented by the good horse is connected to a moral reality. In other words, however intense the desire of soul for the union with the beloved may become, the goodness of soul will direct that desire according to the dictates of modesty.

The evil horse, in thrusting the memory of the pleasures of love before the other members of soul, suggests by this action that this soul has already partaken of such pleasure. But at 256b, Socrates holds open the possibility that soul will never consummate this desire, a state of affairs incompatible with soul having experienced these pleasures and thereby being capable of remembering them. In fact, the reference to memory is a subtle reminder that Socrates is describing human soul, i.e., soul in intimate union with body. The evil horse can thus "remind" the rest of soul of these pleasures even if they have never been experienced, just as a youth can be attracted to erotic behavior without having actually experienced it. The appetitive function of human soul desires union with beauteous bodies, implying that this desire is no less essential to the nature of human soul than the desire to remember the Forms is to that part of human soul that shares in divinity.

At this point, the motion of the beholder's soul, the whole soul, is controlled by the evil horse, and its intent is toward erotic consummation. In other words, the initial vision of the beloved sparks what might be called lust, a form of instantaneous and intense desire, the object of which is immediate sexual gratification. The beholder knows absolutely nothing about the beautiful person before him, but he realizes, as dictated by the evil horse, that he desires to possess that person in the most satisfying carnal way. In a very real sense then, the lover must first capture himself before he can capture the beloved for the sake of their mutual happiness.

Beauty and Memory

Upon beholding the beloved, the memory of the charioteer is returned to "the nature of beauty." The charioteer (then the driver of soul) sees beauty sitting, with moderation, on a holy pedestal. But having seen this, he is now afraid, and falling backward he is compelled at the same time to pull back on the reins so that both horses are on their haunches, the one willingly because he does not provoke the charioteer, the other unwillingly (254b–c).

Socrates is careful to state that the charioteer of the soul remembers the nature of beauty (τὴν τοῦ κάλλους φύσιν)—not just beauty. This locution recalls, again, the technical sense of nature to be defined at 270d–e. That this dimension of beauty is intended becomes clear when the charioteer's vision of beauty includes its intimate connection "with moderation" on a pedestal of chastity. This memory refers to what soul's driver saw while accompanying Zeus during the revolution of the heavens, beholding the things that are, *ta onta*. In this case, when soul saw beauty, soul also saw that beauty is always accompanied with moderation. The experience of beauty thus entails, according to the relation between the realities beauty and modesty as experienced by soul, that the one experiencing it should also behave with moderation. (In fact, failure to moderate one experience of beauty engendered the cicadas from a band of humans, a story Socrates will relate soon after the palinode is concluded.)

The vision of beauty in company with temperance is placed on a pedestal to vivify the stability of the relation, suggesting by this statuary effect a unity of distinct figures and imagistically capturing the metaphysical fact that the Forms are without motion, separate from one another, yet capable of existing in relations to one another by means of the brightness provided by the good. This pedestal is holy because the intimacy between beauty and temperance is readily perceived by divine intelligence but difficult for human sensibilities to ascertain because of the inherent tension between the attraction of beauty, especially when embodied in a human being, and the restraint proper to temperance.[11]

The Training of the Evil Horse

The good horse, ashamed and awed, wets the whole soul with sweat, its struggle against the evil aspect of soul's nature thus affecting the entire soul in its relation to the beloved. And now, the evil horse becomes dominant in reacting to soul's withdrawal. After recovering from the powerful pain of the charioteer's bit, he angrily reviles his fellow horse and charioteer for their cowardice, lack of manhood, and the rupture of their agreement. However, despite the intensity of the evil horse's desire, he yields to a joint appeal to postpone pursuit of the beloved. But when his cohorts, at the appointed time, feign forgetting the realization of desire, the evil horse again reminds them of this agreement. And now the evil horse forces the others to approach the beloved again, urging the same reasons as he gave earlier.

The charioteer is affected as before by the protestations and urgings of the evil horse, only this time his reaction is even more severe—he falls back, pulling the bit so violently that it rips the jaws of the evil horse so they spew blood, and drives his legs to the ground with great pain. Such pain must be experienced by the evil horse many times before it ceases its hubristic behavior and follows the foresight of the charioteer. After this process has been completed, the sight of the beautiful one fills the evil horse with fear and from then on the soul of the lover follows the beloved in reverence and awe (254c–255a).

The horses animating the figure of soul's powers possess the capacity for discourse—for willing, chastising, persuading. And in this case, the evil horse has grounds for complaint, since a prior agreement existed among soul's powers to pursue the beloved in the manner he, the evil horse, had proposed. This agreement, however, illustrates the point, already implicit in the first speech of Socrates, that mutual consent is not sufficient for right action if the agreement lacked proper recognition of the situation by all powers of soul. But despite the intensity of his desire, the evil horse yields to a joint appeal to postpone—not give up—pursuit of the beloved, an action indicating that the evil horse is not entirely opposed to ministrations of moderation and reason.

The fact that the evil horse eventually ceases from this hubristic behavior recalls the hubris so fundamental to soul in the first speech of Socrates. There the only possibility for controlling hubris was stated in terms of opinion aiming at the best. But now soul is in the charge of a charioteer who, when recalling the correct vision of the realities, can diminish the excess desire aroused by the evil horse. The charioteer's response again reveals the natural reaction to the vision of beauty with moderation, but now this response admits of degrees, and it is within the charioteer's power to harness even the most violent desire of soul. But the hubris of the evil horse, although halted, is not eliminated. Such elimination is impossible, given that the principle underlying such hubris is what moves the horse—and soul itself to the extent that its nature includes the evil horse—to advance toward the object of desire.

Once harnessed in this way, the evil horse follows the foresight of the charioteer, with the contrast between foresight (προνόιᾳ) and *dianoia* suggesting that at this, the initial stage in the confrontation between beauty and desire, the charioteer has drawn on the store of memories in order to direct the concerns of soul back to a condition resembling that of its pre-incarnate state. The evil horse "fears" the beautiful one by sensing that the soul will move toward that person in a manner nullifying its kind of motion. Fear is the appropriate feeling— the evil horse anticipates losing his very existence if soul should move in the opposite direction. It is the beauty in the beautiful one which the evil horse fears, beauty in alliance (through the unifying agency of the good) with moderation in contradistinction to beauty as an entry to satisfying carnal desire.

Love and the Good

The lover now begins to act toward, and on behalf of, the beloved, initially by performing various services for him. The beloved receives all these services, "as if from one equal to a god." The lover now is truly in love and not, as did the lover in the speech of Lysias and in Socrates' first speech, pretending not to be. The beloved is "by nature friendly" to the individual who serves him, even though he may have been impressed by fellow students, or others, who had said that it was disgraceful to yield to a lover. For this reason, the beloved may have initially rejected the lover. As time passes, however, his "youth and destiny" lead him to admit the lover into his company. For it is a law of destiny that evil can never be dear to evil and good will always be dear to good (255a–b).

It is in the nature of the beloved to be friendly to the lover, thus possessing a measure of the receptivity necessary in order to react to and act toward the lover so that such friendship can become transmuted into love. The fact that the beloved is naturally friendly to the lover is a function of destiny. For even though the beloved has been swayed by hearing the erroneous speech of Lysias—a clear reference to Phaedrus—to the point of perhaps rejecting the lover, it is destined—given the character of the beloved's soul, which must be on the same level as the soul of the lover in order to be chosen as the object of love by the lover—that the soul of the beloved see through Lysian falseness and accept the lover as, for now, a friend. The fact that the beloved, almost as if in spite of himself, recognizes that the lover's action resembles those of a godlike figure subtly shows his innate affinity for the lover, since both their souls were with the same god when they journeyed to the rim of the heavens to behold the truth.

Destiny decrees that evil is never dear to evil and that good is always dear to good. This dictum has the ring of a fundamental metaphysical principle. Stated abstractly, it says not only that evil exists, but that different things are evil and that these evil things can never be dear (φίλον) to one another, i.e., if juxtaposed in any sense, this shared nature will mutually repel them. On the other hand, anything good will always be dear to anything else which is good—all good things are not only the same in this respect, but they are attracted to one another by virtue of that sameness. Presumably such attraction is a characteristic peculiar to the good. Thus, just or beautiful things are not dear to each other simply by being just or beautiful; they are dear to each other only if they are also good. For if every good thing is attracted to every other good thing, then the result is a totality in which all things defined by goodness not only coexist with one another, but in some sense actively seek to be related to each other. Such desire is illustrated by the beloved's incipient friendliness to the lover—the souls of both are good, and therefore are dear to each other, despite the shell of sinful Lysian discourse which, for the moment, separates them.

Love and Desire

Once the lover is admitted to the company of the beloved, the con-
comitant conversation, intimacy, and good will of the lover so astounds
the beloved that he realizes that the affection of all his other friends and
relatives means nothing compared to the "inspired friendship" of his
companion. The growing communion between lover and beloved continues. Then, when the lover nears the beloved and they happen to
touch, whether in the gymnasium or in general converse, the fountain
of passion which Zeus, when in love with Ganymede, called "desire,"
flows freely toward the lover. Some flows into the lover and some,
when he is filled with this fluid, flows outside him. And just as the wind
or an echo, rebounding from a smooth and hard surface, returns
whence it come, so the "stream of beauty" goes back into the beautiful
one through the eyes, the natural entry into the soul. Once it enters the
beloved, the stream of desire makes the feathers of his soul grow again
and fill the soul of the beloved with love.

Struck with this desire, the beloved is in love but does not know
who he loves. He cannot understand his reaction and, as one who has
caught a disease of the eyes from another, he cannot give a reason for
his condition. He does not realize that his lover is a mirror in which he,
the beloved, beholds himself. Whenever he is with the lover, like him
he is rid of his pain and whenever he is away from the lover, like him he
is stung with desire which he himself inspires. He has an image of love,
a kind of counterlove, but he calls it and believes it to be not love, but
friendship (255d–e).

The lover's intellect is in touch with what truly matters for the
well-being of the beloved, and the beloved's own intellect is sufficiently receptive to this state of well-being to recognize it as superior in
degree, if not in kind, to the friendship not only of his other friends, but
also of his relations as well. The lover has loved, and truly loved, the
beloved, but only at the moment of touch is desire unleashed and the
realization of the full power of love at hand. Socrates says that the desire flooding Zeus in his amatory pursuit of Ganymede also courses
through the lover. But why does this episode highlight the account of

the beloved's capture, given that Zeus had innumerable, and variegated, carnal liasons?

First, Ganymede was the most beautiful youth alive at the time. It
is fitting then that the paradigm of a god's desire for a mortal—the highest god—is exemplified by the most vibrant degree of physical beauty.
Second, Zeus flew down to earth disguised in eagle's feathers to pro-
cure Ganymede, thus illustrating (although in reverse direction) the
winged imagery of soul in pursuit of true beauty. And third, Ganymede
was raised to Olympus in order to be Zeus' cup-bearer. In bringing Zeus
his daily ration of nectar, Ganymede helped provide Zeus with some of
his essential nourishment, just as the vision of beauty, one of the
realities beyond the rim of the heavens, helped define the divinity of
Zeus. The allusion to the Zeus-Ganymede relationship not only joins
the desire of the lover of the beloved to Zeus, the god of philosophers,
thereby connecting the lover's soul to what it saw when in the company
of Zeus during the banquet of reality, but it also epitomizes, in many of
its mythic details, the abstract metaphysical circumstances underlying
the manifestation of love.

Socrates emphasizes the word Zeus used to name this feeling, reminding us that desire has received an etymological analysis with subtle yet clear metaphysical overtones, (i.e., the pun on desire and part
suggested at 251d). The image of desire coursing into the lover from
some external source coheres well with the more abstract notion of soul
deriving its store of reality from its pre-incarnate vision of the realities.
This store has no apparent limits, for when it fills the lover—presumably to a point where desire for the beloved cannot become more intense—than it overflows the lover and rebounds, almost mechanically
(note the images of the reaction of an echo or wind to hard surfaces),
into the eyes of the beloved. The lover thus becomes a conduit for the
desire flowing through him and into the beloved.

The pointed reference to the eyes of the beloved as natural entry to
the soul illustrates, again, that the eyes are reactive receptacles for vision and also the medium through which originate the intellectual
awareness of the Forms. When the feathers of the beloved's soul begin
to grow, the beloved, heretofore in a state of easy friendship with the

lover, is filled with love. The contrast between the beloved before and now should be noted, since it is only because of the entry and passage of desire from the lover toward the beloved that the beloved achieves this new awareness.

The beloved knows that he is in love, but does not know with whom he is in love. The beloved might be expected to connect the eyes of the lover to his own condition, i.e., he would identify the lover as the lover, since the disease he now experiences emanated directly from the lover. But the relationship is more complex. When the beloved looks at the lover, the beloved sees not the lover but himself, as in a mirror. The visual disease of desire has obscured the fact that the beloved loves another and not, as it seems to him, that he only sees himself in the condition of loving.

This remarkable vision of self is congruent with the Platonic emphasis on true education always coming from within rather than from without. The beloved must learn what it means to love, and the way he learns this is first to realize that he himself is in love. Therefore, he does not learn love from the lover, but he learns it from himself insofar as he is placed in a position where love can transpire. This is why, when desire first occurs, the beloved sees himself mirrored in the lover's eyes, and also why the beloved knows neither his condition nor its cause. The beloved confronts Love, as it were, while in the presence of the lover, and he must undergo a period of education in matters metaphysical before he can realize what all that wondrous condition entails for his personal well-being.

Love and Friendship

The beloved desires the lover, but less strongly than the lover desires him. Nonetheless, this mutual desire wins, at least to the point where lover lies with beloved. The lover's unruly horse then has something to say to the charioteer, demanding recompense for his many travails; the unruly horse of the beloved remains mute, but responds to his passion and confusion by embracing and kissing the lover, thereby acknowledging the lover's high-mindedness toward him. As the two lie together, the beloved would not refuse the lover anything, if only the lover requested it; but the good horse and the charioteer of the lover, with "modesty and discourse," oppose this prospect (255e–256a).

Although the beloved discerns, in the midst of passion, the high-mindedness (εὔνουν) of the lover, intimating that the intellect and mind of the lover are in some degree of harmony, the beloved would not refuse the lover anything, if the lover so requested. The beloved's soul is held captive by desire, by the evil horse, and would yield to any carnal wish from the other partner. If therefore the pair is not to fall prey to the physical, the lover must initiate and establish control—even though, as we have seen, the lover desires the beloved with more intensity than the beloved desires him. The good horse and charioteer appeal to modesty and to *logos* in order to counteract the urgings of their third member. Soul saw temperance in intimate connection with beauty when soul beheld the realities (254b); this vision comes into play now, as the soul of the lover recalls the need for modesty when in the presence of desire for beauty. To reinforce this need, the lover uses an account, a *logos*. What the lover says to the beloved concerns, presumably, the relation between carnal desire, which is mutual, and modesty, which is not.

How the lover articulates this relation and persuades the beloved that it should guide their actions is left unspecified. But if both lover and beloved have philosophical souls, then this discussion (which may well become a conversation) must surely be directed by the principles of the highest form of rhetoric in order for the lover to be successful—and, as a result, to allow the souls of both the lover and the beloved to realize their true philosophical nature. We may detect here another anticipation of the need to investigate rhetoric as an essential supplement to the teaching of the palinode about the metaphysics and phenomena of love.

Love and Philosophy

But the lover's high-minded success is not certain, and the next and final stage in the capture saga is a study in contrasting resolutions. Two possibilities are enacted: If the better elements of intellect win, those leading to philosophy, then lover and beloved live a life of happiness and harmony, subjugating soul's evil tendencies and liberating soul for virtue. At the end of mortal life, both are "light and winged," for they have won in one of the three truly Olympic contests. Neither human prudence nor divine madness can confer a greater good than this achievement.

If, on the other hand, the two lead a life without philosophy but yet ruled by love of honor, then in a careless moment, as when drinking, the two evil horses catch their souls offguard and, bringing lover and beloved together, they consummate what the many consider bliss. Once done, the practice continues, but infrequently, since it is not sanctioned by the whole intellect. This pair die as friends, but with less friendship than that displayed in the first example. This condition is maintained when they are in love and afterwards, since the two believe they have exchanged the most binding vows and that it would be sinful to break them, thereby becoming enemies. When they die, they are not winged, but they are eager for their wings to grow, so that the madness of love has amply awarded them. For the law dictates that those who have begun to ascend shall never go into the darkness under the earth, but shall proceed happily in a shining life with each other, and because of their love they will receive equal plumage when they are winged (256b–e).

To lead a life of happiness, the better element of the intellect should prevail. This must mean that the charioteer and good horse win out over the evil horse. But a victory by these elements only leads to philosophy. The better elements of soul must therefore not only subjugate the evil horse, but they must engage the whole soul into motion towards truth. This motion will, as we shall see in the second half of the *Phaedrus*, entail using a particular method. Once this method is mastered and applied, the soul will be orderly (κόσμιον), approximating the condition of soul when it rested on top of the cosmos and beheld the true reality, a condition which, if realized in this life, will constitute virtue and provide happiness.

This pair of souls will have won the first of the three "truly" Olympic contests, reinforcing the fact that the type of soul under scrutiny must be philosophical, for only that type of soul is eligible for liberation after three (rather than ten) thousand-year cycles. If these two souls are successful, they have led a properly philosophical life during the first cycle this type of soul must traverse to be fully winged and "go their way" (249a). The philosopher's way of life must be chosen twice more, and lived with success equal to that of the first traversal, before soul can be fully liberated.

We note, however, that possessing a philosophical soul does not imply that one will act as a philosopher should act. Even the highest level of soul can succumb to the pressure of desire, at least to the extent of guiding life by the love of honor. In this case, the philosophical soul continues to be controlled by love; now, however, it loves only what is proper to the good horse, that part of the soul characterized at 253d as a lover of honor. Thus, the soul of the philosopher has acted according to the degree of reality represented by its good horse. When lover and beloved do indulge in carnal eros, the act is described as what the many consider bliss, the intensity of this experience seen by the many as the highest happiness. Just as the many are essential for the bestowal of honor, so the many deem carnal satisfaction the appropriate climax of all erotic conduct. Although lover and beloved do not often pursue this satisfaction, the fact that they do so at all shows that their sense of reality is contoured, in part, by what the many hold of value. For this reason, the actions of the lover when driven by this derivative sense of reality are not approved by the whole intellect. The charioteer of philosophical soul sees higher reality—and the life of virtue, in concert with carnal abstinence, which this life entails.[12]

Both types of relationship, whether controlled by love of wisdom or love of honor, are now described as friendship. These friendships thus include an essential degree of desire, frequently felt at very high pitch. "Platonic love," a tepid affection without awareness of all the enticements of erotic carnality, does not exist here. For the truly philosophical, this desire is controlled by mutual consent and understanding; for those living according to honor, this desire occasionally erupts into sexual communion. Even in the latter circumstance, however, the palpable presence of Eros does not disqualify the relationship as a type of friendship, although it is, as Socrates says, not as exalted as philosophical friendship.[13]

The second type of friendship possesses a remarkable degree of fidelity, since the friends believe that their bond of love, even though derivative, is equivalent to an oath which would be sinful to break, even when their love is ended. In Socrates' first speech, the lover's first realization that he no longer loved the beloved caused him to retreat from the beloved's presence, thus arousing strong enmity from the jilted beloved. Now, in the palinode, Socrates reintroduces those occasions when love (or, more accurately, friendship) dwindles and dies. At this point, however, the lover and beloved are fully cognizant of what they have experienced when in love, and also how much that experience has meant to their mutual well-being. As a result, when they no longer feel for each other as they once did, they still retain a vestige of that bond—as if they has sworn eternal fealty to one another—to the point where they will never become unfriendly to their former love. Participation in Eros leaves an indelible affect on soul.

The souls of the two friends travel together after death, presumably even if their earthly love for one another had ceased. Their journey is a "happy life," lived "in the light." This refers to that segment of the thousand-year cycle after soul is apart from body, and the light image brings to mind the ambience of the good, and of the prenatal vision of the realities enjoyed by the pair of souls; the richness and variety of this metaphysical experience makes the almost thousand years as happy as it is. This journey into the light, taken in tandem by the two souls, recalls the ascent of soul with a god to see the truth beyond the rim of the heavens, only now the travelers are two souls who have unified themselves after the conclusion of human life, one soul leading and the other being led, but both souls looking in the same direction and seeking the same reality.

If these two souls are to receive wings, then the assumption is that they will choose the philosophical life once again, since only the philosopher's soul can achieve this privileged condition in three cycles rather than ten. If so, they will have to lead this second life loving wisdom rather than, as they did during the first cycle, loving honor, i.e., they must act better as philosophers. Presumably what they learned during the first life will educate the choices they make and the knowledge they pursue during their second cycle.[14]

The Blessings of Friendship

These things, great and divine, the friendship of a lover will give to you, Socrates says to the "dear boy." However, the affection of a nonlover, blended with mortal prudence and bestowing a small measure of worldly goods, will produce in the beloved soul only a meanness of mind, a condition nonetheless praised by the many as virtue. Furthermore, it will condemn soul to float about the earth for 9,000 years and, finally, to wander "mindlessly" under the earth (256e–257a).

The contrast between consorting with nonlover or lover reappears here, reminding the audience how the problem was originally posed. The fact that vulgar virtue is valued by the many is consistent with the dimension of honor circumscribing this kind of activity. The beloved, when in company with a nonlover, will receive a small supply of material goods, but sufficiently public to be recognized by the many, who will admire a kind of prudence combining the satisfaction of carnal appetites and the acquisition of possessions. In contrast, the beloved loved by a lover will receive only intangible—but far more fundamental—services and care.

The soul of the beloved will wander, mindlessly, around and beneath the earth for 9,000 years, i.e., nine thousand-year cycles. At the end of each of these cycles, soul will choose another form of life (249b). The purport of this extended period of wandering is a form of retribution. Such a soul will, in each of its nine thousand-year cycles, choose a form of life which will condemn it to lead a nonphilosophical life, i.e., a way of life without adequate guidance of mind and thus without even the chance of securing the happiness from living in accordance with the realities and the good. These souls will eventually end up under the earth, the place noted at 249a for correction of soul's faults. The period is specified at 9,000 because at the completion of the tenth cycle, soul's wings will be restored (cf. 249a). The punishment for consort with a nonlover is therefore to pass through a series of lives, never even having the chance of seeing the truth. This is an especially heavy price to pay if the soul in question is from the first level, since this soul is not only ineligible for release from body in three (rather than ten) cycles, but also will never actualize its potential for living the life of a philosopher.

The Socratic Recantation: Summary

The palinode, the recantation for the sinful first speech, is now concluded. Socrates says that it has been delivered as beautifully and finely as possible, especially the poetical locutions forced on him on account of Phaedrus. Socrates asks Eros to be kind and gracious to him so that he does not lose the "erotic art" which has been granted to him, nor his powers of sight; also he prays to be considered more worthy "among beautiful things" than he is now. If anything said before struck Love as harsh, blame Lysias, the father of the speech. Socrates prays that Eros can make Lysias cease from such speeches and turn to philosophy as did his brother Polemarchus, so that Phaedrus, Lysias' "lover," no longer hesitates, as he does now, between two ways of life, but may direct his life "simply toward Eros with philosophical discourses" (257b–c).

Socrates addresses Love itself, Eros, announcing that his palinode is now complete. Since the fourth kind of madness distinguished in the palinode is the madness of love, presumably the beauty and excellence of Socrates' speech, including those poetical words Socrates was compelled to use because of Phaedrus, come from Eros rather than from some other divine source. For a different audience, such poetry may not be necessary, or, if it is, it may take a different imagistic form. In general then, the ability to speak about love comes from the same source as the ability to love in the complex cognitive sense Socrates has outlined in this speech.

Socrates also asks Eros not to take away the erotic art he now possesses. This assertion again recalls the *Symposium*, when Socrates says that love is the only thing he understand (177e), and it foreshadows the extended inquiry into art, especially the art of rhetoric and qualifications attendant to great art (cf. 269e–270a).

When Socrates loves, he loves passionately but not randomly; his love is disciplined according to procedural guidelines depending on the structure of an art. This art is quickened by the sight of beauty, which is why Socrates also prays that he be held even more in esteem by things of beauty than he is now. Socrates does not restrict the scope of beauty to beautiful human beings—anything of beauty is special, whether human (for example, Isocrates, who is called beautiful at the end of the dialogue), or natural. Socrates prays to Eros that his esteem by the beautiful be even higher than it is now, implying that for all his receptivity to beauty, human and otherwise, Socrates could become even more sensitive to beauty itself and everything else about reality such sensitivity can reveal. The more different kinds of beautiful objects Socrates experiences, the greater will be his understanding of the realities underlying these objects, an understanding derived from beauty's special presence within the good. Socrates attempts to deflect responsibility for his first speech, which sinned against love, by attributing it to Lysias, who "fathered" that speech by writing the oratory Phaedrus read to Socrates. Such paternity anticipates the doctrine, asserted at 276a–b, that the most effective discourse is the spoken word, the legitimate "brother" of "bastard" writing. Socrates nonetheless responded sinfully to a sinful speech, thus illustrating the seductiveness of spoken language even a lover such as Socrates cannot withstand. In praying that Eros make Lysias cease speaking this way and turn toward philosophy, Socrates implies that Lysias has the capacity for such change, in turn presupposing that Lysias' speech was not altogether sinful, a point made more explicit later (264e).

The final phase of the prayer is directed at Phaedrus. Socrates wants Phaedrus to cease wavering between two ways of life and to direct his whole life simply toward love "with philosophical discourses." What are the two choices Phaedrus has?

One choice is clear—Socrates prays that Phaedrus choose a life seeking love, Eros, with philosophical discourses. This is surely the life of philosophy, but a life which, given Phaedrus' predilection for the written and spoken word, must be accompanied with discourses continually directing and defining that life as philosophical. Phaedrus can be a lover in the highest sense only by following the traces of Eros according to appropriate philosophical language.

But if this is one way open to Phaedrus, then it would follow, given the hierarchy of lives, that the other option must be on the same level, i.e., the first level of soul. This level contains the philosopher, the lover of beauty, and the lover of the Muses (248d). Now Socrates will shortly (259b) describe Phaedrus as a lover of the Muses (φιλόμουσον), evidence supporting that the two ways of life in question occupy the same level of soul. Therefore, Socrates prays that Phaedrus will move from the first level of soul, i.e., from loving the Muses—a love demonstrated in his passion for fine language—to loving wisdom. For what originally attracted Socrates to the speech of Lysias was not so much its content, but the spectacle of witnessing the "divine head" of Phaedrus declaiming that speech (234d)—thus reflecting the fact that (in the language of myth) the head of Phaedrus' soul beheld the realities beyond the heavens.

The fact that Socrates sees Phaedrus as wavering between these two possibilities implies that Phaedrus has already shown at least the capacity for, if not the actual practice of, the philosophical life.[15] Relevant here is Socrates' wish that Phaedrus pursue such a life simply (ἁπλῶς), thus anticipating the important distinction, introduced in the discussion of natures (270d), between simplicity and complexity with regard to the nature of soul. If a particular soul of a certain type has multiple options, this soul should choose the best option and attempt to live by its lights. (This sense of simplicity will be discussed further in the Epilogue chapter).

Socrates prays that Phaedrus pursue Eros with philosophical discourses (μετὰ φιλοσόφων λόγων). But notice that the entire second half of the *Phaedrus* is, structurally, a pursuit of Eros with philosophical discourses, a pursuit with two related dimensions. First, the interplay of discussion between Socrates and Phaedrus is itself a philosophical discourse, as the two men collaborate—with Phaedrus must more active than he has been so far—in rationally analyzing the nature and properties of written speeches. And second, a method is formulated during this discussion for producing a philosophical discourse on any subject, not just the nature of love. To pursue Eros by means of philosophizing is to pursue love through a certain kind of loving, the love of wisdom. But loving wisdom can best be accomplished by employed a certain methodology. Only in this way can the lover of wisdom truly pursue Eros, thereby loving everything possible at the highest level love can achieve.

Phaedrus will embrace Socrates' prayer if he follows and understands what is now to be said, agreeing to live in accordance with the principles embodied by such a life. Phaedrus began the day as a lover of the Muses, especially when they have produced fine language—i.e., Phaedrus had fallen in love with the speech of Lysias, perhaps to the point of inculcating it into his own life. But it is possible, in Socrates' mind, that Phaedrus would end the day as, if not a philosopher, then as one who saw the importance of being as philosophical as possible. The rhetorical half of the *Phaedrus* would end with a prayer, and the discursive half would become a response to that prayer. The unity of the *Phaedrus* thus reduces to a prayer offered and answered, an appropriate structural pivot reflecting the presence of the divine pervading the dialogue.

In the next chapter, Phaedrus' response to the palinode will initiate discussion leading toward clarifying such cognitive and metaphysical love, thereby providing impetus to make that love more accessible, and more intimate, to all those capable of practicing it.

CHAPTER 6

Rhetoric and Truth (257b–262c)

Socrates has completed his second speech on love. It has served as a palinode redressing his sinful first speech on that complex topic. Phaedrus will shortly exclaim that the second speech was outstanding in every way. Why then does the dialogue not just end here, leaving its audience musingly transfixed with rhetorical fineness, with speechifying as it ought to be?

At 276aff, Socrates will argue that speaking is preferable to writing because it affords the opportunity for both clarification and justification of what has been said. In the case at hand, Socrates' palinode had an audience of one—Phaedrus. And although the speech was not written, its extended length and complexity gave Socrates no opportunity to determine what effect, if any, the speech had on that audience. Toward the conclusion of the palinode, Socrates noted that its poetry was included for Phaedrus' sake (257a). Presumably Socrates so shaped the speech as a consequence of his knowledge of Phaedrus' character (thus anticipating one of the requirements for successful rhetoric, stated at 271b). If therefore discussion ensues after the completion of the palinode, then Phaedrus' immediate reaction to this speech will find Socrates equally attentive, for he will learn how the speech struck Phaedrus, and what, if anything, must be added to its extensive mythic descriptions and interlaced metaphysics. That this reaction will be an

urgent Socratic concern follows from the fact that the conclusion of the
speech was a direct appeal to Phaedrus to elect the philosophical life—
Socrates' life—rather than whatever other choice now appears attractive to him.

The Unity of the *Phaedrus*

Here is Phaedrus' initial reaction, in full, to the palinode:

> I join in prayer with you Socrates that these things happen, if
> indeed they are best for us. But for a long time I have been won-
> dering at your speech, how much more beautiful it was than the
> first. I am afraid that Lysias will make a poor showing if he at-
> tempts to compete with it. Indeed, dear sir, one of the politi-
> cians was abusing him calling him throughout his speech a
> speechwriter; so perhaps from love of honor he may refrain
> from writing (257c–d).

When Phaedrus joins Socrates in prayer that "these things" should
transpire, he refers to the very end of Socrates' speech, when Socrates
invites Phaedrus to choose the philosophical life, with all that choice
entails in terms of seeking knowledge of true reality and acting in accordance with that knowledge. But Phaedrus joins in this prayer only
conditionally, i.e., *if* these things are "best for us." The implication is
that Phaedrus is not yet persuaded that the philosophical life is best for
him (as well as for Socrates). Therefore, Socrates must supplement his
palinode with additional discussion to persuade Phaedrus of the goodness of this way of life. The joint prayer connecting applied rhetoric
and theorizing about rhetoric is paralleled at the end of the dialogue,
when Phaedrus will again join Socrates in prayer, at that time to Pan
and the neighboring gods for wisdom and internal beauty. Phaedrus
hesitates now in embracing the philosophical life—then, apparently,
he will not.

How is Socrates to proceed in the task of persuasion? Phaedrus
provides some clues with the rest of his remarks. He tells Socrates that
the beauty of the second speech was greater than the first, which im-

plies that Phaedrus can recognize rhetorical beauty, and that Phaedrus now believes that Lysias will fail to make a good showing in head-to-head competition with the second speech, which reveals (a) that Phaedrus can discern degrees of rhetorical beauty and (b) that Socrates' speech was probably more beautiful than anything Lysias could ever produce. Thus, Socrates now replaces Lysias in Phaedrus' estimation as the primary exponent of oratorical beauty. According to the palinode, beauty is the most palpable Form; the fact that Phaedrus understands the palinode in this respect shows the fundamental kinship of his soul for beauty and, by implication, for all reality of that sort. His next remark, however, reveals certain limits concerning his sensitivity to the beauty in beautiful writing.

In reporting an abusive politician railing at Lysias as a speechwriter and wondering whether Lysias would then refrain from writing out of pride, or love of honor, Phaedrus indicates that he has not yet grasped the propriety inherent in speechwriting. Socrates must therefore instruct Phaedrus about how this activity is an art, an educative process which, it turns out, will require considerable discussion. Notice also that in imputing an action to Lysias based on love of honor (φιλοτιμίας), or pride, Phaedrus has reintroduced the love theme, although in circumstances which reveal that he has misrepresented its relevance. Thus, Socrates must show Phaedrus more about love in order that Phaedrus can recognize that one kind of love, the love of honor, would not properly apply to Lysias as a writer highly regarded in the public eye.

Socrates' prayer was that Phaedrus direct his life simply toward Eros with philosophical discourses. Phaedrus now remarks that for him, the writing of speeches may be rejected if one has love of honor. Socrates must therefore show the relation between the *logoi* of philosophy and the *logoi* of speechwriting. For if Phaedrus can see how writing speeches, any kind of speech, is only a simulacrum of philosophical discourse, then he will realize whether or not love of honor supersedes the love grounding all philosophical discourse.

The demonstration of the structure of speechwriting, and of writing in general will eventually lead Phaedrus to recognize the propriety in living the philosophical life as that life has been depicted in the second speech. This demonstration will appeal to all aspects of the metaphysical hierarchy—the ultimate object of Eros—defining that way of life. The subsequent discursive account would then balance the prior mythic evocation, with Phaedrus receiving two different yet convergent perspectives on the same kinds of reality. Thus, the *Phaedrus*, an ostensibly disjoint juxtaposition of resounding rhetoric and mundane methodology, constitutes a unified account which, on one level, shows Socrates leading Phaedrus to the philosophical life and, on a more general level, describes the nature of the philosophical life to anyone who, resembling Phaedrus in character, would care to be informed about that life. The initial conflict between love of honor and love of wisdom, the goal of the philosophical life, is played out and resolved in the contrast between speaking and writing, both fundamental forms of human communication and each, in its own way, a "labor of love."

Writing and the Love of Honor

Just before the second speech of Socrates, Phaedrus had promised to compel Lysias to write another speech praising the lover (243e); now, however, Phaedrus has lost his initial enthusiasm in requiring Lysias to fulfill that project. Phaedrus surmises that Lysias' love of honor will override his interest in writing speeches on such topics as preferring a nonlover to a lover. The ascription of love of honor to Lysias establishes an immediate thematic link between the second speech of Socrates on love and the rest of the *Phaedrus*. It is, in fact, an elegant paradox. For if Phaedrus' assessment is correct, then Lysias will avoid writing another speech about love precisely because of love, i.e., his own love of honor. A life ruled by love of honor is, as the palinode puts it, "less noble and without philosophy" (256c), but it is a life proximate to the love of wisdom, thus retaining a measure of this most profound love. The analysis of Lysias' reaction to the politician's accusation—an analysis not concluded until 277a, less than two pages before the dialogue ends—will confront the ethereal abstractions of love developed in Socrates' second speech with the concrete reality of Lysias' place within Athenian public life, a confrontation aroused by an opinion of a politician, a professional public man.

The context of inquiry has broadened the scope of rhetoric from the isolated and relatively restricted examples concerning the matter of love to the arena of political discourse. Phaedrus' belief has the politician maintaining a negative view concerning speechwriting, a view based on the possible reputation posterity will assign to those who pursue that activity. Thus, obloquy heaped on speechwriting is not just that it is produced by a sophist, but that it will be known down the ages as so produced. In the course of examining the politician's position, the nature of speechwriting and of rhetoric in general become much more fundamental, not only as defined in the political sphere but in all aspects of life characterized by language.

Socrates indirectly takes up Lysias' defense by questioning whether the critical politician believed what he says about Lysias and the activity of speechwriting. Phaedrus replies that he seemed to, and then substantiates this belief by claiming that the most important men in the cities are ashamed to write speeches and to leave any writings behind, for they do not want to be called sophists. Socrates counters by insisting that the proudest politicians in fact "greatly love" writing and leaving their name on these writings. Phaedrus does not understand, and Socrates explains that any proposed legislation laid before a governing body prominently mentions the name of its proponent, thus showing off his political wisdom. If the legislation is approved, its author is pleased and praised; if it is not approved, he is grieved along with his friends. Surely, Socrates says, this reaction implies that politicians admire rather than deride the profession of speechwriting. For if an orator or king can rival "Lycurgus or Solon or Darius," and attain "immortality" as a writer in the city, he thinks himself, while living, to be equal to the gods, an opinion which will be shared by posterity when they examine his writings and their political effects (257d–258c).

The love of honor which Phaedrus has supposed would motivate Lysias to stop writing speeches because of criticisms of politicians is now opposed by Socrates' insistence that politicians in fact greatly love the business of writing speeches and handing them down to their constituents, and even beyond. The relation between the politicians and the written word thus mirrors the nonloving lover and the beloved in Lysias's speech, for in both cases, the protagonists in fact love what they explicitly say they do not love. Socrates has adroitly collected the attitude of the politicians into the matrix of love analyzed in the rhetorical portion of the day's discussion. This conflict can be resolved only by examining love at a more fundamental level than that denoted by the words of such lovers.

These politicians, described by Socrates as most proud, will be akin to Lysias in valuing honor, the principal capital of the proud. Once again, the development of the dialogue's main argument continues to be animated by love, even if the love of the politicians for writing speeches is hidden by their public repudiation of it as sophistical. Furthermore, the ascription of wisdom to political writings elevates this degree of love—at least by intent—to that approaching the philosophical, the love of wisdom. The extent to which all members of a polity are affected by laws instituted at the behest of their lawmakers is the extent to which this approach to speechwriting is as comprehensive—and as practical—as possible. The political repercussions of the analyses of speaking and writing in the *Phaedrus* are not manifestly tendered. It is important to keep in mind then that Socrates begins the discursive treatment of speaking and writing by connecting these activities to the art of politics. In this respect, the *Phaedrus* is no less political than the *Republic*, and its metaphysics no less crucial to the overall import of the dialogue than that of the earlier work.

The Problem of Writing

After hearing Socrates' approach to political authorings, Phaedrus infers that a politician could not be against Lysias just because Lysias writes speeches, for then the politician would run counter to self-interest, i.e., the politician passing legislation (in written form) bestowing legal wisdom on his constituency. Socrates then concludes it is "clear to all" that writing speeches is not shameful in itself; the disgrace is in speaking or writing badly and disgracefully (258d).

The conclusion of this introductory section is noteworthy in two respects: first, Socrates' appeal to everyone's conviction recalls that same epistemic optimism when, in his first speech, he distinguished between the two primary capacities of soul (237d). But the thinking here seems no less suspect than that employed in Socrates' original division of soul's nature. Thus, Phaedrus has inferred that the politician would be inconsistent in rejecting the speechwriting of Lysias since he himself wants to be a speechwriter. But strictly speaking, it does not follow from this inconsistency that speechwriting is not intrinsically shameful, as Socrates has concluded. A crucial distinction nonetheless emerges from this discussion, i.e., between an activity and how that activity is performed, a distinction allowing Socrates to inquire into the latter.

The second point is that the conclusion of the argument refers to writing or speaking. Up to this point (258d), only writing has been mentioned. Socrates has disjunctively added speaking without justification, a significant move if essential differences obtain between writing and speaking. The point may be that the two activities are coextensive at this juncture in the sense that the distinction between writing as such and writing well (or badly) can also be made for speaking, and that establishing this distinction is, for now, essential in order for the discussion to proceed.

Socrates then asks whether they want to question Lysias concerning the method of writing well or badly. In fact, Socrates extends the proposal by asserting that this inquiry should be directed at anyone who has or will write anything, either public or private, verse or prose, whether by a poet or a private person (258d).

This extension of the scope of the inquiry shows that Socrates intends to scrutinize principles pertaining to any kind of writing, regardless of its form or the professional status of its author. Presumably specific differences among types of writing will require that these principles be adapted—e.g., the formal considerations for an epic poem will be altered when applied to a speech in a law court. But regardless of such individual differences, the assumption is that all forms of writing share and are defined by one set of principles. These principles will be developed at a level of extreme generality, befitting the mythic generality in Socrates' second speech.

Furthermore, this statement of the problem continues the implicit application of the method of collection which has characterized the discussion so far. What began as an isolated observation concerning a speech about love then became an inquiry about speeches in political settings; now the subject matter of speeches has become as comprehensive as possible. Socrates has collected all instances of writing in order to determine the nature of the art of writing. From this perspective then, it would be anomalous for Socrates to pose the problem of the nature of writing without developing that problem according to methodological considerations which, we will be assured, are essential for such an investigation.

Phaedrus' response to Socrates' proposal is in character. He says that one may live for no other pleasure than pursuing the art of writing, especially since such pleasures involve no prior pain and are not for that reason called slavish (258e). The pleasure Phaedrus refers to, in not arising from an antecedent pain (as do a number of bodily pleasures), is mainly, if not entirely, intellectual. Therefore when Phaedrus prefaces this observation by asking rhetorically what else one should live for, he implies that this type of discourse is, for him, the highest kind of pleasure. Thus the ensuing discussion, if duly philosophical, is an intrinsically pleasant exercise and will, if pursued properly, contribute to if not constitute the highest form of happiness. Phaedrus' hedonism here is especially refined, showing he is capable of exemplifying the claim made toward the end of the dialogue, i.e., that employment and practice of the dialectical method will make its possessor as happy as humanly possible (277a). The pleasure Phaedrus feels at the prospect of philosophizing about the nature of writing is the same pleasure experienced by anyone who properly philosophizes about any subject. And it is precisely the same kind of pleasure, derived from ultimate metaphysical concerns and shared by gods and mortals, that was hymned with such fervor in the Socratic palinode. Phaedrus' enthusiasm for philosophical discussion also shows that he has the best kind of soul, for only a soul having seen many of the realities would feel excitement at the thought of the far-reaching speculative inquiry Socrates has just proposed.

The Story of the Cicadas

Socrates asserts that there is, it seems, adequate leisure to question the nature of good and bad speaking and writing. He then begins, seemingly out of the blue, an extended story concerning the cicadas who have been chirruping since the arrival of the two men at this place by the Ilissus (cf. 230c).

This account of the cicadas (259ad) has received various explanatory comment. According to Thompson, Socrates invents a myth by way of encouraging Phaedrus' "philosophic ardour." Hackforth designates three purposes for the account: "first, to provide a temporary relaxation of the reader's mind by means of a charming little myth; second, to appeal, under cover of a warning by Socrates to Phaedrus and himself against lazy-mindedness, for a renewal (or continuance) of the reader's attention; and third, to indicate the immportance and difficulty of the task ahead by appealing for divine support." And for De Vries, the account represents "a relaxing intermezzo" which Plato introduces in order to alert his readers to "serve the Muses in the right way."[1]

By scholarly consensus, the account of the cicadas is a myth, and it is believed to be one of only two myths which is Plato's own creation.[2] However, Socrates never explicitly says that this story is a myth (unlike his first speech, which is called a myth both at its beginning and its end, and his second speech, which is referred to as mythical, in part, at several key junctures). The account of the cicadas begins with a neutral "it is said." Now if this account is indeed mythical, then the sense of the story should be determined in relation to those portions of the dialogue explicitly designated as mythical. In this way, the mythical dimension of the dialogue as a whole will display a consistency of vision commensurate with the rigor of the dialogue's more discursive phases.

The Birth of the Muses

If Socrates and Phaedrus were to doze, lulled by their own lack of discussion, the singing cicadas would laugh at them as if they were slaves,
slumbering like sheep. If, however, they are seen discussing, oblivious
to the charms of their Siren song, then perhaps the cicadas will grant
the gift bestowed by the gods on them to give to those who merit it.
Phaedrus interrupts, saying that he knows nothing of this gift and he
asks Socrates to explain (259b).

Socrates gently criticizes Phaedrus for being a lover of the Muses
but not knowing about these things. He then recounts the story: It is
said that these cicadas were once men, before the Muses were born.
When the Muses were born and their song appeared, some men were so
overwhelmed with pleasure from hearing their song that they too began
to sing. Forgetting food and drink, they sang until, unaware of their
condition, they died. From these men, the race of cicadas began. The
cicadas have a gift from the Muses—they sing continually from birth
and, upon their death, they report to the Muses who, among men, has
honored them. For instance, the "poets of love" are endeared to Erato;
and, in general, each Muse bestows its own favors on those who have
been reported as honoring them. Calliope, the oldest Muse, and
Urania, next to her in longevity, receive the reports concerning those
philosophers who have worshipped them, the Muses most concerned
with heaven and with "discourses divine and human," and whose
sounds are the most beautiful. Thus, Socrates concludes, there are
many reasons why they should talk and not sleep (259c–d).

The key to the import of the cicada account is to determine the
"gift" of which Phaedrus has not heard, as well as the conditions for receiving this gift and the consequences once it has been received. One
commentator has asserted that the gift "Socrates ironically seeks
through the intermediaries who chirp above them is the strength to re-
sist their charms."[3] But this is incorrect. Socrates states, with little or
no trace of irony, that the gift depends on the report the cicadas give to
the Muses telling them of those individuals who have honored the
Muses by practicing, with grace and excellence, the art of that Muse.
Then, as a result of such honor and the report of the cicadas, the human

artist is made more endearing to that divine Muse. If therefore the artist has been drawing inspiration from the Muse to perform that art, then becoming more endeared to this Muse will presumably imply that the protagonist will become even more adept, or more gifted, at that art than before.

That the cicadas function in this way is indicated shortly thereafter, when Socrates proposes to Phaedrus that they examine Lysias' speech and Socrates' rhetorical response to that speech for purposes of locating something in them showing art and the lack of art (262c). Phaedrus agrees, and Socrates asserts that by good fortune the discussions contain an example of how one who knows the truth can lead on his audience with playful words. Socrates then adds that the local deities cause these words, and "perhaps" too the "prophets of the Muses" who sing above their heads have granted this gift—for Socrates does not share in the art of speaking (262d).

The cicadas are posited as providing the source, or at least a source, of the Socratic speeches. Furthermore, the entire discourse, both the first and the second speech of Socrates, can be credited to the gift of the cicadas. This becomes clear at 265c–d, when Socrates, in discussing how the discourse changed from blame (i.e., the first speech) to praise (i.e., the second speech), refers to the discourse as, on the whole, a playful jest. Thus, one who knows the truth can lead on his audience by playing in words (προσπάζων ἐν λόγοις—262d); in fact, Socrates has done precisely this in the "playfully sporting" (παιδιᾷ πεπαῖσθαι) language of the two speeches considered as one discourse (265d).

The cicadas, prophets of the Muses, can present the gift of inspiration for Socrates' speeches. Four of the nine Muses are named in the account of the cicadas—Terpsichore, Erato, Calliope, and Urania. But which Muse (or Muses) have come into play in the cicadas' report on behalf of Socrates?

It would appear that Socrates, as philosopher, must have been inspired by the Muse (or Muses) appropriate to philosophy. That this is the case may be inferred, but only by implication from other passages. At 248d, it was said that the soul of the philosopher has seen most of the

truth. And, at 250c, Socrates identified his own soul (as well as that of
Phaedrus) as one which "follows in the train of Zeus," the deity who
sees the most truth. These souls seek companions of a philosophical nature, for this kind of loving friendship is the special privilege of the
souls who follow Zeus (252e). If therefore Socrates is a philosopher,
then the appropriate Muses are Calliope and Urania—the Muses who
receive the report concerning those who live as philosophers—since
Socrates is about to philosophize about the nature of rhetoric. But was
Socrates *just* philosophizing in the palinode, the more complex rhetorical effort?

Calliope and Urania are, according to Socrates, the Muses most
concerned with the heavens and with accounts dealing with the divine
and the human. Now Calliope and Urania are traditionally the Muses of
epic poetry and astronomy respectively. Strictly speaking then,
philosophy does not have its own Muse, or even its own set of Muses;
rather, philosophy has Muses with a combined bailiwick governing
philosophy's proper province. Furthermore, Socrates has described
these Muses as having the most to do with this province and that their
music, when they are duly inspirational, is the most beautiful (259d).
The suggestion is that Calliope and Urania inhabit the apex of a continuum constituted by the Muse understood as one set. If so, then in a
sense all the Muses are concerned with philosophy, but Calliope and
Urania are most and best concerned with it.

Let us pursue this line of thought. Calliope is described as the
"eldest" of the Muses and Urania as next to her, i.e., next eldest. According to tradition, the Muses were all sired by Zeus. Thus, Calliope,
the eldest, is the first-born Muse and Urania, next to Calliope, is the
second-born Muse. As such, they are the Muses most proximate to
Zeus, their progenitor. Now at 246c, Zeus was described as a "great
leader in heaven" and as "arranging all things and caring for all
things." When therefore Calliope and Urania are designated as the
Muses most concerned with "heaven" and with discourses on "the divine and the human," they are aligned with Zeus in terms of the
heavenly scope under their control and for the care of the two dominant
domains of reality under Zeus' aegis—the gods and human beings. Cal-

liope and Urania are the most philosophical Muses because they control access to matters closest to the specific governance of Zeus, their father and leader. Furthermore, if all the Muses derive their existence from Zeus, then there is a sense in which all the Muses participate in the philosophical dimension governed by Zeus inasmuch as they serve the ends of Zeus' universal control, each Muse in its own way. Thus, to follow and emulate any one of the Muses is ultimately to follow Zeus, and we may expect the souls of Socrates and Phaedrus, followers of Zeus, to have an affinity for the Muses.

One of the nine Muses is Erato, the Muse attending to the poets of love (259d). If therefore Socrates' palinode was executed as beautifully and well as possible, then it is possible that this aspect of its fineness was due, in part, to the inspiration of Erato, who helped shape the lines of love poetry describing the desire and eventual unity of lover and beloved. If continuity of function spans all the Muses, then the poeticisms of Socrates' second speech, as inspired by Erato, are an essential (if metaphysically dependent) part of the philosophical dimension of that speech. That the poet has seen something of the truth has been implied when the poet, and any other kind of imitative artist, was located on the sixth level in the list of souls (248e). Thus, the love poetry in the second speech does invoke the truth (whether or not it is completely successful in this regard), and to that extent it coheres with and indeed augments the distinctively philosophical evocation of the truth.

Socrates concludes the account of the cicadas by insisting that there are many reasons why he and Phaedrus should continue to discuss the matters at hand. The first reason is to ward off the lull of the cicadas' continual drone. But Socrates realizes that if he has practiced activities governed by more than one Muse, then his discourse should be attentive to whatever Muses have played a role in his artistic efforts. Thus, there are as many reasons to talk about the Muses as there are Socratic activities inspired by those Muses. In philosophizing as well as possible about the products of inspiration granted to Socrates by the Muses, Socrates will fortify his access to such products whenever the need for them arises.

It is, of course, not sufficient simply to keep talking; rather, the discussion must concern appropriate subjects and be developed in an appropriately philosophical way. Only if subsequent discussion is pitched in the correct keys and with the right themes will Socrates, and Phaedrus as his philosophical companion, be in a position to receive the gift of those Muses whose inspiration is needed in order to understand the nature of good writing and speaking and to apply that understanding to effective rhetoric.[4]

The Muses and Philosophical Inspiration

The continuity of the Muses as they affect the practice of philosophy and the fact that they represent different degrees of insight into truth produce important implications for understanding the unity of the *Phaedrus*.

Socrates hypothesized that the philosophical dimension of the second speech was as good as it was because of the effective presence of the "prophets of the Muses." It has been argued that he was granted that gift because of philosophy he had already done. Socrates himself gives evidence of this philosophical perspective when, at the beginning of the first speech, he entreated the Muses to assist him in speaking in such a way that Socrates, now considered wise by Phaedrus, will be found still wiser once the speech has been concluded (237b). If the wise Socrates does become wiser, then it will be under the aegis of the Muses—and, in part, from the intercession of the cicadas who continue to sing overhead. Although the first speech will be less successful in wisely depicting the nature of love, it nonetheless contains features— the use of collection and division—essential to attaining wisdom. In this respect, Socrates has philosophized well; the singing cicadas, observing Socrates' art, will report this instance of it to the appropriate Muses, securing for Socrates the gift of inspiration which will fund the resplendent philosophical vision of the second speech.

Socrates' second speech, the palinode, concludes at 257b. At 259e, immediately after the account of the cicadas, Socrates embarks on a discussion of good and bad speaking and writing. Now if this discussion is philosophical, then the continuing intermediary function of the cicadas should make this discussion even better, in a strictly philosophical sense, than the philosophical dimension enunciated during the palinode. In other words, the same type of inspiration that seeded the philosophy embodied in the second speech will, intensified by the very excellence of that speech, also germinate a discursive treatment of what was said during that speech. And this analysis will, by dint of the Muses' inspiration, clarify and extend the philosophical elements of Socrates' oratory.

It may be noted, however, that Socrates' hope that what they will say will be found endearing to the Muses (as reported to them by the cicadas) implies that the discursive development will be incomplete. For if it were a finished account with no need for revision or addition, then there would be no room for improvement; any hope for endearment—and the additional inspiration which may ensue—would therefore be otiose. The best Socrates and Phaedrus can do is philosophize about rhetoric in such a way that the cicadas will report their progress to Calliope and Urania, who will then endow future study with even greater insight, and so on. Recall, however, that Calliope and Urania depend on Zeus for the capacity to inspire in philosophical matters. As a result, even if Socrates and Phaedrus gained as much inspiration as possible from these two Muses, whatever they said, both now and later, would establish them as lovers of wisdom, philosophers, rather than wise. As Socrates notes at the end of the dialogue (279d), the epithet "wise" belongs only to a god.

The account of the cicadas subtly brings out the inspirational limitations of the Muses. The beginning of the account states that the cicadas were once human beings and that these humans existed before the birth of the Muses. Strictly speaking, if inspiration from the appropriate Muse (or Muses) was essential to the successful pursuit of philosophy, then those humans who preexisted the birth of the Muses would have been cut off from even the possibility of being truly philosophical. By implication then, the philosophical life can be practiced without direct assistance from the Zeus-begotten Muses (just as human life itself could be fulfilled without, say, the gift of Promethean fire).

The background circumstances underlying the generation of the cicadas also attests to the derivative quality inherent in the song of the Muses. After the generation of the Muses, some men were so enthralled with the pleasure of their song that they forgot to eat and drink, i.e., they forgot to tend to this aspect of their nature as human beings. These men "died ere they felt themselves to be dying" (in Thompson's elegant rendering, p. 89) and from them originated the *genos* of cicadas. Thus, the very existence of this kind of creature depended on human beings behaving in certain ways.

To be enamored of the Muses to such an extent that one ceases to be concerned with the body is a vice rather than a virtue, and the fact that human beings who lived their lives this way were reborn as cicadas testifies to this one-dimensional and inferior mode of existence. Even the onset of death was, so to speak, subhuman, for they were so unaware of the rich complexities of life as a union of body and soul that they died unaware that they were dying. A rebirth in this lower form is a punishment, not a blessing. For most individuals, the song of the cicadas sedates rather than stimulates. In a natural setting the *Phaedrus* has characterized as of great visual beauty, the aural song of the cicadas can lull the intellect to such an extent that anyone present falls asleep, a kind of living death. This is why Socrates compares the sound of the cicadas to that of the Sirens, who lured unwary mariners to their destruction.

To demythologize the cicada story in this way juxtaposes artistic inspiration with the metaphysical schema underlining the *Phaedrus*. In relating the cicadas to the Muses, the Muses to Zeus and Zeus (as a deity) to the reality beyond the heavens, Plato subtly directs the tradition of divine inspiration toward a purely metaphysical source of fructification. The story of the cicadas is therefore something more than a charming intermezzo. For if this account is connected to the metaphysical and mythic dimensions of the *Phaedrus* as a whole, it becomes a beacon illuminating the unity of what is often called culture, of which philosophy—with the grandeur Plato envisioned for it—is the leading component.

Rhetoric and Truth

As the cicadas continue their song, Socrates says he and Phaedrus should discuss when speaking and writing are and are not well-executed. (Again, no distinction is drawn between speaking and writing— presumably the subsequent account will, unless otherwise specified, pertain to both types of discourse.)

If, Socrates asks, a speech is to be good and well-formed, is it necessary that the intellect of the speaker know the truth about the subject matter of that discourse. Phaedrus replies that he has heard that knowing the truth is not essential; rather, knowing what seems just to the many would suffice rather than knowing what is "good and noble." In short, persuasion comes from what seems true, not from what is true. The words of the wise must be heeded, Socrates says, and he suggests that they examine this position (259e–260a).

According to Socrates, knowledge of the truth is essential in order that the speech be both good and beautiful. What a good speech is has not yet been determined, but if good includes being persuasive, then one might question (a) whether a good speech need necessarily be beautiful, and (b) whether a beautiful speech will also be persuasive. It would seem that different principles of rhetoric would be needed to achieve different rhetorical ends. Nonetheless, Socrates claims that knowing the truth is necessary to produce both characteristics, rhetorical beauty as well as rhetorical effect.

Phaedrus has apparently not thought a great deal about the relation between rhetoric and truth, for his response to Socrates is a report on what he has heard, presumably from authorities—what seems just or good or noble to the many will suffice, and truth is not necessary to achieve persuasion. For Phaedrus, merely expounding an opinion according to certain rhetorical devices is sufficient to produce the desired reaction in one's audience. Socrates insists that the wise must be questioned concerning this position, and he will give reasons to show that these currently popular protagonists of rhetorical theory have not really understood the relevant principles—suggesting by this lack that they have reduced an art to a craft and, as a result, that they may be unable consistently to engender either beauty of rhetorical form or the desired persuasion in their audience.

The Challenge of Opinion

Socrates begins the analysis of rhetoric by considering a hypothetical attempt at persuasion: Suppose that he, Socrates, is trying to persuade Phaedrus to acquire a horse for use at home and in battle. Suppose also that neither of them knew what a horse was, but that Socrates knew that Phaedrus believed a horse to be a donkey. Phaedrus interjects that these suppositions are ridiculous, but Socrates says "not yet." As Thompson notes (p. 91), the full absurdity of this example has yet to be developed, but Phaedrus' interruption signals that even the introduction is, for him, ridiculous. Socrates' response, denying absurdity at this point, indicates that although Phaedrus and Socrates themselves may never be so confused, such confusion may rule when the cast of characters is different or when discussion concerns a different subject.

Socrates continues the example by further supposing that he urged the acquisition of this quadruped in all seriousness by praising the virtues of a donkey, both in battle and in matters agrarian. Phaedrus now says that this situation is very ridiculous, and Socrates wonders aloud whether it is preferable to be ridiculous than clever and an enemy. One could be ridiculous yet well-intentioned; this is better for all concerned than if one is clever (δεινόν) but an enemy to one's audience, presupposing that the speaker is thought friendly but is really of another mind altogether.

This ridiculous example is now generalized: if an orator, unmindful of good and evil, attempts to persuade a polity ignorant in the same way, not by calling a donkey a horse, but by calling evil good, and by using the skewed opinions of the multitude has them imitate what is evil, no good crop will issue from such oratorical seeds (260b–d). A cavalry riding into battle on donkeys will be both ludicrous and short-lived—as would be the polis believing it was good to have its cavalry so equipped. And if both speaker and audience are ignorant of good and evil, there is little hope that whatever is said can halt the eventual decay of the populace. The orator, cannily reacting to a studied feel for opinions, may win rhetorical victory but hardly one of consequence if the polis is ruined as a result.

The image of the orator sowing seeds is thus not haphazardly chosen; it continues the theme of sustenance introduced in the account of soul's vision of reality beyond the heavens and also intimates that what is spoken is itself in some sense alive. The characteristics of life will become essential to Socrates' analysis of both speaking and writing. Spoken words will grow once they have been disseminated, and without being properly formed such discourse will not produce a good crop in its soil—the souls of a human audience.

The Art of Speaking: Rejoinder and Criticism

Socrates now admits that his thinly veiled abuse of the art of speaking was perhaps excessive. He then personifies that art and listens to its rejoinder. The art of speaking says that it does not insist on ignorance of the truth for its prospective practitioners, but it does pride itself on the fact that lacking this art, a knowledge of the truth will get an individual no nearer to mastering the art of persuasion. Socrates' response is to insist that this position represents discourse not as an art but as a craft without art. Arguments are approaching, Socrates says, that will show this criticism to be the case. Phaedrus plays along with the image of living accounts, and Socrates beckons the arguments to appear and to persuade the fine young Phaedrus that unless he pays sufficient attention to philosophy, he will never speak effectively on anything (260d–261a).

The challenge extended to Socrates by the art of rhetoric is forceful and must be clearly stated. The personified art of speaking insists that, ideally, the prospective orator should first discover the truth and then consult the art of speaking to learn how to express the truth most effectively. However, knowing the truth will, by itself, not advance the knower in the fine art of influencing others. In Socrates' example, even if the speaker did know that the donkey was not a horse, he would be unable by possession of that fact alone to persuade his audience about the wisdom of purchasing either animal.

In short, this self-styled art of speaking sees itself as different from whatever comprises knowledge of the truth. It follows then that such speaking is an art—if it is an art—for reasons other than those that characterize truth. Socrates does not deny that this approach to speaking can contribute to producing persuasion. What he denies is more fundamental, i.e., that it is possible to separate truth from the art of speaking. The particular art of speaking pleading its case before us is, in fact, no art at all. Craft is present here—not art, since for Socrates art depends necessarily on truth. Once it has been established that this art of speaking is no art, Socrates will show that the persuasion which this craft claimed, as an art, to be able to produce independently of knowing the truth will not necessarily occur. If so, then there will be all the less reason to seek expertise in such a craft.[5]

The Definition and Scope of Rhetoric

Socrates now characterizes the whole nature of rhetoric as a certain art of leading the soul by means of words or discourses, not only in courts of law and other public places, but in private situations as well. Furthermore, this extension implies that rhetoric is the same art whether it concerns small things or great things. Is this, Socrates asks Phaedrus, what he has heard about rhetoric?

The apparent boundlessness of rhetoric circumscribed in this way unsettles Phaedrus, who has heard only that what is said and written in law courts and spoken in public meetings are proper instances of rhetorical art. Socrates asked whether Phaedrus has not heard of the rhetorical works composed by Nestor and Odysseus while at leisure in Troy, or the treatise by Palamedes. Phaedrus confesses ignorance, unless, he asks, Socrates intends to disguise Gorgias as Nestor and Thrasymachus or Theodorus as Odysseus. Socrates says perhaps, and then tells Phaedrus to forget them, whereupon he embarks on a different argumentative tack (261a–c).

It has just been asserted that the intellect of the speaker must know the truth; now, however, it is asserted that the whole nature of rhetoric is leading the soul by means of words or discourses. If the intellect is not identical to soul (by virtue of soul's tripartite nature), then rhetoric rightly defined will entail that the intellect structure a discourse so that soul, a complex unity, is led toward some conviction. This characterization of rhetoric thus presupposes understanding the nature of soul and describing various forms of discourse suitable for persuading soul, the whole soul, to accept a certain position. This understanding of nature is implied here; Socrates will make it explicit later.

According to Socrates, rhetoric is leading the soul by means of words. But leading the soul toward what? Phaedrus, a lover of the Muses, will perhaps appreciate the end toward which rhetoric should be directed. And such understanding may, *mutatis mutandis*, be generalized. Although not all speakers are philosophers, the extent to which nonphilosophers approach the vision of philosophy with discourse based on knowledge rather than opinion is the extent to which this discourse will have salutary effects on both speaker and audience. Socrates may have this much wider audience in mind in characterizing rhetoric as broadly as he does at this point.

De Vries comments (p. 204) that the humor in visualizing Nestor and Odysseus composing treatises on rhetoric should not be overlooked. But there is a serious point as well. When Phaedrus attempts to associate the personages in this Socratic jape with real figures, i.e., leading authorities in rhetoric, Socrates dismisses the attempt as of no consequence. Why then did he name Nestor and Odysseus as producing such treatises when there is no evidence in Homer that they ever contemplated doing such a thing? Recall, however, that both Nestor and Odysseus were extremely eloquent. Thus, their treatises on rhetoric are their speeches. Socrates is pointing to the fact that skilled rhetoricians—even mythic ones—must have some sort of theoretical glimmer of what they are doing before they speak. So in their idle moments, i.e., when not actually speaking, Nestor and Odysseus are envisioned as reflecting on, and writing about, how to be eloquent. Whether or not they were ever depicted as actually doing so is irrelevant. Phaedrus has seemingly missed the point in attempting to shift the identities, which is why Socrates does not want to pursue this little skit. But Nestor and Odysseus are no less theoretical for being only expert rhetoricians than those rhetoricians who have studied, and written about, this art.[6]

The approach Socrates takes to convince Phaedrus that this extension of the art of rhetoric is legitimate should also be noted. Socrates' procedure here, at 261b–c, is a direct anticipation of the method of collection (as stated at 265d). Thus the kind of dispute found in law courts is added to the kind of dispute found in political meetings. These disputes rest on opposition—the just and the unjust, the good and its opposite, etc. When this kind of contention is then added to the works of Zeno, it becomes evident to Phaedrus that the contention present in legal and political contexts is the same sort of contention found in Zeno's thought, a form of discourse which both in mode of presentation and immediate effect appears far removed from the practical arenas of law and politics. Socrates says, in summarizing these diverse forms of discourse, that if they do indeed represent the art of rhetoric, it will be "one" art. Referring to the unity of this putative art introduces the notion that when disparate things or activities are collected and then examined for features of identity, it is possible to see one Form or common nature which can then be properly divided according to the joints of that nature.

Rhetoric and Opposition

Socrates has presented a wide variety of rhetorical examples to illustrate the broad conception of this art. And he has said that arguments, *logoi*, are approaching which will show that, by contrast, the art of speaking Phaedrus describes is deceiving us in purporting to be an art. These arguments may be divided under two heads: the proper scope of rhetoric with respect to opposition, and the dependency of rhetoric on truth.

Phaedrus has admitted that rhetoric is found in law courts and in political situations, but he hesitates in accepting Socrates' broader notion of this activity. Socrates then asks whether the participants in these contexts "contend in speech." Phaedrus agrees. Socrates broadly generalizes such contention—it is concerned with the just and the unjust. A master of this art will make the same thing appear to the same audience at one time just and, if desired, at another time unjust. Similarly, the public speaker will make the same things appear to the polis to be good at one time and its opposite at another time. Finally, Socrates cites the "Eleatic Palamedes," Zeno, whose art of speaking makes the same things appear to his audience both like and unlike, one and many, at rest and in motion (261b–d).

Phaedrus acknowledges that as far as he is concerned, the art of speaking and writing occurs only in courts of law, and speaking only in public assemblies. Socrates must therefore show Phaedrus that the scope of rhetoric is much more extensive. Socrates begins by referring to courts of law because Phaedrus has just admitted that rhetoric is found in this arena of discourse, i.e., contention concerning the just and the unjust. And Socrates does not say merely that the master rhetorician can convince audience A that X is just and then convince audience B (where no member of A is also a member of B) that X is unjust. He asserts that this rhetorician can convince audience A that X is just and also convince the same audience that the same thing, X, is unjust. But why can Socrates say this?

The facts of a case in law are, presumably, the same for both parties in the dispute. The difference emerges not from these facts, but from how to interpret them in light of the law. One party will say that the facts are emblematic of justice; the other party will say that these facts display injustice. But the facts are the same for both parties. Practitioners of the law must become skilled in arguing that a given set of facts represents one of two opposed evaluations. If, however, the same practitioner had been engaged by the other party in the suit, then this same practitioner would look at the same set of facts from exactly the opposite standpoint. And even if this possibility were rarely or never actualized, the practitioner representing one side of the dispute must be able to anticipate what the practitioner representing the other side will say in order to prepare an adequate defense and, if required, counter argument. Socrates' assumption is therefore that a rhetorician in a law court must be capable of arguing either side of the issue. If so, then one rhetorician could take the same set of facts and make them appear to the same people as just and then unjust.

Socrates next makes a parallel assertion about political speaking, i.e., that it will make the same things appear to the polis to be good at one time, the opposite at another time, a claim which again follows Phaedrus' original belief concerning the scope of rhetoric. There are, however, significant differences between speaking in a law court and before a polis. For example, speaking in a law court is necessarily contentious, whereas speaking before a polis may not be. But the extension is not without justification; thus, it could be argued before the polis that, say, a raid on a seaport both would and would not justify retaliation on the part of the aggrieved city. And, in general, the phenomenon of the same politician urging opposite courses of action in parallel sets of circumstances is not unknown.

The final example, that of Zeno the Eleatic Palamedes, extends the scope of rhetoric far beyond that Phaedrus had initially admitted. And including the distinctive subject matter of Zeno's artistry—like and unlike, one and many, at rest and in motion, all notions of considerable abstractness—has the force of a conclusion by way of generalization. There are kinds of opposition distinctive to law courts and political assemblies, but Zeno's art can produce the most general types of opposition for things in any context. Thus, if the art of rhetoric has the characteristics that Phaedrus agrees belong to speaking in law courts and political settings, then Socrates has shown him that he should broaden his notion of rhetoric so that it encompasses all forms of discourse which include these characteristics. In a sense then, Zeno becomes the paradigm rhetorician, given what he can do in producing instances of opposition in the broadest range of contexts. In legal discourse, the opposition, e.g., between the just and the unjust, is represented by distinct parties, each standing for one of the two opposites. It is, however, the fact of this particularly fundamental opposition that is crucial, not the incidental circumstance in which the poles of opposition are represented by different protagonists.[7]

In the transition from law courts and political meetings to Zeno, the Eleatic Palamedes, a purely metaphysical conflict arises between notions of extreme generality. The works of Zeno, which formed a pivotal place in the structure of the problems presented in *Parmenides*, were adroit manipulations of general terms leading an audience to find the same things subjected to opposite properties. The unlimited pervasiveness of this kind of rhetoric establishes Zeno's version of it as distinctively foundational. The shift from law and politics to metaphysics shows that the ultimate source of the problematic nature of rhetoric lies in the appropriate scrutiny of abstract notions. As a result, to determine the nature of rhetoric is to determine the metaphysical ground for the possibility of rhetoric.

Including Zeno as the primary exponent of rhetoric is the final phase of the first *logos* showing that the supposed art of speaking is not an art. This *logos* has established the full scope of rhetoric. The question then becomes how truth relates to this understanding of rhetoric, particularly with respect to persuasion.

Rhetoric and Truth

Socrates now generalizes these reflections on movement between opposites: the art of contention—if indeed it is an art—is found not only in courtrooms and politics, but is one and the same in all kinds of speaking. This art would be the capacity "to make out everything to be like everything else, within the limits of possible comparison" (Hackforth's translation, p. 124) and also to be able to reveal the attempts of others to do the same thing. When Phaedrus does not understand this difficult claim, Socrates begins to explain by asking, first, whether we are deceived when the differences between things are great or small. The latter, Phaedrus says, and Socrates then points out that someone intending to deceive and not be deceived must know the similarities and dissimilarities between things. If he does not know the truth about a given thing, he will be unable to recognize in other things whether they are more or less like what he does not know about that thing. Such a speaker, being deceived about the truth concerning things, will not have the art of making his audience pass from one thing to its opposite by leading them through likenesses, nor will he be able to avoid being deceived himself. Socrates concludes that one who does not know the truth but merely chases opinions will attain a ridiculous art of speech—in fact, no art at all (261e–262c).

Socrates' conclusion about this art, that it can produce all manner of resemblances between all manner of things, leaves Phaedrus at a loss. And upon reflection, his bewilderment is justified. For if the generality in Zeno's rhetoric is paradigmatic, then an orator possessing this art can make any one thing seem to be like (and unlike) any other thing. It may be noted that such absolute universality renders this understanding of rhetoric derivable from the good, in particular its function of "holding all things together." For to say that any one thing could be likened to any other thing presupposes that all things share at least one property. And if this property is sheer undifferentiated existence, then the good establishes the possibility of such a property.

But there are limits to the possibility of establishing similarities between things. And these limits are set by the fact of difference. Let us assume, as Socrates suggests, that a speaker intends to mislead his audience about something. Now given that things are different, a speaker can successfully mislead an audience only if the speaker knows the degree of resemblance and dissimilarity between this thing (event, proposal, etc.) and that thing. The more X resembles Y, while remaining distinct from Y, the more likely we are to be misled about claims made concerning either X or Y; the less X resembles Y, the less likely we are to be misled since the difference between the two things is wide (whereas in the first instance the difference between them is narrow). Donkeys certainly resemble horses, so it is more likely that we can be misled about donkeys and horses than about horses and, say, chariots.

If, as Socrates points out, the speaker who intends to mislead does not know the degree of resemblance and dissimilarity, then he may end up merely deceiving himself. If Socrates truly thought that a donkey was a horse, he could mislead Phaedrus only by persuading him that a donkey was not a horse. But by intending to misleading Phaedrus, he not only reinforces his own self-deception, since in fact a donkey is not a horse (although Socrates believes that it is), but he also and completely contrary to his intent persuades Phaedrus of the truth, i.e., that in fact a donkey is not a horse. Therefore, in order to avoid the possibility of deceiving himself in his attempt to mislead others, the speaker must know the truth about a given thing.

Furthermore, such deception has a definite strategic shape, since deception is easier when the differences between things are smaller. The transition between one thing and its opposite is facilitated therefore if the speaker moves gradually, by taking advantage of smaller differences, then precipitately, by covering the relevant type of opposition in a few expansive steps. The restriction on producing resemblances is established according to opposition; the relevant degree of resemblance is defined by those resemblances constituting the continuum joining both opposites.

The appeal to rhetoric which intends to deceive not only establishes the dependency of successful rhetoric on truth, it also calls to mind the hypothetical lover in Lysias' speech, and the attempt to persuade the beloved that he should favor the nonlover rather than the lover. But that lover—posing as a nonlover—can achieve this end only by deceiving the beloved about the nature of love. Now according to Socrates' theory, the lover must know the truth about love, for only under this condition could the lover know how to structure a speech showing that one should not favor the lover (one opposite) but rather the nonlover (the other opposite). The fact that Lysias' speech is flawed formally suggests that the lover in this speech does not know the truth about love, for if he did then he would not have produced a malformed speech to secure the end intended.

The presence of opposition is also crucial to the rhetoric currently under study. For Socrates will soon say that his own two speeches were opposites—one favoring the nonlover, the other the lover, and he will then discuss how his discourse could pass from one opposite to the other. Presumably then Socrates was in control of the truth about love, assuming that he not only convinced Phaedrus of what he said but also that he did not deceive himself in the process. In addition, Socrates' critique of the popular conception of rhetoric as deployed according to the continuum of opposition sanctioned the examination of both his speeches as one discourse. (The metaphysical reasons for this important procedural gambit will become evident as Socrates continues to discuss the nature of writing.)

The Socratic critique of the approach to rhetoric outlined by Phaedrus is completed at this juncture (262c), but there is a provisional character in the analysis which should be brought into the open. Phaedrus' understanding of rhetoric reduces it to a craft, not an art. Socrates gradually replaces this craft with a rhetoric grounded in what he asserts to be art. Notice, however, that after generalizing rhetoric with respect to contentiousness, Socrates says "if indeed it is an art" (261e). Socrates is cautious precisely because his approach to rhetoric as an art depends on knowing the truth. If therefore the truth is not known completely, then it would be premature to claim the ability to describe rhetoric as an art, given this prerequisite for art (presumably *any* art). The problematic status of knowing the truth (as evoked in the palinode) becomes evident later, when Socrates asserts that all great arts require speculation about nature (269e). If rhetoric is one of the great arts—and surely it is, since according to Socrates it controls the persuasiveness of discourse at all levels—then rhetoric requires speculation about nature. But if this speculation misses the mark somehow, then this gap measures the extent to which rhetoric remains at some distance from enjoying the status of an art.

The conditions placed on rhetoric with respect to knowing the truth should be kept in mind throughout the rest of the dialogue, since they will direct the course and content of that discussion. In following these conditions, Socrates will eventually articulate the doctrine of natures. This key metaphysical doctrine is the discursive counterpart of knowing the truth mythically described by Socrates in the palinode, and it should come as no surprise that its development is commensurately long and complex.

CHAPTER 7

Rhetoric and Dialectic (262c–266d)

After discussion has shown the dependency of the art of speech on truth, Socrates asks Phaedrus whether they should examine the speech of Lysias, and also what Socrates said, to see whether anything there shows the presence and absence of art. Phaedrus agrees, saying that the discussion has become too abstract without examples (262c).

The Synoptic Perspective

Socrates remarks on the seeming good fortune that the two speeches contained a sort of paradigm of how one who knows the truth can lead on his hearers with "playful words." Socrates says that the local deities have caused this phenomenon; also, the prophets of the Muses, who continue to sing over the heads of the discussants, have perhaps granted this bestowal. Socrates insists that he himself had no part in producing the available paradigm, since he does not share in the art of speaking (262d).

For Hackforth, the two speeches Socrates refers to, represented in Greek by the dual, are "Lysias's speech and *both* Socrates's regarded as one" (pp. 125–6, n1—italics in text). There are, however, problems with this interpretation,[1] and another approach will be followed here.

It is possible that the dual, following Hackforth (and others), could refer to Lysias' speech (as lacking art) and both Socrates' speeches (as having art). The dual would thus emphasize that all three speeches will be examined with respect to art. The problem with this reading is that Socrates also says that the two speeches contain an example of how one who knows the truth can playfully lead on an audience. So if the dual is taken to include the speech of Lysias, then it would follow that Lysias also knew the truth.

If, because of this implication (which Hackforth does not discuss), Lysias' speech cannot be included in the dual, then the dual must refer only to Socrates' two speeches. This interpretation is supported by Socrates' subsequent speculation about divine sources of inspiration, since these sources could come into play only for the speeches he himself uttered. Also relevant is Socrates' final self-effacing remark, that "I have no share in the art" of speaking, suggesting that it is his divinely inspired words—not those of Lysias—that represent the paradigm for those who know the truth. (The sense in which Socrates' first speech is emblematic of truth will be clarified below, since according to Socrates this speech sinned against love.)

Truth and Inspiration

This introductory interlude is also important for situating the function of inspiration both with regard to what Socrates said in his two speeches and also what he is about to say in discussing those speeches.

If the local deities (identified later, at 263d, as Pan and the Nymphs, daughters of Achelous) have indeed caused these speeches, then such inspiration may be derivative, since these deities were not listed in the palinode as divine sources of inspiration. Furthermore, Socrates' supposition that the cicadas may have helped in producing the speeches suggests that the inspiration of the Muses, for whom the cicadas are agents, differs in degree, not in kind, from the inspiration of the lower-order gods. If, however, the cicadas *were* inspirationally active, then the philosophical content of Socrates' two speeches will have been established, since (as noted in the story of the cicadas) some of the Muses have a direct link to philosophical wisdom. The difference between the local deities and the cicadas in terms of inspiration should also be noted. For if both sources of inspiration were present but operating in sequence, then Socrates' second speech may have been better than the first because of the qualitative difference in the respective sources of inspiration.

The fact that the cicadas continue to sing overhead suggests that they will continue to inspire Socrates even now, as he examines the inspired oratory which he spoke. In reviewing what was said, Socrates realizes that this rhetorical feast contains a paradigm of how one who knows the truth can lead an audience to realize the truth for themselves. If truth here names the complex metaphysical schema depicted in the second speech, then the one knowing the truth sees as much reality as the highest type of soul enumerated in that speech. Socrates reported this vision only by virtue of divine inspiration. Now, more detached and reflective, Socrates will nonetheless recreate the truth in retroactively analyzing this rhetoric. We may expect therefore an account of the speeches advancing into metaphysical regions commensurate with the range displayed by the speeches themselves. Socrates' explication of a paradigm of the truth may be no less splendid, in a relatively prosaic way, than the soaring chords of the palinode's hymn.

Phaedrus asks for examples to clarify the discussion. But examples of what? Socrates has just said (262b) that only those who know the nature of things will possess the art of making an audience pass from one thing to its opposite by leading them through the intervening resemblances while also avoiding deception. Thus, the examples of the art of speech Phaedrus requests would appear to be whatever procedures empower and facilitate this transition from opposite to opposite, a feature essential to the art of rhetoric as a whole. The present inquiry will thus, in this one sense, encompass all three speeches as a unity, since this rhetorical movement characterized by opposition— from favoring the nonlover (Lysias and Socrates' first speech) to favoring the lover (Socrates' palinode).

The Art of Rhetoric: Agreement and Division

Socrates' first step in assessing this complex rhetorical unity is to ask
Phaedrus to read the beginning of Lysias' speech. Phaedrus does so,
but Socrates interrupts by asking whether they had just agreed to point
out what lacks art in these discourses. However, Socrates does not immediately criticize Lysias' speech; instead, he outlines a seemingly
parenthetical line of thought which becomes the first step in his revisionist account of the art of rhetoric.

Socrates asserts that it is evident to everyone that we agree in some
things of this sort and disagree in others. Phaedrus thinks he understands, but he requests that Socrates make his point more clearly. Socrates gives examples: whenever someone says "iron" or "silver," we all
have in mind the same thing, whereas if someone says "justice" or
"goodness," we disagree, not only with each other but also with ourselves. After hearing these examples, Phaedrus sees more clearly what
was meant by the two classes Socrates has introduced.

Socrates now asks which class is liable to produce deception in an
audience, i.e., toward which class is rhetoric more powerful. Obviously, Phaedrus replies, doubtful matters. Socrates concludes that
someone formulating the art of rhetoric must make a division, according to a method, in order to recognize the class about which we are
necessarily in doubt and the class about which we are not. Phaedrus
notes that the one grasping this would have a fine class in mind. From
such discernment, Socrates says, one could readily sense in which of
the two classes the subject matter belongs (263a–c).

The content of rhetoric must be established according to method.
Note that the method proceeds by division (διηρῆσθαι), that what is
produced is a class (εἴδους), and that Socrates is describing what must
be done, initially, in order to develop "the art of rhetoric." The terminology suggests that the method is collection and division. Now if
the only method for arriving at truth sanctioned in the *Phaedrus* is collection and division, then Socrates would surely have to use that
method if the problem is determining an essential feature in the structure of rhetoric. Furthermore, at 266b, after the statement and applica-

tion of collection and division, Socrates asserts that these procedures are necessary for speaking and thinking. So if Socrates is currently speaking the truth about developing the art of rhetoric, then he is simply following his own recommendation in applying collection and division to that development. Finally, after Socrates states the distinction concerning agreement and disagreement, Phaedrus asks for a clearer explanation. But the clarity (σαφέστερον) Phaedrus seeks is also mentioned (σαφὲς) in the description of collection, at 265d. Socrates' subsequent explanation thus replicates collection in that the clarity Phaedrus desires is identical to that produced by collection and division.

What then has Socrates collected? Just as his first speech began by appealing to what is clear to all (237d), so also here Socrates gathers opinions, held by everyone, about "things of this sort." These things are the potential subjects of rhetoric. But we have seen Socrates extend the subject of rhetoric to include virtually every possible type of discourse and theme. This extremely large and heterogeneous class is then divided, as described above, according to whether agreement or disagreement obtains concerning the sense of the words comprising that class.

A number of important implications may be drawn from this initial step in determining the art of rhetoric. First, the agreement concerning the class of undisputed things does not presuppose anything like exhaustive knowledge of what has been so divided. Socrates is saying only that certain names (e.g., those of metals), do not result in disagreement when they are spoken (i.e., we normally do not dispute whether a piece of metal is iron or silver). But such consensus does not imply that we know all there is to know about iron or silver. An ostensive definition can produce agreement (although not knowledge) about many kinds of tangible things; however, intangible things—as important to human affairs as they are general and abstract—cannot be so specified. As a result, their very names engender disagreement among those who hear them.

Socrates says that people are necessarily in doubt concerning the class of disputed terms. The modality of necessity here seem puzzling. One could maintain, for example, that people dispute about certain terms simply because they are not sufficiently informed; if they were

better informed, then it is possible that they would agree about goodness and justice as they now agree about iron and silver. But if, as Socrates has said, we are necessarily in doubt about, say, goodness, then
vestiges of this doubt may remain, regardless how profound our knowledge of disputed terms may become. This condition is especially
noteworthy if the metaphysical grounds for that knowledge are, and
must remain, speculative.

Finally, Socrates describes the recognition of the difference between these two classes in terms of perception. Thus, one senses
(αἰσθάνεσθαι) that a given term belongs to one or the other of the two
classes, i.e., one has a sort of intuitive recognition of the term's class
specification (just as, earlier, one could sense the presence of beauty in
a beautiful thing). This recognition becomes more prominent later, in
discussing success in rhetoric (cf. 271e).

Definition and Inspiration

Socrates asks Phaedrus to which class love belongs. Clearly to the
doubtful class, Phaedrus replies, since Socrates could declaim that
love both harms the beloved and is also the source of our greatest
goods. Phaedrus thus shows a firm grasp on the oppositional structure
of Socrates' two speeches taken as a unity (additional evidence that
Phaedrus continues to grow in the philosophical understanding of discourse). After applauding Phaedrus' insight, Socrates then asks
whether he defined love at the beginning of his discourse—he was so
"inspired" that he no longer remembers. Phaedrus replies that Socrates
did define love, and that it was finely done. Socrates now thanks the
source of this definition, Pan and the Nymph daughters of Achelous,
and expresses the view that they were much more artistic in discourse
than Lysias (263c–d).

The definition Socrates refers to is that developed in the first
speech (237c–238c), just before Socrates interrupts the speech to advise Phaedrus that he will become frenzied once the discourse continues. Socrates says that he has forgotten this definition, a convenient
lapse since this definition consummated the rhetorical sin against love

(and the fact that Phaedrus has just applauded its fineness shows that he still has something to learn about being properly philosophical). However, the fact that Socrates refers to this definition, and to its place at the beginning of the speech (singular), suggests that even though the definition was sinful, it legitimately exemplified aspects of the art of rhetoric, particularly with respect to method.

The Critique of Lysias' Speech

Socrates asks Phaedrus whether Lysias has defined love at the beginning of his speech, thus compelling his audience to consider love as one thing. Lysias could then compose the entire discourse in light of that definition. Upon Socrates' request, Phaedrus rereads the beginning of Lysias' speech, and Socrates concludes that Lysias not only does not define love but he does not even begin at the beginning. Socrates compares the progression (or, perhaps, regression) of Lysias' speech to someone swimming on his back and upstream (i.e., from the end to the beginning). For Socrates, Lysias' beginning is what the lover would say at the end of a speech to his beloved. Phaedrus agrees that what Lysias says here is a conclusion (263e–264a).

Socrates' critique is persuasive, for Phaedrus, originally enraptured with the speech, now readily agrees with the structural criticism just made.[2] The fact that Socrates can judge the start of the speech to be an end rather than a beginning presupposes that Socrates can see the whole speech according to more correct rhetorical form (i.e., more correct according to Socratic principles), with beginning and ending where they should be, given Lysias' premises. Socrates' own first speech, which includes a partial reorganization of Lysias' speech, attests to this formally correct vision. Notice also that Lysias has structured this speech in reverse order, turning one opposite (the end of a speech) into the other opposite (the start of that speech). This basic structural flaw illustrates the dialectical legerdemain practiced, with abstract terms, by Zeno. If therefore Phaedrus is still impressed with this speech, then his rhetorical sensibilities are not in tune with the presence or absence of such formal opposition.

Socrates then asks Phaedrus whether any reason can be adduced to explain why the parts of Lysias' speech have been arranged as they are. Socrates, who "knows nothing" about these matters, felt that they just came out willy-nilly, and he asks whether any rhetorical necessity ordered Lysias' speech. Phaedrus confesses that he lacks the expertise to plumb Lysias' mind for such information (264b–c).

But it would appear that if the speech is well-articulated, it should display the requisite form without any need to trace its structure (or lack of same) to an intention hidden in the mind of its author. Lysias not only reversed the start and end of this speech, but in his confusion concerning opposition he also garbled the intermediary points between those extremes. Once opposition has become rhetorically disordered in this way, then following the resulting speech is like swimming upriver backwards.

Socrates then compares Lysias' speech to the inscription supposedly marking the tomb of Midas the Phrygian, written so that its four lines can be arranged in any order (264d–e). This *logos* has, in effect, no proper beginning and end. Such formlessness runs counter to what, for Socrates, characterizes living discourse—it must be organized as a living body, with head, feet, middle, and members fittingly related to each other and to the whole. If Lysias' speech is malformed, then it could never rightly lead an audience to act according to its recommendations. Socrates' critique never addresses whether the content of Lysias' speech is true of false. The critique is strictly formal, based on the rhetorical premise that the parts of a speech will show a beginning and an end, these parts based on defining the principal subject matter and then arranging all other parts of the discourse according to this definition.

Socrates' Speeches: Recapitulation and Madness

After demonstrating the formal faults of Lysias' speech (and its consequent lack of art), Socrates now turns to his own speeches, referring to them in the plural (264e) because, as Hackforth correctly notes (p. 131, n1), the two speeches are to be contrasted. He will be looking for things which those who wish to pursue discourses (λόγων) might well consider. Again, Socrates does not distinguish between spoken and written language; presumably the points considered will apply to both types of discourse.

Socrates first notes that his two speeches were opposites—one affirmed that the lover, the other the nonlover, should be preferred. But soon he will refer to the two speeches in the singular, when he proposes to Phaedrus that they examine how the speech moved from censure to praise (265c6) and also when, after stating the method of collection and its necessity for definition, he mentions the definition of love just secured and how it gave the speech clarity and consistency (265d7). Thus Socrates moves from referring to his two speeches as a unity (through the dual at 262b) to indicating that they are, in fact, two speeches (when seen as opposites) to taking the two opposed speeches as one speech (insofar as it shifts from censure to praise and as it displays clarity and consistency). By seeing his two speeches as opposites in this sense, Socrates shows how they straightforwardly realize the kind of relation so fundamental to Zeno's thought. If therefore Socrates can illustrate how the transition between opposites was structured in his own speeches, he will have gained insight into the ways Zeno executed the same transition concerning matters of utmost generality.

Phaedrus now observes that Socrates' development of this pair of opposite theses was done manfully (ἀνδρικῶς) and Socrates quickly replies that he thought Phaedrus would speak the truth and say madly (μανικῶς). This response is more than a clever pun, for Socrates reminds us that he was inspired in both speeches. And it is well to recall that if the cicadas chirping overhead continue to inspire Socrates, then his description at 265aff of the procedures animating his two speeches may be no less inspired, in its own way, than those speeches themselves. In other words, Socrates may see more clearly now both the philosophical form and content of what he had said, reflecting that greater vision in this description.

Socrates asks whether they said that love was a kind of madness. Phaedrus agrees. Socrates does not specify where this claim was made. In fact, love was said to be madness (μανίας) in both speeches—at the end of the first speech, when the madness of the lover is replaced by *nous* (241a), and, more obviously, as the fourth division of madness, identified as such toward the beginning of the palinode (245c). Socrates can therefore be taken as reporting now, at 265a, what had been said, literally, in his two speeches. However, he may be doing more than merely echoing the content of these speeches.

It was also affirmed, says Socrates, that there are two kinds of madness, one derived from human illness, the other a divine release from customary conduct (265a). This claim is clearly about both speeches, given that the first kind of madness (from human illness) did not play a part in the palinode. But this observation makes it plain that Socrates is not reminding Phaedrus of what had been explicitly said in the two speeches. This is shown by the fact that Socrates refers to Forms (εἴδη) of madness, since in the first speech Socrates did not identify the *hubris* of human illness as a kind or Form of madness. Thus, Socrates is reflectively interpreting the two speeches, examining them as a unity from a clearer metaphysical perspective revealing what they share in terms of class distinctions.

Socrates does not now pursue the Form of madness concerned with human illness, but he does say that four divisions of the second Form, divine madness, were made. Each division was ascribed to a particular deity—prophecy from Apollo, mysticism from Dionysius, poetry from the Muses, love—the best of these four types—from Aphrodite and Eros. The passion of love was then described, in which there was "perhaps" some truth and perhaps things said which led away to something other than truth. The speech as a whole was plausible, a myth chanting a measured and playful hymn to Eros, the protector of youths and the master of both Phaedrus and Socrates. Phaedrus reiterates his pleasure at having heard this speech (265a–c).

Hackforth notes (p. 131, n2) that the identifications of these deities are "inexact, inasmuch as Apollo and Dionysius were not in fact mentioned at 244B–D." Hackforth might also have pointed out about the palinode that Eros—but not Aphrodite—is identified as the source of love, the fourth type of madness. Why is Socrates exact here, in recapitulating the speech, and "loose" during the speech proper? Perhaps because Socrates continues to be inspired and now sees more clearly the connection between the types of madness specified in the palinode and their respective divine origins. For example, in naming both Aphrodite and Eros as sources of love, the fourth and highest type of madness, Socrates aligns goddess with god, desire with fulfillment— the result a more unified divine simulacrum of the mortal power of love's attraction and consummation.

In the story of the cicadas, Calliope and Urania, the Muses of philosophy, provided inspiration with respect to "accounts concerning the divine and the human" (259d). Now, when Socrates identifies the deities inspiring each of the first two types of madness ('and Aphrodite for the madness of love), he is applying precisely this type of philosophical inspiration to the details of the palinode, i.e., that portion of the speech describing the divine sources of madness. Therefore, what Socrates says at 265b need not be a literal report of what he had declaimed at 244b–d; it could be a subtly inspired and philosophically more precise assessment of that portion of the speech. The account of the cicadas has established conditions linking the rhetorical splendor of the palinode with the more rarified analyses of the dialogue's concluding section, and Socrates illustrates this connection with his current remarks.

When he was inspired while uttering the palinode, Socrates had said that he must tell the truth about the truth (247c); now, under a more sober inspiration, he admits that what was said in that speech may not have been altogether true. That the whole palinode must be examined is implied when Socrates refers to it at 265c1, in consecutive words, as both *logon* and *muthikon*. As *logos* and saying the truth, the palinode is reliable; as *muthos*, it must be reexamined to determine what in its metaphysics requires additional thought.

The Art of Rhetoric: Principles and Definition

Socrates now proposes that they consider how the discourse changed from blame to praise. Phaedrus asks for clarification and Socrates says that although the speech as such was playful, there were by chance two

principles which, "if one could artfully seize their power," would not
be ungratifying to learn (265d). The two principles (εἰδοῖν) will be
identified as collection and division. But why does Socrates so guard-
edly introduce them at this point?

Socrates says that it would not be ungratifying if we could artfully
(τέχνη) seize these principles. Socrates is certain that collection and
division are essential to the art of speechmaking; he is somewhat hesi-
tant about artfully learning those procedures. Presumably then the artful manner in which we should pursue these procedures is not identical
to the art of rhetoric itself, or at least to that part of rhetoric (to be called
dialectic) currently under scrutiny. What sense of artful does Socrates
have in mind? At the end of the palinode, Socrates prayed to Eros that
he not lose the art of love. Thus, Socrates knows at least one art. But if
Socrates is adept at this art, then he must realize the nature of the objects of love. According to the palinode, these objects are the *ousia*
beyond the rim of the heavens.

Specifying the objects of love is relevant to the intended sense of
artfully learning collection and division. Later, Socrates posits as an
axiom that all great arts demand speculation and high discussion about
nature (270a). It follows that if collection and division comprise dialectic and if dialectic is itself a great art (as part of the art of rhetoric), then
learning how to practice collection and division will require speculation and high discussion about nature. It would also follow that if the
art of love is a great art, then it too requires such speculation and high
discussion. Now Socrates has provided precisely this kind of speculation in the palinode, in the soaring description of the nature of soul and
its love of true reality, the ultimate object of love. This description included comprehension of the realities (the Forms) and the good through
the active agency of mind. Therefore, Socrates knows that he must pursue the same kind of speculation—a condition essential to any great
art—in order to learn artfully how the principles of collection and division produce knowledge of things.

It is not accidental then that the account of division contains no less
than three cognates of nature, *phusis*, in a very compressed section of
text (265e2, 266a1, 266a3). Thus artfully dividing something presup-

poses knowing the nature of that thing. And such knowledge will, as we shall see, require speculation and high discussion about nature in general. The conditional element here is crucial—i.e., if collection and division can be artfully learned. For if practicing the art of love entails mastering collection and division, then Socrates is wise to qualify the possibility of artfully learning these procedures if this method depends on speculative discourse concerning nature, mind, and the good. Any discussion of the principles Socrates is about to identify as essential to the art of rhetoric will remain incomplete until complemented by such speculation. The fact that the inspired Socrates himself had to resort to myth to satisfy the requirement for "high speculation" in describing the nature of soul as it loves reality attests to his own limited understanding of nature with respect to collection and division, essential components in the great art of rhetoric.

Collection and Division

The first principle exemplified in Socrates' two speeches is "seeing a dispersed plurality under one Form in order to make evident by definition whatever one would wish to explain." Socrates illustrates this process by referring to what he had said just now in defining love. Whether this account is "good or ill," it allowed "the discourse" to be clear and consistent (265d).

The example Socrates intends, the claim made just now (νυνδὴ), is apparently the one pronounced at 265a, that "love is a kind of madness." As we have seen, love was referred to as madness in both the first speech and the palinode. Hackforth notes that the reference to madness in the first speech is more or less casual (p. 133, n1). But Socrates has said that only by chance do the two speeches illustrate collection and division. Therefore, even if the reference to madness in the first speech is casual, the claim that love is a kind of madness applies to both the first speech and palinode. The dispersed pluralities are then the pair of references to love as madness occurring within the first and second speeches.

The Form which defines love is madness. This characterization illustrates collection by establishing a unity spanning two different speeches. Even if these speeches are diametrically opposed, their subject matter can be clarified and made consistent if the speeches are collected under the proposition love is a kind of madness. But the fact that collection occurred by chance in the two speeches reinforces the need to learn collection as artfully as possible, for collection has been illustrated only in the most rudimentary way by what Socrates has said at this point.

Whether the reference to collection in Socrates' second speech (249c) anticipates the process described at 265d has been questioned on the grounds that no mention of division, the correlate process to collection, appears in the palinode.[3] This connection is intended, however, and it brings out an important feature of collection. At 249c, Socrates is speaking of soul prior to becoming related to body, in particular, the conditions which must be met before soul can animate human body. Socrates says that a human must understand "according to a Form" what has been gathered from many perceptions into one Form. Thus, when the soul of a human does gather together disparate perceptions according to one Form, it does so because soul—prior to any relation to human body—had seen these very Forms. Collection is accomplished by an intuition paralleling the direct experience soul has of the Forms, the "things that are." Soul can gather dispersed pluralities into one unity only if soul has at some point seen the appropriate unity and can then discern that unity both as one Form and as instantiated in several (or many) particulars.

As a result, collection becomes the methodological counterpart to anamnesis, so prominent in several earlier dialogues. In fact, collection presupposes anamnesis, the recollection of direct contact with the Forms as realities. Although division also includes recollection for purposes of selecting and applying the appropriate Forms, it is, in a sense, a derivative phase of dialectic, essential only because human soul has become related to body, its experience of the realities thereby channeled through particular instances of the cognitive powers of soul directly to the Forms themselves. Thus Socrates does not mention division in the palinode (249c) because division can be ordered by rules in a way that collection cannot.[4]

Collection is gathering dispersed particulars under one Form, but precisely in order to define. In other words, the process of subsumption establishes a part/whole relation between the unifying element in the particulars (e.g., love) and the unity of the Form as such (e.g., madness). Once the relevant Form has been identified by collection (the ascending relation, as it were), then the relation between that Form and its constituents parts (the descending relation) becomes one of "cutting," as Socrates puts it. Characterizing love as a kind of madness only partially defines love; as Socrates says, this specification allows an account of love to possess consistency and clarity. Although collection leads to the appropriate Form, another procedure must establish that the desired phenomenon has been exhaustively delimited. The next step is to determine whether that class can be divided according to its natural joints.

First, however, notice that division, as Socrates will describe it, has already occurred during collection. Socrates implies this by saying now (265e1) that division is "cutting again according to the Forms." The reference to again (πάλιν) shows that cutting occurred when, in this case, collecting particulars into the class madness had been cut in such a way as to show that love is one kind of madness (implying that there are other kinds as well). But madness must be cut again, into divine and human sorts, before love can be properly defined. Specifying love as a kind of madness is not a definition; this collection-and-division step demarcates a class, duly limited, from which the nature of love can be derived. (The implied presence of division within collection becomes explicit at 277b, the final statement of the method.)

Note that collection has a heuristic as well as a constitutive dimension. Socrates asserts that the categorization provided by collection produces clarity and consistency whether it is "well *or ill*" (my italics). Thus, even an ill-defined account can still generate clarity and consistency. Consider, e.g., the account of love in Socrates' first speech. It was ill-defined—indeed, it sinned against love—and yet this account pointed the way to the more adequate characterization of the relation between love and madness developed in the palinode. Socrates never denies that love is a kind of madness; he denies only love defined as a certain conception of madness, i.e., (as the first speech has it) *hubris* resulting when desire for carnal expression overwhelms rationality. Thus, collecting love under the Form of desire and then dividing *hubris* into love as a type of desire is a definitional exercise contributing toward the proper definition of love as a condition, divinely sent, to elevate soul toward the truth. Socrates shows this by referring to the preliminary characterization of love as what gave the discourse (ὁ λόγος—265d7) its clearness and consistency. The discourse is both Socratic speeches taken as a unity. Only because Socrates recognized that love is a kind of madness was he able, as far as he could, to direct the first speech toward the nature of love, and to continue (and correct) the development of love as madness in the palinode.

In this regard then, collection functions heuristically in guiding discussion by virtue of the clarity and consistency produced by situating the definiendum under a Form—even if that Form must eventually be replaced by a nature more adequate to the definiendum.

Division and Nature

After briefly stating the structure of collection, Socrates now describes division as cutting something "again according to classes where the natural joints are located." For example, the two Socratic speeches "assumed one Form common to them, absence of reason." Then, just as one body can be naturally divided into two parts, right and left, with parts having the same name, so the two speeches conceived of "madness as naturally one Form in us." This Form was cut, producing a left-hand part which was cut again until "a sort of left-handed love" was discovered, which was justly reviled. The other speech led us to "the right-hand part of madness," finding there a love with the same name but divine, and praising it as the cause of our greatest goods (265e–266b).

According to Hackforth, this description has "serious difficulties:" first, it is not true, as Socrates seems to imply, that a "generic concept of madness" was common to the two speeches. And second, it is not true that "a formal divisional procedure" had been followed in the two speeches.

Hackforth is led to the first denial because he construes the three names for madness used in Socrates' present description as reports on what was said, literally, in those speeches. And since, for example, the divisional aspects of the first speech dealt only with *eros* as a kind of *hubris*, there was no division of madness in any of the three formulations just listed. (Hackforth tempers this criticism by paraphrasing what Socrates would have said if Plato has been a "writer with more concern for exact statement.")

Again, however, it was only "by chance" that Socrates' speeches exhibited an application of collection and division. Thus, Socrates continues to talk about his two speeches—first, insofar as both speeches comprise a unity, and second, insofar as they illustrated the method of division. He continues a kind of second-order discourse, just as he did in illustrating collection by asserting that "love is a kind of madness" can be derived by juxtaposing the two speeches and seeing what is common to them. As a result, Socrates need not employ the same terminology in discourse about these speeches as he did during the speeches themselves.

Consider the second of Hackforth's criticisms first, i.e., the lack of formal divisional procedures. Hackforth accuses Socrates of showing that *eros* is a species of *hubris*, but "not by successive dichotomies," nor, in the much more elaborate second speech, is the account of *eros* as madness deployed according to a "scheme of successive divisions, whether dichotomous or other" (p. 133, n1).

But what Hackforth expects Socrates to do is not what Socrates explicitly says he will do. Hackforth's error is to assume that the method of collection and division advanced in the *Phaedrus* is an anticipatory duplicate of the method introduced later in the *Sophist* and the *Statesman*. In fact, however, Socrates in the *Phaedrus* tells us what he is doing and why—with key differences between this methodology and the similar method advanced in subsequent dialogues.

Socrates defines division as cutting things according to Forms

along the natural joints. Nothing is said here about dividing dichotomously—rather, divisions proceed according to the thing's nature, i.e.,
an arrangement by classes (or Forms) governed by a unifying principle.
Thus, if a thing has a complex nature, then the appropriate divisions
will isolate and identify all constitutive Forms of that nature, arraying
them side by side as it were, with no apparent generic hierarchy established. From this standpoint, any dichotomy depends on whether or not
the thing's natural joints are dichotomously arranged; if they are not,
then according to Socrates' current theory dichotomous division would
distort the thing's nature. Such division would dismember the nature of
the thing, just as a bad carver would mangle something by slicing it
down the middle rather than at the joints.

   With this preconception out of the way, consider again what Socrates says in describing how his speeches illustrated division. The two
speeches posited "one Form" which was common (ἐν τι κοινῇ εἶδος).
This Form Socrates call "the absence" of *dianoia* (ἄφρον). Now earlier, at 236a, Socrates said in his analysis of Lysias' speech that anyone
arguing that the nonlover must be favored over the lover cannot avoid
citing the unreason (ἄφρον) of the lover. If this assumption is correct,
then Socrates' first speech, adopting the same premise as Lysias, will
embrace the same position concerning the unreason of the lover. And so
it does, since excess eating or drinking, or the pursuit of carnal pleasure over the urgings of opinion concerning what is best, are examples
of actions resulting from unreason as the absence of intellect. Furthermore, to predict the future (as described in the palinode), e.g., is the
same as the actions mentioned in the first speech in that it too requires
displacement of reason. The displacement of reason thus becomes the
negative side of *mania*, i.e., what must happen to normal intellection
to establish the possibility that something "out of the ordinary" can
occur, whether for good (the palinode) or ill (the first speech).

   The absence of *dianoia* is therefore a synonym—including in its
sense the diverse instances found in Socrates' two speeches—for that
one Form, madness, which must be divided. And Socrates now tells us
how to make that division, although insufficient attention has been

paid to the analogy he introduces at this juncture. Madness as a Form has natural joints, and, Socrates asserts, these joints are modeled on the configuration of the human body. The body is one, but with left and right side, and parts bearing the same name on each side—e.g., the limbs on both the left and right sides of the body are each called "arm" and "leg." Thus, if "left" and "right" designate the nature of a human body, then just as dividing that one body along these joints will reflect the nature of the human body (in this respect), so will dividing madness into a left side and a right side.

The structure of nature thus becomes crucial for the implementation of division. In the case at hand, however, one might object that (a) left and right are arbitrary, since they are based on perspective, and (b) that such differentiation is too superficial to include as part of a thing's nature. These questions are relevant, and dealing with the metaphysical repercussions would require extensive analysis (see the Epilogue for some preliminary observations in this regard). Recall, however, that Socrates does not claim to have exhausted the nature of madness, only to show that madness has natural joints and is divisible according to these joints. Socrates is aware of the importance of determining how the nature of something should be understood, and he will address this problem in due course.

Madness was originally characterized in the absence of *dianoia*. But at this point in the description of division, madness is named *paranoia*, derangement. According to Hackforth, absence of *dianoia* and *paranoia* are two designations for "the generic concept of madness." This is not incorrect, but Hackforth seems to have overlooked an important shift in emphasis. Madness as absence of *dianoia* was that one Form which is common to the two speeches. But madness as *paranoia* is, Socrates says, "one Form in us by nature." Thus the first designation is about madness as it appeared in the two speeches taken as a rhetorical unity; but the second designation is about madness as one Form existing in us (ἐν ἡμῖν)—not just in two speeches about us. Furthermore, Socrates is careful to add that madness as *paranoia* has a nature (πεφυκὸς and therefore can be divided according to its joints as exemplified in human beings. The word *"paranoia"* is finely apposite for this process, since its prefix ("para-") suggests parts separated yet "beside" each other, just as the left and right side of the body are adjacent.

Hackforth, commenting on this passage, says that "Socrates will point out that the two speeches together divided *eros*" into a "sinister" and a divine type (p. 130, n1). But this is incorrect. At 266a, Socrates says that he cut off the left-handed part, then continued cutting until he found "a sort of left-handed love." Socrates did not divide *eros* into left-handed (and right-handed) types of love—he now points out that the initial division established the "left" side, not of love, but of madness as *paranoia*. This left side is *hubris*, the most inclusive Form identified during the first speech, and it names the state of affairs when desire irrationally drags us toward pleasure and rules in us. *Hubris* has many parts and many Forms. And once secured, it was "again" cut, Socrates says, until the definition of love at 248c was produced. These subsequent "cuts" refer to the various types of *hubris* identified in the first speech, e.g., excessive eating, drinking, etc.

In sum, madness as *paranoia* was divided into *hubris*, the left side of madness, and then *hubris* was itself divided until a definition of a left-handed love was secured. Therefore, left-handed love is not, as Hackforth claimed, derived from a division of *eros*; it is a division of *hubris*, and *hubris*—from the synoptic standpoint of seeing both speeches exemplifying division—is a division of *paranoia*, that synonym of madness accentuating the metaphysical fact that the nature of madness has a left and right side.

When Socrates says that the other speech, the palinode, led us to the right-hand part of madness, he returns to the nomenclature stated in the original collection, at 265a. Madness (*mania*) was named the absence of reason (first) and derangement (second) to indicate, and clarify, the process of division during the sequence of thought beginning in the first speech and moving to the conclusion of the palinode. The right-hand part of madness yields a love with the same name (i.e., "love") as its left-hand counterpart, but the former is divine while the latter is decidedly mortal in its carnality. The sameness of name thus conceals more than it reveals, since the tendency to equate carnal love with love makes it difficult to realize that other and very different activities are also love. (Recall *Cratylus* 440c, where it is stated that no one with any sense will put himself or the education of his mind in the power of names.[5])

Socrates reminds us that both speeches are a unity of opposites when he concludes that the palinode praised the right-hand love just as the left-hand love was properly reviled in the first speech. Socrates had posed as problematic how the discourse passed from blame to praise (265c), and his description of division includes these valuational aspects derived from the strict technical application of division. Presumably this method can establish results which, with respect to truth, can be laudatory or base.

Socrates—the Lover of Method

After concluding this very brief account of the method of collection and division, Socrates describes himself as a lover of these collections and divisions,[6] a love he pursues so that he can become fit "to speak and to think." If Socrates observes someone capable of seeing things naturally collected into a unity and divided into many, then he follows such an individual (and here Socrates cites Homer) "as if he were a god." Whether all those so capable are correctly named, god alone knows, but Socrates has to this point called them "dialecticians" (266b–c).

Collection and division will help make Socrates fit to speak and think; thus, dialectic, if defined as collection and division, is a preparation for but not equivalent to rhetoric as such, i.e., all speaking and writing. Socrates has already pointed to the incompleteness of dialectic when he first examined his own speeches. He referred there to collection and division as something which those who wished to investigate discourse should consider (265a)—Socrates did not promise that an exhaustive account of discourse, and of rhetoric proper, would be forthcoming just by analyzing collection and division. Dialectic is a necessary but not a sufficient condition of rhetoric.

When Socrates says he is a lover of collections and divisions, does this love occur before, after, or during the actual collecting and dividing? If love is evinced either before or after, then Socrates is saying simply that he has become aware of the extensive cognitional range collection and division opens up—a recognition arousing the feeling of love. But if love is coextensive with the actual performance of collection and division, then Socrates (and, of course, anyone else) must be mad (i.e., inspired) in order to know. No one denies that philosophy is hard work. But must we be inspired in order to philosophize? Must we love something in order to reason about it correctly, or even to fabulate it persuasively?

According to the *Phaedrus*, the answer is yes. At the conclusion of the palinode, Socrates asks Eros not to take away the art of love Eros has vouchsafed him (257a). If Socrates' love of collection and division is the same as the art of love mentioned in the palinode, then in embracing these methodological practices, Socrates will approach the totality he described, when duly inspired, in the second speech. Thus, the madness of love inspiring Socrates to such rhetorical (and metaphysical) heights in the palinode is the same madness allowing Socrates to know things according to collection and division. The madness of love inspires Socrates to divide madness so that love is recognized as one of its constituent parts.

Socrates is a philosopher. A philosopher is a lover of wisdom. But gaining wisdom, or at least approximating it, demands the practice of method.[7] Thus, to love wisdom is, at least in the approach Socrates is arguing for here, to love the methods essential for acquiring wisdom. Furthermore, the art of love in the palinode places the soul of the philosopher in intimate contact with mind, the Forms, and the good. If therefore Socrates' avowed love of what he names dialectic is commensurate with the art of love mentioned in the palinode, then we should expect the more prosaic (yet still inspired) analysis of dialectic to appeal to the same metaphysical ultimates. Thus, methodology must establish a counterpart to what intellect as mind can know about the truth, in concert with the Forms functioning in collection and division. The incompleteness of dialectic is important to keep in mind to understand the full metaphysical significance of the complementary account (introduced shortly) of determining natures. This account will complete the theoretical treatment of rhetoric advanced in the *Phaedrus*, as well as elaborate division according to a thing's natural joints. Only when this phase of rhetoric has been revealed and adopted will Socrates "speak and think" in a manner befitting the philosopher.

Socrates follows the individual skilled in the art of collection and division, walking in his footsteps as if he were a god. Socrates suggests, again, that he himself does not know adequately how to practice collection and division, for if he did know there would be no need to follow someone else. Socrates, still inspired, knows in the abstract about collection and division but is not completely confident of his ability to practice it. Others may be better at employing the method than Socrates. If so, then these—not winsome, Muse-loving young men— are the individuals Socrates truly loves, for Socrates loves truth above all and the former can help lead him to see true reality better than he does now. But if none are better than Socrates, then Socrates would follow himself, i.e., what his philosophical soul discerns about the reality hymned in his palinode.

The fact that Socrates' hypothetical dialectician is compared to a deity is also significant. The gods derive their metaphysical substance from the realities and the good. Thus, even this mortal master of method, if divine in such mastery, would be no closer to complete control of the fundamental principles underlying that method than any god. The Homeric passage cited by Socrates is neatly apposite; the image portrays Socrates following in the steps of this metaphysically godlike individual just as the soul of Socrates follows divine soul on its journey to the rim of the heavens to see the truth. Such earthbound emulation only approximates this vision, however, since it extends only partway into the reaches of speculation required to see how intellect functions with respect to the good, the Forms, and the relation between Forms and particulars.[8]

In sum, the problem of the one and the many has been recast into collection (gathering particulars under one Form) and division (cutting the Form or Forms according to the appropriate natural junctures). But as Socrates says, only god knows whether it is right or wrong to name

those who proceed thus dialecticians (266c). A god, existing more intimately with the realities and truth than a mortal, would know better
whether dialectic should include more than collection and division.
Only a god could see the reality of dialectic as such, and thus name correctly the human activity which participates in that reality. Socrates is
not wrong in naming the practitioners of this method dialecticians. But
more must, and will, be said about rhetoric at this fundamental level.

Love and the Unity of the *Phaedrus*

Is Socrates as lover inspired by Eros or by the truth? Madness, as formulated here, is sent by the gods (cf. 244a). But the gods are divine
because of the reality beyond the rim of the heavens. Therefore, inspiration from divine Eros is, ultimately, inspiration from this reality—
the truth. The inspiration required for effective rhetoric using collection and division (as Socrates has done, in various degrees, in both his
speeches) is the same as the inspiration to know and articulate the truth
by using these procedures (as he has done, or at least approximated, in
the palinode) and to describe these very procedures in the abstract (as
Socrates is doing now and in the subsequent analyses of rhetoric). Whoever uses these methods must therefore be inspired. This inspiration
moves the intellect away from particulars and into the domain of the
Forms, i.e., when intellect can see one Form present in many dispersed
things. Such vision is not our customary condition; if we have it, its
source is that dimension of reality accessible only to the highest powers
of soul.

It now becomes clearer how the Eros described in the palinode animates the second half of the *Phaedrus*. Soul loves the beauty in beautiful things. The love of beautiful human beings is especially intense.
But soul, by nature, also loves other Forms, if only it could experience
them as it does the Form beauty. Socrates must therefore find a way to
move soul, the animator of (human) body, toward the Forms. If such
motion can be initiated, then the natural love of soul for complete unity
with the Forms as realities seen within the unifying penumbra of the
good—the most perfect of initiations—occurs when soul revivifies this

primordial experience and sees these Forms incorporated into the world around us.

The stark contrast between the rhetorical and discursive phases of the *Phaedrus* is, of course, fully intended. These converging stylistic opposites show that Socrates inspired by love and Socrates as practitioner (and lover) of collection and division are directed toward the same end—the love of wisdom. The praise of discourse in the second phase of the dialogue reflects, at a "dispassionate" interpersonal level, the more pronounced and palpable Eros uniting lovers. The audience for the *Phaedrus* will be led to wisdom through rhetoric—including myth—and reason. And a sufficiently complex soul will require both techniques to be convinced that Platonic wisdom is worth pursuing, just as Socrates and Phaedrus, each in his own way, require such diverse discourse to be certain of that fact.

CHAPTER 8

Nature and the Art of Writing (266d–274b)

Phaedrus assures Socrates that the procedures described so far are correctly named dialectic. It seems to Phaedrus, however, that rhetoric still escapes them. Socrates is surprised, asking whether anything which pertains to the art of rhetoric has been excluded from what he has just said. If so, they must identify and discuss what still remains of rhetoric. Phaedrus replies: all the techniques mentioned in the books about rhetoric. Socrates recalls one of them, that a discourse must begin with an introduction, and asks Phaedrus whether this is the sort of thing he has in mind—the niceties of the art. Phaedrus agrees (266d–e). Therefore, in order to convince Phaedrus that the principles essential for successful rhetoric have already been introduced, Socrates must analyze the relation between current rhetorical theory and the theory of dialectic advanced so far.

The History of Rhetoric

From 266e to 268a, Socrates recounts an extensive series of rhetorical concepts drawn from leading present and past authorities. Phaedrus intersperses brief comments, showing that he too is well versed in this literature. Both men are less than subtle in sarcastically reviewing this theorizing. The traversal of such literature illustrates that Socrates'

229

hunger for speeches, attested to early in the dialogue, included the philosophy of speeches as well, i.e., theories about how to compose speeches. But these matters are the niceties of the art. Why then consider them?

The reason is that Phaedrus believes that this vast canon contains material relevant to rhetoric and not covered by the methodology considered so far. Socrates' impending rehearsal of the history of rhetoric is a kind of collection, gathered together to be examined in conjunction with dialectic as already described in order to determine what, if anything, must still be said about rhetoric. For if existing theories of rhetoric are but collections of niceties, then such reflection, however essential it may appear to produce persuasion, lacks formal propriety and must be revised in light of the principles of dialectic Socrates has just advanced.[1]

Art and the Preliminaries of Rhetoric

Socrates invites Phaedrus to investigate these details to see what power of art they display. They are extremely potent, Phaedrus says, at least before large audiences. Socrates' investigation of this power begins with examples from other arts. First, he describes someone who, knowing how to apply drugs to cause certain effects on the human body, thereby styles himself a physician. Phaedrus replies that such expertise is incomplete without knowledge of who to treat in this way, when, and the dosage required. If the *soi-disant* physician claimed that the available expertise includes such knowledge, Phaedrus judges that the person would be dubbed mad, lacking real knowledge of medicine.

Similarly, if someone told Sophocles or Euripides that he knew how to make very long speeches about a small point and very short ones about something important, and also how to cause a variety of emotional reactions, this would not qualify that person to teach the art of tragedy without knowing how to coordinate these skills within the discourse, the tragedy, as a whole. Neither Sophocles nor Euripides would, however, berate this individual. Rather, they will act as a musician, meeting someone who thought he knew harmony because he could sound the highest and lowest notes; the musician would gently admonish the person that he knew the necessary preliminaries, but not harmony itself. So also, Sophocles and Acumenus would say that knowing the preliminaries of an art is not knowing the art.

When Socrates then turns to Adrastus or Pericles, acknowledged masters in rhetoric, he combines the theoretical positions of the other masters mentioned with the practical response of the hypothetical musician. According to Socrates, either Adrastus or Pericles is "wiser" than he and Phaedrus, or they are not. In fact, these authorities would censure Socrates and Phaedrus for the ridiculing way they spoke about the luminaries of rhetorical theory. These individuals were ignorant of dialectic and therefore could hardly define rhetoric, given that they knew only its preliminaries. As a result, they could not be blamed for thinking that they need not teach anything more concerning the fundamentals of their art, since they do not know the nature of these fundamentals. Phaedrus concludes this phase of the review by agreeing that all the authorities cited earlier who teach and write about rhetoric are properly characterized as masters only of preliminaries and not basics. But, Phaedrus asks, how then and from whom are we to learn the true art of rhetoric (268a–269d)?

Socrates does not deny that those who control the preliminaries of an art know what, in this limited sense, they are doing; he denies that such technique is derived from true knowledge of the art. Socrates has cited Acumenus and Sophocles, authorities in their respective disciplines. If these disciplines are teachable, then they should be the teachers. Phaedrus recognizes their authority and, without prompting from Socrates, he discerns both the kinds of questions the true art of medicine would ask the practitioners of preliminaries and the presuppositions concerning the principles of the art of tragedy as they bear on a related group of consequences. Phaedrus should then be able to apply the same critical questioning—another sign of his growing philosophical awareness to current rhetorical theory.

The reaction of the hypothetical musician to such incomplete knowledge is revealing. Treating gently the protagonists of preliminaries suggests not only that they can be taught the principles of their art, but also how they should be treated in the process. Presumably a musician in this sense is an informed practitioner of any of the Muse-inspired arts. Thus, the musician is in intimate contact with the Muses, i.e., the divine sector closer to the truth than are the souls of mortals. Since the preliminarists do evince a glimmer of the requisite knowledge of their art, they are on the way toward a degree of knowledge that their souls may be fully capable of attaining. However, whether they attain this knowledge depends on how well their souls have been educated in the metaphysics of truth and the extent to which that education can be recouped and developed.

A pattern emerges from the knowledge the preliminarists display: it involves making people feel warm and cold, long speeches on small matters and short speeches on large issues, striking the highest and lowest chords. In each case, the preliminarist has mastered techniques for producing opposite effects—just as Zeno could make the same things appear both one and many, like and unlike, etc. (cf. 261d). Awareness of such opposites is only a metaphysical preliminary and does not constitute knowledge of the whole art.

The fact that Pericles would censure both Socrates and Phaedrus implies that neither individual has a sufficiently "musical" character to treat properly those who know less about art then they do. The greater wisdom attributed to Pericles apparently endowed him with a more refined metaphysical sensibility, as well as greater kindness toward those less naturally gifted. It would seem then that Socrates has yet to master himself completely, has yet to become duly elevated in his actions and speech to merit the title of "musician."

Art and Nature

Socrates answers Phaedrus' question about the source of true rhetoric by asserting that the power to be a perfect orator is, and perhaps must be, dependent on conditions. Someone rhetorical "by nature" will succeed if this natural talent is coupled with knowledge and practice. However, the method for securing the art of rhetoric is not that of Lysias and Thrasymachus.

Socrates proposes that Pericles be cast as the ideal orator. He then makes a general claim of vital importance for defining rhetoric: "all great arts require discussion and speculation about nature." The required high-mindedness and all-around accomplishment essential for success in any great art seem, Socrates says, to come from these pursuits. Although endowed with great natural skill, Pericles also had the good fortune to chance upon Anaxagoras, who filled him with speculation and taught him "the nature of mind and lack of mind"—subjects, Socrates adds, frequently considered by Anaxagoras. Pericles then derived from such reflection what pertained to the art of discourse (269e–270a).

Socrates implies a distinction here between great and ordinary arts, suggesting that the latter do not require speculation concerning nature. Rhetoric is a great art, since Socrates introduces such speculation as essential to determining its essence. Medicine is another of these arts, and Socrates will soon compare both medicine and rhetoric to learn about nature. One other art mentioned in the *Phaedrus* is worth considering in this regard. We will recall that at the end of the palinode, Socrates entreats Eros not to take away the erotic art granted to him (257b). If therefore the erotic art is a great art—and Socrates can articulate the metaphysical scope of the love of wisdom precisely because he has the erotic art—then this art also requires discussion and speculation concerning nature.

This interpretation of the need for metaphysical speculation is crucial for recognizing the unity of the *Phaedrus*. For if all the great arts mentioned here—rhetoric, medicine, and love—require such speculation, then at least part of what applies to one great art with respect to nature may also apply to any other great art.[2] Speculating about nature in order to determine the structure of rhetoric (which Socrates is about to do) is no less necessary then speculating about nature as part of seeing the truth (which Socrates has done in the palinode)—both phases of the *Phaedrus* are united in requiring such speculation. If Eros leads soul to truth, Eros will also lead soul to what must be seen and done to achieve success—and truth—in rhetoric.

Socrates' palinode, in particular the account of love as the fourth type of madness, clearly exemplifies metaphysical speculation about nature. Consider the parallels between the way Pericles was affected by such speculation and the account of Eros in the palinode.

First, Socrates says that Pericles was taught "the nature of mind and lack of mind."[3] To speculate about nature with respect to understanding a great art is, in part, to speculate about the nature of mind and the opposite of mind (i.e., what lacks mind). And in that section of the palinode where Socrates states the truth about the truth, he asserts that the divine intellect, as well as every other intellect of sufficient capacity, is nurtured on "mind and pure knowledge" (247d). This is the sense of *nous*, mind, that "steers" the soul. Mind can see the highest reality—and the pure knowledge of this reality includes not only full awareness of all the Forms, the things that are, but also the good insofar as it holds together all Forms. To assert that mind governs the metaphysics underlying the structure of Eros is therefore a preeminently speculative claim, especially since what mind knows is approached mythically and therefore in some sense indeterminately.

The second parallel concerns speculation about a specific nature. From speculating about nature in general, Pericles gleaned what is useful to the art of discourse. Socrates will soon say that the art of rhetoric must analyze the nature of soul (270b). If therefore Socrates has speculated about the nature of soul in the palinode's discussion of Eros, then this is speculation essential to determining one nature particularly relevant to rhetoric, i.e., the nature of soul.

As argued in the palinode, the nature of soul is self-motion. The palinode also discloses that soul cares for all that is soulless; furthermore, soul covers the heavens, appearing in many forms, and when perfect it ascends and governs the entire cosmos. When soul has lost its wings, it eventually settles on some earthly body which then appears self-moving because of the power of the soul within it (246c).

This brief account summarizes the most fundamental active and reactive properties of soul when soul is seen from a cosmic perspective. At 270c, Socrates asks whether worthy knowledge can be gathered about the nature of soul, a question that must be answered in the affirmative to determine the art of rhetoric. But surely soul understood as (a) always moving, (b) caring for everything nonsouled, (c) governing the cosmos, and (d) animating all mobile bodies—all properties of soul described in the palinode—is worthy knowledge of soul. Socrates has thus speculated on nature in the palinode, in particular on the nature of soul.

These parallels reveal two distinct but related ways to speculate about nature. The first way evokes nature writ large, as it were—fundamental principles encompassing all living things. The second way is directed at the nature of a specific type of thing (e.g., soul). A metaphysical dependency connects these two ways, since the nature of a particular type of thing will be derived from speculation about nature in its more inclusive, cosmological sense.

According to Socrates, Pericles mastered speculation because of Anaxagoras' tutelage. It may be noted, however, that the accuracy of Socrates' ascription of "mind and lack of mind" as a frequent topic of Anaxagorean reflection has been questioned.[4] But in context, the relevant point is not so much whether the extant texts of Anaxagoras support Socrates, but simply that Socrates finds instruction in mind and lack of mind crucial in determining the art of rhetoric and, by implication, all other great arts. Therefore, even if the historical Anaxagoras only approximated such study, his work would still exemplify reflection on one of the foremost metaphysical subjects.

In fact, a source justifying Socrates' appeal to Anaxagoras' speculation on mind and lack of mind appears in fragment 12 (preserved by Simplicius).[5] Here Anaxagoras speaks of *nous* as "alone by itself," in contrast to "all other things," which are all mixed together. Socrates' formulation is such that lack of mind (ἀνοίας) could refer either to all living things without mind or to everything, living or nonliving, which lacks mind. But if fragment 12 is Anaxagorean principle, the latter is the sense intended. Although *nous* in Anaxagoras is in some respects corporeal—for which Anaxagoras is roundly criticized in the *Phaedo* (98c–99c)—this *nous* still functions similarly to its Platonic counterpart, for it has all knowledge about everything and it controls all things.

The Socratic counterpart to things which lack mind appears earlier in the palinode (246c), when Socrates asserts that soul, if perfect, governs everything which lacks soul (ἀψύχου). The relation of governance between soul and what lacks soul parallels the relation between mind and what lacks mind. If therefore what lacks mind in Anaxagoras is equivalent to what lacks soul in the palinode, and if this common lack is body, then the palinode evokes this reality by positing body as what soul seizes on when soul loses its wings. The metaphysical origin of body is not addressed in the palinode, but presumably (as noted in chapter 3) body is coeval with soul, its existence no less primordial and fundamental.

In studying these senses of mind and lack of mind, Pericles would have seen close analogues to the two polar constituents of the Platonic universe shaped in the *Phaedrus*. Socrates does not identify how Pericles applied this study to the art of discourse, but perhaps he reflected on the nature of soul in order to proceed with art in giving soul the desired virtue through appropriate discourses. Thus, the high-mindedness Socrates claimed will be exhibited by those who speculate about nature reflects Pericles' awareness of *nous* at its most basic level. And the all-around accomplishment that also results from this study shows that mind and lack of mind jointly encompass the universe. Knowing this polarity will therefore affect whatever particularity becomes subject to cognition, as well as any rhetorical expression based on such knowledge.

Nature and Totality

Socrates now establishes a crucial analogy between the methods of medicine and rhetoric. Both must study nature—the nature of body for medicine, the nature of soul for rhetoric—if they are to proceed with art in either discipline. Socrates then asks whether it is possible to "know anything worthy" about "the nature of soul" without also knowing "the nature of the whole." Phaedrus replies that if Hippocrates the Asclepiad is to be believed, knowledge of body also requires this method. Socrates agrees with the Hippocratic position, but adds that they cannot rest content with authority—let us see, says Socrates, what "Hippocrates and a true account" reveal about nature (270b–c).

The pivotal question from this passage concerns the sense of whole (ὅλου) required to secure knowledge of the nature of soul. According to Hackforth, what Pericles took from Anaxagoras "was not a doctrine, but a method of viewing things, of viewing anything," i.e., to look to "the 'nature' revealed in a whole, rather than to the character of its parts" (p. 149). Accordingly, Hackforth takes whole in a restricted rather than an absolute sense.[6] Thus, "Plato is not saying that the doctor and the orator must know the nature of the universe, but that they must know the general character of the object that their art deals with, the nature of body as a whole, or soul as a whole" (p. 150). Hackforth then translates 270c as "do you think it possible to understand the nature of the soul satisfactorily without taking it *as a whole*" (my italics).

Given that at 270b, Socrates explicitly contrasted knowledge of the nature of body with knowledge of the nature of soul, it might seem that whole at 270c would mean whole soul. But why does Plato so elliptically make this important point?

According to the mythic section of the palinode, soul is composed of parts or functions. Therefore, to know soul as a whole, as Hackforth puts it, is to know all possible interactions between (and among) all functions of soul. But these interactions do not exhaust the structure of the whole soul. For soul is also affected by what is other than itself. Therefore, to know the nature of the whole soul presupposes knowing the extent to which everything other than soul will affect soul, whether for good or ill.

Two textual considerations support this implied sense of totality with respect to the nature of soul. First, the method of determining a thing's nature (which Socrates is about to state) includes showing "how a thing acts and is acted upon, and by what" (270d). No restrictions are placed here on how the thing can act and, importantly, on what can act on that thing. Thus if nature in "the nature of the whole" at 270c is understood in the technical sense defined at 270d, then determining the nature of soul presupposes analyzing how everything other than soul will affect soul. And second, this sense of totality has already been applied: the first step in proving that the madness of love has been given for our greatest benefit is to determine the nature (φύσεως) of divine and human soul, by seeing how it acts and is acted upon (245c). The active/passive terminology at 245c and 270d is virtually identical, strongly suggesting that Socrates has already applied in his inspired palinode the theoretical considerations formulated later in the dialogue (when, according to the interpretation of the cicadas argued above, Socrates remains philosophically inspired).

Let us examine this application in order to recognize the metaphysical boundaries of this totality. After stating the need to determine soul's nature (245c), the discussion of soul's self-motion immediately follows, and then Socrates introduces (246a) the image of winged horses and driver to account for the "composite nature" of soul's powers. This account describes soul affected by what exists beyond the heavens, i.e., the realities and the good, as well as (for human soul) matter and evil. Therefore, if knowing the nature of the whole soul entails knowing soul with respect to everything which can affect and be affected by soul, then Hackforth's translation of 270c implies an appeal to totality if this translation is to be compatible with other doctrines in the dialogue.

Given this implication, it would seem preferable to translate the passage literally, i.e., "without the nature of the whole." Socrates does not say that knowing the nature of soul requires knowing the whole universe (the sense Hackforth believes is not intended). Socrates says that no worthy knowledge of soul is possible without the nature of the whole. But this does not imply that each entity in the universe must be known as a necessary condition for knowledge of soul. The relevant sense of whole is to the metaphysical principles underlying reality— the things that are, the good, matter—as, e.g., adumbrated in the palinode. These dimensions of reality will produce worthy knowledge of soul because only these dimensions will define the limits of what soul can do and what can affect soul.

According to Phaedrus, Hippocrates advanced this method in order to know the nature of body. Hackforth takes the point to be that the doctor must know "the nature of body, what 'body' in general is, as distinct from the particular bodies, with their individual peculiarities, that he has to treat" (pp. 149–50). But, again, Hackforth overlooks that body in general exists, necessarily, in relation to other things. This point should be taken in conjunction with the fact that other commentators on Plato's use of Hippocrates, seeking to determine whether any texts in the Hippocratic corpus can verify what Socrates says about method at 270d–e, have questioned whether such verification is possible.[7] However, Socrates says to Phaedrus that they should "see what Hippocrates and a true account" say about nature, implying that Socrates will blend the writings of Hippocrates with an account based on the truth.

Let us briefly examine Hippocratic practice to determine whether it coheres with this description of method. The Hippocratic texts are strongly critical of philosophical abstractions (instead of specific recommendations) in diagnosing and treating patients. Thus (e.g., in *Ancient Medicine*), Hippocrates notes that no absolute heat or cold can treat a given illness.[8] Furthermore, various types of hot thing are applicable for medicinal purposes, and since each type causes different reactions depending on the original condition, it would be a mistake, perhaps a fatal mistake, to prescribe something hot just because the malady appeared to require heat.

But rejecting treatment of an opposite condition by its opposite hardly implies the rejection of all philosophy. For, again in *Ancient Medicine*, the overall medical condition of the body is determined in terms of (a) everything that body experiences, both diet and climate; and (b), the doctrine of the four humors, powers common to all bodies and having their seat in nature.[9] Thus, diseases are caused not just by bodily disturbances, but also by atmospheric and climactic conditions, i.e., natural settings. And nature can reorder these irregularities by restoring harmony among the four humors.

Thus the Hippocratic rejection does not imply the rejection of all philosophy, if by philosophy is meant a concern for totality—the same concern animating the mythic speculation of the Socratic palinode. Totality for Hippocrates' understanding of body differs metaphysically from the Platonic totality determining the nature of soul. Hippocratic totality is bounded by nature defined empirically according to processes which, although transcending individual bodies, exist in nothing other than bodies. Nonetheless, all human bodies are subject to *all* these process. As Phaedrus puts it, the method Socrates cites as necessary for determining the nature of soul remains the same, in principle, as that for determining the nature of body for medical purposes in Hippocrates—analyzing a thing in relation to everything other than and relevant to that thing.

The Structure of Nature

Socrates now describes (as a rhetorical question) a general method for determining natures:

> In considering the nature of anything, must we not consider first, whether that in respect to which we wish to be learned ourselves and to make others learned is simple or multiform, and then, if it is simple, enquire what power of acting it possesses, or of being acted upon, and by what, and if it has many forms, number them, and then see in the case of each form, as we did in the case of the simple nature, what its action is and how it is acted upon and by what.

Phaedrus responds, "it is very likely," and Socrates adds that any other method would be like the progress of someone blind; surely, Socrates says, whoever pursues any study according to art should not be compared to someone who is blind or deaf (270d–e).

Someone who is blind cannot see, an impairment which as a rule severely cripples progress in an inquiry. The method of determining a thing's nature avoids this procedural blindness. The analogy to vision and its lack should be connected to the light imagery in the palinode's description of truth. The investigator into the nature of something will see what has informed that thing by the reality "illuminated" beyond the rim of the heavens. And of course the light imagery again suggests the good.

This concern for totality underlines the tacit ֽ.
tion between determining a thing's nature according ֽ.
described and collection and division. The two methods n.
dependent of one another, with the method concerning natֽ.
duced solely to describe the nature of soul, a problem relevaֽ.
rhetoric. Thus, division according to Forms represents one analytical
procedure: determining a thing's simplicity or complexity and then
how the thing acts and is acted upon is another.[10]

But arguments show that this separation is not intended. First, Socrates introduces the method of natures by referring to "the nature of
anything," implying that the method applies to things other than soul.
And second, when Socrates introduced division, he said that a thing is
divided according to its natural joints (265e). This appeal to nature is
thus crucial to division. At that point, however, Socrates did not discuss how natural (πέφυκε) should be understood. But the explicit discussion of nature at 270d–e should be connected to its implicit use at
265e, since division *presupposes* knowing a thing's nature as a prerequisite for dividing correctly the parts of the thing. Socrates separates the introduction of the method of nature from that of collection
and division because determining the nature of something depends on
seeing the totality described in the palinode, and such vision can, for
Socrates, be evoked only through myth. The textual separation between the two methods establishes distance between a primarily analytic method and one which, although possessing analytic features (e.g.,
the active/passive rubric), is based ultimately on high-minded speculation.[11]

Teaching the Art of Rhetoric

After stating the method of natures, Socrates reminds Phaedrus that the
purpose of rhetoric, of which this method is a part, is to produce persuasion in the soul. He then enumerates three conditions to be met before anyone can seriously teach the art of rhetoric: first, soul must be
described with perfect accuracy so that its nature can be seen as "one
and the same" or, like the body, of multiform character. For this, Soc-

ates says, is what we call explaining its nature. Second, the nature of soul must be specified in terms of how its acts and how it is acted upon. Third, the types of soul and speeches must be classified and related to one another, showing why one kind of soul is necessarily affected by certain kinds of speech and why other kinds are not.

These three steps are excellent, Phaedrus remarks, and Socrates concludes that only if this regimen is followed will anything be spoken or written with art. Those who have written the rhetorical treatises Phaedrus has heard are deceptive although, Socrates insists, they know soul very well. However, these authorities must speak and write according to the method Socrates has outlined before we will believe that they write with art (271a–c).

The enumeration of these conditions should be noted. At 270d, Socrates says that determining a thing's nature includes numbering its respective parts. In numbering each of the three steps, Socrates intimates that he is giving the nature of rhetoric, i.e., the three parts of rhetoric as a complex unity.

Note then, with regard to the first step, that in the palinode Socrates had said that describing the form of soul would require a long and divine narrative (246a). Now, however, Socrates insists that the nature of the soul must be fully described. And the alternatives given for that nature are puzzling. The teachers of rhetoric must determine whether soul is one or many. But surely soul is like the body in having, as the palinode teaches, distinguishable functions. Therefore either the palinode should not be taken seriously and the nature of the soul remains indeterminate, or the differentiation of soul in the palinode is accurate, but whether soul can maintain its unity as a whole of parts has yet to be resolved. If the palinode's account of soul is not a complete fabrication, the latter alternative seems more plausible. Either way, however, the problem of the one and the many again arises, and in an especially crucial context.

Socrates also contends that those who have written treatises on the art of rhetoric know the soul very well but keep their knowledge hidden. If Socrates is ironical here, then the intended sense becomes virtually the opposite of what he says (i.e., that the currently hailed experts in rhetoric do not know the soul very well at all). But if Socrates means that these theorists do have knowledge of soul, but hidden knowledge, how does he know they in fact possess it?

The evidence may be found in the very existence of their treatises. What they say concerning rhetorical technique is correct—as far as it goes; current rhetorical theory is only a craft, but an effective craft. Therefore, if the authors of these procedures did not know the nature of soul, they could not have formulated such an array of effective rhetorical devices. These authors must then know the nature of soul, at least knowing what language human beings typically find persuasive. An essential condition for successfully applying the method of dialectic is not the recreation of all rhetorical techniques *ex nihilo*; such labor is neither feasible nor necessary. The various niceties of current rhetorical theory will suffice as long as they are restructured according to appropriate methodology and metaphysics.

This proviso concludes Socrates' treatment of how to teach the art of rhetoric. Next he examines how to practice this art. Applying and teaching the art of rhetoric differ, since successfully teaching rhetoric and successfully practicing it need not be coincident.

Practicing the Art of Rhetoric

Phaedrus desires more information on the method that must be practiced before rhetoric can become art. Socrates says it is not easy to say the exact words of this method, but he will tell how one must write in order to proceed as much as possible according to the principles of art. Socrates then amplifies, from 271d to 272b, the three-part outline given at 271a–b:

The student of rhetoric must know how many types of soul there are, since these types will determine types of people. Then the student must do the same with classes of speech, and be able to categorize each speech under the appropriate class. To determine the types of soul, the student must apply the second condition stated at 271a (i.e., how soul acts and is acted upon). Presumably the number of classes of speech will comprise the presently existing classes. Socrates does not advise fashioning new type (or types) of discourse—additional evidence that existing rhetorical conventions adequately produce persuasion.

The student must then study the action and reaction of all types of individuals with all classes of speeches. Such study again applies the second condition, as well as the third, i.e., the adaptation of speeches to individuals to establish efficacy or its lack. In addition to knowing these classes, the student must be able to sense which type of person is present; without this ability, theoretical knowledge remains abstract and, in practical affairs of the moment, virtually useless. During the time rhetoric is being formulated, the student must recognize the types of individual described in rhetorical theory, and also be able to deliver a certain kind of speech to achieve a specific end, whether action or belief.

And there is more. The student must know when to keep silent, i.e., when any kind of discourse, regardless of formal perfection, would serve no purpose. Here the importance of "sensing" the nature of one's audience becomes apparent, for if speech should not be uttered, then presumably the reason depends on the character of the audience. They may be dull, or bright but perverse—many possible combinations of natures would command silence from a prospective speaker. Knowing when to keep such silence would seem therefore to require extensive experience with a wide variety of human beings. In fact, gathering such experience may presuppose actually speaking when silence would have been best—and then suffering the consequences, in whatever form they may take.

The admonition to maintain silence is potentially ambivalent, for it could be adapted to sanction an elitist style of interpreting any complex writing—even, and in some cases especially, Plato's own dialogues. The adaptation would take this form: Plato says one thing but he really means something else, perhaps a meaning directly opposite from what the text appears to say. This esoteric meaning is silent to those lacking the appropriate insight into the text. This silence is not the absence of discourse, but rather a shield for significance parallel to, but hidden from, more public dimensions of meaning. The problem with this appeal to systematic silence is obvious. For if the surface meaning of the text can be readily denied to establish the silent meaning, then the text can mean whatever the interpreter wants it to mean. It is not evident that the *Phaedrus* would endorse a silence susceptible to such unlimited development.[12]

Be that as it may, once all such knowledge, both theoretical and practical, has been secured, then and only then will the art of rhetoric be finely and fully mastered. Anyone who speaks or teaches or writes without any one of these conditions, and claims to do so with art, should not be believed.

Probability and the Good

Socrates now personifies the author of the rhetorical treatise he has just sketched, asking himself and Phaedrus whether they agree with its dictates or whether some other way must be sought to account for the art of speech. This is the way, Phaedrus says, but it seems extraordinarily difficult. Socrates agrees, and insists that everything said must be examined to see whether a shorter path might be taken rather than this long road. If Phaedrus has heard anything, Socrates urges him to report it. When Phaedrus admits he can recall nothing relevant, Socrates offers something he has heard from those conversant with rhetoric.

Socrates, now acting as wolf's advocate (in his phrase) in responding critically to the position just stated, has heard it contended that one need not carry this matter back to first principles, as he and Phaedrus have done. All that must be said is that no one really cares for truth in the courts. From this perspective then, artistry in speech, the whole art of rhetoric, depends solely on probability. Phaedrus recalls that this point was mentioned before (i.e., at 259e).

Socrates vivifies this rejoinder by an example purportedly held by Tisias, a rhetorician whose theories, Socrates asserts, Phaedrus had studied carefully. This example involves both parties in a lawsuit lying to make their respective cases appear more probable. After Phaedrus agrees that Socrates has fairly represented Tisias' position, Socrates sardonically deems it an awesome art, and he sketches a response to Tisias and whoever else would champion rhetoric based on deception.

Tisias thus exemplifies this kind of rhetorical theory, as Lysias did for an equivalent kind of rhetorical practice.

Probability was accepted by the many because of its likeness to truth, but as Socrates has argued, the one who knows the truth is most likely to discover probabilities. If therefore Tisias has anything else to say about the art of discourse, we will listen; otherwise, we will believe what has just been said—a person must classify the natures of the audience as well as divide things according to their Forms and gather things under one Form. Only in these ways will one reach the highest human possibility in the art of speech. Much effort must be expended to achieve this goal, and the wise individual will undergo this regimen not for speaking and acting before human beings, but to be capable of speaking what is dear to the gods and also to do everything as much as possible for the sake of what is dear to them. For those wiser than we are say that one having sense (*nous*) would not act to please fellow slaves, except as a secondary consideration, but rather masters who are "good and from the good." If the path to seeing this kind of rhetoric is long and arduous, it is so in order to realize great ends, not those which Tisias seeks. But even such goals will be best attained in this way—if one still wishes to pursue them.

Phaedrus' reaction is that Socrates' response has been finely said—if only one could do it that way. But, Socrates insists, to pursue noble things is itself noble, including as part of nobility the acceptance of whatever may happen while seeking it. Phaedrus agrees, and Socrates concludes that they have said enough about the art of speaking and what lacks that art (272b–274b).

In introducing the personification of the relativist position attributed to Tisias, Socrates refers to what his own account as a treatise (συγγραφεύς); strictly speaking, it is not a treatise, since Socrates has said, not written, the program for successful rhetoric. But the account is tantamount to a treatise in that it simply stands there—monolithic, unchallenged, unexamined. Therefore, in order to enliven this account, Socrates personifies it, then confronts this personification with a real-life protagonist, the theoretician Tisias. The emergent image is of a series of personal confrontations between a proponent of the true theory of rhetoric (and an inquirer into truth) and someone representing an approach to rhetoric based on the sufficiency of probability. Socrates simulates the head-to-head discussion he will advocate as surpassing the written word—including all treatises—in its capacity to approximate truth.

In comparing the Tisian response to a wolf's advocate, Socrates recalls the lover envisioned as a wolf devouring the lamb, the beloved, poetized in his first speech (241d). This was sinful love, and the "vulpine" critique Socrates will mount is directed against a theory of rhetoric no less sinful than the definition of love in the first speech. According to Tisias, both parties in a criminal lawsuit should lie to make their respective cases more persuasive, advice based on the theory that understanding what probably happens will be more effective than what truly happened. Whereas in the Lysian speech and Socrates' first speech, only one party—the hidden lover—is advised to dissimulate, Tisias counsels both sides to lie. A wondrously hidden art, Socrates says, since the position of each party, if based on a lie, will invite the opponent to invent another lie in order to refute the original false position. The upshot is an endless round of charge and countercharge, with no way out given that the theory never endorses an appeal to truth at any point.

Socrates begins his response by noting that the many accepted probability only because it bears a likeness to the truth; and, as we have already shown, those who know the truth can best discover likenesses. In other words, knowing the truth is essential even on Tisias' principles, for only such knowledge provides a speaker with likenesses considered most probable and therefore most effective. An advocate following Tisian theory will fail to persuade an audience against someone who knows the truth; the latter will know how to construct what is more probable while the former knows only what is probable. This outcome seems obvious to Socrates, but he will listen to anything else Tisias may say about the art of discourse, again anticipating the live interchange between divergent positions concerning the truth on a given issue, the paradigm of philosophical discourse. Without a rejoinder from Tisias, Socrates will rest content with what was said just now, and he lists the results of the previous inquiry into the method of rhetoric—taking account of the natures (φύσεις) of his audience, dividing things according to Forms, and gathering particulars under one Form.

The wise person will seek such knowledge not only to speak as well as possible, but to act as well as possible, and in all things, so that both discourse and actions are dear to the gods. The distinction between speaking and acting is crucial in broadening the scope of rhetoric. Speaking is one kind of action and Socrates now contends that all kinds of action other than speaking also require implementation of collection and division.

Moreover, the injunction to act in order to please the gods, not our fellow humans, indirectly connects human beings and true reality. The gods are divine only because of their relations to the truth; therefore to act in order to please the gods is to act in accordance with the truth. Collection and division thus represent far more than correct strategy for persuading a human audience. The method of dialectic also becomes a prerequisite for right action, and the happiness that results if we act to please the gods.

For Socrates, those wiser than we are say that someone having good sense will act not to please their fellow slaves, but their masters, the gods, who are "good and from the good." Socrates is a philosopher. Therefore, someone wiser than Socrates will be more knowledgeable about the thing philosophers should know. Philosophers should know the truth. Thus, having good sense (νοῦν ἔχοντα) is not a vague appeal to common sense, but should be understood in the metaphysical context of *nous* described in the palinode's account of truth. This interpretation is further attested to when Socrates calls the gods good and from the good (ἀγαθοῖς τε καὶ ἐξ ἀγαθῶν) the same phrase used in the palinode (246b) to describe the horses and driver mythically representing divine soul. This important metaphysical formula implies (as argued in chapter 3) that divine soul is intrinsically good, deriving this nature from the good as such. The reoccurrence of this phrase suggests that those wiser than Socrates say what they do because they have a clearer—less mythically defined—grasp of the good; they can see that the divine nature is "good and from the good" and how mind, *nous*, allows discernment of this most fundamental aspect of truth. To "have *nous*" in this sense is to see the good better than Socrates, to discern more adequately the relation between the divine and the good, and to transform that awareness into action so that life can be lived on a higher plane of perfection than if life were governed solely by whatever intellect (*dianoia*) divines of the truth.

Socrates concludes this treatise by advising Tisias that to follow the trail of the principles of rhetoric should be done for great ends, ends Socrates will soon identify. Yet even if Tisias desired derivative ends, i.e., mastery of rhetoric and prestige from that success, he should follow the argument laid down in the Socratic approach. Tisias, and all theorists of rhetoric, may not have the kind of soul capable of seeing that the public prizes won by successful rhetoric are more glitter than good. But they are advised to follow the trail of Socratic dialectic in any case, for it is the best way whatever their ends may be.

Socrates has proclaimed something very fine (παγκάλως) says Phaedrus, if only it were possible. But, Socrates replies, it is noble (καλὸν) to strive for noble things (καλοῖς), regardless of outcome. If Phaedrus recognizes the full import of what Socrates has been saying, then his spirit is indeed philosophical, for he has arisen from the intense but unreflective experience of literary beauty to an awareness of the loveliness of all reality insofar as dialectic reveals its structure. The word for noble (καλὸν) is the word for beauty. Thus the immediate appeal of the beautiful, so crucial to the experience of love analyzed in the *Phaedrus*, is akin to the more protracted and complex character of pursuing rhetoric as a whole. If the trail of the beautiful is followed to its metaphysical completion, then we will see beauty related to all other realities within the unifying penumbra of the good—a preeminently noble vision of reality.

At the end of the *Phaedrus*, Socrates prays that he be *kalon* within (279b), and the fine ambivalence between beauty and nobility will receive additional significance from the view, expressed here, concerning the inherent nobility in striving to be noble regardless of circumstance. Our own share of nobility will be determined by how seriously we seek this vision by following the directions of Socratic dialectic. We may or may not succeed in this quest. If we fail, it may be either because we are insufficiently skilled for such endeavor or, perhaps, because destiny blocks our attainment of this end. But in any case the nobility derives from the effort, not the result. And everyone can make this effort, whether philosopher, poet, merchant, or even those lower on the hierarchy of types of soul.

With this noble sentiment, Socrates concludes his inquiry into discourse with respect to art. What has been said is sufficient, he affirms. This sufficiency has been deployed oppositionally, i.e., Socrates has analyzed discourse at both extremes—the speech of Lysias and its failure to implement even the most basic principles of order, and his own rhetorical efforts, with their chance manifestation of the principles of dialectic essential to the art of rhetoric. However, the inquiry into the nature of rhetoric, and the conduct which that nature implies for its practitioners, has not yet been completed. The day's discussion concludes with Socrates' final statement on rhetoric as discourse and as writing when both activities are seen from the metaphysical perspective developed in the dialogue.

CHAPTER 9

Writing and Wisdom (274b–279c)

The analysis of the art of speaking has concluded. Socrates now poses the final problem addressed during this noble colloquy.

The Problem of Writing

There is, Socrates asserts, propriety and impropriety in writing, how it should and should not be done. He then asks Phaedrus whether he knows how to act or speak concerning discourses in a way pleasing to god. Phaedrus says no, and asks Socrates whether he does. In answer, Socrates relates something he has heard from those who lived long ago; as to its truth, only they know. But, Socrates immediately adds, if we discover for ourselves whether it is true for ourselves, we should not care about human opinion, and Phaedrus agrees (274b–c).

Socrates restates this problem in very general terms, asking how one should act or speak about discourses in order to be dear to god. Thus the scope of discussion now includes how we should act toward discourses. In this way, Socrates will make explicit the truly educative function of rhetoric. This inquiry will show how one should behave toward rhetoric in order to be most pleasing to god. We must please the gods because they are higher than we are—but we must also keep in mind the fundamental metaphysical reasons why the gods are where they are in the first place.

Socrates appeals to something he has heard from those who lived before, presumably the ancients. Earlier, Socrates had shown considerable reverence for what the ancients had said, apparently because they had privileged insight no longer shared by the moderns. But now, equipped with the dialectical method and a vision of truth, Socrates tenders to Phaedrus the possibility that they themselves can discover the truth about discourses. If so, then human opinion—even the privileged opinions of the ancients—no longer carries the influence it once did. This shift in attitude indicates Socrates' confidence in the methodology he has advanced, and it also forewarns the reader that what Socrates is about to relate to Phaedrus should be established by independent inquiry based on Socratic methodology. Such inquiry is all the more crucial, given that Socrates will relate a *logos* bearing all the trappings of a *muthos*.

The Prophecy of Thamos

Socrates heard that Theuth, one of the ancient gods, was at Naucrates, in Egypt. This god invented numbers, arithmetic, geometry, astronomy, draughts, dice, and most importantly letters. The king of Egypt was the god Thamos, called Ammon in Greece. Theuth sought Thamos' permission to distribute these letters throughout Egypt, but Thamos, who passed judgment on all Theuth's inventions, rejected the dissemination of letters. Thamos said it would not be an elixir of memory, as Theuth contended, but would induce forgetfulness since those who had letters will not exercise their memory. They will put their trust in writing, in characters apart from themselves, rather than in the memory animating these characters. The elixir is not of memory but of reminding, and the Egyptians would have only an opinion of wisdom, not true wisdom. They will read many things and seem to know many things, but they will in fact be ignorant and hard to associate with, since they will only appear, and not be, wise.

Socrates' report ends at this point and Phaedrus responds by chiding Socrates for making up discourses about Egypt, or any country he feels like. Socrates points out that the very first prophecy was, it is said, words from an oak tree sacred to Zeus. People then, seemingly not as wise as the young are now, listened to an oak or a rock as long as it spoke the truth. Phaedrus seems to think that it makes a difference who speaks and where the speaker is from rather than whether what is said is true. Phaedrus acknowledges the rightness of Socrates' rebuke, and admits that what the Theban said is accurate. Whoever thinks that any art in words has been left in writing and that whatever written is clear and certain will be simple and ignorant of Ammon's prophecy; written words serve only to remind the one who knows the matters about which the words are written (274c–275d).

The first prophecy was, according to Socrates, spoken by a Zeus-favored oak tree. In the natural order, oaks do not speak because they are not capable of speaking. But this example emphasizes the point that the origin of discourse is not relevant. Even if an oak tree startles us by speaking, the wise will listen to what is said (since one never knows through whom, or what, a god may speak)—then determine its truth or falsity. For Socrates, truth can be divulged by a divinely inspired tree as well as by an enraptured human.

In this case, we are told that the god Theuth, inventor of letters, also invented basic forms of mathematics, as well as draughts and dice. The latter are instruments of play and controlled by chance; the former are principles of order, typically used for serious ends, and invariable in their interrelations. The two classes of invention are opposites in these respects, although the fact that Theuth fashioned both implies that they both display divinity despite the fact of opposition. Human nature may be better off with numbers, but it may or may not be better off with letters. Thus, the products of opposition, even from a divine source, must be examined with care.

The fact that one god must consult, and then discourse with, another god is striking. In Socrates' palinode, the gods act but are never depicted as speaking, whether with each other or to mortals. And the fact that discourse in the Theuth account involves praise and blame suggests that divine activity is not justified by itself alone. Thamos,

king of the gods, must appeal to something other than divinity to legis-
late the rightness of things produced by his peers. Thus, when the two
gods discuss, Thamos must use a *logos* to convince Theuth that the invention of letters is not automatically good. In fact, this *logos* shows
that letters produce the opposite of what Theuth intended, since those
using letters will forget what their souls could recollect because they
unquestioningly trust the letters standing before them. Their wisdom is
only apparent, and in fact characterized more by its opposite, ignorance and intractability. And note that Thamos makes this point by
speaking, illustrating the strength of the spoken word against the inherent weakness of letters at their (mythic) point of origin.

Ammon is the chief deity in this story, and one might have thought
that divine decree would not have allowed Thamos' letters to be disseminated. But letters have become public. The story does not detail
how letters bypassed the negative verdict of Ammon and became common coin, but the implication is that the gods are not omnipotent in
such matters. Note then that Ammon's description of the effect of letters is a prophecy. If this prophecy has come to pass, then people do not
trust the written word more than the thoughtful justification of what it
says. The value of the written word has been assumed for millennia; but
perhaps language in this form is a mixed blessing insofar as the pursuit
of wisdom depends on the ability of living language to direct that pursuit, as Socrates now indicates.[1]

The Character of Writing

Phaedrus agrees with the prophecy of Ammon, and with the description
of writing as a tool of remembrance. Socrates then compares writing
with creatures represented in paintings. These creatures stand like living beings, but if you question them, they remain silent. Just so with
writing—the words appear to speak, and to speak with prudence, but
if they are questioned from a desire to learn about what is said, they repeat one and the same thing forever. Furthermore, once a word is written, it goes everywhere, both to those who know and to those who have
no interest in knowing, and it does not recognize to whom it should

speak and to whom it should not. Such words, frozen in their sameness, always need their father for protection, since they have no power to protect themselves. Phaedrus agrees completely.

Socrates now contrasts writing with another kind of discourse, the brother of writing, yet more powerful than it. This is language written in soul, able to defend itself and to know to whom it should speak and to whom it should be silent. Phaedrus asks whether that is the living word of the one who knows, of which the written word is justly called an image. Socrates heartily agrees (275d–276b).

Socrates' criticism of writing is based on the premise that writing has a strange characteristic—just as creatures painted as alive cannot answer a question, so writing always says one and the same thing if interrogated. Writing is dead discourse, since it cannot respond to questions and defend the sense incorporated in the written words. However, Socrates does not say that writing inherently falsifies what is said, nor does he contend at this point that writing represents a necessarily incomplete expression of truth (in the expanded critique of writing to be offered shortly, Socrates does move very close to this position). Writing can say what is true—as Socrates said "the truth about the truth" in his palinode. The initial problem with writing is that when confronted with another account, or by someone who does not understand what the writing says, it cannot either defend itself against the opposing view or explain itself to the interested but unseeing spectator.

What has been written can, presumably, be defended in such a way that any competing view is shown to be inadequate. There would then be no need to revise whatever had been originally written (except perhaps to forestall objections of alternative views). In the same way, although to anticipate all the questions that could be asked of a written work is doubtless impossible, one could conceivably answer all such questions without having to alter what had been written originally. Thus, neither defending nor explaining a piece of writing need entail a revision or extension of that writing.

Socrates also notes that written language can be publicized indiscriminately and speak to those whom it should not, either because they are not interested or because they do not have the requisite capacity for understanding. This point suggests that some people should not read some writings, a consequence which seems unpalatable since it runs against democratic sensibilities. It may be noted that this consequence can also be derived from the hierarchy of souls described in the palinode; thus, e.g., only those souls should read philosophy who have the capacity for seeing what is said. If writing is read by those who are averse to understanding the intended sense, such understanding remains possible—if the writing were explained and defended. But since accompanying every piece of writing with a living advocate is not possible, it is better (or at least simpler) to maintain that whoever requires such an advocate should not read that writing. For Socrates, it is better to be unaware of something written than to read—and misunderstand—that writing.

The contrast between writing and speaking is couched in terms of life and living things—the brother of writing is language written in the soul of the learner, and Phaedrus adds that writing is an image (ἔιδωλον) of language written in the soul. This terminology suggests a participation relation between the reality manifested by the written word in comparison with the reality of words existing in the soul. Thus, the meaning embedded in writing is not totally unreal (e.g., the speech of Lysias), just as anything participating in a Form is not totally unreal. But the degree of life manifested by the written word is less than that manifested by words which, existing in the soul of a living human, are capable of correction, clarification, development, and above all, transmission to the souls of others.

The Gardens of Letters

Socrates now introduces an analogy between language and another kind of living thing. The sensible husbandman, the husbandman who has *nous*, does not plant seeds so that they come to fruition in eight days; he follows the art of husbandry and waits the required eight months until the seeds reach natural maturation. Similarly, one knowing "the just and the good and the beautiful" has no less sense (*nous*) about his seeds than the husbandman. This individual will not sow these seeds with a pen, using words which neither can defend themselves by means of a logos nor adequately teach the truth.

The gardens of letters, as Socrates calls them, will be planted for amusement, and as reminders for one's old age. When others refresh themselves with banquets and such things, the writer will review what has been written. A noble enterprise, interjects Phaedrus, who also mentions those who find equivalent entertainment in "spinning stories" about justice and the other things Socrates has cited. Socrates agrees, adding that truly serious discourse is even more noble than such written diversions, in particular when the art of dialectic is planted in the right kind of soul along with knowledgeable accounts which will help both the one who has these accounts and the one who planted them. This fructification will engender other individuals capable of such instruction, and the entire enterprise makes those having such knowledge and producing such instruction "as happy as is humanly possible" (276b–277a).

Socrates compares the husbandman who "has sense" (*nous*) with those who "have sense" (*nous*) in their knowledge of the just, good, and beautiful. On one level, the parallel could refer to mere common sense. But in the palinode, Socrates proclaimed that true knowledge is visible only to "mind" (*nous*) and that divine intelligence and all other souls capable of such vision are nurtured on mind and knowledge. Also, mind is described there as "the pilot of the soul." Now the husbandman, located on the seventh level of soul (248e), has seen truth seven levels removed from truth seen by the philosopher. But the husbandman has seen truth. Thus what he has seen will steer his soul to act appropriately—as a husbandman.

The husbandman may be tempted to expedite the natural growing process; but if he is serious about what he is, then he would follow the art of husbandry and be pleased with the results once the natural period of fruition was fulfilled. That the art of husbandry requires this procedure exemplifies the highest kind of knowledge open to a husbandman *qua* husbandman—thus Socrates can say that the husbandman has *nous* because knowing the difference between artificial and real art in matters agrarian presupposes the highest good sense for someone practic-

ing this art. The way in which even a husbandman has metaphysically
experienced the truth is overlooked if *nous* is taken as good sense without the rationale for its goodness, i.e., the husbandman's unique feel
for that aspect of the totality of nature realized in the techniques required to make things grow from the earth. Even if husbandry is not a
great art, its status as an art presupposes an awareness of nature analogous to the understanding of nature requisite for the great arts. The
pleasure the husbandman feels with the results of his art measures the
love resulting when anything, whether animate or otherwise, has been
acted upon from the standpoint provided by knowledge of the truth, in
this case knowledge of acting toward seeds so they grow to their natural
fruition.

Socrates says that one who has knowledge of the just, good, and
beautiful must surely have an equivalent degree of *nous*. To know in
this sense is to conceive the Forms insofar as mind, or *nous*, sees them
as realities existing on the most fundamental metaphysical dimension.
Only if soul has a high degree of *nous* can soul approximate knowledge
(ἐπιστήμας) described in the palinode—seeing realities, the Forms,
and, by the glimmer of the good vouchsafed to soul, envisioning relations between and among Forms and participants in Forms.

Socrates extends the husbandman image by asserting that a more
noble type of discourse plants the art of dialectic in the souls of others.
We know now that the art of dialectic includes collection and division
insofar as division depends on determining a thing's nature. But to
know a thing's nature means to know a thing as fully as possible—and
to speak about what one knows—according to the complete metaphysical vision of the palinode, the truth about the truth. Now in planting
the art of dialectic in another, rhetoric must be used to order the educational discourse according to the nature of the audience. But since the
one learning the art of dialectic will also pass on that learning, then
planting the art of dialectic includes planting the art of rhetoric—as
well as the metaphysics grounding the possibility of practicing this
great art.

The vision animating the promulgation of this method will bestow
the highest degree of happiness possible for humans. The fuller our

knowledge, the happier we will be. The strictly intellectual character of this happiness is striking—suggesting that sheer knowledge, without any support from material means, will guarantee human happiness. However, Socrates will modify this apparent intellectualism when he offers his final prayer at the conclusion of the day's discussion.[2]

Socrates compares the pleasures of writing with the amusements of others, specifically citing banquets, and Phaedrus extends the comparison by noting the higher pleasure of those who "spin stories about justice and those other things of which you speak." It is more noble to amuse oneself with writing than with banquets, but for Socrates, it is even more noble to have serious discourse with others, using the method of dialectic. It follows that it is more noble to discourse with someone about the issues discussed at a banquet than to write a report about that discussion. Thus, when Socrates mentions banquets (συμ-ποσίοις) as an inferior pleasure, we may infer that writing about a banquet—e.g., the *Symposium*—is commensurately inferior to talking about what was discussed at that banquet.

Phaedrus reinforces this intriguing exercise in Platonic self-criticism. His examples of higher pleasure are spinning stories (μυθολογοῦντα) about justice, and all the other things Socrates talks about. The *Republic* is about justice. Is the *Republic* a myth, a spun story? It is if myth is understood as employed throughout the *Phaedrus*, i.e., an account concerning fundamental matters which must be seriously examined and rethought (recall, for example, the good—the metaphysical core of the *Republic*—represented through sun imagery). Furthermore, any other Platonic dialogue modeled after the discourse of Socrates is, as a written pastime, no less mythic in this sense.[3]

The reference to banquets occurs at 276d8; the reference to spinning stories about "justice" occurs at 276e2. The proximity is not happenstance; the references are to Plato's own writing. The *Symposium* and the *Republic* are generally considered Plato's finest literary works. Plato agrees with this evaluation, but he also realizes the implications of the position developed in the *Phaedrus*. Written language, however profound and beautiful, is a pale reflection of what can be accomplished through discussion directed by the appropriate method. Plato tells us (although obliquely) that his best writing falls under the critique of writing Socrates is advancing.[4]

Consider the *Symposium*. In structure, it is a written representation of a series of speeches. Save for the interlude between Socrates and Agathon, this writing does not detail any discussion of these speeches. It is good to speak about love. But it is far better to have such speeches and then discuss them. And it is even better if, during this discussion of the speeches, the participants evolve a method showing how further speech can express the truth. Behold then the *Phaedrus*. The *Phaedrus* stands as a critique of the *Symposium* simply from the former's narrative structure. The *Phaedrus*, although no less written than the *Symposium*, is writing which represents how we should act with respect to writing about love and, by implication, to writing about any other subject.

Lysias Revisited

Socrates now says that they can address the criticism of Lysias as a speechwriter (a point originally posited by Phaedrus at 257c, immediately after the completion of the palinode), and to analyze the speeches delivered so far to see which were with and without art. Socrates repeats that the latter inquiry has been clearly shown, and Phaedrus asks to be reminded.

The Need for Method

Socrates summarizes: one must know the truth about each thing spoken or written. This means defining everything, then having defined it, to cut it again according to classes "until further division is impossible." In the same way, the nature of soul must be understood, and simple speeches directed at simple souls, complex and harmonious speeches to complex souls. Only when these procedures have been executed will one become competent, by nature, in the art of discourse, whether the purpose of that art is to instruct or to persuade. Our entire discussion, Socrates says, has taught us this requirement (277b–c).

According to Hackforth (p. 165, n1), the "entire discussion" Socrates refers to is "probably" that part of the dialogue immediately after the conclusion of the palinode, when Phaedrus asks whether speech-writing is inherently base. But there is another way to take this internal reference.

At 270b, Socrates asserted that the method of natures was essential in determining the nature of soul. But to know the nature of something, including the nature of soul, is to study that thing in terms of the metaphysics revealed in the palinode's mythic discussion of the nature of soul. Thus, the "entire discussion" Socrates refers to must also include that portion of the palinode, since only there does Socrates describe the limits of nature. Furthermore, when Phaedrus asks for a reminder of both what has and lacks art, surely Lysias' speech should be included, since it well illustrated how a discourse lacked rhetorical art. It would seem then that the "entire discussion" points to virtually the whole dialogue, not just to that part where methodology was specifically addressed.[5]

The final summary of *Phaedrean* methodology must therefore be interpreted in light of the entire dialogue, in particular the mythic vision of the palinode. Thus, when Socrates begins by stating that one must know the truth about each thing spoken or written, truth should be understood in the metaphysical sense defined in the palinode, i.e., that each thing be known not only according to its formal structure, but also from the standpoint of what mind discerns about that thing within the totality adumbrated in the palinode. To know the truth about a given thing, we must define that thing, then cut it again until further division is impossible. The allied processes of collection and division are here combined, making it clear that to collect things under a Form initiates definition. For example, instances of manic behavior, including those that are amatory, have been collected under madness. But other kinds of madness exist. Therefore, to say that love is a kind of madness is initially to divide madness into one Form, the madness of love, and to separate it from all other Forms of madness.

But the thing so defined is not yet known according to the truth. It must be cut "again"—implying (as argued in chap. 7) that it had been cut during the initial phase of definition—until "further division is impossible," i.e., when all Forms constituting the thing are enumerated. This completeness will be secured only if the thing is seen in relation to everything toward which that thing can act and be acted upon. But this is precisely to determine the nature of the thing as stated at 270d. Therefore, Socrates can stipulate now that division must be exhaustive because he has envisioned totality, i.e., the conditions circumscribing the attainment of complete division. And these conditions are described only in the palinode's mythic and metaphysical vision of the composite natural powers of soul.

The summary next asserts that the nature of soul must be understood "according to the same considerations" (κατὰ ταὐτά). Determining the nature of soul follows the same procedures as exhaustively defining a given thing. In principle then, determining a thing's nature is identical to the definition produced by collection and division. For consider: the first step in determining a thing's nature stipulates its simplicity or complexity. However simplicity and complexity should be understood, a simple thing as one thing cannot be subjected to division; a complex thing, a unity comprised of a multitude of Forms, cannot be additionally divided, i.e., all the Forms comprising the unity of the thing are enumerated. Thus the completeness marking the division of a thing's constituent Forms is the same as that characterizing the nature of either a simple or complex thing. Determining a thing's nature is therefore identical to dividing that thing according to Socrates' new stipulation (i.e., until further division is impossible.)

The method of natures added two vital dimensions to collection and division; first, direction—informing the investigator to look at how the thing acts and is acted upon to determine where the thing should be divided; second, totality—a complete division of the thing based on examining relations between that thing and all other realities, whether material or formal, capable of affecting it.[6]

This complex method must be employed whether one intends to instruct or to persuade. The distinction between these two types of discourse seems clear, since one can instruct without persuading or persuade without instructing. Thus, the discussion of soul's immortality at 245c–246a instructs Phaedrus in soul's nature, but is not necessarily persuasive. Hence the development of the mythic figure, beginning at 246a, which perhaps persuades Phaedrus without instructing, at least not in the way instruction is produced from the taut terms of the argument preceding that extended figure.

But the sharpness of the distinction between instructing and persuading soon begins to blur, since an instructive account can be persuasive without mythic afterthought, and a myth can instruct while persuading without a discursive "head" preceding it. But if the palinode, e.g., is read as a coherent blend of instruction and persuasion, then it is reasonable to suppose that the same rhetorical principles underlie this variegated account. Thus, persuasion need not involve different principles of discourse than those necessary for instruction, and this is the position Socrates asks us to consider.

According to Socrates' final summary, rhetoric will be successful only if the thing to be known is divided exhaustively. But how often is such knowledge secured? Consider two examples from the palinode: Is madness divided into all its constituent Forms? And are there nine and only nine types of soul? If neither division is exhaustive, the palinode is rhetorically defective. And yet Socrates' second speech seems to be particularly fine rhetoric.

I suggest that at 277b–c, Socrates is describing limit conditions for rhetoric, the ideal state of affairs which, if satisfied, will show how speaking well is a consequence of having complete knowledge.[7] It may be assumed, given human finitude, that these conditions will rarely (if ever) be met. But all relevant conditions affecting the practice of rhetoric must be identified, regardless whether the actual practice of rhetoric in light of those conditions is good, bad, or humdrum. The extent of human perfection will be measured by approximating the vision of totality, by how close our discourse can come to what we think and know is the truth.

This concern for limit conditions has been anticipated at several key junctures earlier in the dialogue. Thus, at 230a, Socrates announced that he does not yet know whether he is a more complicated and furious beast or a godlike and more simple living thing. But it would tell against Socrates' self-awareness if he knew that soul could be defined by simplicity or complexity yet could not determine whether his own soul was simple or complex. One may infer then that at 230a, Socrates is presenting limit conditions for determining the nature of human soul—a continuum of possibilities along which all instances of human soul could be located (leaving it open whether his own self-ignorance was sincere or ironic).

The second appearance of limit conditions is the cosmological structure of the myth, in particular the fact that the truth is located beyond the rim of the heavens, beyond the spatiotemporal boundaries circumscribing common experience. Such mythic specification compels us to think through, in conceptual terms—and to the best of our abilities—the totality depicted in this way.

The third limit condition appears when Socrates points out that the art of rhetoric could, in its fullest development, make all things become like all other things, to the limit of possibility. The context concerns grounding similarity in truth, for only by such grounding could things different from but resembling one another be determined as truly different. The art of rhetoric could meaningfully treat any one thing to be like any other thing if all things are, in some sense, identical to one another and can be spoken of in ways derived from this identity. But such extreme abstractness suggests that Socrates has in mind a metaphysical dimension that can be articulated only by an uninformative appeal to, say, reality—e.g., if all things are real in some sense, then all things can be said to be like one another by virtue of sharing in this identity.

The fourth limit condition is implied in the description of the method of natures. If knowing the nature of something requires knowing how that thing acts and is acted upon, the presumably all such relations must be specified. It would follow that to know each thing is to know the active and passive relations between that one thing and everything else. Not to consider any one of these relations discounts the possibility that this relation will affect the nature of the thing to be known. But surely such comprehensive knowledge is a practical impossibility—we cannot know how any one thing acts and is acted upon by every other thing. The point then is that we should be aware of totality in determining the nature of a specific thing, even if practical limitations curtail what can be known about that nature.

A fifth limit condition emerges in the recommendation that successful rhetoric should address a simple soul with simple speech and a complex soul with complex speech. The assumption is that all souls fall into one of these two classes and that no other relevant class exists.[8] But if an audience includes both types of souls, then it will be impossible to speak effectively to this audience (assuming that concurrent simple and complex speeches are mutually exclusive). One more category of speech (at least) seems required to cover the possibility that in a mass audience, both types of soul will be present. If so, then simplicity and complexity merely indicate disjunctive limits (limits which, in some instances, may not be empirically sufficient for effective rhetoric).

Noting the limit condition pertaining to exhaustive division, as the final phase in Socrates' discursive retrieval of the metaphysical vision of the palinode, reveals an important feature in the structure of this part of the dialogue. When Socrates is asked by Phaedrus to repeat a point or position stated earlier, he always adds a new element to the original position. It is important to recognize that this gradual refinement of the overall teaching of the dialogue results from the continuous interchange between Socrates and Phaedrus. The more they discuss rhetoric, the closer this ongoing account comes to situating the art of rhetoric within the limits of totality circumscribed in the metaphysics of the palinode.

It is asserted at the end of the dialogue that discussion is preferable to writing, and the written word of the *Phaedrus* shows this priority by having the art of rhetoric, both in the methodology of collection and division and in the determination of the nature of soul, become progressively more precise through the discursive activity of Phaedrus and Socrates. It is this discussion that eventually discloses the nature of rhetoric—not an isolated challenge to produce a beautiful speech (i.e., a monologue) on a certain topic. Furthermore, the fact that the conversation between Socrates and Phaedrus has ended need not imply that everything relevant to determining the nature of the art of rhetoric has been said.

The Propriety of Writing

After summarizing, for the final time, the complete art of rhetoric, Socrates also repeats the correct response to the question whether writing is intrinsically noble or disgraceful. If Lysias, or anyone, ever wrote or shall write, publicly or privately, anything believing that this writing is certain and clear, then it is a disgrace to the writer. For not knowing the difference between a waking or sleeping understanding of just and unjust, good and bad, is, in truth, disgraceful, even if everyone applauds such ignorance. Phaedrus agrees.

The correct attitude toward writing is that much in it is necessarily playful, that neither prose nor anything in meter should be taken seriously, since the best such efforts merely remind us of what we know. Only words concerning justice and beauty and goodness spoken by teachers for the sake of learning, and truly written in the soul, will be clear and perfect and worthy. These words are the speaker's only legitimate progeny—first, what is in the speaker, if such words are found there; second, their descendants or brothers which may have arisen in other souls. By comparison, no attention should be paid to other kinds of words. Whoever adopts this attitude toward writing is the type of individual Socrates and Phaedrus pray they might become. Phaedrus echoes this wish and prayer (277d–278b).

Socrates specifies a single positive function for the written word— it can remind us of what we already know. In fact, the drama of the *Phaedrus* at this point illustrates this very need. When Socrates recalls what has been said about the art of rhetoric, Phaedrus asks to be reminded; then, when Socrates mentions that the propriety of speaking and writing has been stated not long ago, Phaedrus interrupts with a "What?" Phaedrus has forgotten both points, although given their complexity, he can hardly be faulted. The point is that the remembrance (ὑπομνησόν) Phaedrus requests from Socrates at 277b4 is an instance of the remembrance (ὑπόμνησιν) Socrates cites at 278a1 as the singular virtue of writing.[9] For if these accounts had been transcribed as spoken, then Phaedrus would not now have to be verbally reminded of them.

Although spoken discourse may be higher than written discourse for reasons stated in *Phaedrus*, it is necessarily fugitive. And if things spoken are long and difficult, then forgetfulness is virtually unavoidable. In such circumstances, writing becomes essential as a record of what was said, especially if what was said is asserted as true. If the Socratic analysis of the art and propriety of rhetoric were true, then Phaedrus may well have forgotten it—unless what was thought and spoken had also been written. For if it were written, then Phaedrus—and posterity—could be reminded of the truth. The writer Plato thus practices what the speaker Socrates preaches. The *Phaedrus*, a written critique of writing, represents, in written discourse incorporating spoken discourse, one important reason why writing must be preserved.

The earlier critique of writing (274d–e) is expanded here. Socrates includes under the present analysis all forms of writing, past and future, produced by professional or amateur authors. Although many instances of writing are not intended to be true or profound, but merely to convey information, these instances fall under Socratic strictures no less than serious writings.

Anyone who writes believing that the writing is either certain or clear is, Socrates says, disgraced. These two misconceptions should be distinguished. A piece of writing may be clear enough, but this is not to say that it cannot be made clearer. This characteristic holds not only for writings misunderstood because inadequately or incoherently expressed, but also for well-developed writings. The assumption is that written language is inherently opaque—such opacity can be reduced but never entirely eliminated.

The second problem has more drastic consequences. For if to say that writing does not have great certainty implies that it cannot represent truth, then it seems impossible to write the truth. This lack of stability can, however, mean not that writing always remains some distance from truth, but merely that it never stands firm against attacks. If truth is fragile, then it must be protected by active defense, especially since its being written implies, according to considerations just discussed, that it could always be clarified.

The fact that Socrates prays that he and Phaedrus become imbued with the propitious attitude toward writing implies that both men presently lack this attitude. Phaedrus' initial bedazzlement with Lysias' speech show why he should pray for this end. But why must Socrates pray? Socrates has said that he does not know whether he is simple or complex; if this uncertainty remains even marginally true, then Socrates' hunger for speeches, attested to at 230e, may still be out of hand. After all, we have just seen Socrates counter one written speech with yet another speech—not with critical discussion of that speech. Is he certain that he will react to the next written speech in a manner pleasing to the gods? Better then to pray for the requisite self-control which may not be readily in Socrates' power to implement when the occasion demands.

The Legacy of Composition

After this final assessment of written language, Socrates says to Phaedrus that they have entertained themselves about discourses long enough. He then urges Phaedrus to tell Lysias that he and Socrates heard words in a holy place which they were told to repeat to Lysias and whoever composed speeches, to Homer and whoever wrote poetry (with or without musical accompaniment), and to Solon and whoever penned political words called laws. If these individuals have written with knowledge of the truth, can support this writing with discussion, and can show by their own speaking that written words are of small value, such an individual should not be named speechwriter, or poet, or lawmaker. Although this person should not be called wise, for that epithet belongs only to a god, the person may be called a philosopher, a lover of wisdom, a fit title for a human seeker of such ends. Someone, on the other hand, who does nothing better than write words and then tinker with them can only be addressed properly as poet, writer of speeches, maker of laws. Phaedrus agrees with this assessment (278b–e).

Socrates has gathered the leading exponents of three different arts—Lysias in oratory, Homer in poetry, Solon in lawmaking—as well as anyone else who practiced one or the other of these arts. And the radical character of Socrates' subsequent challenge should be noted. For if a Lysias, Homer, or Solon were to produce rhetoric, poetry, or laws according to the truth, then it is not evident that they would have written what in fact they did. If their writings were fashioned in light of the truth, then what posterity has recognized as great linguistic art in these forms might have been very different. Socrates thus proposes the possibility of a complete revision of these areas in Greek literature and law, a revision following upon the dictates of the truth. The implication for lawmaking is especially striking, for the entire fabric of Greek life might have been different if Solon had codified laws on the basis of the truth (assuming that Solon's principles and truth are not identical).

This remarkable revisionist implication, if carried far enough, render rhetoric, poetry, and lawmaking virtually indistinguishable from philosophy. But even if these literary exemplars did not so revise their work, the possibility that they could discuss and defend it in light of the truth implies that each of them is a lover of wisdom—a philosopher—as well as orator, poet, or lawmaker. This possibility is in a way no less radical than the first, since Socrates envisions Homer (e.g.) to be as brilliant philosophically as he was poetically. Without this capacity, Homer would just be Homer, a poet of great skill but ultimately someone who tinkers with words to achieve a certain effect, without the knowledge of the truth enabling his poetic discourse to be great art and also consonant with, and revelatory of, the truth. Socrates' recommendation here shows all the more the great confidence he has in the structure of reality he has seen, and portrayed, in his speeches as well as his retrospective study of them.

The fact that Phaedrus is charged with announcing this message to these great literary figures suggests not only that Phaedrus has understood everything said about the art of rhetoric and its dependence on the truth, but also that he has the capacity to defend the position if Lysias and company should dispute, or request clarification of, the Socratic injunction to rethink the metaphysical principles underlying their literary pursuits. Even partial success in this project (if, for Homer and Solon, it could have transpired) would testify to the philosophical nature of Phaedrus' soul.

Socrates Prophesies

After Phaedrus hears what Socrates wants him to tell his friend Lysias, Phaedrus asks what Socrates intends to do with his own friend. Socrates asks "what friend?" and Phaedrus responds "the beauteous Isocrates." Socrates replies that Isocrates is still young, but he is willing to prophesy about him. To Socrates, it seems that he has a nature higher than that represented by the author of Lysias' speeches as well as a nobler character. In fact, Socrates will not be surprised if he excels all others in discourses or, if this pursuit does not satisfy Isocrates, a more divine source will drive him to even greater heights. For, Socrates contends, there is something naturally philosophical in his intellect. This is what Socrates will convey from these deities to his favorite, Isocrates, and he urges Phaedrus again to send the aforementioned message to his favorite, Lysias (278e–279b).

Socrates' prophecy has occasioned a large literature concerning Plato's thoughts about Isocrates as rhetorician.[10] However, the prophecy also serves other purposes in the philosophy of the *Phaedrus*.

Phaedrus refers to the Isocrates as the beauteous (καλόν), presumably as much an epithet for his rhetorical products as for any physical comeliness he may have possessed. Socrates offers a prophecy concerning this exemplar of beauty. If this prophecy follows the discussion of madness in the palinode, then Socrates must be inspired in order to deliver it rightly. And should the prophecy come to pass, then Isocrates will emulate Socrates in pursuing wisdom. Furthermore, Socrates testifies to his self-knowledge in seeing Isocrates as potentially transcending the realm of rhetoric and becoming properly philosophical, since only one who has seen the truth witnessed by a philosopher can recognize an equivalently philosophical vision in another individual, whether or not such vision is ever realized. In the same vein, Socrates refers twice to the nature of Isocrates, first in comparison with Lysias, second as a prerequisite for his incipient command of philosophy, and the technical sense of nature should be kept in mind. Socrates sees Isocrates' body and soul acting and interacting so that he will speak and live according to the truth granted this kind of intellect.

The Prayer of Socrates

Phaedrus agrees to relay Socrates' prophecy to Lysias. He then says that it is time to leave, since the heat of the day has abated. Socrates asks whether a prayer to the deities would be appropriate, and Phaedrus agrees. Socrates prays to Pan and all other gods of this place that he be made beautiful within and that whatever external things he possesses be friendly to this inner self. He prays also that he may think the wise man wealthy and that he has such wealth as the virtuous man is capable of enduring. For Socrates this prayer is enough. Phaeus asks to share in the prayer as well, for friends share all things. Socrates says "let us go," and with that terse remark the dialogue ends (279b–c).

Earlier, when it was almost noon, Phaedrus had used the heat of the day as added inducement for Socrates to remain in the shade and continue the discussion (242a). That discussion included the palinode and the extensive treatment of method and the nature of rhetoric. Now at 279b, the heat has subsided and Phaedrus is ready to leave. The hottest period of the day was coincident with the most speculative phase of the palinode, when Socrates described and discussed the nature of truth. The sun's heat reflected the intensity of Socrates' metaphysical vision, and the source of that heat recalled the heavenly image for the good, the source of all being and knowledge.

Socrates proposes a prayer to Pan and all other local deities. But why pray to Pan and not to Zeus, identified earlier as the god of friendship? Pan is the god of forests and shepherds; as such, he represents whatever local deities rule the sylvan splendors where Socrates and Phaedrus have spoken. That Socrates has these gods in mind is indicated by the appeal to the gods of this place. Socrates is praying to a circumscribed dimension of divinity, thus reflecting the scope of what Socrates is praying for.

Socrates prays that he may be made beautiful ($\kappa\alpha\lambda\tilde{\omega}$) within. As the most manifest Form, beauty typically refers to predominantly sensible instances. The present context is primarily moral in character, but the manifest character of *kalos* should be taken in the same way, as clearly visible in moral situations and in Socrates' own moral choices.

In this way, Socrates will more readily achieve self-knowledge, since if he knows himself as beautiful within, then he should be able to connect that recognition to as many other formal realities as his prenatal soul beheld.

The noble beauty Socrates requests from deity depends on how he views himself "from within." When he then prays that his possessions be friendly (φίλια) with the inner man, everything depends on the nature of the inner man. If the inner man is wise, there will be harmony between soul and possessions; if the inner man is not wise, conflict may erupt between what Socrates is and what he possesses. The metaphor of friendship joining the inner man with his possessions is an image for friendship in the highest philosophical sense; the nature of an individual with appropriate self-knowledge will love possessions in a way benefiting the soul, directing it to the highest possible happiness.

Socrates next requests that he think the wise man is wealthy. It does not follow that Socrates thinks himself wise; he asks only for expansiveness of soul sufficient to recognize the nature and value of wisdom. Whether he will achieve such wisdom is left open. And, in fact, Socrates does not pray for wisdom. This pattern continues in the final phase of the prayer when Socrates asks for only as much wealth as the man of temperance can bear.[11] Socrates does not say that he is temperate but that a temperate man will have so much wealth—and no more, the amount of wealth depending on the degree of temperance animating one's soul. Socrates appeals to the importance of wisdom and temperance, but he does not say that he has either; the relation between the possession of these virtues and the amount of external possessions consonant with them must also be left open.

The very fact that Socrates prays for wealth may appear anomalous, almost signaling a lack of moral character. This part of the prayer may, however, complement the *Phaedrus'* concerted emphasis on knowledge as the substance of human happiness. The temperate man needs money—as, indeed, do we all—to satisfy basic human needs. Presumably the most knowledgeable individual will be wise, and being wise, will also be temperate. This individual will then be capable of handling the right amount of wealth to satisfy all the practical cares coincident with loving wisdom and temperately realizing that love.

By tradition, Socrates was impoverished, and therefore he would fully realize the need for money. But as a philosopher, he would also know that this need must be directed by higher concerns—and his prayer is that both desiderata be fulfilled. Socrates has grown in self-knowledge as the day has passed. But he has done so under divine inspiration. Now, as day ends and he is no longer under the direct sway of deity, he prays in such a way that his own nature remains hidden behind the fundamental importance of wisdom and temperance in ready alliance with just the correct amount of material wealth. Socrates also illustrates the principles of rhetoric just advanced; since he does not fully know his own nature, his prayer reflects that indeterminacy. He does know, however, what the philosopher's soul should desire if it truly loves reality and that is wisdom.[12]

After Phaedrus wishes to be included in the prayer, he adds, as an apparent afterthought, that friends share all things. This remark, a Pythagorean adage, may be taken on several levels. First, Phaedrus sees himself as Socrates' friend and therefore eligible to share in whatever Socrates has. Second, Socrates and Phaedrus exemplify only one kind of friendship, i.e., that between philosophers, lovers of wisdom. But if friends have all things in common, then all friends share in all things—all human beings who participate in true friendship can share in those things philosophical friends participate in to the highest degree. All friends share not just external benefits of friendship as socially manifested as well as internal feelings of satisfaction; they also have access to the highest degree of reality. This reality—the Forms and the good binding the Forms to one another and to everything else—is most open to those friends who are philosophers. But in principle it is open to all levels of friendship (as indicated, e.g., by the palinode's nine types of soul having seen measures of truth).

Socrates and Phaedrus will return to the city, where each man will meet friends who have other friends, etc. The city is, in one sense, grounded on friendship. As Aristotle might have put it, only a beast or a god would not have at least one friend. The Pythagorean dictum allows the bond of friendship between any two individuals—whether philosophers or not—to have all things opened to them, and of maximizing their mutual happiness through this communion of concerns. As long as friends discourse, as long as friendship draws its reality from the love hymned and discussed in the *Phaedrus*, the friends so bound will enjoy one another and the reality underlying this intimacy in a manner exemplifying the friendship of philosophers loving each other and reality to the highest degree.

In this respect, the Pythagorean adage offers a precise summary of the day's discussion. Phaedrus was enamored by a speech about love, read the speech to Socrates, Socrates responded with a speech of his own, then retracted that speech and offered another; finally the two men spent some time applying the account of reality in the second speech to rhetoric and the meaning of success in rhetoric. Phaedrus now knows much more about love, the particular rhetorical theme stimulating the day's linguistic adventures. He knows that the highest love is friendship, that the highest type of friendship is philosophical friendship, and the metaphysical reason why—only the soul of the philosopher has seen the most reality. If Phaedrus is receptive to all the implications in "friends share all things," then he is more philosophical than his words and actions have so far betokened.

The dialogue concludes with Socrates saying "let us go" (Ἴωμεν). Socrates and Phaedrus, initially apart from one another, have met by chance early in the morning. But they are returning to the city as a pair, joined by a bond of friendship perhaps stronger than it was that same morning, and surely more secure by virtue of everything said about friendship during the day. This security has been established by being open to divine inspiration and then retreating from the intense vision engendered by that inspiration in order to codify this vision against past and current theorizing concerning the nature of rhetoric. The movement away from the safety of the city into the country and then back to the city reflects the rhetorical movement into the wilds of myth and then back into discursive restraint. Socrates epitomize this process aspect of this discussion with one word—the *Phaedrus* as a whole represents a complex, beautiful, and noble counterpart to this movement.

Concluding Comment

In our time, the written word is everywhere. And it is not an exaggeration to say that texts, both literary and philosophical, have assumed a reality characterized by monolithic self-determination. This reality does not allow current interpreters of these texts to move outside them in order to see their connections, if any, to the nonverbal world. Reading the *Phaedrus* provides much food for thought for anyone willing to scrutinize and evaluate this conviction. For Plato, writing is subservient to speaking, and both writing and speaking are servants of the truth. But truth exists as a dimension of reality apart from fields of discourse. This otherness stands as a fixed certainty, even for those continuing to whirl in interpretive maelstroms pursued, apparently, only to spawn one more interpretation of one more text.

The *Phaedrus* depicts a drama of human beings talking about the most intense kind of experience within a metaphysical hierarchy that preserves this intensity while elevating it toward the highest reaches of reality. This transition, if achieved, will make us happy precisely because it directs the almost limitless energies of love toward approaching, and restoring, our cognitive vision of reality, the ultimate ground of human happiness. This study has attempted to demonstrate that Plato envisioned love, and discourses about love, as convergent routes toward possessing such happiness.

To love in the sense argued for in the *Phaedrus* involves thinking and speaking an abstract language which, as the *Parmenides* puts it, will be dismissed by many as idle chatter. It is a fascinating example of the prophetic vision of the *Phaedrus* that it anticipates, and would endorse, the currently popular understanding of philosophy as conversation—as long as this conversation is properly ordered. For the *Phaedrus* also teaches that philosophers cannot just talk; they must take great care to talk rightly about the right things. And it is practicing the idle chatter proper to dialectic that will help us see the metaphysical truth spoken in the *Phaedrus*.

Two consequences may be noted if one conceives philosophy as conversing about interesting topics and nothing more. First, the interpretation of the *Phaedrus* argued in this work will be dismissed as a hopelessly antique exercise. Second, philosophy itself cannot become more than talk about talk. But if, against this approach, philosophy is seen as a unique love for a unique wisdom which, if pursued, will make us better human beings, then we ignore this understanding of the *Phaedrus* at the risk of overlooking a unique approach to happiness. Such happiness—love animated by metaphysical discourse—remains a prospect worth thoughtful consideration.

Method and Metaphysics in the *Phaedrus*

Discussions of the *Phaedrus* often observe that it contains only a rudimentary version of collection and division,[1] a method that was to become a primary concern of the *Sophist* and *Statesman*. However, the development of this method in the *Phaedrus* is sufficiently detailed to warrant inquiry into some of its assumptions and principal consequences, especially as exemplified within the *Phaedrus* itself. This Epilogue, a recapitulation and speculative development of what has gone before in this study, is such an inquiry. The points made here may help situate the *Phaedrus* in relation to the metaphysical discussions in the *Parmenides*, *Sophist*, *Statesman*, and *Philebus*. They will also focus attention on those aspects of the metaphysics of the truth not explicitly integrated into the account of rhetoric rendered in the discursive phase of the dialogue.

Collection

Socrates' truncated account of collection at 265d–e may be expanded as follows. The particulars collected are dispersed, and there may be many of them. They are then gathered so that they can be seen under one Form. The various members of the dispersed plurality will differ among themselves, whether in few or many respects. However, running through these differences will be one characteristic which all members of that plurality share. Also, this characteristic is not accidental; rather, it must be essential to each member of the plurality, since it will be the locus for what defines that thing as a member of that plurality. Collection is not merely gathering things into an aggregate, but involves an intuitive seeing of unity in the midst of diversity. These unities are the Forms, as instantiated in particulars. This vision is intellectual, and discerns the formal identity that underlies the perceptible exterior of a group of things exhibiting individual dissimilarity.[2]

But how does such intuitive seeing proceed? What are we to look for and how will we know when we find it?[3] The answers to these questions depend, in part, on the character of the Forms, and of reality in general, underlying collection. Thus, collection (which, as developed in the *Phaedrus*, already involves division) is problematic because division is problematic by virtue of its relation to the nature of the Forms.

Division and Nature

Division is deployed according to a thing's natural joints. From 265e to 266a3, the phrase "by nature" appears three times to describe (a) where the joints are to be divided, (b) how the joints of one kind of thing, human body, are divided, and (c) how madness, as a Form, is found in us. As already noted, these references are not stylistic reinforcement. Rather, they serve a definite metaphysical function, having been concentrated at this crucial phase in the account of division to anticipate the doctrine of natures (advanced later because of the speculative character of that doctrine) and the essential relation between this doctrine and the allied procedures of collection and division. In fact, rules of procedure for applying collection and division follow from nature insofar as nature pertains to the products of collection and the process of division. Collection and division thus presupposes determining a thing's nature as a prerequisite for deciding where the parts of that thing should be divided.

Formal divisions of a thing depend on the meaning of nature. Socrates advances a theory of natures at 270d–e. The following reflections assume the primacy of this account. The theory of natures will be examined as it stands, followed by discussion of a series of problems with respect to division insofar as division is based on a thing's nature.

Nature

Here again is the statement of the theory of natures:

> In considering the nature of anything, must we not consider first, whether that in respect to which we wish to be learned ourselves and to make others learned is simple or multiform, and then, if it is simple, inquire what power of acting it possesses, or of being acted upon, and by what, and if it has many forms, number them, and then see in the case of each form, as we did in the case of the simple nature, what its action is and how it is acted upon and by what.

The Range of Nature

Socrates says that this method applies in determining the nature of anything. Therefore, although the context in which the method of natures is introduced concerns the nature of soul, the statement of the method implies that things other than soul will have a nature. But will all types of particulars have a nature? If not, are there criteria for determining which particulars have a nature and which do not? For if something must have a nature in order to become subject to division, then a thing without a nature cannot be divided and, presumably, cannot therefore be known. Assuming then that knowledge of all things is possible via collection and division, then dividing a thing according to its natural joints implies that all things must have a determinable nature. (The importance of this assumption cannot be overemphasized, since it seems prima facie plausible that things could exist without having this technical sense of nature.)

Nature and the Forms

Does a Form have a nature? According to the *Phaedrus*, the answer is yes, an answer tendered both in the mythic section of the palinode and in the discursive sequel. First, in the palinode, Socrates speaks of the driver of soul remembering "the nature of beauty" standing "with modesty" on a pedestal of chastity (254b). Beauty here is the Form beauty, and although the reference to nature may be taken as merely intensive, the fact that the Form beauty is depicted in a relation to both modesty and chastity suggests that this usage of nature anticipates, by way of illustration, the doctrine of natures to be introduced later. Thus, the Form beauty has a nature such that it can exist in relation to something other than itself, i.e., to act and be acted upon (in senses discussed below).

Second, at 265d, collection is said to produce an idea (ἰδέαν). Now if this idea is a Form, then when Socrates describes division of this Form—a process, recall, controlled by nature—as proceeding according to Forms (κατ' εἴδη), the Form must have a nature allowing it to be so partitioned. In general then, a Form has natural joints no less than entities participating in Forms.

Simplicity and Complexity

According to the theory of natures, the first step in defining the nature of something is to determine whether it is simple or complex. However, Socrates does not indicate how this step should be understood. Some preliminary speculation in this regard may therefore be useful.

The doctrine of natures does not assert that a simple or complex thing will necessarily include active and passive features (although all things, whether simple or complex, may display these features). Presumably a thing can exist as, say, simple and lack further specification of any sort. It may be noted, however, that the *Parmenides* hypothesizes that something (i.e., unity) could have being but no other property, and then explores the paradoxical consequences that follow (142ff). We may assume then that simplicity cannot refer to sheer undifferentiatedness. Another reason against this possibility is that the method of natures situates a simple thing with respect to active and passive considerations, suggesting that a nature characterized by simplicity must be at least capable of acting toward something other than itself and also being acted upon by something other than itself.

How would simplicity and complexity pertain to a Form if a Form has a nature? The simple/complex disjunction suggests that a given thing is one or the other but not both. Now if complex means multiform (as suggested by the Greek word—πολυειδές), then a Form could be complex if divisible into a plurality of Forms. Thus, if madness is a Form, then madness is complex, since there are (at least) four types of madness, each itself presumably a Form. But if complex means multiform, then the obvious parallel is that simple means monadic. Thus a Form would be simple if it were not divisible into any other Forms. If, e.g., prophecy, as a Form, could not be divided into any other Forms, then prophecy would be simple in the sense required.

However, the contrast between simplicity and complexity becomes more intricate if we consider Socrates' remark at 230a, when he speaks of his supposed inability to determine whether he is, by nature, more complex or "more simple" (ἀπλούστερον). The phrasing suggests that simplicity and complexity admit of degrees. Now a Form cannot admit degrees of simplicity if simplicity refers to Form's monadicity. Thus, any Form is no more or less a Form, *qua* one Form, than any other Form. If therefore complexity means multiplicity of Forms, then simplicity cannot mean monadicity if simplicity and complexity are parallel and determine properties from the same perspective.

Simplicity and complexity pertain to the nature of anything which has a nature. The *Phaedrus* emphasizes how these properties pertain to soul. Thus, at 271a, Socrates says that the art of rhetoric will describe "the nature of soul"—whether it is one and all alike or whether, like the body, it has many Forms. Examining what is said about determining soul's nature will suggest an approach to simplicity and complexity when applied to entities other than Forms.

At 246a, the nature (φύσεως) of soul is said to be self-motion. This conclusion is part of the proof of the immortality of soul. Socrates then says that the form (ἰδέας) of human soul, expressed in an image, is constituted by three distinct powers. Since all human souls have these powers, tripartition is essential to soul's nature. But if every soul is tripartite, then simplicity and complexity cannot be defined as above, i.e., for the Forms, since both simple and complex souls are identical in being tripartite. Thus, a soul with a simple nature cannot be monadic, for even a simple soul must be tripartite in order to be a soul. At 277c, Socrates says that one skilled in the art of rhetoric will deliver elaborate discourses to complex souls and simple ones to simple souls, strongly suggesting that some souls will be simple while other souls will be complex. The problem then is to determine how one tripartite soul can be simple and another tripartite soul can be complex.

A clue to the relevant sense of simplicity appears at the end of the palinode (257b), when Socrates wishes that Phaedrus no longer hesitate between two ways of life, but direct his life simply (ἀπλῶς) toward love with philosophical discourse. This qualification suggests that simplicity (and, correlatively, complexity) may be understood in terms of function. In the same vein, consider 248d–e, when Socrates lists nine levels of soul distinguished by how much truth they have seen in their preembodied existence. Presumably each soul will fall into one of these classes. If therefore one soul exhibits conduct befitting just that class, then it is simple; by contrast, a complex soul would display a range of behavior exemplifying soul's membership in more than one class.

Witness Socrates: in the mythic phase of the palinode, he describes his soul as that of a philosopher (250b). However, elsewhere in the dialogue, he also describes himself as a lover of beauty, a seer, and a poet. The lover of beauty is in the same soul-class as the philosopher, but inhabiting a lesser degree of that class. The seer is in the fifth class while the poet belongs on the sixth level (248e). In sum, Socrates sees himself (or, more accurately, his soul) as exhibiting two degrees of the first level of soul as well as both the fifth and sixth levels.

Now consider Phaedrus. At 250b, his soul is allied with that of Socrates as both mythically follow in the train of Zeus (implying that Phaedrus has the soul of a philosopher). Later, however, Socrates refers to Phaedrus as a "lover of the Muses" (259b). Now a Muse-loving soul occupies the lowest rung of the first level of soul (248d) while the lover of wisdom, the philosopher, occupies the highest rung of this level. Thus, it appears that Phaedrus wavers between the lives of philosophy and love of the Muses.

If these two ways exhaust the possibilities for Phaedrus' soul, then that soul is simple in the sense described. A simple soul remains within the range of conduct appropriate to that soul's experience of truth. If, by contrast, Socrates exemplifies one sense of complexity intended by the simple/complex of rubric, then complexity refers to soul displaying a range of behavior cutting across the divisions established by the nine levels of soul. When Socrates is a poet, then he acts as a poet in terms of what a poet sees of the truth; when he is a seer, he acts as a seer; when he is a philosopher, he acts as a philosopher. If all these levels presuppose three different apprehensions of the truth, then the extent to which Socrates ranges over these levels is the extent to which his soul is complex, i.e., varying in applying the truth it has experienced. And yet it is one and the same soul throughout, with, according to the myth, a single vision of truth.

Earlier, Socrates had said that the nature of soul is self-motion. Such self-motion would, for soul marked by simplicity, coexist with whatever Forms will allow soul to remain "one and all alike" (271a). Complex soul coexists with Forms in such a way that the soul becomes variegated, undergoing changes to which the simple soul is not subject. Self-motion is thus a necessary but not sufficient condition for the nature of soul. The nature of soul will be sufficiently determined when (and, perhaps, if) all Forms fulfilling its native simplicity or complexity are specified. When Socrates says that a complex soul requires a complex and harmonious discourse (277c), the appeal to harmony reflects the fact that a complex soul has divergent strains that must be coordinated and, if possible, unified by variegated yet rhetorically unified discourse.

According to the method of natures, everything with a nature is either simple or complex. How can simplicity understood in this analogical sense be applied to things other than soul? If something can be simple and still be composed of parts, then one way to determine simplicity for this thing will depend on how it displays unity with respect to function. As a result, a direct connection obtains between simplicity and unity. Furthermore, if simplicity admits of degree (as it does with respect to soul), then something composed of parts can be more simple only if that thing can remain one thing and yet display a varying degree of simplicity. If therefore a thing's unity guarantees that it will be of this kind and no other kind, then unity becomes essential to that thing's nature. The very notion of nature presupposes a sense of unity preserving the sameness of kind requisite for a nature to exist at all.[4]

And unity becomes even more fundamental with respect to complexity. A complex thing is constituted by a plurality of Forms. Socrates illustrates this complexity by appealing to the human body, saying that it is composed of many Forms. But the unity of human body, as one type of body, is different from the unity of any other type of body. The leg of a human differs from the leg of a horse not just because of its length or shape, but because the nature of a human differs from the nature of a horse; the differences between similar parts depends, ultimately, on differences between distinct natures of which those parts are members. Determining simplicity and complexity therefore presupposes a fundamental sense of unity, especially since some things are complex, existing as ensembles of distinct Forms.

Republic VII, 525a, asserts that the study of unity is vital in leading soul to true being; the study of unity will be pursued at great length in the *Parmenides*. And the *Phaedrus* develops a doctrine of natures which show, by implication, why the study of unity is so essential.

Since the nature of a thing guarantees that the thing is unique as a type, this nature is distinct from the sum of the determinable parts (i.e., Forms) of that thing. Thus nature becomes no less metaphysically ultimate than Form or instance of Form, since the nature of a thing represents a diverse set of Forms existing as a separate and unique type of being. As a result, nature is metaphysically privileged (a characteristic noted below when interpreting division).

Active and Passive

Once the thing has been determined as either simple or complex, then it must be analyzed in terms of how it acts and is acted upon. It might appear that this determination does not require specifying a thing's Forms, since all we need do is notice whether or not, e.g., a tree acts or is acted upon in its relation to other things, or, with respect to itself, whether the branches and leaves of a tree act or are acted upon by each other. However, Socrates obviates this gambit by having simplicity and complexity determine how the thing is active and passive. Thus, active and passive characteristics must be derived from the thing's nature and formal structure, and cannot be accounted for simply by observational appearances.

How then is a Form active and passive? If the Forms act causally, then they fund particulars with whatever reality they possess by participation; if Forms ground predication, then they actively "give a name" to whatever is so spoken. Forms are also active in blending with other Forms (as beauty blends with temperance). In contrast, Forms are passive, or acted upon, to the extent that dependency relations obtain between or among them; thus beauty is passive as acted upon by a Form other than itself, e.g., temperance. Also, Forms are acted upon in being known by human beings. This might seem a type of passivity too obvious to state. If, however, a Form existed, yet was unknown, then it could not be acted upon in this way (in fact, there is no reason even to hypothesize, let alone to grant existence to, such an entity).

Determining precisely how these active and passive considerations apply to Forms in order to preserve their canonic immutability will lead directly into the classic problems of participation. The relevant point is that these functions of a Form may be placed under the active/passive rubric, thereby justifying that a Form has a nature in the technical sense specified in the *Phaedrus*.

Nature and Totality

As stated, the active/passive condition is without limit—in theory, anything can act or be acted upon by anything else. In fact, of course, such undifferentiated boundlessness is curtailed by the nature of the thing. Thus, the plane tree will act upon Socrates and Phaedrus because its nature includes producing shade, but the tree will not be acted upon by two men just sitting beneath it because its nature does not have the capacity to be so affected. However, the generality of this condition points to an important metaphysical presupposition. If a thing can act and be acted upon by widely distant, and disparate, entities, then the nature of that thing is determined only when examined against a backdrop of totality. In theory, the nature of a thing is incomplete unless that thing is seen in relation to all other things, with active and passive responsives fully described. Thus, natures differ, but the conditions under which natures are determined are identical for all natures— conditions ultimately bounded by totality.

This important point was anticipated by Socrates at 261e, when he described the limits of rhetoric as that art—if it is an art—which allows one to make out everything to be like everything else, within the limits of possible comparison. The sense of this vexed passage is replicated by the active/passive phase of the method of natures with respect to totality. For in determining all the Forms which constitute the nature of a thing, the thing must be seen as like or unlike all other relevant things. The qualification, "within the limits of possible comparison," reflects the fact that the Forms defining the nature of X will differ at some point from the Forms defining the nature of Y; as a result, the likenesses and unlikenesses establishing the nature of X will not apply to the likenesses and unlikeness establishing the nature of Y. Thus, e.g., the constitutive Forms of madness will be determined through active and passive considerations differing from the constitutive Forms of other entities. But it is essential to defining each nature in light of active and passive considerations to see that nature as like and unlike everything else, i.e., with respect to totality.

Another important inference may be drawn. The implied presence of totality brings out that the active/passive condition is heuristic as well as constitutive. To determine a nature, the thing must be situated in as many contexts as possible. The more contexts examined, the greater the knowledge of the thing's nature. The only way to tell whether a thing acts toward and reacts to some other thing is to place that thing in a given context and then observe the results. Only if all the relevant ways a thing acts and is acted upon are determined can that thing be divided, accurately, according to its natural joints.[5]

This heuristic function, in concert with the implied presence of totality, reveals the powerful empirical dimension of the method of natures. Determining a thing's nature requires observing that thing in the most varied set of conditions possible. A given thing is thus connected not only to a potential multiplicity of Forms, but also (in theory) to all spatiotemporal particulars—a remarkable metaphysical richness. Furthermore, a thing's nature also includes an essential process dimension, since the active/passive consideration is directed at the thing in all phases of its existence. For example, the nature of "being in love" will be defined by how the person acts just as much as it will be by what happens to the person as a result of the objects animating that love.

This heuristic function also pertains to Forms. Just as a particular thing must be situated in many contexts to see whether and how it acts and reacts, so also a Form must be related to other Forms to see whether relations (logical or metaphysical) will issue from such juxtaposition. This implication anticipates the blending of the Forms, a conspicuous concern in the *Sophist*. Not all Forms will blend with one another, just as not all things will actively or passively relate to other things. But to determine the nature of a Form or a particular kind of thing, the entity in question must be subjected to concentrated study—logical and metaphysical analysis for Forms, empirical scrutiny culminating in formal specification, or division, for kinds of particulars.

Nature and Division

Implications from the theory of nature described above are essential to interpreting division.[6]

1. According to Socrates, the subject of division is divided in harmony with its natural joints. Thus, since the differentiation of parts is controlled solely by the nature of the thing, there is no reason to expect a genus-species arrangement of the Forms comprising that nature. Furthermore, there is no indication whatsoever that division must proceed dichotomously, as recommended in the *Sophist* and *Statesman*. There will be as many cuts in dividing the thing as dictated by the natural unity of the thing divided. Apparently then the Forms coexist

with each other, but not as species in relation to species, since this suggests that the collected Form subject to division was a genus.

2. It has been argued here that division of a Form produces a Form, not a class term with properties perhaps other than those of Forms in the canonic sense. The principal Form analyzed in Socrates' first speech is *hubris*. Now at 238a, *hubris* is said to have many Forms and many parts. Clearly then the relation between the multiplicity of Forms in *hubris* and *hubris* itself is not the same as the relation between the multiciplicity of parts in *hubris* and *hubris* itself. Thus, a Form of *hubris* must differ from a part of *hubris*.

In the first speech, *hubris* is divided into gluttony, drunkenness, and the other types of excess desire (238b). These types are Forms of *hubris*, since they give their names to those who have these excesses— e.g., an individual who is a glutton is named glutton because that person partakes of the Form gluttony. Thus, the distinction between Form and part concerns the perspective taken on division. A Form divided produces other Forms, but these Forms as results of division are parts of the Form so divided. Gluttony therefore is both a part (of *hubris*) and a Form (exhibiting the same properties as *hubris*); and *hubris* has many Forms and many parts as the source of such divisions.

Another example of a part of a Form appears at 266a, when Socrates refers to the left-hand part (μέρος) of madness. In this case, the parts of madness are indicated by the "left-" and "right-" designation; but the parts as such denote Forms. Thus, the left-hand division of madness refers to a part of madness; but *hubris* (i.e., the left-hand part of madness) refers to a Form of madness. In this case then, *hubris* is a part of madness if considered as the left-hand side of madness; but *hubris* itself is a Form having its own nature and capable of being divided into other Forms.[7]

3. If a Form has both Forms and parts, then how is the unity of the Form preserved? The subject to be divided must be one thing while being divided into its constituent Forms. If, however, division of a Form according to its natural joints produces parts that are themselves Forms, then the notion of nature becomes even more complex, since it

must encompass the unity of an entity with metaphysically distinct components (i.e., Forms and parts).

This sense of unity helps clarify some questions concerning the active/passive phase of the method. For example, if a thing is complex, i.e., composed of multiple Forms, does each constituent Form have distinctive active and passive characteristics or only the thing as a unity, so that the different Forms constituting that thing blend, establishing the relevant active and passive properties for the thing as a whole?

It seems that for some natures, each constitutive Form has its own active and passive considerations. Thus, the arm of a human being will act and be acted upon in ways which differ in some respects from any other part of the body placed in similar situations. However, if the body as a whole has active and passive considerations which differ from those of any one (or several) of the parts of the body, then unity again becomes crucial. Only by seeing a complex thing as a unity can the properties of that thing as one thing be determined.

In view of this aspect concerning nature, it may be noted that the first hypothesis of the first deduction of the *Parmenides* examines whether part and whole apply to unity (137c–d). If complexity, however it should be understood, implies parts, then this hypothesis of the *Parmenides* is directed at the same aspect of the thing as the initial characterization of a thing's nature in the *Phaedrus*. The subsequent topics pursued in the *Parmenides*—e.g., limit/unlimited, shape, motion/rest, same/different, equal/unequal, older/younger/same age—are also extremely general. But these categories are all ways, spanning a variety of contexts, a thing can act or be acted upon.

Furthermore, whereas the *Phaedrus* assumes that natures exist, presupposing that unity exists as essential to nature, the *Parmenides* examines the consequences both if unity exists and if it does not. From this standpoint, the promulgation of a theory of natures in the *Phaedrus* is simply "high-minded speculation," unbuttressed by discursive justification. The *Parmenides* addresses this point by considering what would follow if unity (and nature as a kind of unity) does not exist. In this respect, the *Phaedrus* and the *Parmenides* are, recalling Cornford's image, very near neighbors indeed, with part of the former's implied metaphysics an explicit concern of the latter. The *Parmenides* is, in a sense, an extended commentary on the theory of natures in the *Phaedrus*. The fact that individual arguments advanced under a given category in the *Parmenides* may or may not be valid does not tell against this application. An appeal to nature—and its resident sense of unity—involves *aporiae* which must be analyzed before division with respect to acting and being acted upon can proceed. Determining a thing's natural joints is, as the *Parmenides* forcefully demonstrates, an extremely complex matter.

4. In the final summary of the method of division, Socrates asserts that the thing must be divided exhaustively (277b). The relevance of this condition emerges in the division of madness in the palinode, since there may be other types of madness—e.g., Ares as the inspiring deity for a type of madness found only in combat (reflected in the idiom "he fought like a man possessed").

The rationale for appealing to exhaustivity is clear; if the subject were not so divided, then the nature of the subject remains partially undefined. The indeterminate residue could then affect the accuracy of whatever portion of the nature has been divided.

The appeal to exhaustibility is a limit condition; as such, it represents an ideal which may never be realized in practice. But the doctrine of natures establishes a set of factors from which this possibility may be deduced. For if the ways a thing acts and is acted upon can be determined in all respects, i.e., in a context circumscribed by totality, then it is theoretically possible to determine all the Forms constituting that thing. That exhaustiveness is crucial for division is attested to by the fact that this condition is specified in both the *Sophist* (253d–e) and *Statesman* (287c). The theory of natures in the *Phaedrus* provides this context, with its implied appeal to totality in determining how a thing acts and is acted upon.

5. Division according to a thing's nature does not always produce a neutral balance of members. Thus, e.g., *hubris* (as the ground of left-handed love) and *mania* represent the left- and right-hand joints of

paranoia. But there is also a valuational aspect to this division; just as the right-hand side of the body is usually privileged in terms of overall control, so also the right-hand side of *paranoia* is higher than the left-hand side. This valuational component also emerged in the palinode's division of madness when Socrates said that love was the best of the four kinds of madness identified in that division.

It appears that division is not always "value-neutral." But how are these evaluations determined? The point is not addressed in the *Phaedrus*, but there is an implied consequentialist standard. Thus love is a better Form of madness because its proper employment produces the highest degree of human happiness, thereby becoming more valuable than other Forms of madness. However, a metaphysical dimension is also available for grounding such evaluations. For if the good is present to all the Forms, then it is possible that a given division is good or not good (or displays some degree of goodness). That love is the best Form of madness can be justified on the basis of how it better displays the good than any other division of madness.

There are, however, obvious problems with this implication. If, for example, every division has a penumbra of the good, then all divisions are in some sense good; it would be difficult therefore to determine, from the standpoint of the good as such, how one division was better than another. The problem appears to be one of establishing criteria for determining when division results in such evaluations, given that these results derive from an ultimate metaphysical source. This implication is particularly crucial since it intimately connects collection and division with the good. The question then arises whether the good, with its suffused yet pervasive presence in the *Phaedrus'* metaphysics, also animates the more prosaic refinements of collection and division developed in later dialogues.

NOTES

Introduction

1. F. M. Cornford, *Plato and Parmenides* (London: Routledge & Kegan Paul, 1939), p. 64.

2. In commenting on *Phaedrus* 242c8–d, C. J. Rowe notes, without elaboration, that Plato paraphrases this poem by Ibycus in the *Parmenides*. See *Plato: Phaedrus*, translation and commentary by C. J. Rowe (Wiltshire: Aris & Phillips Ltd., 1988). p. 166.

Chapter 1 (227a–237b)

1. The dramatic function of Phaedrus becomes evident only if his character is allowed to reveal itself during the conversation (the approach adopted in this study). Thus, Charles Griswold excoriates Phaedrus and fails to appreciate what Socrates sees in him—Charles L. Griswold, *Self-knowledge in Plato's Phaedrus* (New Haven: Yale University Press, 1986), pp. 25, 158. A more balanced account of Phaedrus' character may be found in G. R. F. Ferrari, *Listening to the Cicadas; A Study of Plato's Phaedrus* (Cambridge: Cambridge University Press, 1987), pp. 4–9, 39, 229. Martha Nussbaum also has considerable sympathy for Phaedrus' virtues. See chapter 7 of her *The Fragility of Goodness* (Cambridge: Cambridge University Pres, 1986), passim. See also G. J. De Vries, *A Commentary on the Phaedrus of Plato* (Amsterdam: Adolf M. Hakkert, 1969), pp. 5–6.

2. For discussion of these rites, see I. M. Linforth, "The Corybantic Rites in Plato," *University of California Publications in Classical Philology* 13 (1946): 121–62.

3. See also the detailed description of the location by the Ilissus in W. H.

293

Thompson, *The Phaedrus of Plato* (London: Wittaker & Co., 1868) p. 10. For additional discussion of the setting, see Griswold, pp. 33–6. Also relevant are the following: Ferrari, pp. 16–21; R. E. Wycherley, "The Scene of Plato's *Phaidros*," *Phoenix* 17 (1963): 88–98; Kenneth Dorter, "Imagery and Philosophy in Plato's *Phaedrus*," *Journal of the History of Philosophy* 9 (1971): 279–88; and A. Philip, "Récurrences thématiques et topologie dans le *Phèdre* de Platon," *Revue de métaphysique et de morale* 86 (1981): 452–76.

    4. R. Hackforth, *Plato's Phaedrus* (Cambridge: Cambridge University Press, 1952), p. 26; W. J. Verdenius, "Note on Plato's *Phaedrus*," *Mnemosyne* 4 (1955), p. 268. (Unless otherwise indicted, all subsequent references to Hackforth are to his *Phaedrus* translation and commentary.)

    5. For other interpretations of the Boreas myth, see Léon Robin, *Phèdre, Platon: Oeuvres completes*. Vol. III, Pt. 3 (Paris: 1933), p. 6, n1; Hackforth, p. 26; see also Griswold, pp. 36–44.

    6. For additional commentary on the Typhon, see Ronna Burger, *Plato's Phaedrus: A Defense on a Philosophic Art of Writing* (Tuscaloosa: University of Alabama Press, 1980), p. 129, n25; also Griswold, pp. 39–41.

    7. De Vries (p. 57) discusses the occasions when Socrates did leave the city.

    8. For discussion of the authenticity of the speech attributed to Lysias, see Hackforth, pp. 16–8, and Paul Friedländer, *Plato*. Vol. 3 (Princeton: Princeton University Press, 1969), p. 510, n5. Rowe (note) pp. 142–5, is also helpful.

    9. See Robin, Notice, pp. 64–8, who asserts that the speech is ordered into four main sections.

    10. For different perspectives on the import of Lysias' speech, see Stanley Rosen, "The Non-lover in Plato's *Phaedrus*," *Man and World* 2 (1969), pp. 432–6; Griswold, pp. 45–51; Ferrari, pp. 88–95; and Nussbaum, *Fragility*, pp. 205–8.

    11. Griswold (p. 254, n5) agrees with the ascription of irony. See also De Vries, p. 75. But cf. Robin, Notice p. 31, who sees the references as anticipations of Socrates' second speech.

    12. For other explanations of Socrates' covered head, see De Vries, p. 82; Burger, p. 134, n7; Griswold pp. 55–6.

    13. See also Griswold's interpretation of Socrates' shame, pp. 56–7.

Chapter 2 (237b–244a)

    1. For discussion of the Lygians, see De Vries, p. 82.

    2. Since Socrates will assess his first speech as "sinful," Hackforth (p.

37) denies that the Muses truly inspire this speech, presumably because he does not understand how the Muses could inspire a sinful product. Hackforth does not see the ascending scale of inspiration underlying the speeches in the *Phaedrus*; thus he could not envision the Muses to be only partially correct and superseded by a higher type of inspiration. See also Burger (p. 32) for the various sources Socrates identifies as causing his first speech.

3. For other interpretations of *muthos* in this context, see Robin, p. 18; Hackforth, p. 50; De Vries, p. 103.

4. Commentators typically do not interpret much of the detail of Socrates' first speech as exemplifying collection and division, but when, at 265d, Socrates says that his two speeches "by chance" illustrated collection and division, he intends that more of the speech has been structured in this way than the particular examples he cites at that point. My discussion shows some of this structure (including the importance of the doctrine of natures in this regard).

5. A metaphysical perspective denied by De Vries (p. 84), who would translate *idea* with some "vague" and "nonphilosophical" terms.

6. For commentary on the notion of parts, see the Epilogue.

7. The "popular" reading of these terms is held by De Vries, p. 99, and Verdenius, p. 274. Griswold (p. 63) describes the introduction of the terms as "another step forward in developing a vocabulary of self-knowledge," but he does not pursue any metaphysical implications.

8. For De Vries (p. 100), it is "more likely" Socrates had a proverb in mind with the same import as the poetry he apparently creates; for Thompson (p. 34), the line is doubtless Plato's.

9. A more direct allusion to the *Symposium* will appear later in the *Phaedrus*—see ch 9.

10. For an interpretation of the *Phaedo* emphasizing the importance of mind and the good to the metaphysics developed in that dialogue, see my *Myth and Metaphysics in Plato's Phaedo* (Susquehanna: Susquehanna University Press, 1989), esp. ch 8.

11. Burger (pp. 41–3) notes the connection between the appeal to Simmias and the *Phaedo*, but without drawing the implications made above. See also Paul Friedländer, *Plato*. Vol. 3, p. 220.

12. For commentary on the function of life in the final proof for the immortality of soul in the *Phaedo*, see *Myth and Metaphysics in Plato's Phaedo*, ch 11. Cherniss endorses the relevance of life in this proof in interpreting the account of soul's immortality in the palinode (245c–246a). See Harold Cher-

niss, *Aristotle's Criticism of Plato and the Academy.* Vol. 1. (Baltimore: John Hopkins University Press, 1944), p. 436.

13. Cf. De Vries, p. 110.

14. Sources on this point include Hackforth, p. 53; and Robin, pp. 29–30.

15. For discussion of this point, see Griswold, p. 21.

16. Griswold (p. 72) has also noted that the first three kinds of madness are represented in this interlude.

Chapter 3 (244a–247c)

1. For Thompson, p. 39, all proper names are significant; but cf. De Vries, pp. 113–4, and Rowe, p. 171, both of whom have reservations on this point. See also Nussbaum, p 211 (and pp. 472–3, n23).

2. As Socrates notes elsewhere (with, perhaps, tongue in cheek), even a very slight permutation of a word's letters will sometimes give an opposite sense (*Cratylus*, 418b).

3. Rowe (pp. 170–1) takes both etymologies to be "deliberately fanciful." For another interpretation of the purpose of this etymologizing, see Ferrari, pp. 114–7 (and p. 257, n9).

4. For additional discussion of this type of madness, see I. M. Linforth, "Telestic Madness in Plato, *Phaedrus* 244DE," *University of California Publications in Classical Philology* 13 (1946): 163–72.

5. For a useful summary of questions and problems, both philosophical and philological, pertaining to this argument, see T. M. Robinson, "The Argument for Immortality in Plato's *Phaedrus*." In *Essays in Ancient Greek Philosophy*, eds. J. Anton and G. Kustos (Albany: State University of New York Press, 1971): 345–53. For other interpretations of the argument, see Griswold, pp. 78–87; and Ferrari, pp. 123–5.

6. This interpretation of the metaphysics underlying the structure of the palinode will be argued in greater detail in chapter 9.

7. R. S. Bluck, *Plato Phaedo* (New York: Bobbs-Merrill, 1955), pp. 31–2, n4.

8. But compare *Timaeus* 34c, which claims that the demiurge created soul older than body (suggesting that soul has a point of origin).

9. Representative recent sources endorsing the tripartite character of

soul as determined in the *Republic* include: Rowe, p. 177, and (with reservations) Griswold, p. 94 and Ferrari, pp. 200–1 (also p. 275, n92).

10. See also Verdenius, p. 277, and De Vries, pp. 126–7 (and sources cited).

11. This concerted emphasis on the good should be noted in view of the dominant opinion that the good does not appear in the palinode (Cf. e.g., Martha C. Nussbaum, " 'This Story Isn't True': Poetry, Goodness, and Understanding in Plato's *Phaedrus*" in *Plato on Beauty, Wisdom, and the Arts*, eds. J. M. E. Moravcsik and P. Temko (Totowa: Rowman and Littlefield, 1982, p. 122, n32; and Griswold, p. 86. See also below, chap. 5, n11.

12. The purpose of Socrates' conclusion here has not always been understood. Thus, Martha Nussbaum asserts that "we are even told that our very ideas of the divine life and the divine intellect are themselves human fictions, based on the experience of being confined within the limits of a human way of life" ("Story," p. 110). To support her claim, Nussbaum translates 246c–d and then concludes:

> We speak only of what we have, as humans, seen and thought. We make up gods that look like us ("Story," p. 111).

What Nussbaum does not say about 246c–d is that it concludes a discussion, clearly demarcated, which Socrates begins by asserting that he must try to say "how a living being is called mortal or immortal." As we have seen, this problem, stated at 246b, is immediately followed by Socrates' description of the cosmic scope of soul's activity in all its forms. Now soul makes a being exist as living. Thus, the problem posed at 246b is not about existence; it is about the reliability of discourse concerning two different types of existing things. For Socrates, both gods and humans are "living beings." A mortal living being is called mortal by virtue of being a compound of body and soul (246c). By contrast, immortal is said without an account established by reasoning—we imagine god to be an immortal living thing having soul and body, these things joined together for all time. Thus we do not make up the existence of a god, just as we do not "make up" the existence of a mortal living being. What we make up is god having a body and soul joined together for all time. What we do not know or adequately understand is not whether the gods exist, but how to render divine existence—formed as it is entirely by vision of the realities (cf. 249c)—intelligible to our limited cognitive processes. Plato is therefore not guilty of the mammoth impiety ascribed to him by Nussbaum.

(See also the related discussion in "Recollection: The One and the Many" in chapter 4 below.)

13. Griswold obviates this problem by denying that the chariot ever appears in the myth. See p. 93 (also p. 262, n28).

14. Ferrari understands human soul to be "prone" to corruption (p. 276, n98), but apparently he does not see the intimacy between this propensity and matter; thus, he asserts (p. 128) that it is "merely contingent" that soul sustains "our natural cosmos."

Chapter 4 (247c–250d)

1. For discussion on translating this phrase, see John Sallis, *Being and Logos; The Way of Platonic Dialogue* (Pittsburgh: Duquesne University Press, 1975), pp. 144–5.

2. Rowe, p. 180, has also observed this apparent peculiarity.

3. Martha Nussbaum's interpretation of this passage is crucial for her inclusion of the *Phaedrus* as a text illustrating "the fragility of goodness." But it is also fundamentally misconceived. Here is her main contention:

> We are told that all other souls follow with difficulty, held back by the nature of their horses. Although the best souls do get their heads above the rim, they experience so much trouble that their vision is disturbed. "They scarcely discern the things that are" (248a5). The Greek here is ambiguous, permitting either the interpretation that they succeed in getting a full view, though with difficulty, or the interpretation that they get only a very restricted and blurred sort of view; but later evidence clinches the case in favor of the latter interpretation, for "all" are said to return "imperfect (*ateleis*) in the contemplation of being," and all are fed with the "food of opinion," instead of the nectar and ambrosia of the gods (248b).

Nussbaum then concludes by asserting that since the soul of the future philosopher saw only "the most" and is never said to have seen "all," or to have seen "fully," then [no] human soul has had the full divine vision" and "all are nourished with opinion" ("Story," pp. 109–10).

But consider the contrast Socrates draws at 248b between those souls scarcely seeing the realities and those souls seeing some realities and not others. Both types of soul comprise the class of best soul, since Socrates says that a soul following deity and seeing "any" of the realities will be free from harm until the next period (248ᴄ). Thus, whether a soul sees all, some, or only one of the realities, it will be safe during the period it follows a god and beholds true reality beyond the heavens.

The contrast between the two classes of best souls shows, by implication, what "scarcely" must mean. For if one class sees some of the realities and not others, then the other class must see *all* the realities. If they did not, there would be no real contrast between the two types of best soul, since all souls in the best class would see only some of the realities and not others. But if so, then Socrates could have said of both classes of soul that "they see some things but not others."

On this interpretation, the ambiguous "scarcely" must qualify the way all the realities are seen, not how many are seen. But recall that the mere fact that soul sees any of the realities—however obscurely they may be seen—provides these souls with a continued safe journey with a deity. Nussbaum seems to think that if the soul of the philosopher does not see all the realities a god sees and as clearly as the divine vision, the philosopher sees no reality whatsoever and is doomed to dine on nothing but opinion. But she has misunderstood the careful demarcations in types of soul and has failed to connect these demarcations with relevant passages occurring shortly afterwards in the myth.

This use of *mogis* is finely glossed in the *Republic*, Book VII. Socrates is telling Glaucon about the import of the allegory of the cave, and he says "that in the region of the known the last thing to be seen and hardly [*mogis*] seen is the idea of good, and that when seen it must needs point us to the conclusion that this is indeed the cause for all things of all that is right and beautiful, giving birth in the visible world to light, and the author of light and itself in the intelligible world being the authentic source of truth and reason, and that anyone who is to act wisely in private or pubic *must have caught sight of this*" (517b–c—my italics; Shorey's translation). It is clear here that "scarcely" refers to the actual apprehension of the idea of the good, but not in a way that will give the apprehender a complete vision of that idea. If the idea of the good can be seen, then it is reasonable to believe that so can all other less accessible ideas.

Nussbaum defends consigning the souls of philosophers to nourishment solely on opinion as follows:

> It is barely possible that the "all" here refers only to those who did not get heads up over the rim. But in this case the story is strangely incomplete: We are never told how the philosophical souls return, or how they are nourished. ("Story," p. 123, n41).

However, it is essential that this "all" refers just to those souls. If it did not, then the souls mentioned at 248b4 would get their heads up over the rim and become, at the very least, souls having seen some realities and not others. There would then be no difference between the lower level of best soul and the level of soul nourished solely on opinion, rendering otoise Socrates' careful distinction between them.

Consider now the two problems Nussbaum has posed. First, the fact that we are not told how the philosophical souls are nourished is problematic only if it is true that these souls are where Nussbaum has consigned them. For if they are not, then the souls of future philosophers are fed just as are the souls of the gods—on "mind and pure knowledge" (247d). And, in fact, Socrates knows full well that some nondivine souls can receive this nourishment—that is why, at the beginning of his description of divine nourishment, he adds parenthetically that this nourishment also fulfills "the intellect of every soul capable of so receiving it" (247d). Socrates is anticipating the division of soul into the two types of best soul; and souls in these classes see the same kind of things as the gods see (only to a diminished degree, i.e., the scarcely already discussed).

As for the first problem, the reason we are not told how the philosophical souls return is, simply, that they do not return—as long as they continue to see at least some of the realities. If they do not so continue, then they fall beneath the rim and feed on opinion, as do all other nonphilosophical souls, until such time as they manage, while in the company of a god (i.e., Zeus), to poke their heads above the rim again and see the realities. The myth is straightforward on this point.

Nussbaum's misunderstanding of this passage leads to equally serious misreadings of the method of collection and division as well as the function of happiness with respect to dialectic. See the following notes for discussion: n7 below; ch5, n12; ch7, n8; ch9, n2.

4. Other sources agreeing with Hackforth on this point include De Vries, p. 143 and Rowe p. 181. See also n7 below.

5. For attempts to explain the ordering of the hierarchy of lives, see Hackforth, pp. 83–4, and Rowe, p. 181.

6. For discussion of soul's fall and reincarnation, see R. S. Bluck, "The *Phaedrus* and Reincarnation," *American Journal of Philology* 79 (1958): 156–64 and D. D. McGibbon, "The Fall of the Soul in Plato's *Phaedrus*," *Classical Quarterly* n.s. 14 (1964): 56–63. See also Ferrari, pp. 133–9.

7. For Nussbaum, certain kinds of erotic relationships "are argued to be fundamental to psychological development and an important component of the best human life" (*Fragility*, 201). There is, however, no argument to this effect in the *Phaedrus*. At 251a, Socrates will describe the experience of one who is "newly initiated" when he sees "a godlike face or form that well recalls beauty." Thus, what strikes the lover is the fact that this individual, the future beloved, is an image of beauty, not that the beloved is a human being. with a complex psychology and diverse personal history. This point is important because it shows that the lover is attracted to an instance of beauty as an earthly instance of the Form beauty—the most palpable Form, as Socrates says (250e)—thereby allowing the lover entry into the radiance and happiness of experiencing true reality by connecting the experience of an instance of true beauty to as many other realities as his soul beheld, ultimately to all realities if soul saw all realities. This instance of beauty may be a beautiful human—but nowhere does Socrates say that it must be.

As additional evidence, consider 249a, Socrates' description of the highest kind of human soul, the members of which can regain their wings after the third period of a thousand years (rather than ten such periods) and "go their way." Nussbaum quotes this passage and says: "Here it makes no difference whether we refer to the highest human type as 'the one who philosophizes without guile' or 'the one who pursues the love of a boy along with philosophy' (249A)" (*Fragility*, p. 220). But, as we have just seen, it makes an essential difference to distinguish between these two types. The first type genuinely, honestly—without guile of any sort—loves wisdom wherever it may be found, i.e., in whatever images of true reality might be discernible to his soul, whether they be images of beauty, goodness, justice, etc. This distinction establishes the real possibility that the philosopher could see wisdom as clearly as anyone can see it (indeed, perhaps better) without having to pursue that vision with another human being (whether beautiful or otherwise). If so, then Nussbaum is incorrect to claim that the *Phaedrus* "argues" the essential need for erotic relationships. Such relationships are found in the highest class of human beings, but they are not necessary for membership in that class and they are not necessary for the successful pursuit of philosophy.

Consider also a remark by Nussbaum in a different context:

Everything we know about Socrates outside of this dialogue testifies that he never did, in fact, go mad with *eros*. The passion and wonder of his pupils were answered with a coolly ironic distancing (*Fragility*, p. 232).

Why did Socrates not revel in the rapture of *eros*? Precisely because
Socrates was a philosopher of the first type, i.e., someone who did not need
the company of a young man in order to philosophize. True enough, Socrates was powerfully moved by human beauty. But he was also powerfully
moved by natural beauty, as he clearly shows in his rapturous description
of the locale by the Ilissus (230b). But what Socrates truly loved was wisdom, and to achieve that end he would talk to anyone, whether that individual was Adonis-like in figure or someone less ideal in physical appearance.
Other individuals inclined toward philosophy would, however, doubtless require the other approach. Hence, in part, the *Phaedrus*. Cf. Ferrari,
pp. 149–50, on whether the philosopher must love a human being to be a
philosopher.

8. A contrast noted by Rowe, p. 183.

9. This reading of Phaedrus' character is additional evidence against the
severe judgment of Griswold (cf. ch1, n1).

10. And N. Gulley concurs—see Norman Gulley, *Plato's Theory of
Knowledge* (London: Methuen, 1962), p. 124.

11. The interpretation of the "brightness" of beauty's earthly instances
has aroused dispute concerning whether Plato intends these instances to
resemble more closely the Form beauty or whether the point is that their
appearance is more immediately evident. Ferrari disagrees with both interpretations (pp. 142ff). He notes that "Socrates' suggestion that not only
are the likenesses of beauty brighter, but even the Form of beauty shone more
brightly than the other Forms" allows the inference that since "beauty in this
world has the function of directing attention to the totality of values, its Form
might well be represented as illuminating all the others. . . ." (p. 264, n15;
cf. pp. 262–3, n5). Ferrari is well on the way to seeing that the brightness of
beauty's instances reflects the brightness of the Form beauty, and that what
this means is that beauty, both as a Form and in its instances, is the most accessible reality for gaining entry to and integrating all other Forms within the
embrace of the good. Thus, the "brightness" does not concern the relation between instances of beauty and the Form beauty, but between the Form beauty
(including all instances of that Form) and the good. All Forms are illuminated by the good, but beauty can be seen in this way more readily than any
other Form.

12. An approach preferable to Thompson's who also attempts
such exegesis (pp. 59–60) but by appealing to passages in other dialogues.

Chapter 5 (250d–257b)

1. Lovers of beautiful things will find this premise congenial, particularly with respect to what beautiful art can convey about reality and truth. But insofar as this claim about beauty rests on an undefended assertion, it embodies a position requiring considerable analysis of its psychological and epistemological presuppositions. To note the essential link between beauty and the good only inaugurates such an analysis. See Ferrari, pp. 140–50.

2. The account given in this section is not intended to do justice to the complex psychology embedded in Socrates' mythic description of erotic desire. In this regard, Ferrari's discussion should be consulted (pp. 150–67), although it may be noted that he does not attempt to connect his analysis to the metaphysics underlying this segment of the myth. The metaphysics of love is crucial for determining the details in any psychological analysis of the lovers. (See, for example, ch4, n1 and n12 below on Martha Nussbaum's reading of the psychology of the lovers.)

3. Thompson, p. 66, Hackforth, p. 99, n3, and De Vries p. 159 agree, with varying degrees of certitude, that the lines are Platonic.

4. What the lover should say to the beloved to make him more Zeus-like is also discussed, with regard to Martha Nussbaum's interpretation, in ch7, n8.

5. It is important to see the different relations between the various gods and the reality beyond the heavens, since these differences affect the subsequent history of human souls when they behold reality while in company with the gods. For Nussbaum, "only the god-souls have a full and complete view of all the forms in the circuit, as they stand on the rim of the universe" and they alone have "the full divine vision" ("Story," p. 109). This seems to mean that all the gods see all the Forms. But there is evidence that this is not the case. First, the gods are ranked, with Zeus first and all the rest deployed into eleven squadrons (247a). How is this ranking determined? Consider 249c, when Socrates says that the vision of true reality is what makes the gods divine (a passage Nussbaum does not discuss). But if all the gods are divine only because of their vision of reality and Zeus is the leader of the gods, then presumably Zeus has seen more reality than any other deity. Second, when Socrates contrasts the lives of souls following Zeus and Ares, he begins by observing that all human souls act toward themselves and others in accordance with the nature of the god with whom they saw reality. But those following Zeus can "bear a heavier amount of the winged burden" than those following any other god. Furthermore, the souls who are the "servants of Ares" are prone to become murderous and self-destructive if wronged by a

mortal lover (252d). But if the gods are divine only by seeing reality, the suggestion is that serving a bellicose deity will lead humans to such flawed behavior just because that deity has a less extensive vision of reality than does Zeus.

This contrast between Zeus and Ares can be relevantly generalized. At 248d–e, Socrates listed a ranked series of types of life, ranging from the philosopher at the top to the tyrant at the bottom. Now if the philosopher is ranked first because the philosopher's soul has seen the most, then all other types of life are animated by souls having seen less than the soul of the philosopher. But all human souls see reality only in the company of a god (248c). It may then be inferred that all other human lives are ranked below the life of the philosopher because the souls of these humans accompanied gods who themselves saw less reality than Zeus, the deity leading the souls of future philosophers (250b). And since the order is ranked, from the first through ninth, then the gods leading souls at these consecutive levels may also be ranked according to the degree of vision each god experienced. The picture that emerges from these considerations is a continuum of divine nourishment defined by degrees of more and less depending on the nature of the individual deity, rather than, as Nussbaum seems to understand it, a full and complete complement of reality for each and every god.

For discussion of the possibility that all souls have the capacity to become philosophers, see M. Dyson, "Zeus and Philosophy in the Myth in Plato's *Phaedrus*," *Classical Quarterly* 32 (1982): 307–11.

6. Hackforth, p. 101, notes the presence of love among all the classes lower than the philosopher, adding that such love will be "defective." But this is so only in comparison to the capacity for love defining the souls of philosophers. For other types of soul, love may well be perfect in the sense that the actions of lover and beloved will meet the standards set by the reduced vision of reality possessing these types of soul. Thus, the poet will not love to the extent that the philosopher will love, but only because the soul of the poet beheld less reality than the soul of the philosopher. See comments of John M. Rist, *Eros and Psyche; Studies in Plato, Plotinus, and Origen* (Toronto: University of Toronto Press, 1964), p. 19. See also n14 below.

7. The connection between the good and evil horses and the *idea* of the first speech has also been noted by Griswold, p. 96.

8. Thompson (p. 72) and Hackforth (p. 103, n1) deny that "true opinion" should be taken in a technical Platonic sense; De Vries (p. 166) suggests translating the term as "general renown."

9. See Ferrari, p. 273, n80) for another explanation of the absence of a description of the charioteer.

10. Once again, my account of this passage will emphasize the metaphysical dimension underlying the complex psychological interaction between lover and beloved. For commentary from the latter perspective, see Ferrari, ch. 6, although the cautionary remark concerning the connection between metaphysics and psychology mentioned in n2 above should be recalled.

11. This passage is relevant to Nussbaum's denial that the good appears in the *Phaedrus*: "The absence of an ascent to a unitary vision of the good may be connected with the fact that the *Phaedrus* nowhere introduces the form of the good, nor says that the good is something unitary." Furthermore, the "forms appear, even by the gods, to be seen one by one, without the sort of overall ordering that the Form of the Good would provide" ("Story," p. 122, n2). Apparently Nussbaum discounts the passage at 246e where Socrates characterizes the divine as "beauty, wisdom, goodness (*agathon*) and all such things." Beauty is designated as a Form at 250b; if therefore goodness is metaphysically parallel to beauty and wisdom in this passage, then Socrates has introduced "the form of the good," and in a context of considerable importance—it is named as one of the realities that makes the gods divine.

Furthermore, consider the fact that the intellect of the lover sees, via memory, the true nature of beauty, i.e., the Form beauty, but he sees it with modesty on a pedestal of chastity. Modesty and chastity are distinct from beauty—a distinction known all too well by soul's evil horse. But here, when soul's intellect is seeing the Form beauty, soul is also seeing a close intimacy between beauty and these other properties. There is the strong suggestion then that the two properties are, if not themselves Forms, then the appearances of Forms, as Socrates describes them at 250c. Thus if we follow the mythic image, beauty and modesty are not seen "one by one" (as Nussbaum describes soul's vision of all Forms); rather, they are seen with each other, the pair resting atop a pedestal representing chastity. Nussbaum has denied that "the overall ordering that the Form of the Good would provide" appears in the *Phaedrus*. But how then are we to account for the finely relevant ordering of the Forms beauty, modesty, and chastity for the intellect of the lover beholding the beloved and sorely tempted to satisfy the drive of soul's evil horse?

12. The guiding function of the intellect in the love of philosophers must be noted. Thus, Nussbaum has claimed that in the *Phaedrus* the "intellectual element," if alone and "itself by itself," will be "doomed to the niggardly life of mortal self-possession," and that it is not "necessary and sufficient for the

apprehension of truth and for correct choice" (*Fragility*, p. 222). But it is the intellect of the philosopher which alone has wings, putting the philosopher in constant touch with the realities (249c). It follows then, *contra* Nussbaum, that the intellect decides the destiny of the two lovers with respect to happiness, since the intellect is that part of soul that can recall the realities in their purity, the same realities that make the soul of the beloved godlike in the first place.

This error has important implications in several of Nussbaum's inferences describing how lover and beloved behave while loving. For example, Nussbaum says that

> Plato's lovers choose not to have intercourse with one another, even though they express their love regularly in physical caresses that stop short of this (cf. 255b)—because they feel that the extreme sensual stimulation involved in intercourse is incompatible with the preservation and awe for the other as a separate person. Appetite is curbed not by contemplative intellect, but by the demands of the passions that it has awakened (*Fragility*, p. 217).

As we have just seen, however, it is precisely what Nussbaum calls the "contemplative intellect" that must win out over the darker sides of soul in order to prevent this kind of intercourse. The passions, once aroused, will continue to demand what it is in their nature to demand. Furthermore, since the intellect, the best part of soul, is (for philosophers) in continuous touch with the realities, it is precisely in virtue of its "contemplative" phase that such self-control is achieved. Thus, if there is "preservation and awe" in this action, it is "for the other as a separate person" only to the extent that the other person shares in, and reciprocates, the lover's vision of the realities. The soul of the lover stands in awe of the realities and of a godlike image of those realities— not simply of the sheer presence of a particular human being as human.

13. H. L. Sinaiko suggests that the contemporary stigma against male homosexual love can be eliminated for the *Phaedrus* account of lovers because it is possible, and even illuminating, to "translate" the homosexual language of the three speeches into heterosexual terms and thus to think of the "beloved" as a "beautiful young woman." Sinaiko admits that this is a "violation" of the text. Furthermore, such interpretation has odd consequences if it is recalled that in the *Phaedrus*, true love for philosophical souls requires complete carnal abstinence. It would follow, e.g., that a husband and wife, both aspiring to be philosophers, must either abstain from sex or, if they did indulge their desires,

be barred from a degree of wisdom attainable on condition of abstinence. I suggest therefore that the temptation to reduce what is, for some, an odious aura of the *Phaedrus'* position be resisted. It is precisely the intensity of male-to-male eroticism which must controlled—yet cultivated—to orient such pairs of souls toward reality. It does not appear that the place of an equivalent heterosexual intensity for this philosophical program can be determined from the *Phaedrus* as it stands.

14. The description of the conduct between lover and beloved has engendered a sizable literature concerning the relation between Platonic love (in the sense developed in the *Phaedrus*) and a modern conception of the term. It may be noted that Plato's approach is to "cosmic Eros," a union of Eros and dialectic (the phrase is from Z. Diesendruck, *Struktur und Charakter des platonischen Phaedros* (Wein-Leipzig: W. Braumüller, 1927), p. 32). How "democratic" this approach can become, e.g., toward loving a person as a unique individual (with a medley of good and bad points), would not be easily determined. The question that seems most relevant to this concern is that even if a more personalistic type of love can be developed, what ultimate purpose will that love serve, especially if both lovers are philosophers? The issue then becomes whether personalistic love (however defined) is complete in itself or whether it too requires a more elevated approach to love. If the latter, then the *Phaedrus* account of love, for all its ostensible impersonality, may well be worth careful study.

Selected sources on this topic include: Gregory Vlastos, "The Individual as an Object of Love in Plato," in *Platonic Studies*. 2d ed. (Princeton: Princeton University Press, 1981): 3–42; A. H. Armstrong, "Platonic *eros* and Christian *agape*," *Downside Review* 82 (1961): 199–208; Drew Hyland, "*Eros, epithumia,* and *philia* in Plato," *Phronesis* 13 (1968): 32–46; L. A. Kosman, "Platonic Love," in *Facets of Plato's Philosophy.* Ed. W. Werkmeister. *Phronesis.* Suppl. vol. 2. (Assen: Van Gorcum, 1976): 53–69; A. W. Price, "Loving Persons Platonically," *Phronesis* 26 (1981): 25–34; G. Santas, "Passionate Platonic Love in the *Phaedrus,*" *Ancient Philosophy* 2 (1982): 105–14; David M. Halperin, "Platonic *Eros* and What Men Call Love," *Ancient Philosophy* 5 (1985): 161–204. See also Nussbaum, *Fragility,* ch7, *passim* and Ferrari's response to Vlastos, pp. 182–4.

15. Socrates' proposal is additional evidence that as far as he is concerned, Phaedrus has a soul that has seen "the most," i.e., it belongs to the highest class of human soul.

Chapter 6 (257b–262c)

1. Thompson, p. 87; Hackforth, p. 118; De Vries, p. 193. See also the discussions in Griswold, pp 165–8 and Ferrari, pp. 25–34. My account emphasizes the function of the cicadas (or the point of the cicada story) in connecting the inspiration for Socratic rhetoric on love with the inspiration to talk about that rhetoric in a way which recoups the metaphysical core of Socrates' two speeches.

2. See P. Frutiger, *Les Mythes de Platon*, (Paris: F. Alcan, 1930), p. 233.

3. Burger, p. 73.

4. Among recent interpreters, Griswold and, to a lesser degree, Ferrari posit an overly sharp separation between dialectic and rhetoric, and I suggest that this reading of the cicada story and its implications offered here more accurately portrays the relation between the two forms of discourse. See also the discussion of rhetoric in chapter 7.

5. The *Gorgias* (454e) distinguishes between two types of persuasion, one producing belief without knowledge, the other knowledge. This distinction is apparently no longer relevant to the *Phaedrus* approach to rhetoric. For more general discussion of persuasion in rhetoric, see George Kennedy, *The Art of Persuasion in Greece* (Princeton: Princeton University Press, 1963).

6. See also Thompson, p. 96, and Hackforth, p. 123, n3 for additional discussion of the Homeric allusions.

7. The need for rhetorical skill in mastering opposition is noted by Aristotle, *Rhetoric* 1355[a]12ff.

Chapter 7 (262c–266d)

1. Additional sources taking the dual to refer to all three speeches include: De Vries, p. 206; Griswold, p. 177; Ferrari, p. 61 (also pp. 244–5, n41). An interpretation similar to mine may be found in V. Tejera, "Irony and Allegory in the *Phaedrus*," *Philosophy and Rhetoric* 8 (1975): 71–87, esp. pp. 78–9; Rowe (p. 197) also argues against taking the dual to refer to all three speeches.

2. See Ferrari, pp. 45–59, on how Socrates' criticism of Lysias' speech does not reflect its distinctive subtlety (a point already noted by Thompson in his comments on 264 a–e).

3. See, for example, Griswold, p. 116.

4. Collection, as a separate phase of dialectic, will be discussed again in the Epilogue.

5. For Nussbaum, the "method of division is a method of analyzing and classifying our conceptions" ("Story," p. 111). This method contains "appeals to what, more comprehensively, we say and do, how we see things" ("Story," p. 112). Thus, the method "appears to be inseparable from the linguistic and interpretive practices of contingent mortal beings, their ways of structuring the world" ("Story," p. 112). The "godlike philosopher is now not the one who can give accounts of transcendent and stable forms, but one who can practice supremely well and seriously a method that, in one way or another, is the method on which our ordinary speech itself implicitly relies" ("Story," p. 113). In a word, the method of division is defined by "anthropocentrism" (*Fragility*, p. 474, n42).

Recall, however, 249e, where Socrates asserts that a human being must understand an *eidos* by collecting perceptions into a unity through reasoning and 249e, when it is stated as a "law of nature" that "every human soul has seen *ta onta*, otherwise it would not have entered into a human being." In the first passage, Socrates calls the Form an *eidos* because at this point he is describing what a soul must do after it animates a human being, i.e., it must deal with perceptions and it must collect these perceptions into a unity through reasoning. The account at 248e concerns what soul saw prior to animating a human being. At that point, there are no perceptions, and reasoning is not required—soul simply "sees" what is real.

Nussbaum claims that the method in the *Phaedrus* must concern itself with language, the way we talk. But at 249c, Socrates explicitly says that soul lifts itself above "what we now call being." Thus the proper object of knowledge exists in a way transcending the things we commonly talk about as being real. The same beclouding effect of language was already mentioned at 247e, when Socrates described knowledge of the Forms proper to the gods and any other soul capable of such vision. There he asserts that "true knowledge" does not have a beginning and does not vary, as does the kind of awareness associated with one of the other of "the things we now call beings." It is hardly likely then, when Socrates has turned his attention to a method for recouping that original metaphysical vision, that he will commend to philosophers a method which deals only with language and conceptions.

6. A description of himself in relation to collection and division repeated at *Philebus*, 16b.

7. But cf. Ronna Burger (p. 144, n39):

It is easier to understand Socrates' abstract analysis of the principles
of dialectics as a standard for evaluation of the claims of the rhetoricians than as an account of the way Socrates himself proceeds in conversation, or of the way in which the Platonic dialogue is constructed
as an imitation of Socratic conversation. The various accounts of the
principles of dialectics presented in several Platonic dialogues do not
seem to be identical with each other, insofar, perhaps, as each is implicitly colored by the context of the discussion in which it arises; at
the same time, however, it is never immediately obvious how each of
these formal and abstract analyses is exemplified in the conversation
it is presumably intended to clarify.

In response, it may be noted that although the various accounts of dialectic
in the dialogues may, if strung together serially, produce conflicting positions,
this type of global interpretation is not relevant to what Socrates means by
dialectic in a given dialogue, e.g., the *Phaedrus*. Also, although it may be
granted that the way Socrates applies the method to his own speeches in the
Phaedrus is not "immediately obvious" (witness all of Hackforth's misconceptions), the difficulty of application does not warrant giving up the attempt to re-
produce such application—the primary problem is following correctly the
directions Socrates himself provides. And, finally, the beginning of Burger's
remark carries the sense that because it is easier to apply Socrates' "abstract
analysis" of collection and division to, say, the speeches of other rhetoricians,
we may forego taking seriously what Socrates has explicitly said—i.e., that he
must practice this method in order to speak and to think. Such practice will involve Socrates in complex metaphysical issues, but these issues (which include those raised in the *Parmenides*) are much more fundamental and crucial
to human knowledge and happiness than whatever wisdom is gleaned by
evaluating the speeches of others through collection and division. Socrates
takes metaphysics seriously—this is one reason why he wants divine blessing
for the name he has given to the method for understanding and speaking truly
about reality.

8. Nussbaum comments on the first part of Socrates' summation of collection and division at 266b, but she omits mention of the last part, i.e., when Socrates says that whenever he thinks anyone can see something naturally collected
into unity and divided into many, he "follows him and walks in his footsteps as if
he were a god." The fact that Socrates is willing to abandon his own practice of
the method in order to follow someone who can use it better than he can shows
that when Socrates describes himself as a "lover" of the method, what he really

loves is the method. Thus Socrates is attracted to other human beings only insofar as they can assist him in revivifying his own vision of reality.

The relation between love and method has important implications for understanding the appropriate behavior between lover and beloved. Consider what Nussbaum has written on this point:

> If we ask what sort of understanding this is and what truths the lovers can tell, we get a complicated answer. No doubt they will know some general truths about characters of a certain type. But some of their truths may well be more particular and more like stories. And some of their knowledge of habits and ways may reveal itself not so much in speeches as in the intuitive understanding of how to act toward the other person, how to teach, how to respond, how to limit oneself (*Fragility*, p. 218).

Does Socrates ever give any indication what lover and beloved say to one another? First of all, the description of lover and beloved pertains to souls who are followers of Zeus (250b) and who have seen many of the realities beyond the heavens (251a). Now followers of Zeus "seek for one of philosophical and lordly nature, and when they find and love him, they do all they can to give him such a character" (252e). But to give the beloved a Zeus-like character is to make the beloved see, as far as humanly possible, what Zeus saw. Now Zeus is the leader of the gods (246e). And what makes all the gods divine is beauty, goodness, wisdom and all such things (246e). It follows then that giving the beloved a Zeus-like character will be educating the beloved in precisely those things that have made Zeus Zeus, and that have made the soul of the beloved (as well the soul of the lover) a follower of Zeus—beauty, goodness, wisdom, and all such things. Thus, lover and beloved will not tell story-like accounts to one another (at least not *qua* philosophical lovers); nor will they enter into discussion over "intuitive understandings" of how they can get along better with each other by being more open, less selfish, more caring, etc. What they will talk about are precisely the realities that have attracted them to each other in the first place—beauty, wisdom, goodness, and all such things. They will, in short, philosophize. And from this discussion will come happiness.

Nussbaum also asserts that the beloved is valued "as a separate being with his or her own self-moving soul—not as something to be held, trapped, or bound by any philosophical *technē*" (*Fragility*, p. 218). This denial is aimed at collection and division, and the point seems to be that this method has no place in the loving activity of the lovers toward each other. But recall that Socrates has said that he is a "lover" of these collections and divisions. And he also says why he loves these exercises in *technē*—so that he can speak and think (266b). If therefore Socrates were to love another person, then any discourse Socrates would direct to that individual would hardly eschew this method—indeed, if the method is essential for arriving at truth, then Socrates' discourse would be carefully informed by this very method because only in this way would what is said between lovers aid the beloved to become truly Zeus-like.

Chapter 8 (266d–274b)

1. For historical background of rhetorical figures, see Hackforth, pp. 139–40; De Vries, p. 233; Kennedy, pp. 54ff. Aristotle notes that the existing records of rhetoricians preserved only a small portion of their art (*Rhetoric*, 1354a3).

2. Rowe (p. 205) translates speculation (μετεωρολογίας) as "babbling" (following De Vries, p. 233), suggesting (if not implying) that he would not take what is said to be philosophically relevant, much less crucial. Burger would translate "idle talk and meteorologizing about nature." She adds:

> With this ironic description of Periclean rhetoric and its theoretical foundations, Socrates seems to suggest that the fitting teacher of "the truly rhetorical and persuasive art" would have to exhibit the combination of an interest in the political power of persuasion with an interest in the study of nature. Socrates himself, who rejects both these aims and claims to possess only knowledge of his own ignorance [here Burger cites *Apology* 18b–c, 19b–c, 23b] necessarily brings into question the teachability of this true art of persuasion.

Although Socrates does say he knows only his own ignorance in the *Apology* texts Burger cites, he also claims to understand about the art of love (*Symposium*, 177e). And since Socrates has been the mouthpiece of speculation about the nature of love in the palinode, as well as avowedly asserting that he is a "lover" of collection and division as integral to dialectic, there is no reason whatsoever to bring "into question the teachability of this true art of persuasion." It is, in fact, a great art; as such, it will require speculation. But the Socratic palinode, both in its content and its rhetorical form, has given us a model for such speculation, as we shall see.

3. Translating, with De Vries, "lack of mind" (not Hackforth's "folly") to preserve the essential opposition in this context.

4. See Hackforth, p. 150–1, on the accuracy of Plato's description of Anaxagoras in this context. See also Rowe, pp. 204–5.

5. The fragment appears in G. S. Kirk and J. E. Raven, *The Presocratic Philosophers* (Cambridge: Cambridge University Press, 1957), pp. 372–3.

6. Sources agreeing with Hackforth on this meaning of "whole" include Verdenius, p. 286; De Vries, pp. 234–5; Ferrari, p. 76 (also 247–8).

7. See P. Kucharski, "La 'methode d'Hippocrates' dans le *Phèdre*," *Revue des études Grecques* 52 (1939): 301–57; R. Joly, "La question Hippocratique et le témoignage de *Phédre*," *Revue des études Grecques* 74 (1961): 69–92; J. Mansfield, "Plato and the Method of Hippocrates," *Greek, Roman and Byzantine Studies* 21 (1980): 341–62.

8. Hippocrates, *Ancient Medicine*, XIII.

9. Hippocrates, *Ancient Medicine*, XX, XXIV.

10. A view of Trevaskis, p. 124, seconded by De Vries, p. 238.

11. An exposition and critique of the doctrine of natures is undertaken in the Epilogue.

12. See, e.g., these remarks by Griswold (p. 221), who contends that the Platonic dialogues

> announce their deeper message only to those readers able enough to find it. To those unsuited to philosophizing, the Platonic dialogues are closed books.

One could infer from this principle that any interpretation of the *Phaedrus* which differed from Griswold's would render its author a nonphilosopher. And, more generally, those authors who write about Plato steadfastly adhering to the tenet that Socrates frequently means something other than what he says (with, in the context of this study, the corollary that Plato did not really believe in the importance of metaphysics, of thinking and speaking about "the things that are") tend either to translate ostensibly metaphysical claims into some other arena of significance or simply to ignore them. (See also ch9, n6). For discussion (with documentation) of irony in Plato, see Griswold, pp. 9–16.

Chapter 9 (274b–279c)

1. For additional commentary on Thamos' prophecy, see the Excursus in Burger's monograph, pp. 109–14; Griswold, pp. 202–7; and Ferrari, pp. 215–20.

2. It is nonetheless crucial to notice the essentially "rationalistic"

character of happiness in the *Phaedrus*. Failure to see this point has led Martha Nussbaum to a number of fundamental misconceptions. As she reads the *Phaedrus*, the best life "for a human being is found not by abstracting from the peculiarities of our complex nature, but by exploring that nature and the way of life that it constitutes" (*Fragility*, p. 221). When we do explore that nature, we will love, but "these lovers love one another's character, memories, and aspirations" (*Fragility*, p. 220). As a result, unlike "the life of the ascending person in the *Symposium*, this best human life is unstable, always prey to conflict" (*Fragility*, p. 221). Hence the fragility of goodness. And it is not difficult to see why this fragility results, since the extent to which Nussbaum's lovers grasp the good depends on how well they can sustain a relationship circumscribed exclusively by opinion and the bounds of their individual, often erotically volatile, personalities, and experiences.

But let us review what the *Phaedrus* has said about happiness. The gods are "happy" while they attend to their duties and behold the blessed sights in the heavens (247a). The souls of humans are "happy" when they follow deities and behold the realities beyond the rim of the heavens (250b–c). Just before the description of the capture of the beloved by the lover, Socrates says that if this capture is accomplished as he is about to describe, the capture will bring happiness from the inspired one to the loved one (253c). Again, those souls who have, by virtue of occasional sexual congress, not led a perfect philosophical life, will nonetheless "lead a happy life in the light as they journey together" (256d), a journey begun only upon the release of the lovers' souls through death. Thus, when Nussbaum says that human lovers "grasp the good and true not by transcending erotic madness, but inside a passionate life" (*Fragility*, 220), we must disagree. Only by embracing the realities seen, and described through dialectic and rhetoric, will soul grasp the good and the true and everything else that soul saw when it existed apart from body. These sights are the truly blessed and beholding these sights constitutes human happiness.

3. But cf. De Vries, p. 256, on *muthologonta* at 276e.

4. The allusion to the *Republic* has been noted by Thomas Szlezak, *Platon und die Schriftlichkeit der Philosophie: Interpretationen zu den frühen und mittleren Dialogen* (Berlin, 1985), p. 14 (quoted in Rowe, p. 212).

5. Other sources criticizing Hackforth on the extent of this reference include De Vries, p. 260 and Ferrari, p. 282, n31.

6. These aspects of the essential connection between the doctrine of natures and the method of collection and division also show the dependency of both rhetoric and dialectic on the metaphysics "hymned" in the palinode. A

tradition of interpretation denies this dependency. Thus G. E. L. Owen claims that the tripartite soul and the Forms have nothing to do with rhetoric (G. E. L. Owen, "Plato on the Undepictable," in *Exegesis and Argument. Phronesis.* Suppl. vol. 1. (Assen: Van Gorcum, 1973), p. 350). This position has been taken over, unargued, by Ferrari, who says that the arguments in the second part of the *Phaedrus* "shun such deep metaphysical waters and are more pragmatic in spirit" (p. 249, n3); as a result, the second part of the dialogue is not as important as the first for determining "the philosophical life" (p. 280, n16). And, in a similar vein, Griswold puts forth the following reading. He distinguishes *three* different sense of *epistēmē* in the *Phaedrus* (p. 261, n23) and asserts in this regard that "the palinode itself must be retracted" p. 117), i.e., that the account of knowledge in the myth is intended to be superseded. To demonstrate the inadequacy of the method leading to this knowledge (an inadequacy which Plato fully intends), Griswold lumps together five distinct descriptions of method occurring form 266c to 274b—completely ignoring dramatic context—then shows how they are mutually inconsistent (pp. 186–97). Griswold concludes that "the art of thinking is subordinated, in the *Phaedrus*, to the artless path of dialogue" (p. 175, also p. 178), and that "the problem is to determine *how* we are to talk in order to fulfill the palinode's aims" (p. 165, italics in text).

I submit that for Plato, there is only one *epistēmē* (not three), that the palinode presents a complete metaphysical vision and should not be retracted, that the various descriptions of method elucidate this vision and that they differ in order to bring out its distinct features, and that we are to talk about the aims of the palinode precisely according to the rules stated by the method of dialectic, including the doctrines of natures and collections and division. It may be noted that if Griswold's interpretation is correct, then the primary purpose of the *Phaedrus* is to have us talk about the most fundamental philosophical matters—but without even the semblance of the art of dialectic (indeed, any art) that Socrates has been at such pains to expound in the second half of the dialogue. Griswold's approach is therefore a particularly unfortunate way of stating the "silent" sense of the *Phaedrus*.

7. The ideal character of the Platonic approach to rhetoric is discussed by George Grote in *Plato and the other companions of Sokrates*. Vol 2. New York: Burt Franklin, 1973 (1888), pp. 248–53. See also Burger, p. 108, who notes the "demand for complete knowledge of the whole, together with complete knowledge of all types of human perspective on that whole." She concludes, however, that this sense of totality "seems to be nothing but an "ideal"

standard by which to measure, not only the rhetoricians' claim to teach an art of persuasion, but also the actual procedure of Socratic conversation and, further, the Platonic imitation of that conversation." But this ideal standard may be precisely what is required as a limit condition in order to see the full import of love in the philosophical sense advanced in the *Phaedrus*.

In a related vein, Ferrari notes the overlap between the list of nine types of human life (248c) and the ranking of the gods at 253b. Thus, the "follower of Ares, for example, would seem to belong, if anywhere, in the second rank with the 'warlike' king and general 248d4; but that is where we put the follower of Hera also." Ferrari concludes that such discrepancies are "only to be expected" if, as Ferrari contends, "Plato wants to sharpen the fuzziness of human character with the artificial sharpness of these division" (pp. 267–8, n40). Although human character may be inherently "fuzzy," our analytic descriptions of human nature should not rest content with equivalent fuzziness. Another way to take the "artificial sharpness" of these divisions is that they represent an ideal to be striven for whenever the method of collection and division is employed, even (and, perhaps, especially) when this method is directed at peculiarly recalcitrant types of reality such as human beings. (This approach will not appear feasible for those who deem collection and division an unworkable method contaminated by "bad" metaphysics.)

8. But cf. Hackforth, (p. 161, n1) on *poikilia*, the word for complex, differing from the manifold nature of soul (271a–b). The assertion is not argued. See also Rowe, pp. 212–3.

9. Phaedrus' remembrance in this regard is noted by Ferrari, pp. 207–8.

10. See, for example, the following: R. L. Howland, "The Attack on Isocrates in the *Phaedrus*," *Classical Quarterly* 31 (1937): 151–9; G. J. A. De Vries, "Isocrates' Reaction to the *Phaedrus*," *Mnemosyne* 6 (1953): 39–45; J. A. Coulter, "*Phaedrus* 279a: The Praise of Isocrates," *Greek, Roman, and Byzantine Studies* 8 (1967): 225–36; H. Erbse, "Platons Urteil über Isokrates," *Hermes* 99 (1971): 183–97; see also Friedländer, vol. III, p. 514, n34.

11. For discussion of the ambiguity concerning Socrates and money in the last clause of the prayer, see Thompson, p. 148, De Vries, p. 266, and Rowe, p. 217.

12. For additional discussion of Socrates' prayer, see: T. G. Rosenmeyer, "Plato's Prayer to Pan—*Phaedrus* 279b8–c3," *Hermes* 90 (1962): 34–44; A. Motte, "Le pré sacré de Pan et des nymphes dans le *Phédre* de Platon," *L'antiquité classique* 32 (1963): 460–76; D. Clay, "Socrates' Prayer to Pan," in

Arktouros: Hellenic Studies Presented to B. M. W. Knox (Berlin: de Gruyter, 1979); 345–53.

Epilogue

1. See, for example, Natorp, cited by Stenzel with qualified approval in J. Stenzel, *Plato's Method of Dialectic*. Trans. by D. J. Allan. (New York: Arno Press, 1973, p. 150. See also Gulley, p. 122.

2. The intuitive factor in seeing what is one among many is brought out by F. M. Cornford in *Plato's Theory of Knowledge*. (London: Routledge & Kegan Paul, 1935), pp. 183, 186. For discussion of alternative ways of interpreting collection, see Gulley, p. 121. And Sayre has noted the link between collection and recollection (*anamnesis*); see Kenneth M. Sayre, *Plato's Analytic Method* (Chicago: University of Chicago Press, 1969), p. 219, n4.

3. The lack of criteria for correct collection has been noted in Nicholas White, *Plato on Knowledge and Reality* (Indianapolis: Hackett, 1976), p. 121. And in a related difficulty, White has observed (p. 123) that collection and division lacks the element of an initiating hyptheis, a methodological requirement stated in the *Phaedo* and *Republic*. For White, this "leaves an important gap" in the methodology advanced in the later dialogues. See also the related comments in J. A. Philip, "Platonic Diairesis," *Transactions of the American Philological Association* 97 (1966): 335–58, esp. p. 339.

4. The development of this sense of nature shows that Griswold is shortsighted in arguing that no *epistēmē* of soul is possible if there is no *idea* of soul (p. 89). For even if soul does not have one specific Form, soul has a distinct nature which, presumably, can be divided so that soul as such can be known. See also Griswold's denial that the *Phaedrus* gives any answer to the question of what "nature" means (p. 184), a denial also asserted by Thompson, p. 124.

5. The active/passive factor appeared already in the methodology advanced in the *Phaedo* (97d), and the same factor will recur in the *Theatetus* (156a) and *Sophist* (247e–248d).

6. For a useful statement of the kinds of problems arising from the Platonic approach to division, see J. A. Philip "Platonic Diairesis," pp. 327–8. For more general discussion, see Gilbert Ryle's criticisms in "Dialectic in the Academy," in *New Essays on Plato and Aristotle*. Ed. R. Bambrough. (New

York: Humanities Press, 1965): 39–68 and John Ackrill's response, "In Defence of Platonic Division" in *G. Ryle: A Collection of Critical Essays*. Eds. O. P. Wood and G. Pitcher (Garden City: Doublyday, 1970); 373–92. And for further discussion, see the following: A. C. Lloyd, "Plato's Description of Division" in *Studies in Plato's Metaphysics*. Ed. R. E. Allen. (London: Routledge & Kegan Paul, 1965): 219–30; J. Stannard, "Socratic eros and Platonic dialectic," *Phronesis* 4 (1959): 12034; Roland J. Teske, "Plato's Later Dialectic," *Modern Schoolman* 38 (1961): 171201; J. R. Trevaskis, "Division and its Relation to Dialectic and Ontology in Plato," *Phronesis* 12 (1967): 118–29; J. M. E. Moravcsik, "Plato's Method of Division," in *Patterns in Plato's Thought*. Ed. by J. Moravscik. (Dordrecht: Reidel, 1973): 158–80; J. M. E. Moravcsik, "The Anatomy of Plato's Divisions," in *Exegesis and Argument*. *Phronesis*. Suppl. vol. 1. (Assen: Van Gorcum, 1973): 324–48; S. M. Cohen, "Plato's Method of Division," in *Patterns in Plato's Thought*. Ed. J. Moravcsik. (Dordrecht: Reidel, 1973): 181–91.

7. Cf., against this interpretation, the view of Gulley (p. 111) and Trevaskis (p. 124), i.e., that division according to natural joints need not result in Forms. It would apparently follow that if part of a Form is not itself a Form, then the metaphysics of division has at least four elements—Forms, instances of Forms, natures, and parts of natures not themselves Forms. The problem then of the status of particulars (noted by Stenzel, p. 156) becomes all the more crucial, since it is an individual entity which, upon the fact of division, serves as the locus for these metapysically heterogeneous elements.

BIBLIOGRAPHY

This bibliography contains works relevant to the scope of this study. It is divided into: editions of and commentaries on the *Phaedrus*; books on themes treated in the *Phaedrus*; articles on the *Phaedrus* or on issues discussed in the *Phaedrus*.

Editions of and Commentaries on the *Phaedrus*

Burger, Ronna. *Plato's Phaedrus: A Defense of a Philosophic Art of Writing*. Tuscaloosa: University of Alabama Press, 1980.

Burnet, John. *Platonis Opera*. Vol. II. Oxford: Clarendon Press 1901.

De Vries, G. J. *A Commentary on the Phaedrus of Plato*. Amsterdam: Adolf M. Hakkert, 1969.

Ferrari, G. R. F. *Listening to the Cicadas; A Study of Plato's Phaedrus*. Cambridge: Cambridge University Press, 1987.

Fowler, H. N. *Phaedrus*. Vol. I (Loeb Library). Cambridge: Harvard University Press, 1914.

Griswold, Charles L. *Self-knowledge in Plato's Phaedrus*. New Haven: Yale University Press, 1986.

Hackforth, R. *Plato's Phaedrus*. Cambridge: Cambridge University Press, 1952.

Helmbold, W. C., and W. G. Rabinowitz. *Plato's Phaedrus*. Indianapolis: Bobbs-Merrill, 1956.

Jowett, Benjamin. *Collected Dialogues*. Vol. III. Oxford: Clarendon Press, 1953.

Robin, Léon. *Phédre*. In *Platon: Oeuvres completes*. Vol. III, Pt. 3. Paris: Collection des Universités de France, 1933.

Rowe, C. J. *Plato: Phaedrus*. 2d ed. Warminster: Aris & Phillips, 1988.

Thompson, W. H. *The Phaedrus of Plato, with English Notes and Dissertations*. London: Wittaker & Co., 1868.

Vicaire, P. *Platon: Phèdre*. Paris: Association Guillaume Budé, 1972.

Books on themes treated in the *Phaedrus*

Allen, M. J. B. Trans. and Ed. *Marsilio Ficino and the Phaedran Charioteer*. Berkeley: University of California Press, 1981.

Aristotle. *Nicomachean Ethics*. In *The Basic Works of Aristotle*. Ed. by Richard McKeon. New York: Random House, 1941.

————. *Rhetoric* (Loeb Library). Trans. John Henry Freese. Cambridge: Harvard University Press, 1926.

Bluck, R. S. *Plato Phaedo*. New York: Bobbs Merrill, 1955.

Cherniss, Harold. *Aristotle's Criticism of Plato and the Academy*. Vol. 1. Baltimore: Johns Hopkins University Press, 1944.

Cornford, F. M. *Plato and Parmenides*. London: Routledge & Kegan Paul, 1939.

————. *Plato's Theory of Knowledge*. London: Routledge & Kegan Paul, 1935.

D'Arcy, Martin C. *The Mind and Heart of Love*. New York: H. Holt, 1947.

Dies, A. *Autour de Platon: Essais de Critique et d'histoire*. 2 Vols. Paris: Bibliotheque des Archives de Philosophie, 1927.

Diesendruck, Z. *Struktur und Charakter des platonischen Phaidros*. Wien-Leipzig: W. Braumüller, 1927.

Dionysius of Halicarnassus. *Dionysius of Halicarnassus, the Critical Essays*. Trans. S. Usher. 2 Vols. Cambridge: Harvard University Press, 1974.

Dover, K. J. *Greek Homosexuality*. Cambridge: Harvard University Press, 1978.

Ferber, Rafael. *Platos Idee des Gutens*. St. Augustin: Hans Richarz, 1984.

Findlay, J. N. *Plato: The Written and Unwritten Doctrines*. New York: Humanities Press, 1974.

Frenkian, A. M. *La méthode Hippocratique dans le Phèdre de Platon*. Bucharest: Imprimerie Nationale, 1941.

Friedländer, Paul. *Plato*. Trans. Hans Meyerhoff. Vols I and III. New York: Pantheon Books, 1969.

Frutiger, P. *Les mythes de Platon*. Paris: F. Alcan, 1930.

Gadamer, Hans-Georg. *Dialogue and Dialectic: Eight Hermeneutical Studies on Plato*. Trans. by P. C. Smith. New Haven: Yale University Press, 1980.

————. *The Idea of the Good in Platonic-Aristotelian Philosophy*. Trans. by P. Christopher Smith. New Haven: Yale University Press, 1986.

Gaiser, Konrad. *Platons Ungeschriebene Lehre*. Stuttgart: Ernst Klett Verlag, 1962.

Gould, Thomas. *Platonic Love*. London: Routledge & Kegan Paul, 1963.

Grote, George. *Plato, and the other companions of Socrates*. Vol 2. 1865 Reprint: New York: Burt Frankin, 1973.

Gulley, Norman. *Plato's Theory of Knowledge*. London: Methuen, 1962.

Guthrie, W. K. C. *The Greeks and their Gods*. Boston: Beacon Press, 1951.

————. *A History of Greek Philosophy*. Vols 3 and 4. Cambridge: Cambridge University Press, 1969, 1975.

Hackforth, R. *Plato's Philebus*. Cambridge: Cambridge University Press, 1945.

Hermeias of Alexandria. *In Platonis Phaedrum Scholia*. Ed. P. Couvreur. 1901. Reprint. Hildesheim: G. Olms, 1971. With additions by C. Zintzen.

Hippocrates. Vol. 1 (Loeb Library). Trans. W. H. S. Jones. New York: G. P. Putnam's Sons, 1923.

Isocrates. *Isocrates*. Trans. G. Norlin. 3 Vols. London: W. Heinemann, 1928.

Jebb, R. C. *The Attic Orators from Antiphon to Isaeos*. New York: Russell and Russell, 1962.

Kennedy, George. *The Art of Persuasion in Greece*. Princeton: Princeton University Press, 1963.

Kirk, G. S., and J. E. Raven. *The Presocratic Philosophers*. Cambridge: Cambridge University Press, 1957.

Moors, K. F. *Platonic Myth; an Introductory Study.* Washington, D.C.: University Press of America, 1982.

Moravcsik, J., and P. Temko, Eds. *Plato on Beauty, Wisdom, and the Arts.* Totowa: Rowman and Littlefield, 1982.

Nussbaum, Martha. *The Fragility of Goodness.* Cambridge: Cambridge University Press, 1986.

Nygren, Anders. *Agape and Eros.* Philadelphia: Westminster Press, 1953.

Pieper, Josef. *Enthusiasm and Divine Madness.* Trans. Richard and Clara Winston. New York: Harcourt, Brace & World, Inc. 1964.

Rist, John M. *Eros and Psyche; Studies in Plato, Plotinus, and Origen.* Toronto: University of Toronto Press, 1964.

Robin, Léon. *La théorie platonicienne de l'amour.* Paris: Presses Universitaires de France, 1933.

Robinson. T. M. *Plato's Psychology.* Toronto: University of Toronto Press, 1970

Rosen, Stanley. *Plato's Symposium.* 2d ed. New Haven: Yale University Press, 1987.

Sallis, John. *Being and Logos; The Way of Platonic Dialogue.* Pittsburgh: Duquesne University Press, 1975.

Sayre, Kenneth M. *Plato's Analytic Method.* Chicago: University of Chicago Press, 1969.

Schleiermacher, F. E. D. *Introductions to the Dialogues of Plato.* Trans. by W. Dobson. 1836. Reprint. New York: Arno Press, 1973.

Sève, B. *Phèdre de Platon.* Paris: Editions Pédagogie Moderne, 1980.

Shorey, Paul. *The Unity of Plato's Thought.* 1903. Reprint. Chicago: University Press of Chicago, 1968.

Sinaiko, Henry L. *Love, Knowledge, and Discourse in Plato: Dialogue and Dialectic in Phaedrus, Republic, Parmenides.* Chicago: University of Chicago Press, 1965.

Skemp, J. B. *The Theory of Motion in Plato's Later Dialogues.* Cambridge: Cambridge University Press, 1942.

Solmsen, F. *Plato's Theology.* New York: Johnson Reprint Co., 1968.

Sprague, R. K. *Plato's Use of Fallacy: A Study of the "Euthydemus" and some other Dialogues.* New York: Barnes & Noble, 1962.

Stenzel, J. *Plato's Method of Dialectic*. Trans. D. J. Allan. 1940. Reprint. New York: Arno Press, 1973.

Stewart, J. A. *The Myths of Plato*. Ed. G. R. Levy, 1905. Reprint. Carbondale: Southern Illinois University Press, 1960.

Vlastos, Gregory. *Platonic Studies*. 2d ed. 1973. Princeton: Princeton University Press, 1981.

———. (ed.) *Plato I*. Garden City, New York: Doubleday, 1971.

———. (ed.) *Plato II*. 1971. Reprint. Notre Dame: University of Notre Dame Press, 1978.

White, David A. *Myth and Metaphysics in Plato's Phaedo*. Susquehanna: Susquehanna University Press, 1989.

White, Nicholas. *Plato on Knowledge and Reality*. Indianapolis: Hackett, 1976.

Zaslavsky, R. *Platonic Myth and Platonic Writing*. Washington, D. C.: University Press of America, 1981.

Articles on the *Phaedrus* or on issues discussed in the *Phaedrus*

Ackrill, J. L. "In Defence of Platonic Division." In *G. Ryle: A Collection of Critical Essays*. Eds. O. P. Wood and G. Pitcher. Garden City: Doubleday, 1970: 373–92.

———. "On *Phaedrus* 265e–266b." *Mind* 62 (1953): 278–9.

Allan, D. J. "Review of *Plato's Phaedrus* by R. Hackforth." *Philosophy* 28 (1953): 365–6.

Armstrong, A. H. "Platonic *eros* and Christian *agape*." *Downside Review* 79 (1961): 105–21.

———. "Platonic love: a reply to Professor Verdenius." *Downside Review* 82 (1964): 199–208.

Barnes, H. E. "Plato and the Psychology of Love: *Phaedrus* 252c–253c." *Classical Weekly* 40 (1946): 34–5.

Baron, C. "De l'unité de composition dans le Phèdre des Platon." *Revue des études Grecques* 4 (1981); 58–62.

324 Bibliography

Beare, J. I. "The *Phaedrus*: Its Structure, the *eros* Theme: Notes." *Hermathena* 17 (1891): 312–34.

Blass, F. "Kritische Bemerkungen zu Platons *Phaidros*." *Hermes* 36 (1901): 580–96.

Bluck, R. S. "The *Phaedrus* and Reincarnation." *American Journal of Philology* 79 (1958): 156–64.

Bonitz, H. "Zur Erklärung des Dialogs Phädros." In *Platonische Studien*. 1886. Reprint. Hildesheim: G. Olms, 1968: 270–92.

Bourguet, E. "Sur la composition du *Phèdre*." *Revue de métaphysique et de morale* 26 (1919): 335–51.

Brown, M., and J. Coulter. "The Middle Speech of Plato's *Phaedrus*." *Journal of the History of Philosophy* 9 (1971): 405–23.

Brownstein, O. L. "Plato's *Phaedrus*: Dialectic as the Genuine Art of Speaking." *Quarterly Journal of Speech* 51 (1965): 392–98.

Bury, J. B. "Questions Connected with Plato's *Phaidros*." *Journal of Philology* 15 (1886): 80–5.

Carter, R. E. "Plato and Inspiration." *Journal of the History of Philosophy* 5 (1967): 111–21.

Chen, C.-H. "The *Phaedrus*." *Studi internazionali di filosofia* 4 (1982): 77–90.

Clay, D. "Socrates' Prayer to Pan." In *Arktouros: Hellenic Studies Presented to B. M. W. Knox*. Ed. G. W. Bowersock et al. Berlin: de Gruyter, 1979: 345–53.

Cohen, S. M. "Plato's Method of Division." In *Patterns in Plato's Thought*. Ed. J. Moravcsik. Dordrecht: Reidel, 1973: 181–91.

Coulter, J. A. "*Phaedrus* 279a: The Praise of Isocrates." *Greek, Roman, and Byzantine Studies* 8 (1967): 225–36.

Courcelle, P. "La plaine de vérité: *Phèdre* 248b." *Museum Helveticum* 26 (1969): 199–203.

Cropsey, Joseph. "Plato's *Phaedrus* and Plato's Socrates." In *Political Philosophy and the Issue of Politics*. Chicago: University of Chicago Press, 1977: 231–51.

Demos, R. "Plato's Doctrine of the Psyche as a Self-Moving Motion." *Journal of the History of Philosophy* 6 (1968): 133–45.

DeRomilly, Jacqueline. "Les conflits de l'âme dans le Phèdre de Platon." *Wiener Studien* 16 (1982): 100–13.

Derrida, Jacques. "La Pharmacie de Platon." In *La dissémination*. Paris: Seuil, 1972: 69–198.

De Vries, G. J. "Colloquialisms in *Republic* and *Phaedrus*." In *Studia Platonica, Festschrift für Hermann Gundert*. Amsterdam: B. R. Gruner. 1973: 87–92.

———."Isocrates in the *Phaedrus*: A Reply." *Mnemosyne* 24 (1971): 387–90.

———. Isocrates' Reaction to the *Phaedrus*." *Mnemosyne* 6 (1953): 39–45.

———. "Mystery Terminology in Aristophanes and Plato." *Mnemosyne* 26 (1973): 1–8.

———. "A Note on Plato, *Phaedrus* 270ac." *Mnemosyne* 35 (1982): 331–3.

Dimock, G. E. "*Alla* in Lysias and Plato's *Phaedrus*." *American Journal of Philology* 73 (1952): 381–96.

Dorter, Kenneth. "Imagery and Philosophy in Plato's *Phaedrus*." *Journal of the History of Philosophy* 9 (1971): 279–88.

Duffy, Bernard. "The Platonic Function of Epideictic Rhetoric." *Philosophy and Rhetoric* 16 (1983): 79–93.

Dumortier, J. "L'attelage ailé du *Phèdre* (246)." *Revue des études Grecques* 82 (1969): 346–8.

Dyson, M. "Zeus and Philosophy in the Myth in Plato's *Phaedrus*." *Classical Quarterly* 32 (1982): 307–11.

Edelstein, L. "The Function of the Myth in Plato's Philosophy." *Journal of the History of Ideas* 10 (1949): 463–81.

Erbse, Hartmunt. "Platons Urteil über Isokrates." *Hermes* 99 (1971): 183–97.

Fisher, J. "Plato on Writing and Doing Philosophy." *Journal of the History of Ideas* 27 (1966): 163–62.

Fortenbaugh, W. "Plato's *Phaedrus* 235c3." *Classical Philology* 61 (1966): 108–9.

Fritz, K. von. "*Nous, noein*, and their Derivatives in Pre-Socratic Philosophy." *Classical Philology* 40 (1945): 223–42; 41 (1946): 13–24. Also in *The Pre-Socratics*. Ed. A. P. D. Mourelatos. Garden City: Anchor Books, 1974: 23–85.

Furley, D. J. "Self-Movers." In *Essays on Aristotle's Ethics*. Ed. A. O. Rorty Berkeley: University of California Press, 1980: 55–67.

Gadamer, H.-G. "Die Theorie der Dialektik im *Phaidros*." ch. 1, pt. 7 of *Platos dialektische Ethik und andere Studien zue platonischen Philosophie*. Hamburg: Meiner, 1968: 66–72.

Greene, W. C. "The Spoken and Written Word." *Harvard Studies in Classical Philology* 60 (1951): 23–59.

Guthrie. W. K. C. "Rhetoric and Philosophy; the Unity of the *Phaedrus*." *Paideia* (Special Plato Issue) (1976): 117–24.

Hackforth, R. "Plato's Theism." In *Studies in Plato's Metaphysics*. Ed. R. E. Allen. London: Routledge & Kegan Paul, 1965: 439–47.

Hall, R. W. "*Psuche* as Differentiated Unity in the Philosophy of Plato." *Phronesis* 8 (1963): 63–82.

Halperin, David M. "Platonic *Eros* and What Men Call Love." *Ancient Philosophy* 5 (1985): 161–204.

Hartland-Swann, J. "Plato as Poet: A Critical Interpretation." *Philosophy* 26 (1951): 3–18; 131–41.

Helmbold, W. C., and W. B. Holther. "The Unity of the *Phaedrus*." *University of California Publications in Classical Philology* 14 (1952): 387–417.

Hoerber, R. G. "Love or Rhetoric in Plato's *Phaedrus*." *Classical Bulletin* 34 (1958): 33.

Howland, R. L. "The attack on Isocrates in the *Phaedrus*." *Classical Quarterly* 31 (1937): 15–19.

Hyland, Drew. "*Eros, epithumia,* and *filia* in Plato." *Phronesis* 13 (1968): 32–46.

Jackson, B. D. "The Prayers of Socrates." *Phronesis* 16 (1971): 14–37.

Jäger, G. *"Nus" In Platons Dialogen*. Gottingen: Vandenhoeck & Ruprecht, 1967.

Joly, R. "La question Hippocratique et le témoignage du *Phèdre*." *Revue des Études Grecques* 74 (1961): 69–92.

Kelley, W. G. "Rhetoric as Seduction." *Philosophy and Rhetoric* 6 (1975): 69–80.

Koller, H. "Die dihäretische Methode." *Glotta* 39 (1961): 6–24.

Kosman, L. A. "Platonic Love." In *Facets of Plato's Philosophy.* Ed. by W. Werkmeister. *Phronesis.* Suppl. vol. 2. Assen: Van Gorcum, 1976: 53–69.

Kucharski, P. "La 'méthode d'Hippocrate' dans le *Phèdre.*" *Revue des études Grecques* 52 (1939): 301–57.

———. "La rhétorique dans le *Gorgias* et le *Phèdre.*" *Revue des études Grecques* 74 (1961): 371–406.

Lebeck, Anne. "The Central Myth of Plato's *Phaedrus.*" *Greek, Roman, and Byzantine Studies* 13 (1972): 267–90.

Lee, E. N. "Reason and Rotation: Circular Movement as the Model of Mind (Nous) in Later Plato." In *Facets of Plato's Philosophy.* Ed. W. Werkmeister. *Phronesis.* Suppl. vol. 2. Assen: Van Gorcum, 1976: 70–102.

Levinson, R. B. "Plato's *Phaedrus* and the New Criticism." *Archiv für Geschichte der Philosophie* 46 (1964): 293–309.

Linforth, I. M. "Telistic Madness in Plato, *Phaedrus* 244DE." *University of California Publications in Classical Philology* 13 (1946): 163–72.

———."The Corybantic Rites in Plato." *University of California Pubications in Classical Philology* 13 (1946): 121–62.

Lloyd, A. C. "Plato's Description of Division." In *Studies in Plato's Metaphysics.* Ed. R. E. Allen. London: Routledge & Kegan Paul, 1965: 219–30.

Mansfield, J. "Plato and the Method of Hippocrates." *Greek, Roman and Byzantine Studies* 21 (1980): 341–62.

McCumber, John. "Discourse and Psyche in Plato's *Phaedrus.*" *Apeiron* 16 (1982): 27–39.

McGibbon, D. D. "The Fall of the Soul in Plato's *Phaedrus.*" *Classical Quarterly,* n.s. 14 (1964): 56–63.

Merlan, P. "Form and Content in Plato's Philosophy." *Journal of the History of Ideas* 8 (1947): 406–30.

Meyer, H. W. "Das Verhältnis von Enthusiasmus und Philosophie bei Platon im Hinblick auf seinen *Phaidros.*" *Archiv für Philosophie* 6 (1956): 262–77.

Moore, J. D. "The Relation between Plato's *Symposium* and *Phaedrus.*" In *Patterns in Plato's Thought.* Ed. J. Moravcsik. Dordrecht: Reidel, 1973: 52–71.

Moravcsik, J. M. E. "Plato's Method of Division." In *Patterns in Plato's Thought.* Ed. J. Moravcsik. Dordrecht: Reidel, 1973: 158–80.

————."The Anatomy of Plato's Divisions." In *Exegesis and Argument. Phronesis.* Suppl. Vol. 1. Assen: Van Gorcum, 1973: 324–48.

————. "Reason and Eros in the "Ascent" Passage of the *Symposium.*" In *Essays in Ancient Greek Philosophy.* Ed. John P. Anton. Albany: State University of New York Press, 1971: 285–302.

Morrow, Glenn. "Plato's Conception of Persuasion." *Philosophical Review* 62 (1953): 234–50.

Motte, A. "Le pré sacré de Pan et des nymphes dans le Phèdre de Platon." *L'antiquité classique* 32 (1963): 460–76.

Mueller, G. E. "The Unity of the *Phaedrus.*" *Classical Bulletin* 33 (1957): 50–3; 63–5.

Mulhern, J. J. "Socrates on Knowledge and Information (*Phaedrus* 274B6–277A5)." *Classica et medievalia* 30 (1969): 175–86.

Murley, C. "Plato's *Phaedrus* and the Theocritean Pastoral." *Transactions of the American Philological Association* 71 (1940): 281–95.

Nussbaum, M. C. "This Story Isn't True': Poetry, Goodness, and Understanding in Plato's *Phaedrus.*" In *Plato on Beauty, Wisdom, and the Arts.* Ed. J. Moravcsik and P. Temko. Totowa: Rowman and Littlefield, 1982: 79–124.

Osburne, H. "Colour Concepts of the Ancient Greeks." *British Journal of Aesthetics* 8 (1968): 269–83.

Owen, G. E. L. "Plato on the Undepictable." In *Exegesis and Argument. Phronesis.* Supple. vol. 1. Assen: Van Gorcum, 1973: 349–61.

Panagiotou, Spiro. "Lysias and the Date of Plato's *Phaedrus.*" *Mnemosyne* 28 (1975): 388–98.

Philip, A "Récurrences thématiques et topologie dans le *Phèdre* de Platon." *Revue de métaphysique et de morale* 86 (1981): 452–76.

Philip, J. A. "Platonic Diairesis." *Transactions of the American Philological Association* 97 (1966): 335–58.

Plass, Paul. "The Unity of the *Phaedrus.*" *Symbolae Osloenses* 43 (1969): 7–38.

Price, A. W. "Loving Persons Platonically." *Phronesis* 26 (1981): 25–34.

Regenbogen, O. "Bemerkungen zur Deutung des platonischen *Phaidros.*" In *Kleine Schriften.* Munich: F. Dirlmeier, 1961: 248–69.

Robinson, R. "Plato's Consciousness of Fallacy." *Mind* 51 (1942): 97–114.

Robinson, T. M. "The Argument for Immortality in Plato's *Phaedrus.*" In *Essays in Ancient Greek Philosophy.* Ed. J. Anton and G. Kustas, Albany: State University of New York Press, 1971: 345–53.

Rodis-Lewis, G. "L'articulation des thèmes du *Phèdre.*" *Revue Philosophique de la France et le l'Etranger* 165 (1975): 3–34.

Rosen, Stanley. "Socrates as Concealed Lover." In *Classics and the Classical Tradition. Festschrift for R. Dengler.* Ed. E. Borza and W. Carruba. University Park: Pennsylvania State University Press, 1973: 163–77.

———. "The Non-Lover in Plato's *Phaedrus.*" *Man and World* 2 (1969): 423–37.

Rosenmeyer, T. G. "Plato's Prayer to Pan—*Phaedrus* 279b8–c3." *Hermes* 90 (1962): 34–44.

Ryle, Gilbert. "Dialectic in the Academy." In *New Essays on Plato and Aristotle.* Ed. R. Bambrough. New York: Humanities, 1965: 39–68.

Santas, G. "Passionate Platonic Love in the *Phaedrus.*" *Ancient Philosophy* 2 (1982): 105–14.

Shorey, Paul. "On Plato *Phaedrus* 250d." *Classical Philology* 27 (1932): 280–2.

———. "On the *Erotikos* of Lysias in Plato's *Phaedrus.*" *Classical Philology* 28 (1933): 131–2.

Stannard, J. "Socratic eros and Platonic dialectic." *Phronesis* 4 (1959): 120–34.

Tejera, V. "Irony and Allegory in the *Phaedrus.*" *Philosophy and Rhetoric* 8 (1975): 71–87.

Teske, Roland J. "Plato's Later Dialectic." *Modern Schoolman* 38 (1961): 171–201.

Tourney, Garfield. "Eros, Plato and Freud." *Journal of the History of the Behavioral Sciences* 2 (1966): 256–72.

Trevaskis, J. R. "Division and its Relation to Dialectic and Ontology in Plato." *Phronesis* 12 (1967): 118–29.

Verdenius, W. J. "Another Note on Plato's *Phaedrus,* 270ac. *Mnemosyne* 35 (1982): 333–5.

———. "Der Begriff der Mania in Platons *Phaidros.*" *Archiv für Geschichte der Philosophie* 44 (1962): 132–50.

————. "Notes on Plato's *Phaedrus*." *Mnemosyne* 4 (1955): 265–89.

Versényi, L. "Eros, Irony and Ecstasy." *Thought* 37 (1962): 598–612.

Vlastos, Gregory. "The Individual as an Object of Love in Plato." In his *Platonic Studies*. 2d ed. Princeton: Princeton University Press, 1981: 3–42.

Weaver, R. M. "The *Phaedrus* and the Nature of Rhetoric." In *Language is Sermonic*. Baton Rouge: Louisiana State University Press, 1970: 57–83.

White, F. C. "Love and the Individual in Plato's *Phaedrus*." *The Classical Quarterly* 40 (1990): 396–406.

Wolz, Henry. "Plato's Discourse on Love in the *Phaedrus*." *Personalist* 46 (1965): 157–70.

Wycherley, R. E. "The Scene of Plato's *Phaidros*." *Phoenix* 17 (1963): 88–98.

INDEX

Absolutes. *See* Forms
Achelous, 22, 204
Active (and passive), 32, 286–7; as
 heuristic, 287; and motion, 82; as
 properties of natures, 104, 137–8,
 282–5; and simplicity, 135; and
 soul, 77–8, 82–7, 96–7, 243
Acumenus, 12, 231
Adrastus, 231
Afterlife (of soul), 117–20, 166–70
Agreement: as condition for truth,
 206
Allegory: as explanation, 19; and
 myth, 19–20; and nature of soul,
 92–3
Allen, R., 125, 318
Ammon, 252
Anacreon, 28–9
Anamnesis: See Recollection
Anaxagoras: and causality, 110; and
 mind (*nous*), 232–7; and Socrates,
 54
Animals: souls of, 95, 96, 112,
 118–9
Aphrodite, 212, 213
Apollo: as source of inspiration, 212
Apology, 1
Appearances: of Forms, 134–8
Arche: See Principle
Ares, 146, 304
Aristotle, 154, 308, 312
Art (*Techne*): and madness, 67–9; and

nature, 214, 232–6; and poetry, 71;
 and rhetoric, 202, 230–2; and
 speculation, 214
Ast, F., 136
Athens, 11, 15, 26; and Socrates, 15,
 274–5, 294

Bacchants, 148
Beauty: and body, 42; and etymology,
 143; experience of, 140–3, 171;
 and Forms, 125–6; and love of, 6,
 13, 114–5; as most evident Form,
 125, 139, 177, 301; and nature,
 158; as noble, 249–50, 272–2; and
 philosopher, 114–5; and recollection, 157–8; and rhetoric, 22–4;
 and Socrates, 23, 171; and soul,
 142–3; and truth, 124–5; and
 wisdom, 139–40, 171
Bluck, R., 296, 300
Body: and beauty, 42; as evil, 100,
 104–5; and gods, 103; and
 knowledge, 237; and pleasure, 40;
 and soul, 83, 85–7, 89–90, 95,
 97–100, 128
Books: and Socrates, 54
Boreas, 17–9, 21–2, 36, 294
Burger, R., 294, 295, 308, 309–10,
 312, 313, 315–6
Burnet, J., 9

Calliope, 184, 185, 187, 189, 213
Centaur, 18, 19
Chariot: and nature of soul, 98–100
Charioteer, 89; and discourse, 165; as divine, 111; and nature of soul, 91, 93, 98–100, 101, 155, 159
Cherniss, H., 295–6
Chimaera, 18–19
Cicadas: and Muses, 62, 115, 204–5; as myth, 183; and rhetoric, 213; story of, 183–90
Collection, 277–8; and dialectic, 214, 223–4, 226, 248, 258; and division, 214, 215–8, 261, 278–9; and Forms, 217–8, 277–8; and the good, 145, 291; as heuristic, 217–8; and love, 44, 140; and madness, 44, 48, 67, 71, 215–9; and method, 35, 219, 241, 223–6, 311–2, 315; and nature, 151, 214–5, 221, 240–1, 278–9, 287–91; and rhetoric, 196, 206–7; and Socrates' first speech, 39–40; and speculation, 241; and truth, 261–2; and unity, 39–40; 225–6; and writing, 182
Continuum: and Forms, 75; and gods, 102; and life, 21; and madness, 73–4
Cornford, F., 3–4, 290, 317
Corybantic rites, 14, 15, 26
Cosmos: and mind, 234–6; and motion, 85; and nature, 236–40; and soul, 95–8
Cratylus, 1, 69, 223, 296

Daimon: and love, 46–7; and Socrates, 33, 54
Darius, 179
Definition: and division, 218; and explanation, 37–8, 208; and

knowledge, 37–8; as ostensive, 207
Delphi, 20, 67, 73
Derrida, J., 2
Desire: as Form, 39, 218; and love, 39, 42, 89–90, 162–4; and nature of soul, 90–2, 105, 159–60; and pleasure, 40, 41–2, 157; and predication, 41–2
Destiny: in afterlife, 117; and evil, 161; and fallen soul, 114–7; and the good, 160–1
De Vries, G., 22, 54, 131, 183, 195, 295, 300, 303, 308, 312, 313, 314, 316
Dialectic: and collection and division, 214, 223–4, 226, 248, 258; and education, 258; and Forms, 214; and the good, 214; and happiness, 248, 257; as incomplete, 223; and love, 224; and mind, 214; and method, 301, 310; and rhetoric, 203–27; and Socrates, 35
Dianoia. See Intellect
Dionysius, 212
Diotima, 55
Dithyramb, 43, 50–1
Divine: and Forms, 100–6; and gods, 101; and the good, 132–3; and love, 55–6; and participation, 100; and Phaedrus, 32; and Socrates, 54; and soul, 78, 86, 94, 96, 98, 100–1, 108–11, 133–4, 153. *See also* Gods
Division: and collection, 214, 215–8, 261, 278–9; and definition. 218; and dialectic, 287–91; as dichotomous, 220, 287–8; and enumeration, 74, 242, 262–3; as exhaustive, 18, 74–5, 261, 263, 265, 290; and Forms, 40–2, 206–7; and human nature, 40; and knowledge, 263; between

Division: *continued*
  lover and nonlover, 38–41; and
  nature, 214–5, 218–23, 262,
  278–9; and recollection, 216;
  and rhetoric, 246; and simplicity
  and complexity, 262; and value,
  223, 290–1. *See also* Collection;
  Dialectic
Dorter, K., 294

Education: and dialectic, 258; and
  love, 146, 149–50, 164; as
  Platonic, 164; and truth, 148–9
Egypt, 252–3
Eidos: See Form
Eleusinian mysteries, 131
Erato, 184, 185, 187
Eros: as god of love, 170–3, 178,
  212–4, 224
Eros: See Love
Eryximachus, 53
Etymology: and beauty, 143;
  philosophical function of, 35–6,
  66, 163, 296; as type of
  madness, 66, 69
Euripides, 230
Evil: and body, 100, 104–5; and
  destiny, 161; and the good,
  160–1; and pleasure, 46–7; and
  soul, 104–5, 111, 113, 116–7,
  124, 153–4, 155, 298
Excess (*Hubris*), 41–2, 141, 159–60,
  222, 288, 290; and form of soul,
  152; and love, 219
Explanation: and allegory, 19; and
  definition, 37–8, 208; and
  probability, 19

Ferrari, G., 293, 298, 302, 303, 305,
  308, 313, 314, 316
Forms: appearances of, 134–8; and
  beauty, 125–6; and collection,

217–8, 277–8; and continuum,
  75; (form) of desire, 39, 218;
  and dialectic, 214; and divine,
  100–6, 147; and division, 40–2,
  206–7; and gods, 56, 86, 103,
  105–6, 122, 147, 161; and the
  good, 67, 75, 77, 110, 130,
  132–4, 137–8, 145, 150, 158,
  291, 305; and happiness, 136–8;
  and knowledge, 78, 108–11; and
  love of, 276; and madness, 14,
  44, 66, 76, 211–2; and method,
  40; and mysteries, 128–30,
  132–3; and myth, 19, 106; and
  nature, 280–1; as one and many,
  225; as part and whole, 41–2,
  288–9; and participation, 132;
  and particulars, 226, 278, 287;
  and perception, 121; and
  philosopher, 121, 125, 273; and
  predication, 41, 285; properties
  of, 134–8; and recollection,
  120–3, 216; scope of, 125; and
  soul, 85, 87, 111–3, 127–8, 283,
  298–300; and truth, 144–5; and
  unity, 120, 225
Friedländer, P., 294
Friendship: blessings of, 169–79,
  273; and love, 46–7, 164–5,
  157–8, 307; and philosophy, 273
Frutiger, P., 308

Ganymede, 162; and Zeus, 162–3
Generation: and cosmos, 84; and
  motion, 83
Genos: See Forms
Gods: action toward, 248, 251; and
  body, 103; and continuum, 102;
  and divine, 101; existence of,
  122, 297–8; and Forms, 56, 86,
  103, 105–6, 121–2, 147, 161,
  251, 303–4; and the good, 66–7,
  225, 248–9; and happiness, 103;

Gods: *continued*
  and heavens, 105–6; and human
  nature, 123, 161; and Plato, 122;
  and knowledge, 98, 108–9; and
  soul, 49–50, 111–3, 123; and
  truth, 144–5; and wisdom, 189.
  See also Divine
Good (*Agathon*): and collection and
  division, 67, 145, 291; and
  destiny, 160–1; and dialectic,
  214; and divine, 132–3; and evil,
  160–1; and Forms, 67, 75, 110,
  130, 132–4, 145, 150, 158, 241,
  305; and gods, 66–7, 225,
  248–9; and happiness, 136–8;
  and husbandry, 256–8; and
  light, 130; and love, 66, 75,
  133–4, 145, 160–1; and
  madness, 66–7; and medicine,
  238–40; and mind, 52–3, 53,
  66, 77, 110, 134, 138, 234, 295;
  and mysteries, 130–8; nature of,
  161; and nature, 240, 258; and
  opinion, 38, 40; partial
  knowledge of, 133; and
  particulars, 151; in *Phaedo*, 110;
  and probability, 245–50; and
  Republic, 133, 299; and
  rhetoric, 200; and soul, 93–5,
  238; and speculation, 225
Gorgias, 194
Gorgias, 1, 308
Gorgons, 18, 19, 21
Greece, 26, 33, 67
Griswold, C., 293, 295, 296, 298,
  302, 304, 308, 313, 315, 317

Hackforth, R., 18, 29, 33, 48–9, 60,
  66, 73–4, 113, 119, 126,
  128–31, 183, 203–4, 210, 215,
  218–20, 222, 237–9, 260–1,
  294–5, 303–4, 308, 312–4, 316;
  and nature of soul, 89–92, 94,
  99–100, 114

Happiness: and dialectic, 248, 257;
  and Forms, 136–8; and gods,
  103; and the good, 136–8; and
  intellect, 166; and knowledge,
  259, 275; and love, 149–50,
  157, 166, 291; and metaphysics,
  276; and method, 313–4; and
  philosohpy, 125, 274; and soul,
  168–9; and wisdom, 276
Harmony: and motion, 84–5
Heavens: and gods, 105–6; and soul,
  105–6; and time, 106
Helen, 57
Hera, 148
Hestia, 101, 102
Hexameter, 43, 50–1
Hippocrates, 236–40, 313; and
  philosophy, 239–40
Homer, 56–8, 61, 143–4, 268, 308;
  as philosopher, 269; and truth,
  57–8; and wisdom, 58
Homosexual love, 306–7
Honor: and form of soul, 154; love
  of, 167, 177–80; and politicians,
  177, 180
Horses: form of, in palinode, 151–6;
  and nature of soul, 87–95,
  98–100, 155–6; and soul of
  gods, 110–1, 153
Hubris, *See* Excess
Human nature, 40; and gods, 123,
  161; and life, 21; and rhetoric,
  21; and soul, 40; and unity,
  39–40
Husbandry: as art, 258; and the good,
  256–8; and mind, 257–8; as type
  of life, 257
Ibycus, 3–6, 54, 62
Iliad, 57–8
Ilissus, 30, 43, 51, 140, 293–4
Immortality: as personal, 119; proof
  of soul's, 56, 77, 88, 95–100
Inspiration: and madness, 42–4; and
  Muses, 35–6, 43, 62, 70,
  188–90; and Nymphs, 204, 208;
  and philosophy, 224

Intellect (*dianoia*): and beloved, 45–6; and happiness, 166; and knowledge, 109–10, 121; and madness, 220–1; and mind, 68–9, 78, 108–9, 153; and nature of soul, 121, 220–1; and philosopher, 121

Ion, 1

Irony: in Plato, 224–5; and Socrates, 13

Isocrates: and Socrates, 270

Justice: as Form, 109, 117–8

Knowledge: of body, 237; and definition, 37–8; and division, 263; as Form, 109; and Forms, 78, 108–11; and gods, 98, 108–9; of the good, 133–4; and happiness, 259, 275; and intellect, 109–10, 121; and method, 8, 315; and mind, 108–9; and myth, 109; and opinion, 39, 113; and perception, 130; as recollection, 120–3, 216; and rhetoric, 14; of soul, 234–5, 237–8

Language: and method, 309

Law: and politicians, 179–80; and rhetoric, 196–9; and truth, 247

Learning: love of, 23

Leisure: and love, 11–4

Life: and continuum, 21; and human nature, 40; and motion, 81–2; and soul, 98

Light: and the good, 130

Likeness: and truth, 199–201

Love: of beauty, 6, 13, 114–5; and collection and division, 44, 140; definition of, 42, 44, 208–9; and desire, 39, 42, 66, 89–90, 157,

162–4; and dialectic, 224; and divine, 55–6; and education, 146, 149–50, 164; and excess, 219; of Forms, 6, 127–8, 144–5; and friendship, 46–7, 164–5, 167–8, 307; and the good, 66, 75, 133–4, 145, 160–1; and happiness, 149–50, 157, 166, 291; as homosexual, 306–7; of honor, 167, 177–80; and knowledge, 145; of learning, 23; as "left-handed," 35, 38, 218; and leisure, 11–4; and madness, 14, 44, 66, 76, 211–12; and metaphysics, 5–6, 145, 163; and mind, 48–50, 52, 66; of Muses, 127, 172; and natures, 45; necessity of, 13; and nonlove, 38–41, 46, 51, 201; and participation, 147–8, 151; and philosophy, 45–6, 148, 150, 165–9, 305–6; and pleasure, 157; and prudence, 48–50, 140; of wisdom, 23, 172–3, 226–7

Lycurgus, 179

Lysias: and Phaedrus, 12–7, 25, 58–9, 161, 173, 178, 209, 268; and Plato, 28; and rhetoric, 12, 294; and Socrates, 15, 16; Socrates' critique of, 28, 37, 47, 172, 201, 203–4, 209–10, 250, 268; speech of, 13, 24–5; and speechwriting, 179; and truth, 204, 210

Lysis, 2

Madness: and art, 67–9; and collection and division, 44, 48, 67, 71, 215–9; as continuous, 73–4; as Form, 48, 71–2, 215–6, 221–2, 281; and the good, 66–7; having and sharing, 126–8; and intellect, 220–1; and love, 14, 44, 66, 76, 211–2; metaphysics

Madness *continued*
    of, 63, 71–5; and Muses, 43, 70;
    and participation, 124–8; and
    philosophy, 123; and poetry,
    43–4, 70–2, 74, 144; and
    prophecy, 43, 67–9, 72; and
    purification, 61, 70, 72, 144; as
    sickness, 48; and Socrates,
    61–3; types of, 62, 67, 212; and
    wisdom, 66
Mania, See Madness
Matter: and evil, 104; as kind of
    reality, 238
Medicine: as art, 233; and the good,
    238–40
Meno, 1, 79 125
Metaphysics: and happiness, 276;
    and love, 5–6, 145, 163; and
    madness, 63, 71–5; and method,
    277–91; and mysteries, 128,
    131–8; and rhetoric, 7, 199; and
    structure of *Phaedrus*, 3–9, 35,
    42
Method: and collection and division,
    35, 219, 223–6, 241, 311–2,
    315; and dialectic, 301, 310; and
    happiness, 313–4; and knowl-
    edge, 8, 315; and language, 309;
    and metaphysics, 277–91; and
    nature, 240–2, 279–91; and
    Socrates, 223–7; and Socrates'
    first speech, 35, 38–40; and
    soul, 97; and speculation, 241;
    and wisdom, 173. *See also*
    Collection, Division
Midas, 210
Mind (*Nous*): and Anaxagoras,
    232–7; and cosmos, 234–6; and
    divine intellect, 234; and the
    good, 52–3, 66, 77, 110, 134,
    138, 234, 295; and husbandry,
    257–8; and intellect, 68–9, 78,
    108–9, 153; and knowledge,
    108–9, 257–8; and love, 48–50,
    52, 66; and Pericles, 233–5; and

philosophy, 68–9; and rhetoric,
    27, 77–8; and Socrates' first
    speech, 49–50; and soul, 257;
    and wisdom, 68–9
Mortality: and immortality, 94,
    95–100
Motion: as active and passive, 82;
    and cosmos, 85; and generation,
    83; and harmony, 84–5; and life,
    81–2; and soul, 80–7, 97
Muses: birth of, 180–4; and inspira-
    tion, 35–6, 43, 62, 70, 188–90,
    294–5; and love of, 127, 172;
    and madness, 43, 70; and
    philosophy, 114–5, 188–90,
    205, 213; and poetry, 107,
    186–7; and Socrates, 35–7
Muthos. See Myth
Mysteries: Eleusinian, 131; and
    Forms, 128–30, 132–3; and the
    good, 130–8; and love, 150; and
    Orphism, 137; and rightness in
    philosophy, 123; and Socrates,
    128
Myth (*Muthos*): and allegory, 19–20;
    criteria for explanation of,
    17–20; and Forms, 19, 106; and
    knowledge, 109; and nature, 20,
    241; and Plato, 99–100; in
    Republic, 259; and similarity,
    20; and Socrates, 21–2, 36, 51;
    and truth, 56–8; and wisdom, 20

Nature; active and passive properties
    of, 104, 127–8, 282–5; and art,
    214, 232–6; and beauty, 158; and
    collection and division, 151,
    214–5, 221, 240–1, 278–9,
    287–91; and cosmos, 236–40;
    and enumeration of Forms, 151;
    and Forms, 280–1; and the good,
    240, 258; knowledge of, 40,
    287; and method for determin-
    ing, 240–2, 279–91; and myth,

Nature *continued*
  20, 241; and pleasure, 141; and
  simplicity, 135, 280–4; and
  soul, 261, 281–2; and speculation, 233, 235–6; and totality,
  239–40; 285–7; and unity,
  289–90; and wisdom, 75–8; and
  writing, 229–50. *See also*
  Collection, Dialectic, Division
Nestor, 194–6
Nous, See Mind
Nussbaum, M., 146, 293, 297–9,
  301–6, 309–14
Nymphs, 204, 208; and inspiration,
  43, 50

Odysseus, 194–6
Opinion: and the good, 38, 40; and
  knowledge, 39, 113; and nature
  of soul, 113, 152; and particulars, 39; and rhetoric, 191–4
Opposition: between lover and
  nonlover, 37, 51; metaphysics
  of, 198–9, 201; and rhetoric,
  196–9; and Socrates' first
  speech, 45–6, 51
Oreithia, 17
Orphism: and mysteries, 137
Owen, G., 315

Palinode (Socrates' second speech):
  audience for, 60–1; and gods,
  101–6; inspiration for, 64–7,
  187–9; and Socrates' first
  speech, 141, 159; Socrates'
  prayer in, 170–3; and soul,
  151–6, 241; structure of, 76–8
Pan, 176, 204, 208, 271
Parmenides, 62, 75, 125, 275,
  289–90; and structure of
  Phaedrus, 3–9
Part: and Forms, 41–2, 288–9; and
  desire, 163

Participation: and divine, 100; and
  Forms, 132; and love, 147–8,
  151; and madness, 124–8
Particulars: and Forms, 226, 278,
  287; and the good, 151; and
  opinion, 39
Pegasus, 18, 19
Perception: and division, 208; and
  Forms, 121; and knowledge, 130
Pericles, 231, 232–7; and mind 233–5
Persuasion: and argument, 263; and
  Phaedrus, 176–7; and rhetoric,
  193–4, 243–4, 262–3
Phaedo, 1–2, 27, 53, 55–7, 79, 85,
  110, 133, 235, 317
Phaedrus: age of, 60–1; character of,
  13–6, 293; as lover of Muses,
  129, 172–3, 195; and Lysias,
  12–7, 25, 58–9, 161, 173, 178,
  209, 268; and persuasion,
  176–7; and philosophy, 61,
  171–3, 178, 182–3, 208, 231,
  249, 269, 282; and rhetoric, 13,
  26–7, 59–60, 191; and Socrates,
  9, 14–7, 30–4, 52–3, 58–9, 129,
  170–1, 175–6, 273–4; and
  wisdom, 76
Phaedrus: and criticism of poetry,
  71; and *Parmenides*, 3–9; and
  politics, 180; principles of
  interpretation for, 1–9; unity of,
  2–3, 176–8, 188, 226–7, 233; as
  written, 7–8
Philebus, 77, 277, 309
Philosopher: afterlife of, 117–9; and
  Forms, 121, 125, 273; and
  intellect, 121; as lover of beauty,
  114–5; as lover of youths,
  119–20, 301–2; as lover of
  wisdom, 119–20; and pleasure,
  182; and reasoning, 129–30;
  Socrates as, 185–6, 224; and
  soul, 119–20, 142; and unity, 121
Philosophy: as culture, 190; and
  etymology, 35–6, 66, 163, 296;

continued
  and friendship, 273; and
  happiness, 125, 274; and
  inspiration, 224; and love,
  45–6, 48, 150, 165–9, 305–6;
  and madness, 123; and mind,
  68–9; and Muses, 114–5,
  188–90, 205, 213; and Phaedrus,
  61, 171–3, 178, 182–3, 208,
  231, 249, 269; 282; rightness in,
  123; and Socrates' first speech,
  45–6; and wisdom, 172–3, 276
Phusis, See Nature
Pindar, 12
Plato: and gods, 122; irony in,
  244–5; and Lysias, 28; and
  writing, 259–60, 267
"Platonic love," 167
Pleasure: and beloved, 45–7; and
  body, 40; and desire, 40–2, 157;
  and evil, 46–7; as good, 47; and
  love, 157; and nature, 141; and
  philosophy, 182; as principle in
  Socrates' first speech, 38, 40–1
Poetry: as art, 71; and madness,
  43–4, 70–2, 74, 144; and Muses,
  107, 186–7; and poetry, 70–1;
  and Socrates, 44, 51, 62, 107–8,
  187, 282; and truth, 57, 107–8
Polemarchus, 170
Politicians: and honor, 177, 180; and
  law, 179–80; and rhetoric, 198;
  and speechwriting, 179
Predication: and desire, 41–2; and
  Forms, 41, 285
Principle: and nature of soul, 78–87;
  and self-motion, 87
Probability: and explanation, 19; and
  the good, 245–50; and truth, 247
Prophecy: and madness, 43, 67–9,
  72; and Socrates, 43, 61–2, 270
Prudence: and love, 48–50, 140
Purification: and disease, 44; and
  madness, 61, 70, 72, 144; and
  Socrates, 44

Recollection, 5; and beauty, 157–8;
  and collection and division,
  120–3, 216; and Forms, 120–3,
  216
Republic, 1–2, 27, 77, 180; and the
  good, 133, 299; and myth, 259;
  psychology in, 89–92
Rhetoric: and action, 248; agreement
  in, 207–8; as art, 202, 230–2;
  and beauty, 22–4; and collection
  and division, 196, 206–7;
  definition of, 194–6, 213–5; and
  dialectic, 203–27; and the good,
  200; history of, in Greece, 26,
  229–30; and human nature, 21;
  and knowledge, 14; and law,
  196–9; limit conditions of,
  263–5; and Lysias, 12, 294; and
  metaphysics, 7, 199; and mind,
  27,77–8; and opinion, 191–4;
  and opposition, 196–9; and
  persuasion, 193–4, 243–4,
  262–3; and Phaedrus, 13, 26–7,
  59–60, 191; and poetry, 70–1;
  and politicians, 198; practicing
  of, 243–5; and silence, 244–5;
  and Socrates, 26–7; and soul,
  195, 241–3; and speculation,
  202; and speechwriting, 177–8;
  teaching of, 241–3; and truth,
  191–4, 199–202, 233; and types
  of soul, 243–4; and wisdom, 227
Robin, L., 294
Robinson, T., 296
Rosen, S., 294
Rowe, C., 293, 296, 300, 302, 312,
  313, 316
Ryle, G., 317

Sallis, J., 298
Sappho, 28–9
Sayre, K., 317
Schleiermacher, F., 1
Self-knowledge, 8; and Socrates, 15,
  20–3, 29, 32, 36, 270, 272

Self-motion: and nature of soul, 78–87, 97

Shame: and Socrates, 33–4, 294

Sibyl, 61

Silence: and rhetoric, 244–5

Similarity: and myth, 20; and truth, 199–201

Simmias, 52–3, 57, 295

Simplicity: and complexity, 262, 264, 280–4; and natures, 135, 280–4; as property of Forms, 135; and soul, 87, 172, 282–3; and unity, 280, 284

Sinaiko, H., 306–7

Sirens, 190

Socrates: and Anaxagoras, 54; and Athens, 15, 274–5, 294; and beauty, 23, 171; and books, 54; character of, 30–4, and critique of Lysias' speech, 28, 37, 47, 172, 201, 203–4, 209–10, 250, 260; and daimon, 33, 54; as dialectician, 35; as ironic, 13; and Isocrates, 270; as lover, 13, 16, 171, 233, 302; as lover of discourse, 15, 26, 32–3; as lover of method, 223–7; and Lysias, 33–4, 47, 51–2, 171; and madness, 61–3; and Muses, 35–7; and mysteries, 128; and myth, 21–2, 36, 51; and Phaedrus, 9, 14–7, 30–4, 52–3, 58–9, 129, 170–1, 175–6, 273–4; as philosopher, 185–6, 224; as poet, 44, 51, 62, 107–8, 187, 282; prayer of, 176, 266, 271–5; prophecies of, 43, 61–2, 270; and purification, 44; and rhetoric, 26–7; as seer, 53–5; and self-knowledge, 15, 20–3, 29, 32, 36, 270, 272; shame of, 33–4, 294; and speeches, 23, 54–5, 185, 204; and truth, 52, 175–202; and wealth, 272–3; and wisdom, 34, 188–9, 272–3; and writing, 23–4, 29, 55, 268

Solon, 179, 268–9

Sophist, 2, 219, 277, 317

Sophocles, 230–1

Soul: active and passive properties of, 77–8, 82–7, 96–7, 243; afterlife of, 117–20, 166–70; of animals, 95, 96, 112, 118–9; and beauty, 142–3; and body, 83, 85–7, 89–90, 95, 97–100, 128; and cosmos, 95–8; and desire, 90–2, 105, 159–50; and destiny, 114–7; as divine, 78, 86, 94, 96, 98, 100–1, 108–11, 133–4, 153; and evil, 104–5, 111, 113, 116–7, 124, 153–5, 298; as Form, 87–9; and Forms, 85, 87, 111–3, 127–8, 283, 298–300; and gods, 49–50, 111–3, 123; and the good, 93–5, 238; and happiness, 168–9; and heavens, 105–6; and human nature, 40; immortality of, 56, 77, 88, 95–100; and intellect, 121, 220–1; and life, 98; and method, 97; and mind, 257; and nature, 261, 281–2; nature of, 76–89, 93, 95, 105, 129, 151, 155–6, 234–5, 241–2, 261, 264; parts of, 142; in *Phaedo*, 79; of philosopher, 119–20, 142; powers of, 89–93, 97; in *Republic*, 89–92; and rhetoric, 195, 241–3; and self-motion, 78–87, 97; and simplicity, 87, 172, 282–3; as tripartite, 151, 195, 296–7; and truth, 107–38; types of, 115–6, 127, 155, 242–4, 256, 282, 316; and unity, 156

Speculation: and art, 214; and collection and division, 241; and the good, 225; and method, 241; and nature, 233, 235–6; and rhetoric, 202

Speechwriting: and Lysias, 279; and

continued
    politicians, 179; and rhetoric,
    177–8
Statesman, 2, 219, 277
Stenzel, J., 317, 318
Stesichorus, 56–8, 61–2, 64
Symposium, 2, 13, 16, 24, 32, 53,
    55, 259–60, 295

Tartarus, 21
Temperance, 49, 152, 285
Terpsichore, 184
Thamos: prophecy of, 252–4, 313
Theatetus, 317
Theodorus, 194
Theuth, 252–4
Thompson, W., 183, 190, 192, 302,
    303, 304, 308, 316
Thrasymachus, 144, 232
Timaeus, 1, 296
Time: and heavens, 106
Tisias, 245–7, 249
Truth: and beauty, 124–5; and
    collection and division, 261–2;
    and education, 148–9; and
    Forms, 144–5; and Homer,
    57–8; and law, 247; and
    likeness, 199–201; and Lysias,
    204, 210; and myth, 56–8; and
    poetry, 57, 107–8; and probabil-
    ity, 247; and rhetoric, 191–4,
    199–202, 233; and Socrates, 52,
    175–202; and truth, 107–38; and
    writing, 8, 254–6, 267
Typhon, 21, 294
Tyrant: as type of soul, 116, 118

Unity: and collection, 39–40, 225–6;
    and Forms, 120, 225; and human
    nature, 39–40; and nature,
    289–90; and philosopher, 121;
    and simplicity, 280, 284; and
    soul, 156
Urania, 184, 185, 187, 189, 213

Verdenius, W., 2, 18, 48, 68, 295, 313
Vlastos, G., 307

Wealth: and Socrates, 272–3; and
    temperance, 272
White, D., 295
White, N., 317
Wisdom: and beauty, 139–40, 171;
    and gods, 189; and happiness,
    276; and Homer, 58; and love of,
    23, 172–3, 226–7; and madness,
    66; and mind, 68–9; and myth,
    20; and nature, 75–8; and
    Phaedrus, 76; and philosophy,
    172–3, 276; and rhetoric, 227;
    and Socrates, 34, 188–9, 272–3;
    and writing, 251–76
Writing: clarity of, 267; and
    collection, 182; good and bad,
    7–8, 180–3; and love of honor,
    178–80; and nature, 229–50; and
    Phaedrus, 13; and philosophy,
    177; and Plato, 259–60, 267;
    properties of, 251, 254; and
    Socrates, 23–4, 29, 55, 268; and
    speaking, 178, 191, 193, 197;
    and truth, 8, 254–6, 267; and
    wisdom, 251–76

Zeno, 7, 30, 196–9, 209
Zeus, 21, 96, 101–2, 112, 122, 146,
    147–9, 158, 232, 253; as god of
    philosopher, 112, 128–9, 149,
    163, 303–4, 311